Bring it on!

vol.4

Baek HyeKyung

Yen Press

Words from the Creator

I used to sit in front of the T.V. for hours until I had headaches…But lately, I don't even have time to watch it for even an hour. Even still, whenever I watch programs like "60 minutes" that dig up the truth, and other shows that deal with law or romantic problems between couples, I find myself engrossed and glued to the T.V.

These days I've been thinking about writing a story about a normal whiny middle-aged man and wife who become wrapped in an unusual plot. Of course my friends immediately say, "What?! A story about old people? You really are over the hill now. Where did you hide your walker?" >_T

Yeah…the thirties are coming…soon…sniffle…

Ah, the schedules got a bit messy and the book was a little late, so for those of you who have waited, thank you very, very much.

To family, friends, my right and left handman Woo-Wun and Jae-Eun, and my editor… everyone thank you very much~!!

Hye-Kyung Baek

Hae-Kyung's
Loves and Hates

Best Three (Really, really, really love!!)

1) Sexy and kind men and women.

2) Furry mammals. (except humans! ^^;)

3) Limitless lazy vacations.

Worst Three (Really, really, really hate!!)

1) Insects with lots of legs.

2) Poverty.

3) Rudeness, and bad-manners.

* Please understand, I can't even draw them!! T.T

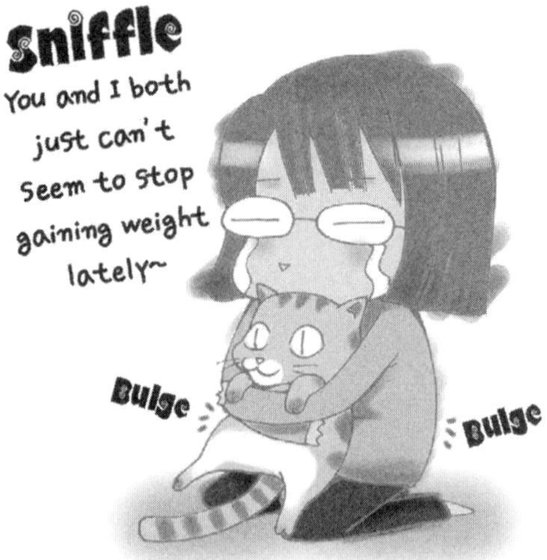
Sniffle
You and I both just can't seem to stop gaining weight lately~
Bulge
Bulge

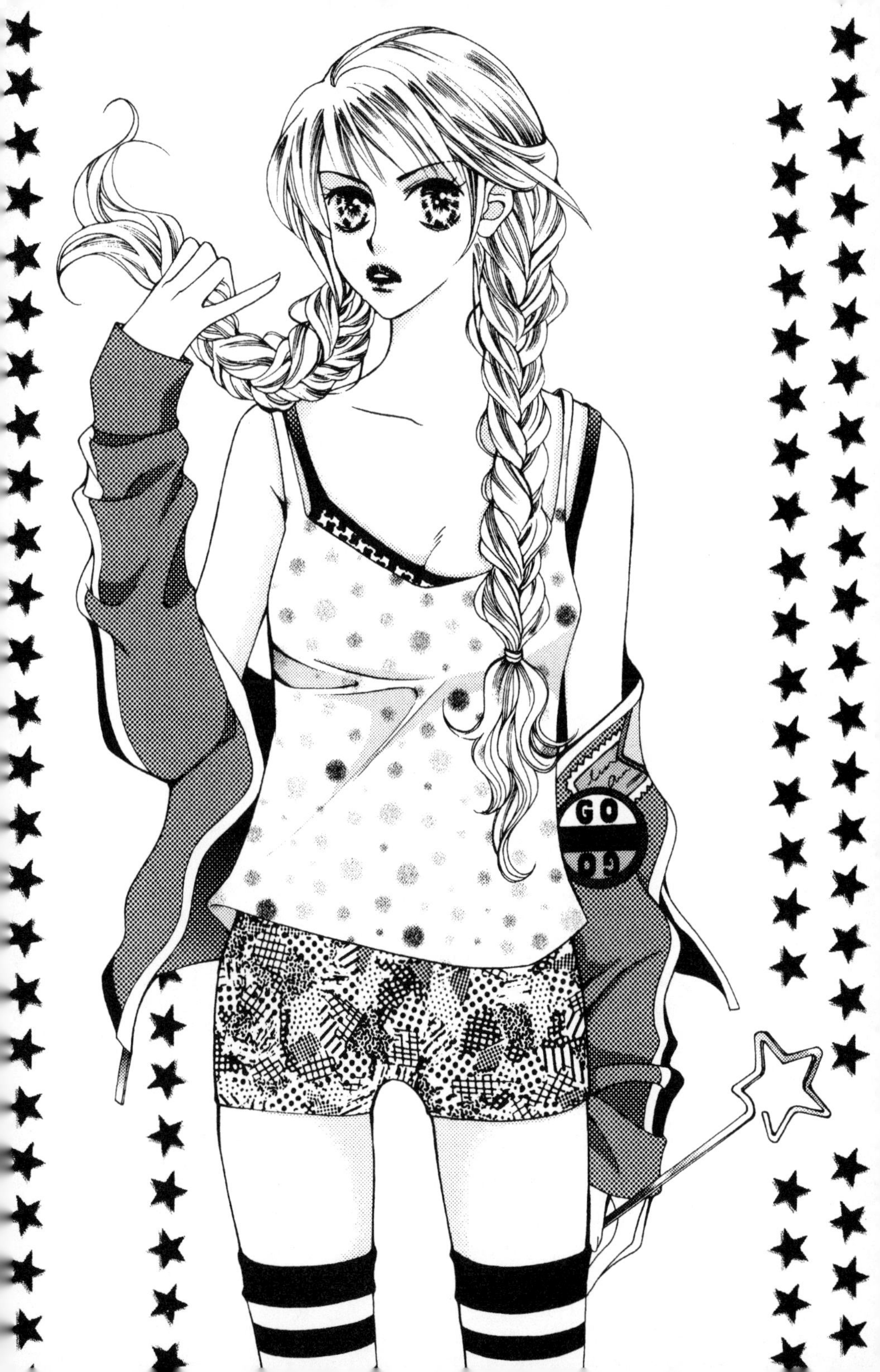
GO
GO

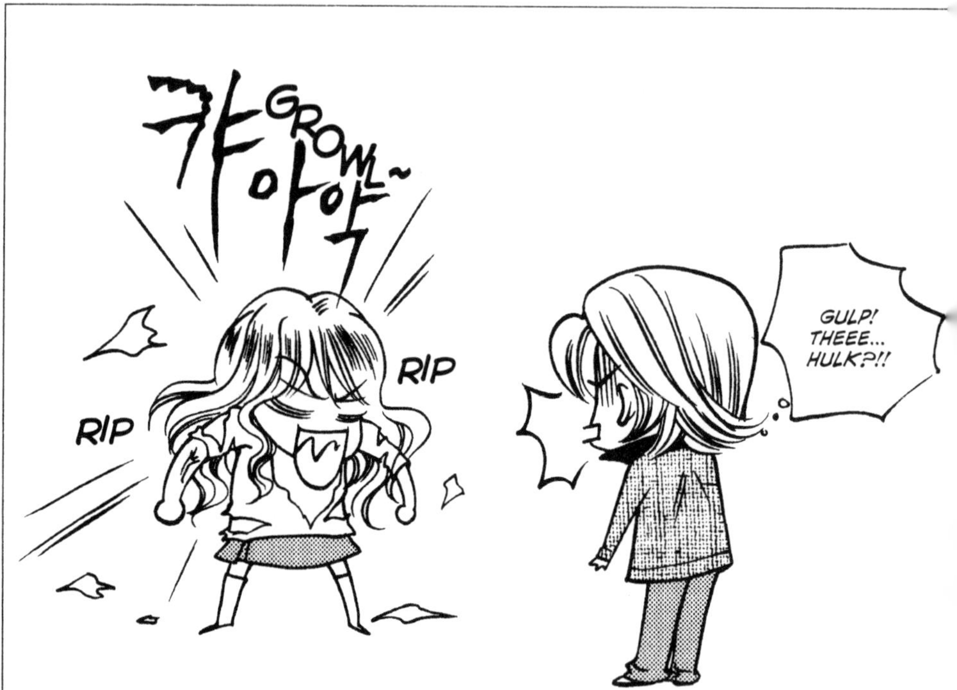
카아악
GROWL~
RIP
RIP
GULP! THEEE... HULK?!!

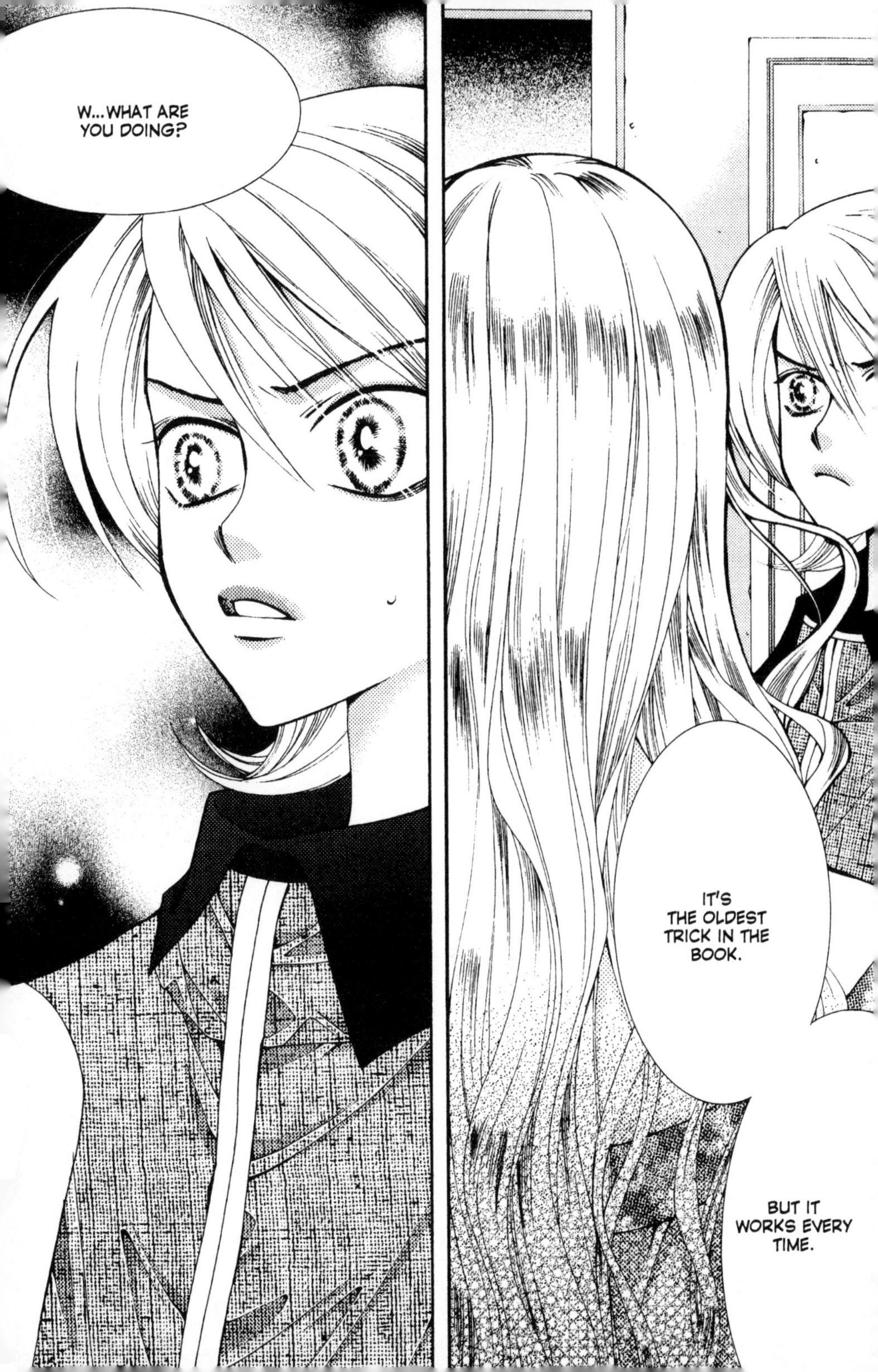
W...WHAT ARE YOU DOING?
IT'S THE OLDEST TRICK IN THE BOOK.
BUT IT WORKS EVERY TIME.

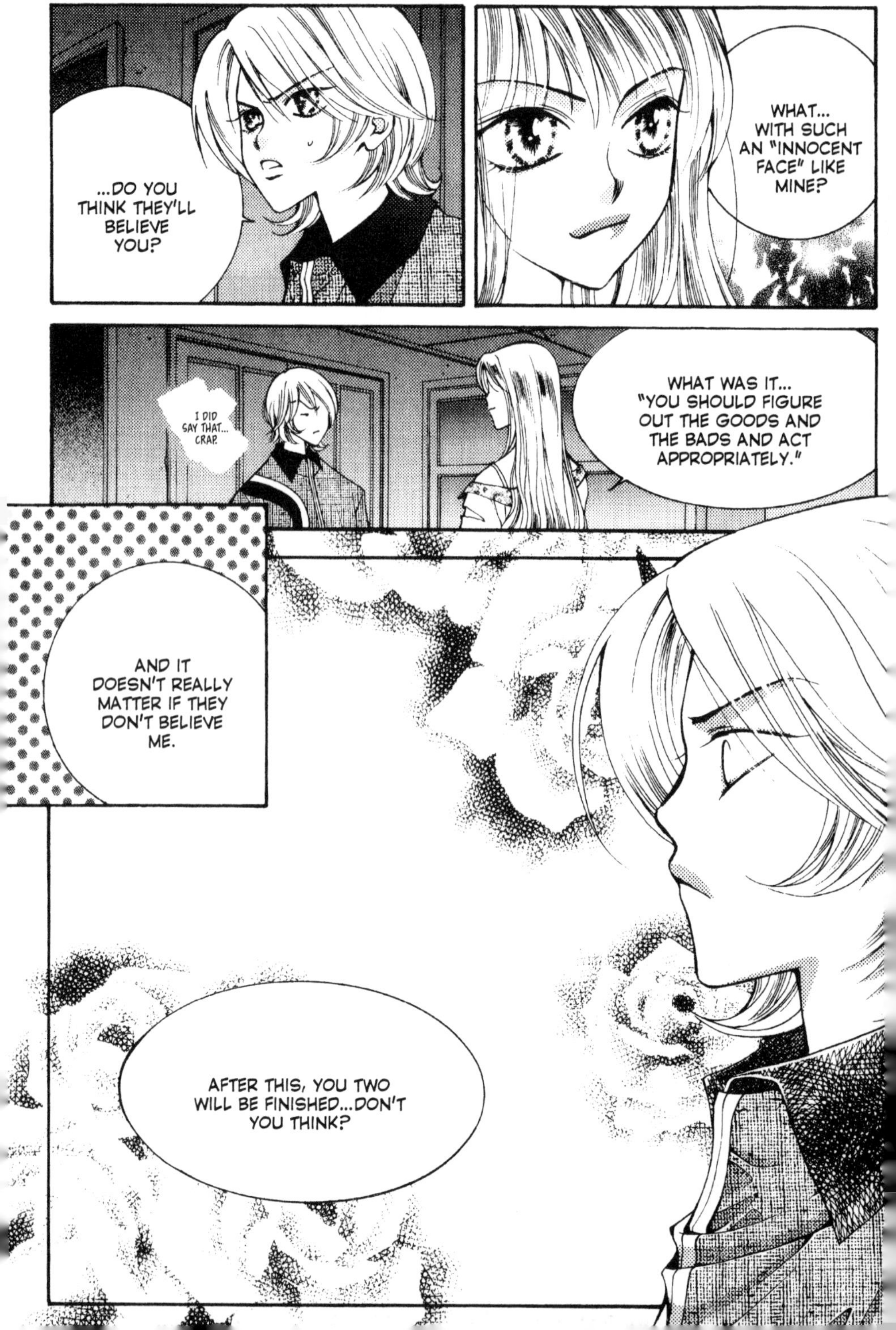
...DO YOU THINK THEY'LL BELIEVE YOU?
WHAT... WITH SUCH AN "INNOCENT FACE" LIKE MINE?
I DID SAY THAT... CRAP.
WHAT WAS IT... "YOU SHOULD FIGURE OUT THE GOODS AND THE BADS AND ACT APPROPRIATELY."
AND IT DOESN'T REALLY MATTER IF THEY DON'T BELIEVE ME.
AFTER THIS, YOU TWO WILL BE FINISHED...DON'T YOU THINK?

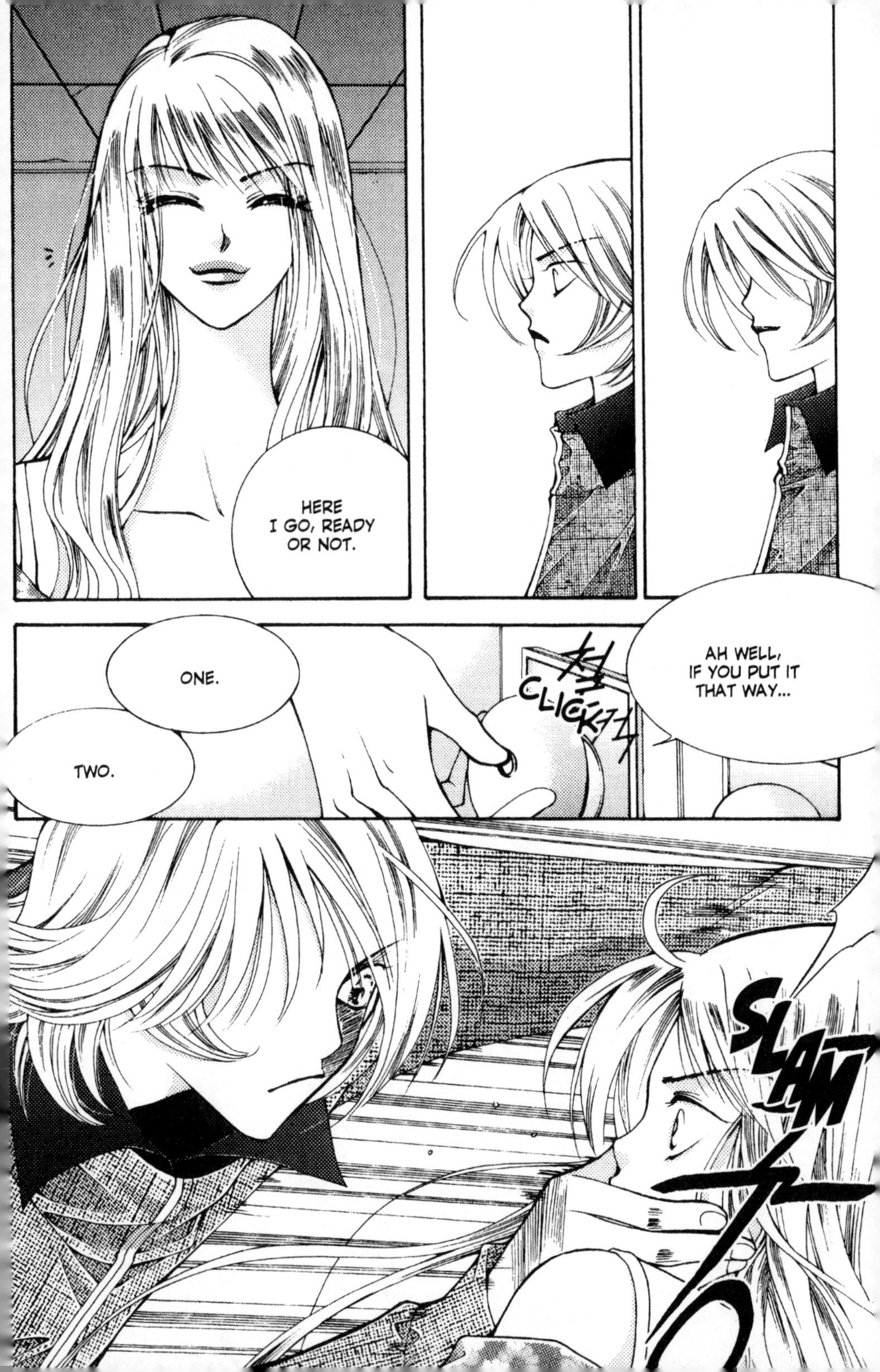
HERE I GO, READY OR NOT.
ONE.
TWO.
CLICK
AH WELL, IF YOU PUT IT THAT WAY...
SLAM

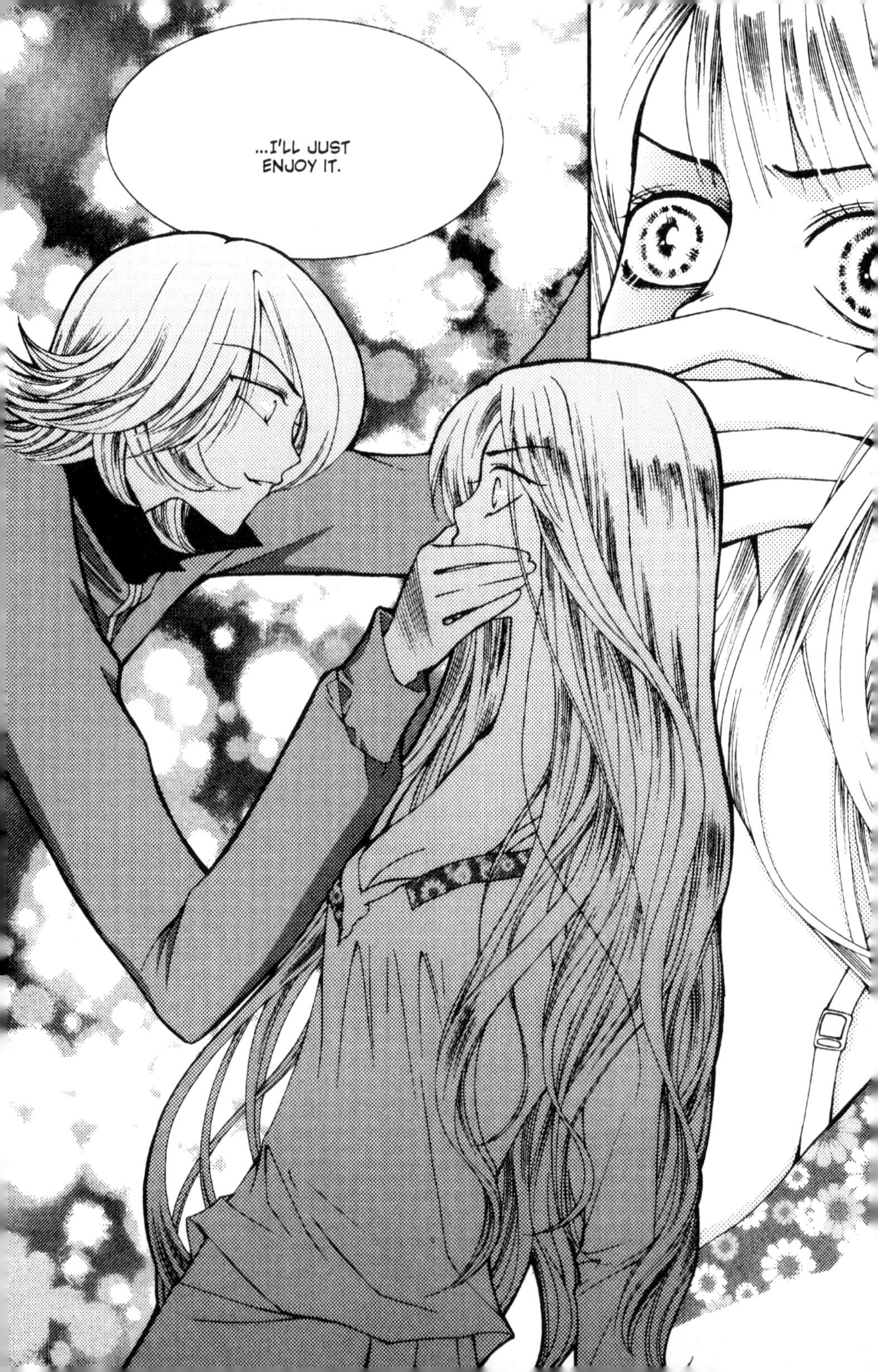
...I'LL JUST ENJOY IT.

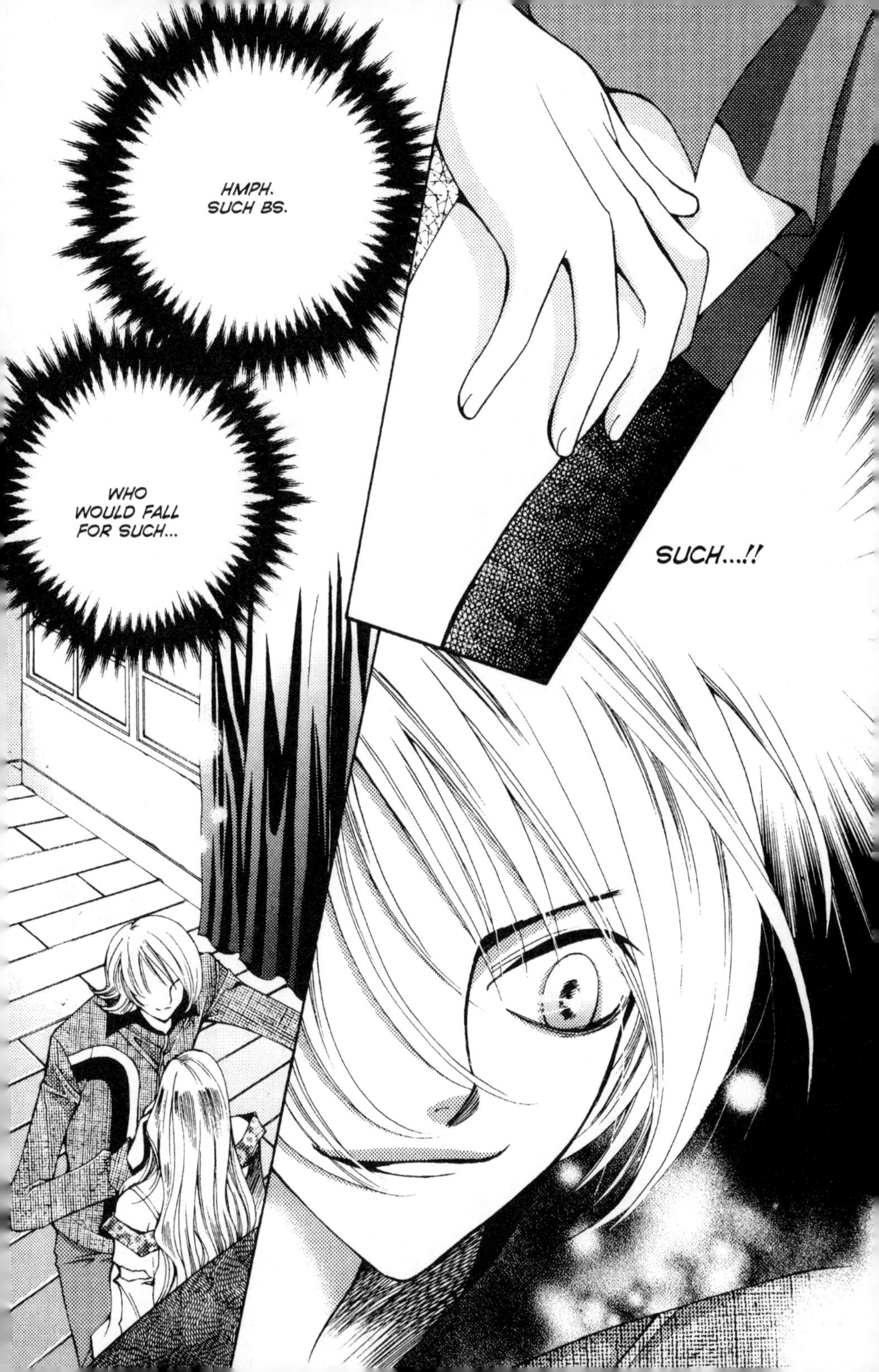
HMPH. SUCH BS.
WHO WOULD FALL FOR SUCH...
SUCH...!!

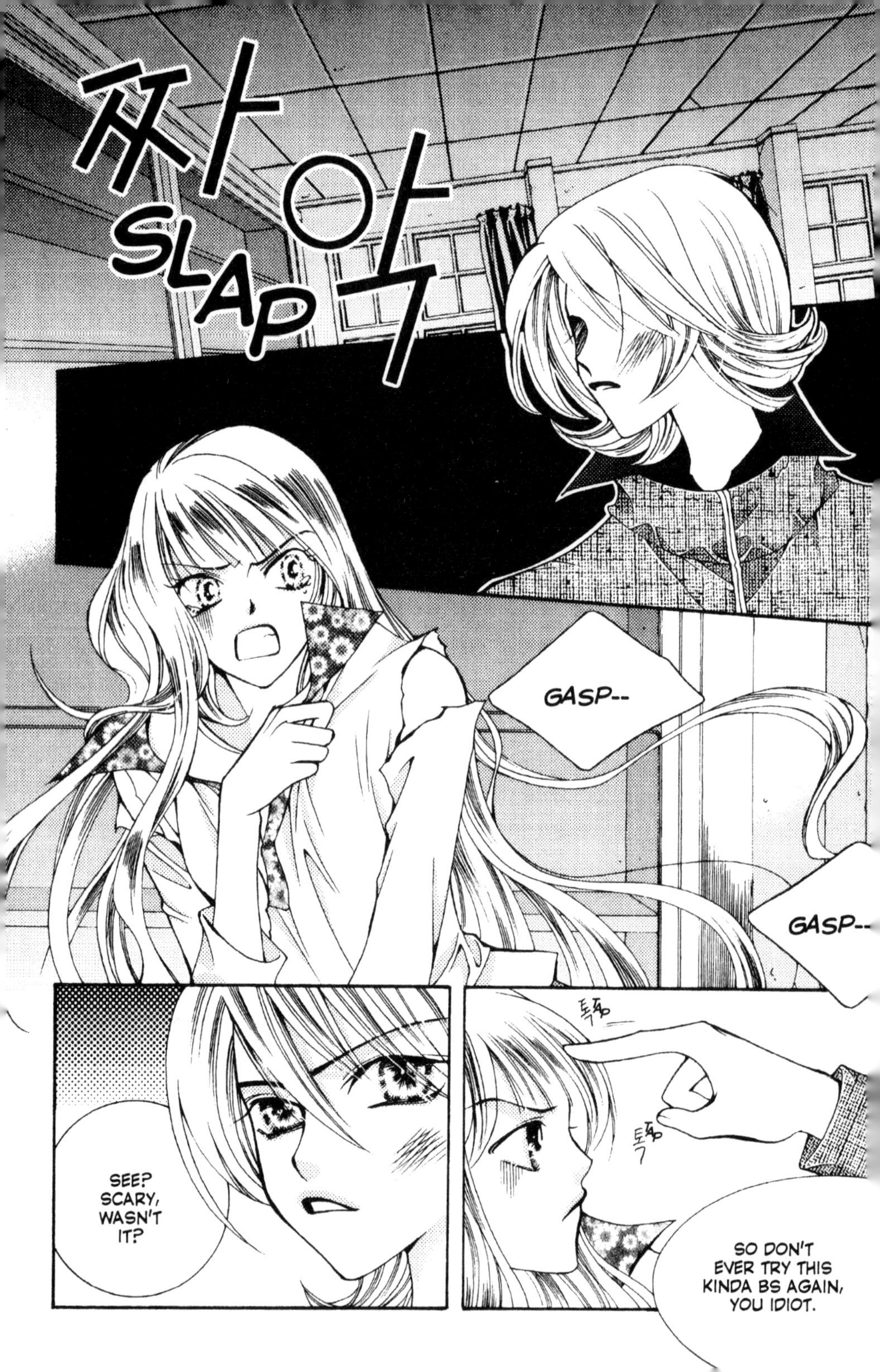
SLAP
GASP--
GASP--
SEE? SCARY, WASN'T IT?
SO DON'T EVER TRY THIS KINDA BS AGAIN, YOU IDIOT.

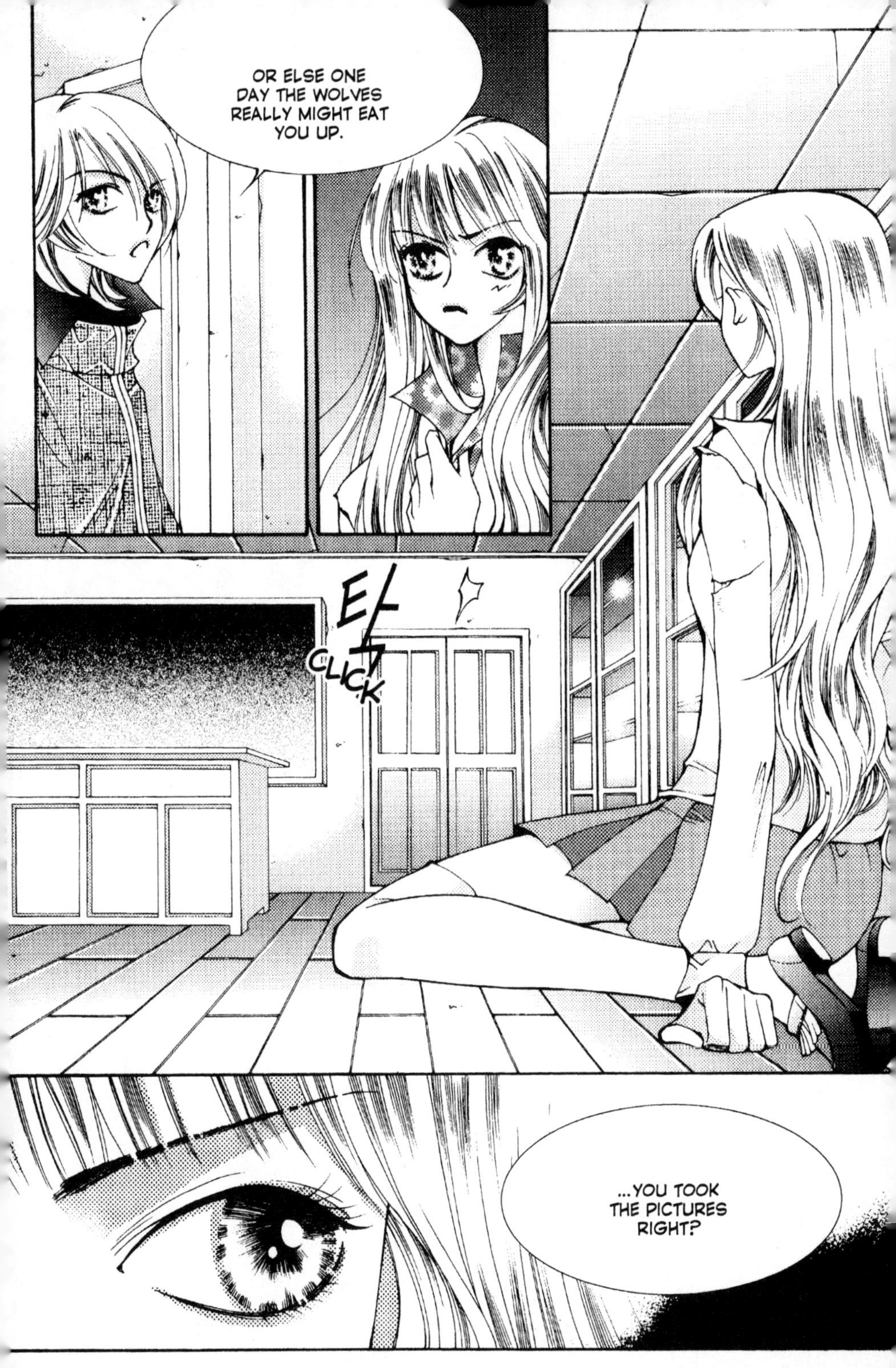
OR ELSE ONE DAY THE WOLVES REALLY MIGHT EAT YOU UP.
CLICK
...YOU TOOK THE PICTURES RIGHT?

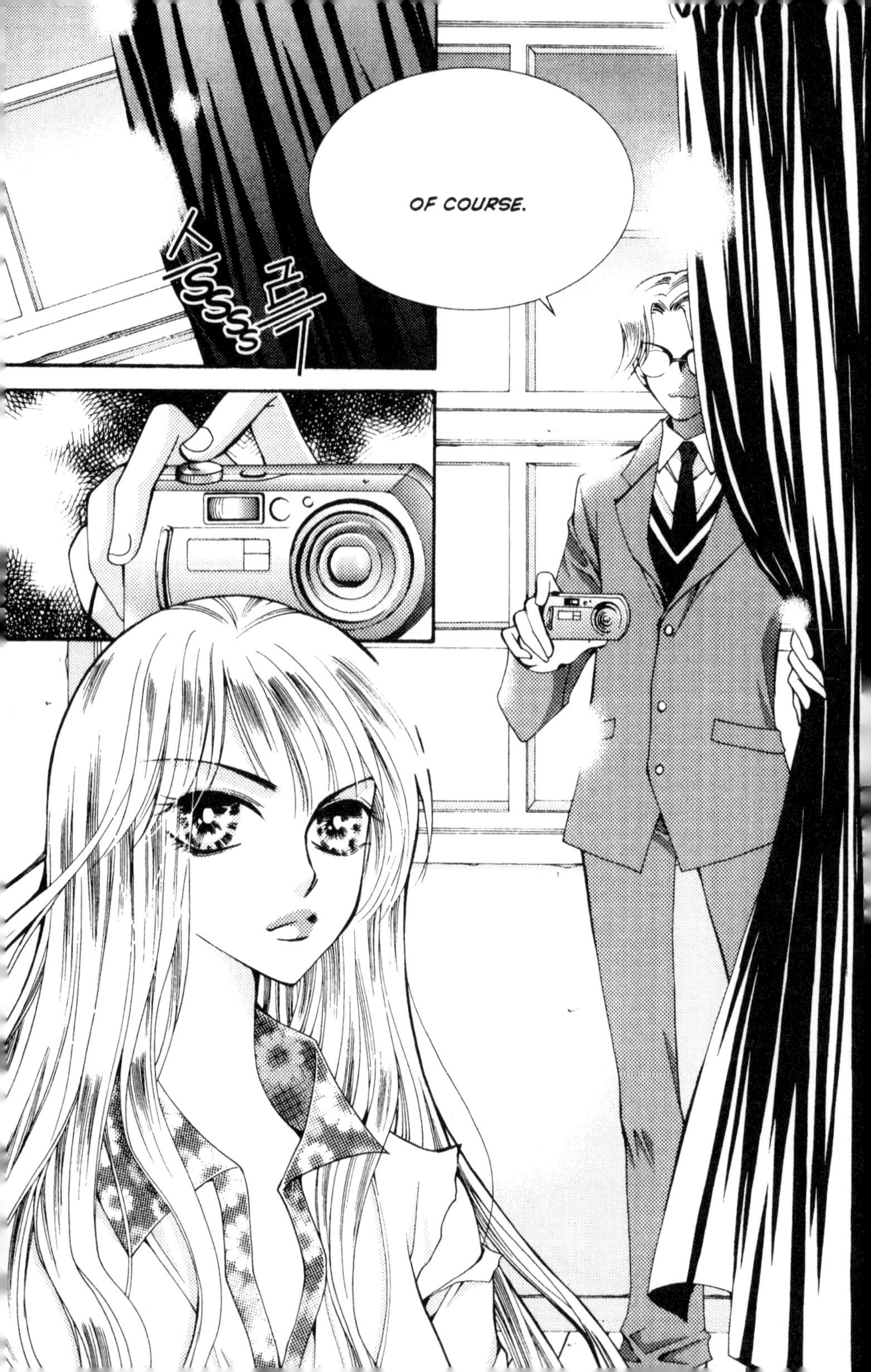
스르륵 SSSS
OF COURSE.

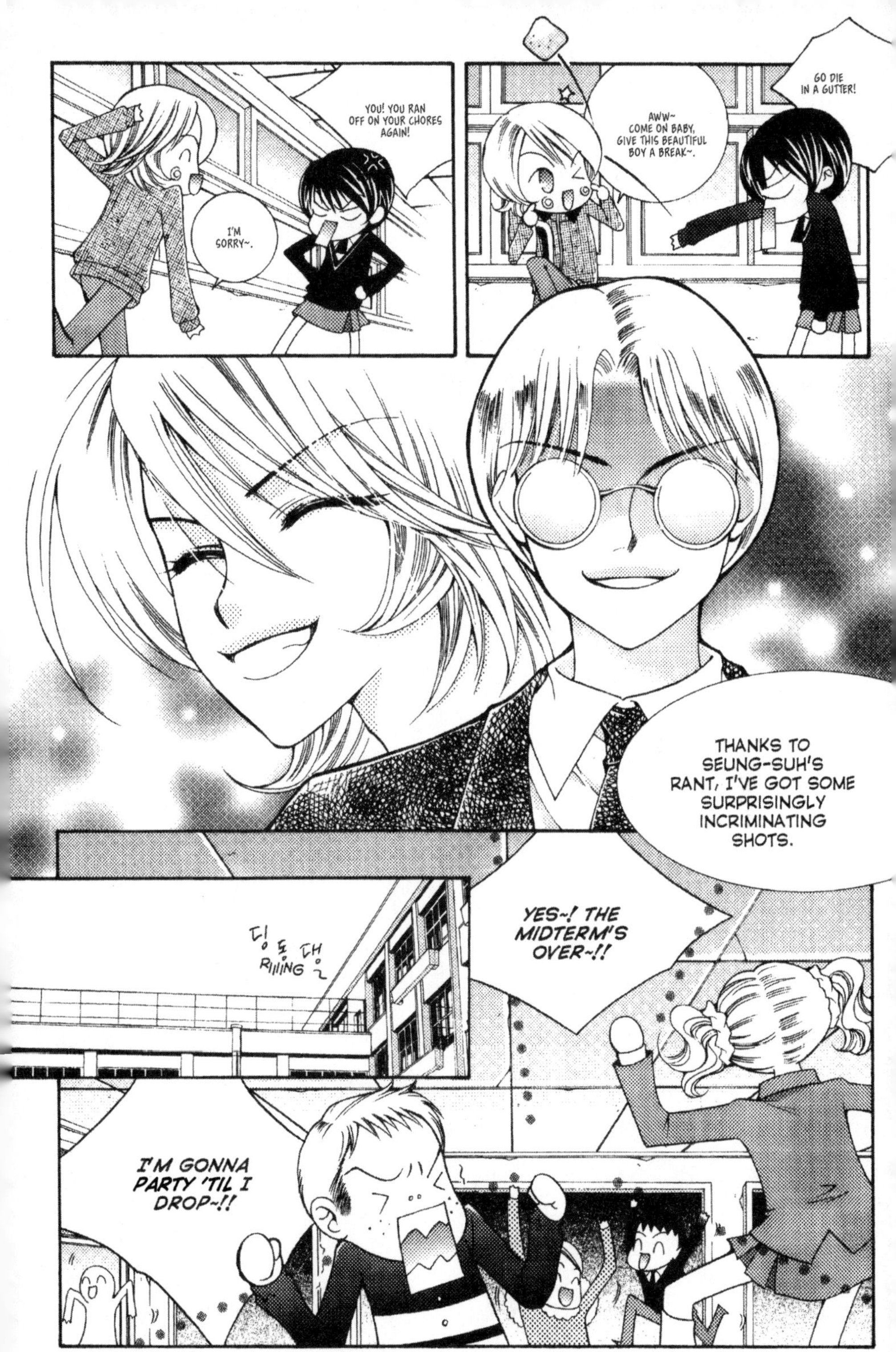
YOU! YOU RAN OFF ON YOUR CHORES AGAIN!
I'M SORRY~.
AWW~ COME ON BABY, GIVE THIS BEAUTIFUL BOY A BREAK~.
GO DIE IN A GUTTER!
THANKS TO SEUNG-SUH'S RANT, I'VE GOT SOME SURPRISINGLY INCRIMINATING SHOTS.
딩동댕
RIIING
YES~! THE MIDTERM'S OVER~!!
I'M GONNA PARTY 'TIL I DROP~!!

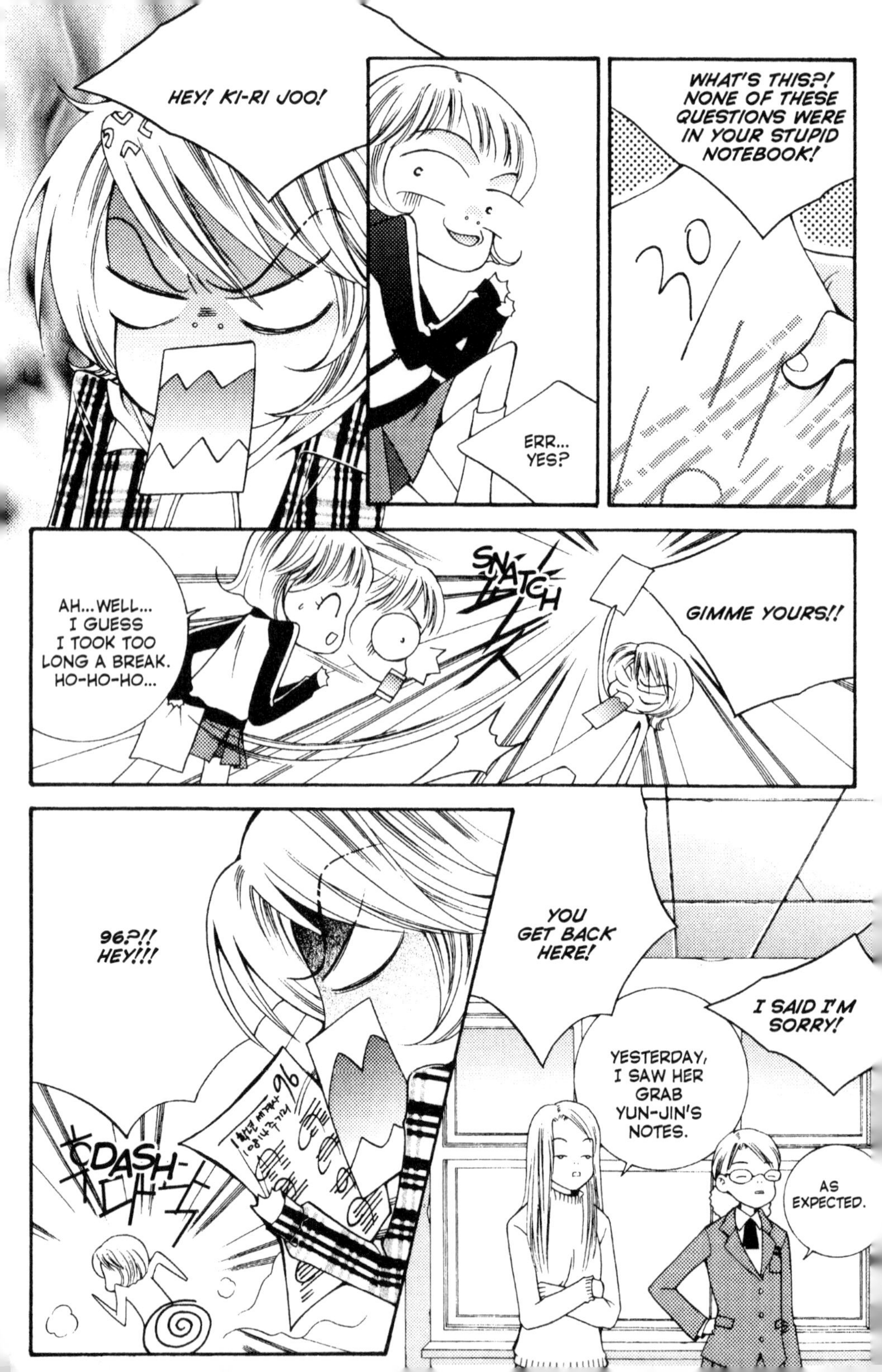
HEY! KI-RI JOO!
ERR... YES?
WHAT'S THIS?! NONE OF THESE QUESTIONS WERE IN YOUR STUPID NOTEBOOK!
30
AH...WELL... I GUESS I TOOK TOO LONG A BREAK. HO-HO-HO...
SNATCH
GIMME YOURS!!
96?!! HEY!!!
96
DASH-
YOU GET BACK HERE!
I SAID I'M SORRY!
YESTERDAY, I SAW HER GRAB YUN-JIN'S NOTES.
AS EXPECTED.

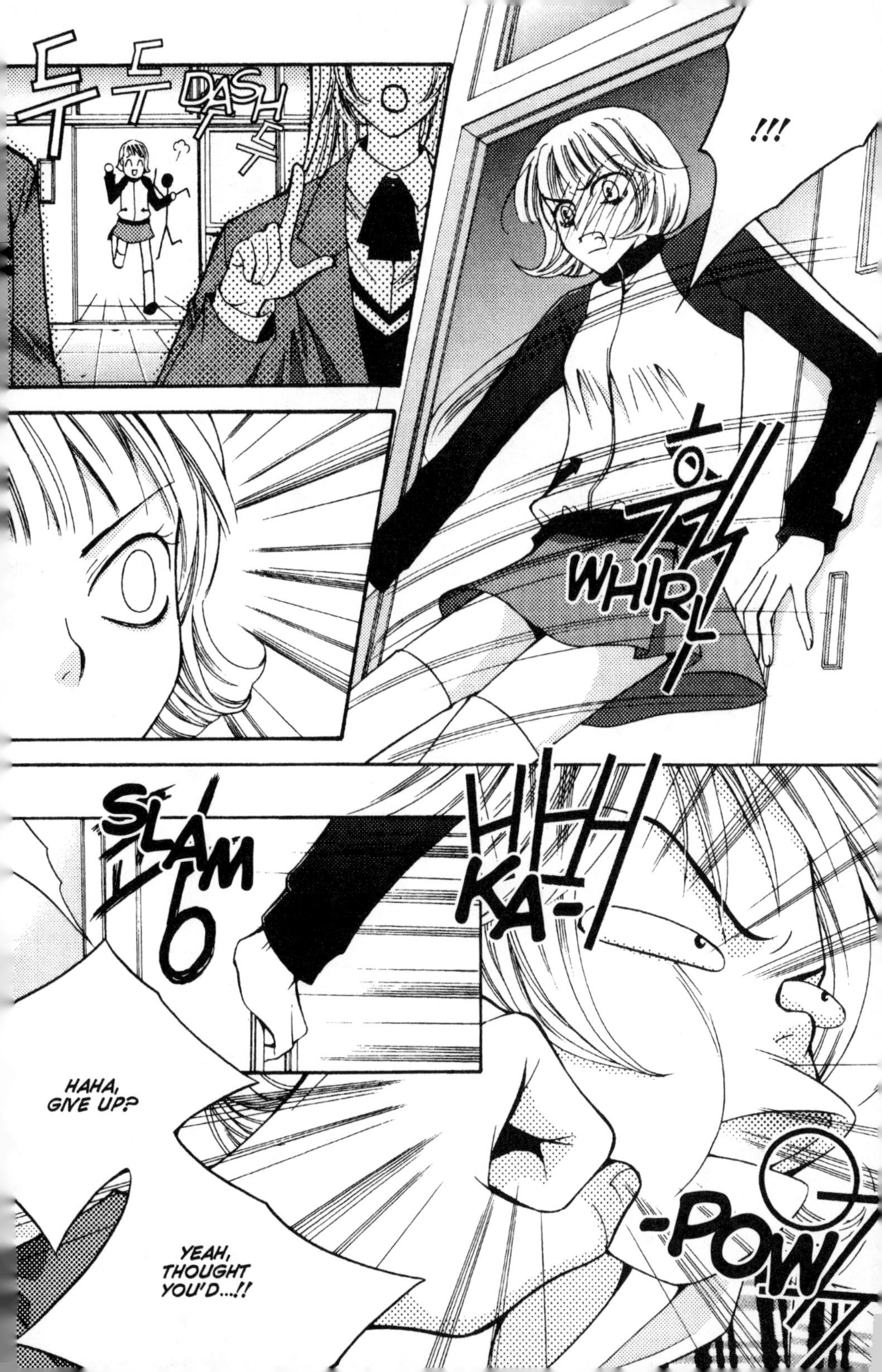
DASH
!!!
WHIRL
SLAM
HHH
KA-
HAHA, GIVE UP?
YEAH, THOUGHT YOU'D...!!
-POW

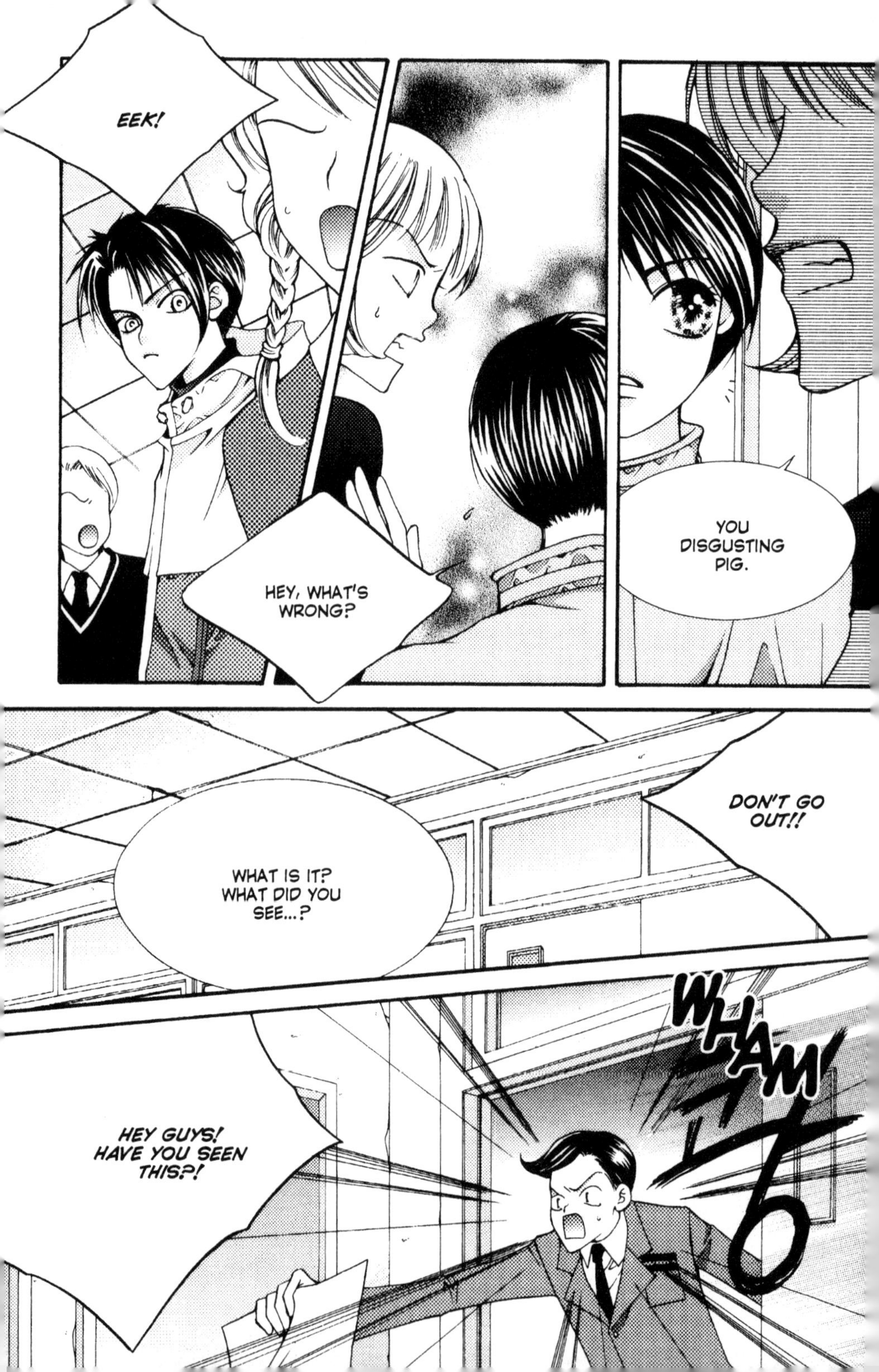
EEK!
HEY, WHAT'S WRONG?
YOU DISGUSTING PIG.
WHAT IS IT? WHAT DID YOU SEE...?
DON'T GO OUT!!
HEY GUYS! HAVE YOU SEEN THIS?!
WHAM

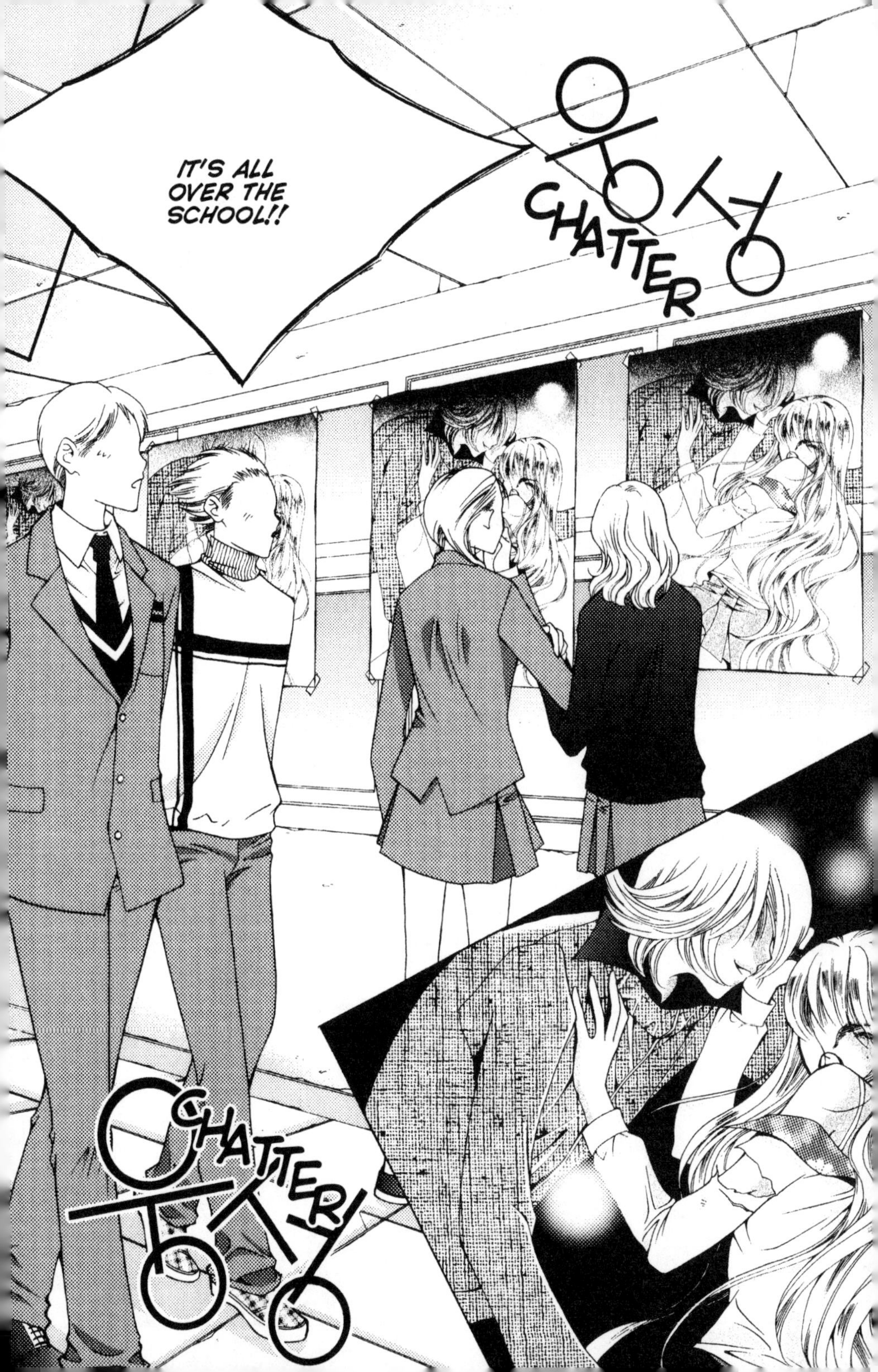
IT'S ALL OVER THE SCHOOL!!
CHATTER
CHATTER!

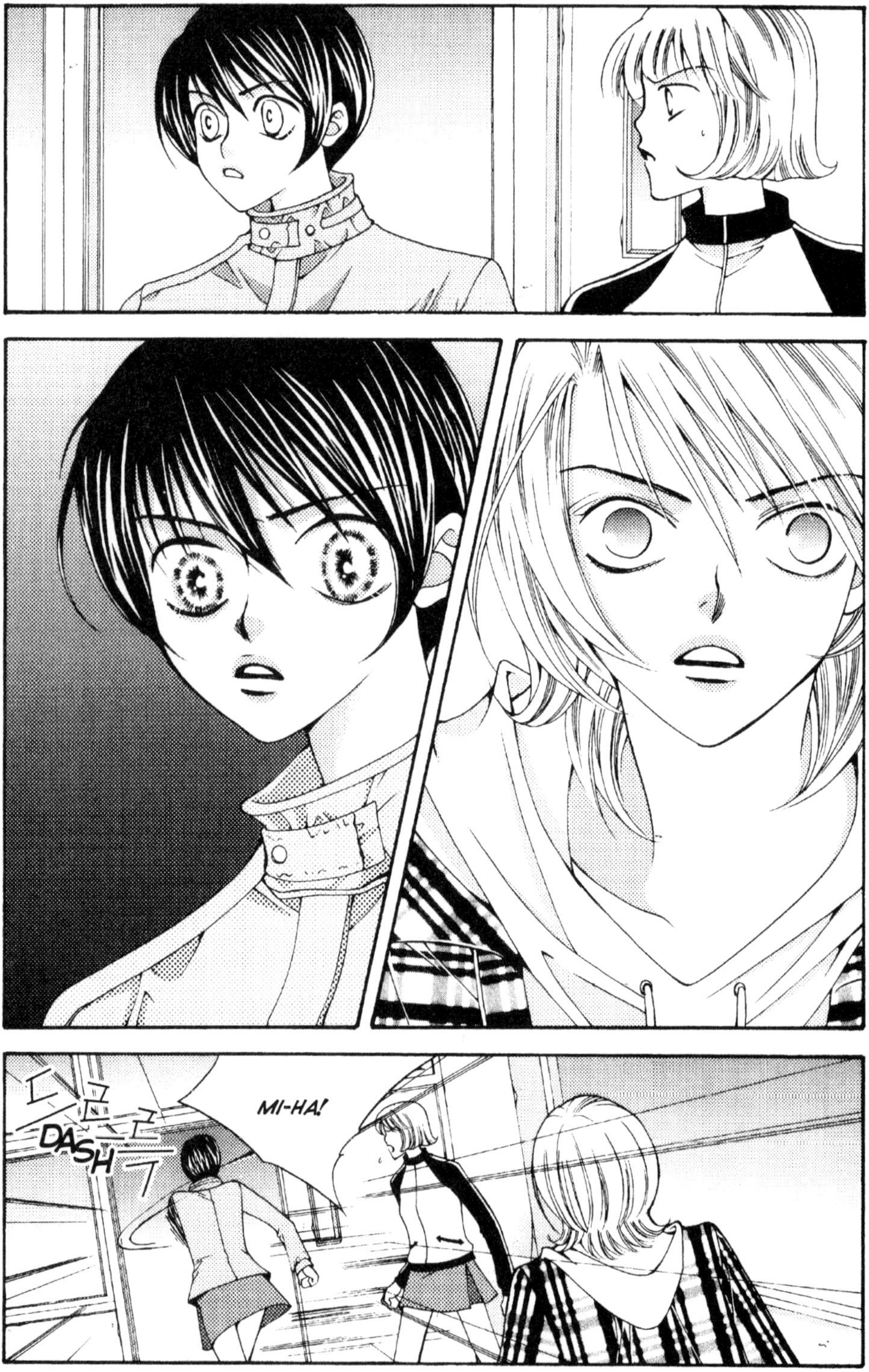
DASH
MI-HA!

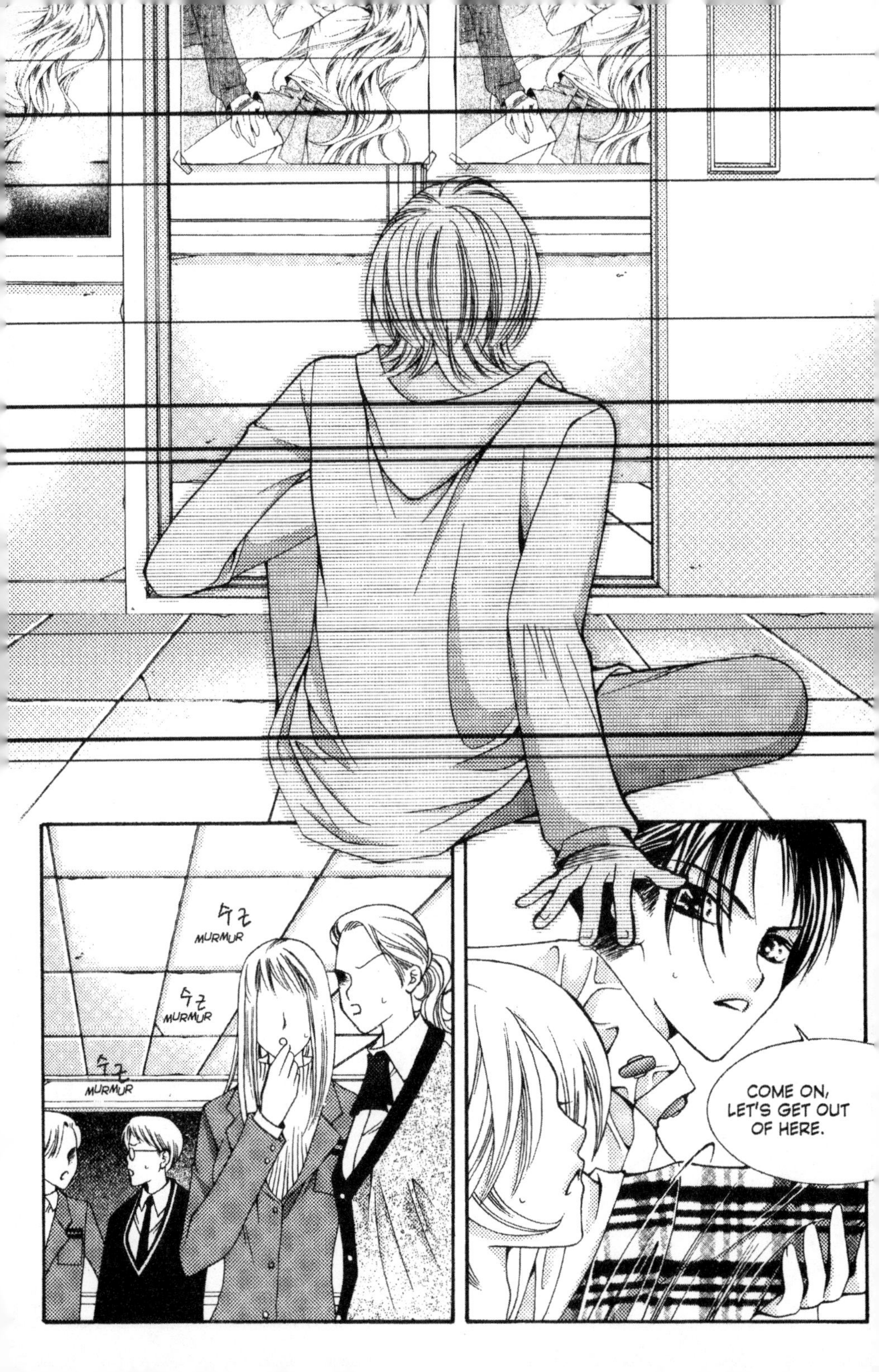
수군
MURMUR
수군
MURMUR
수군
MURMUR
COME ON, LET'S GET OUT OF HERE.

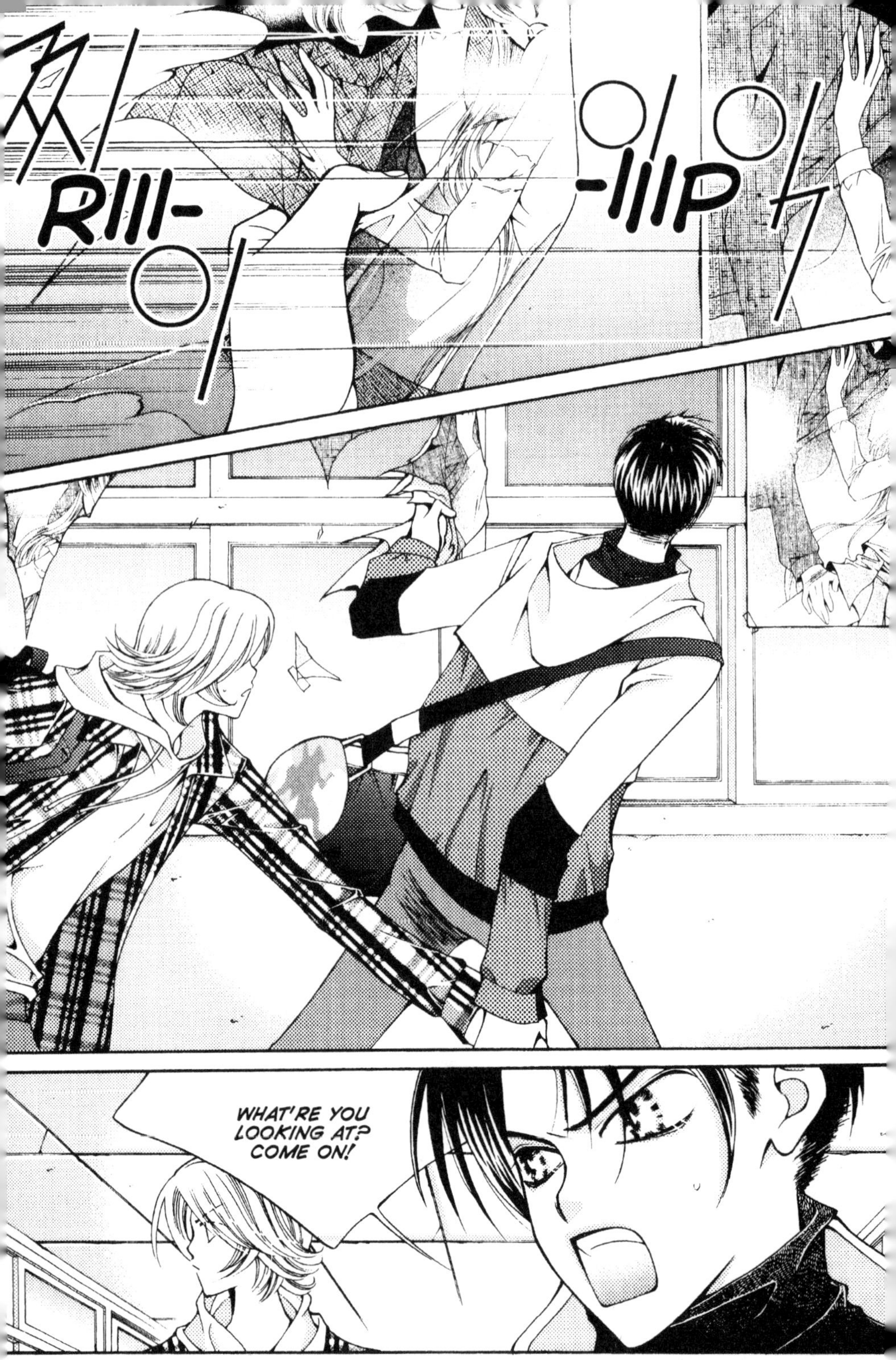
RIII-
-IIIP
WHAT'RE YOU
LOOKING AT?
COME ON!

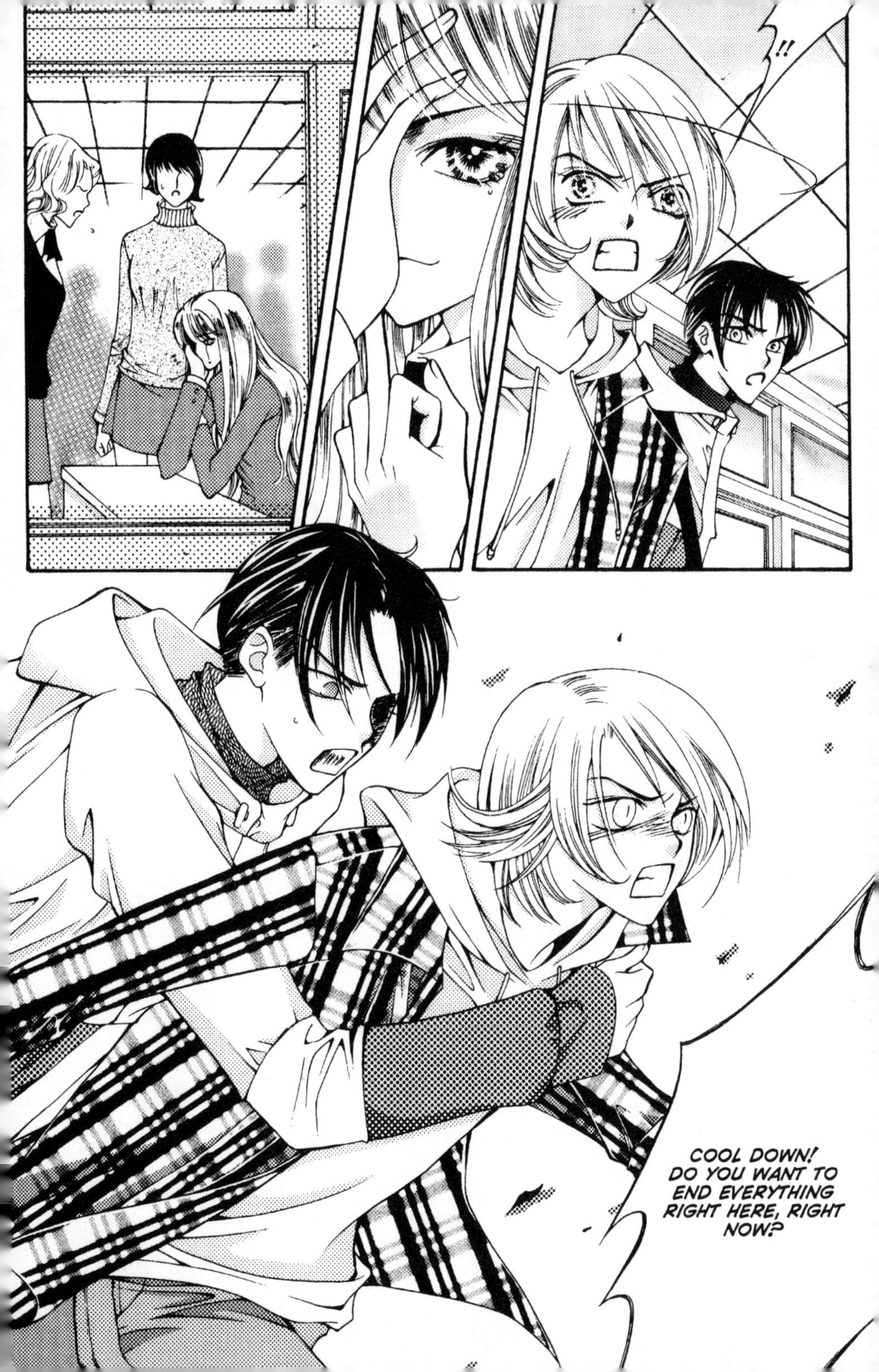
!!
COOL DOWN! DO YOU WANT TO END EVERYTHING RIGHT HERE, RIGHT NOW?

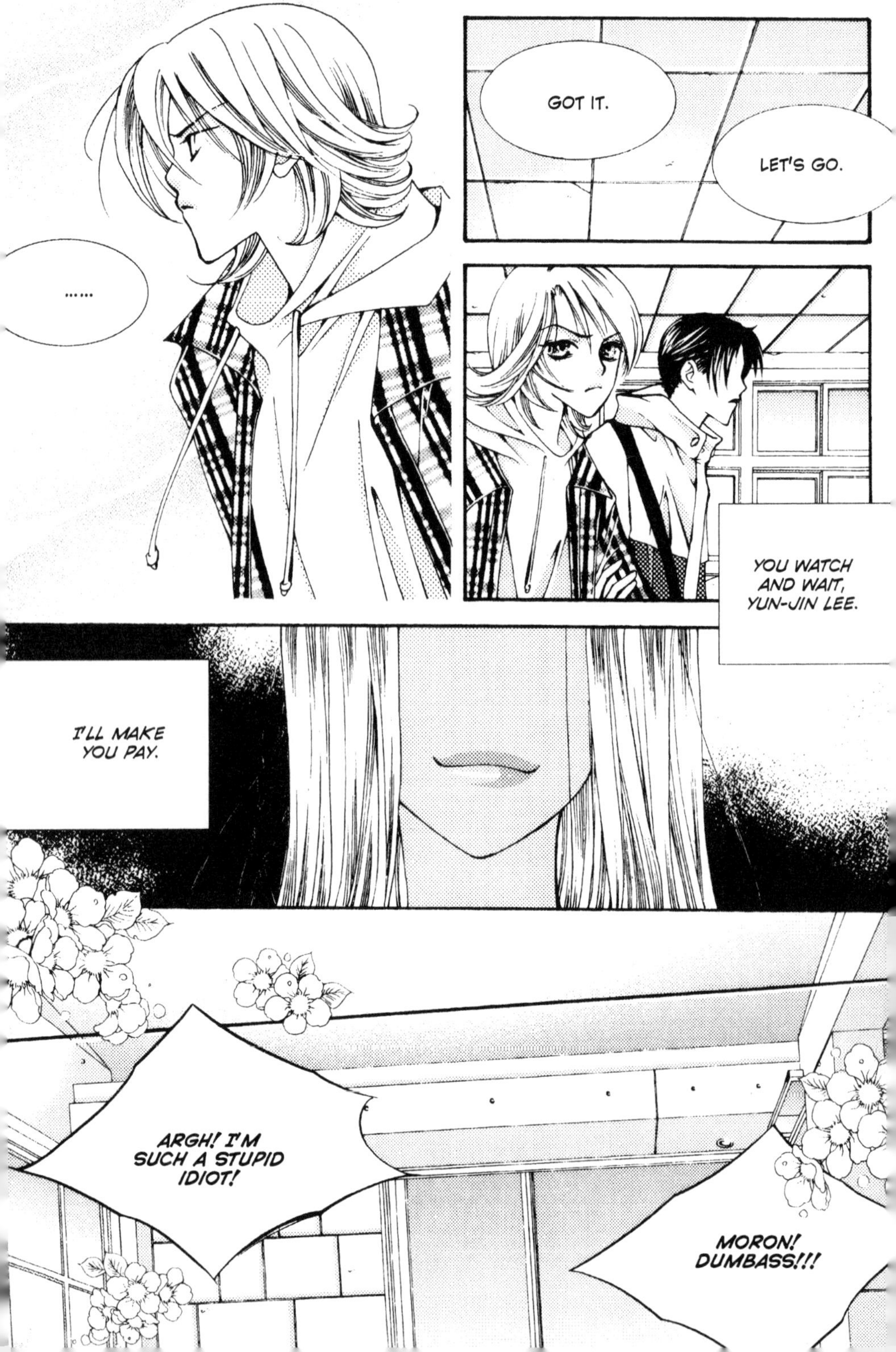
......
GOT IT.
LET'S GO.
YOU WATCH AND WAIT, YUN-JIN LEE.
I'LL MAKE YOU PAY.
ARGH! I'M SUCH A STUPID IDIOT!
MORON! DUMBASS!!!

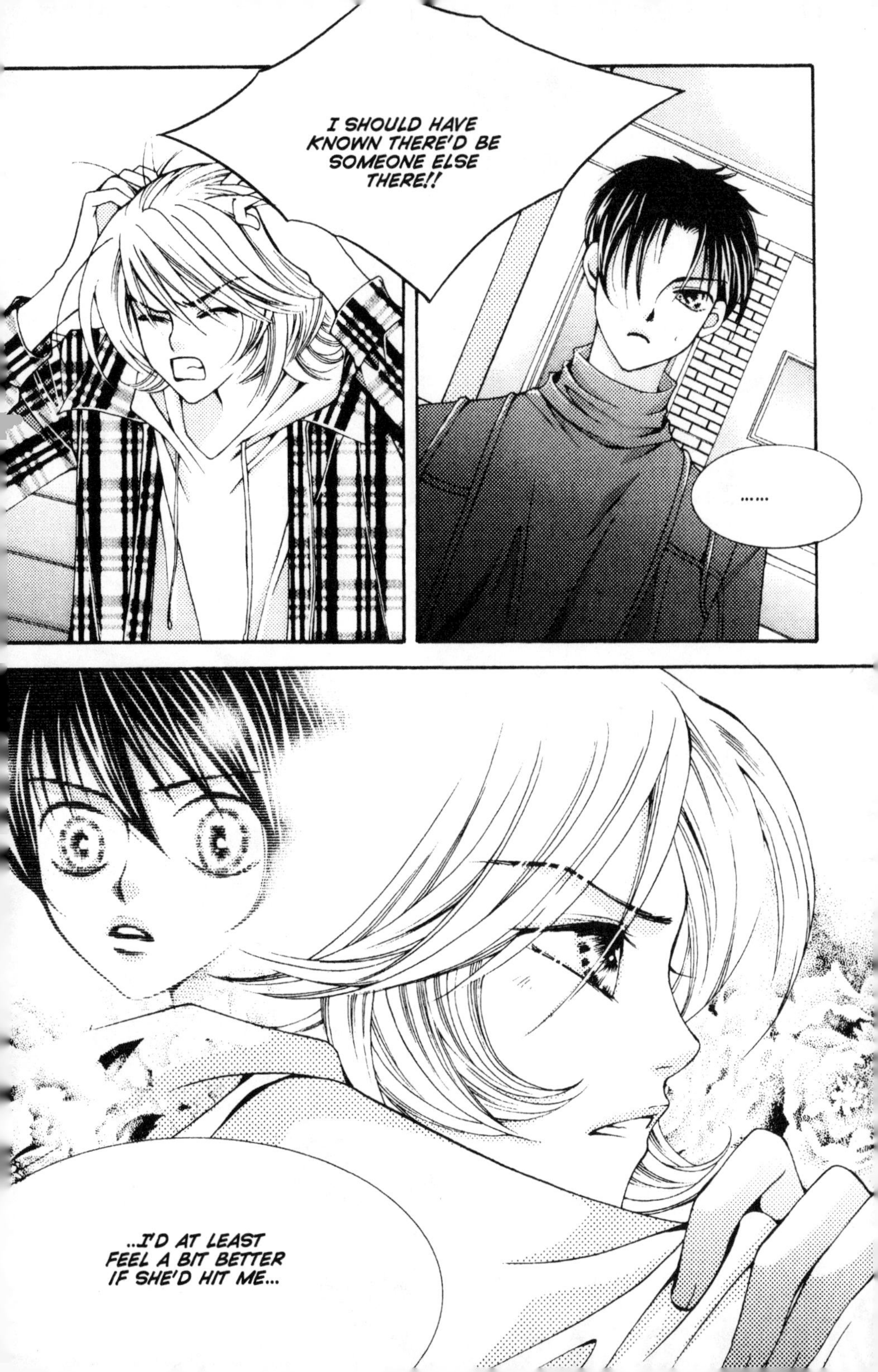
I SHOULD HAVE KNOWN THERE'D BE SOMEONE ELSE THERE!!
......
..I'D AT LEAST FEEL A BIT BETTER IF SHE'D HIT ME...

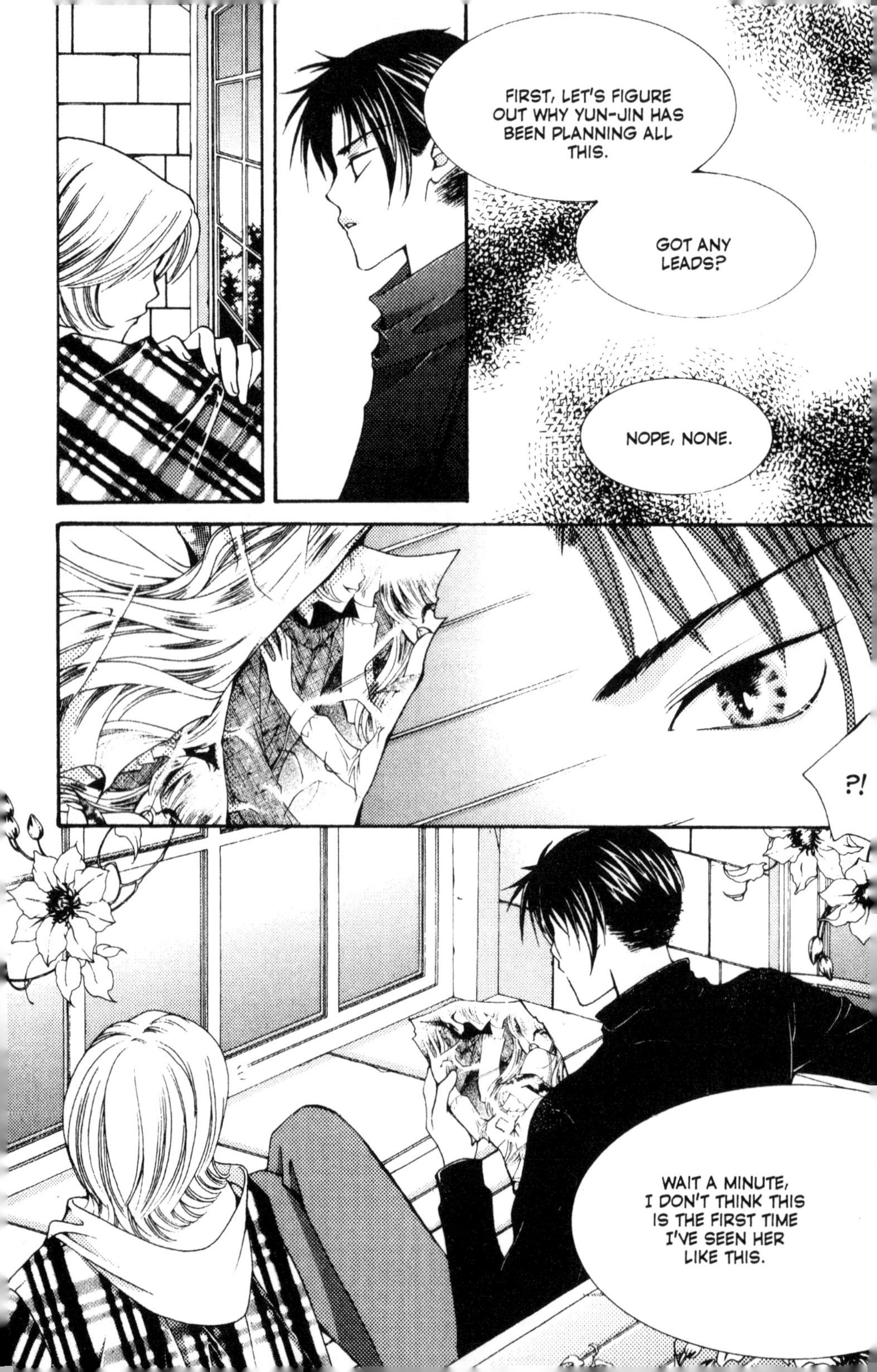
FIRST, LET'S FIGURE OUT WHY YUN-JIN HAS BEEN PLANNING ALL THIS.
GOT ANY LEADS?
NOPE, NONE.
?!
WAIT A MINUTE, I DON'T THINK THIS IS THE FIRST TIME I'VE SEEN HER LIKE THIS.

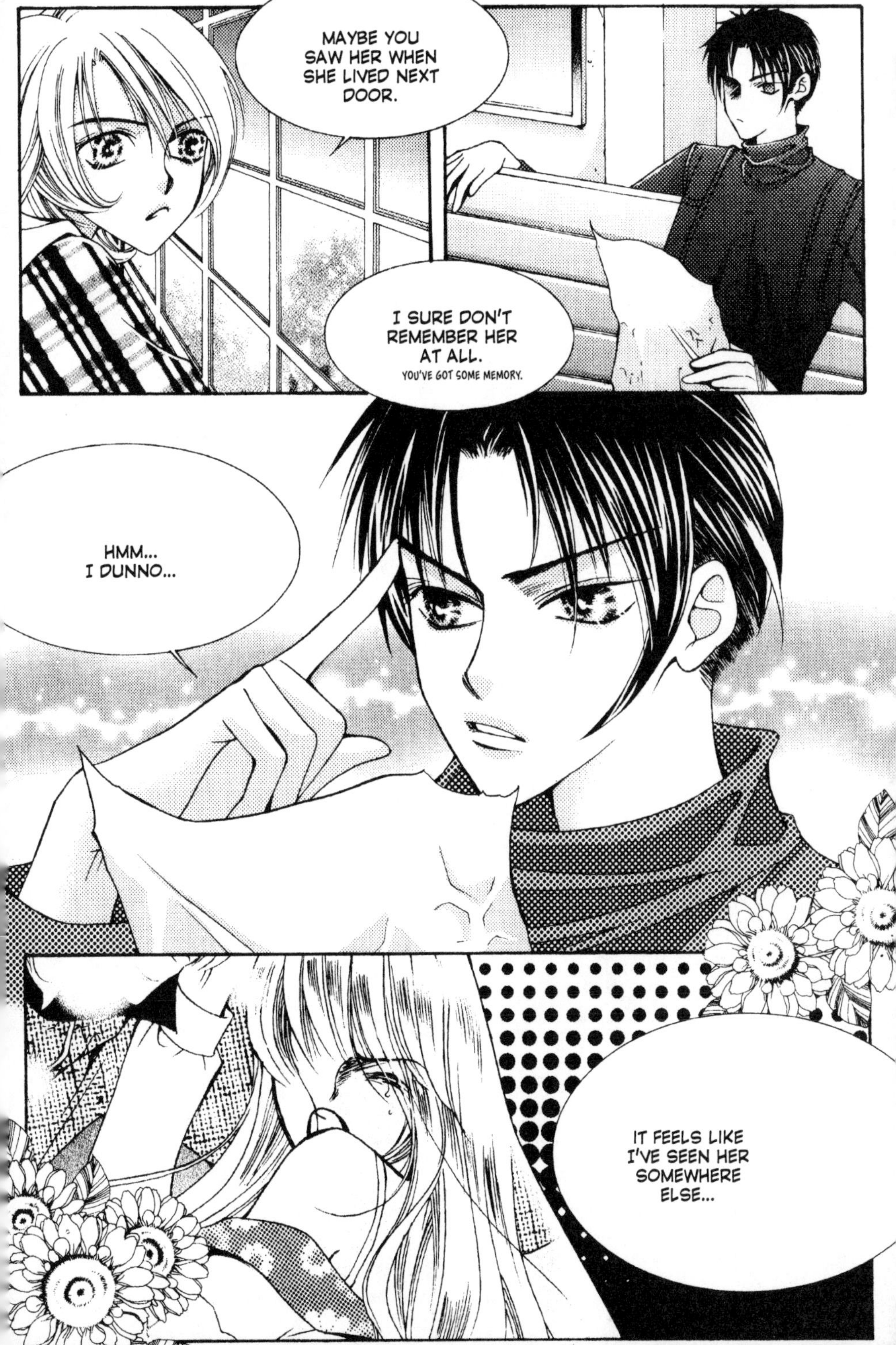
MAYBE YOU SAW HER WHEN SHE LIVED NEXT DOOR.
I SURE DON'T REMEMBER HER AT ALL.
YOU'VE GOT SOME MEMORY.
HMM... I DUNNO...
IT FEELS LIKE I'VE SEEN HER SOMEWHERE ELSE...

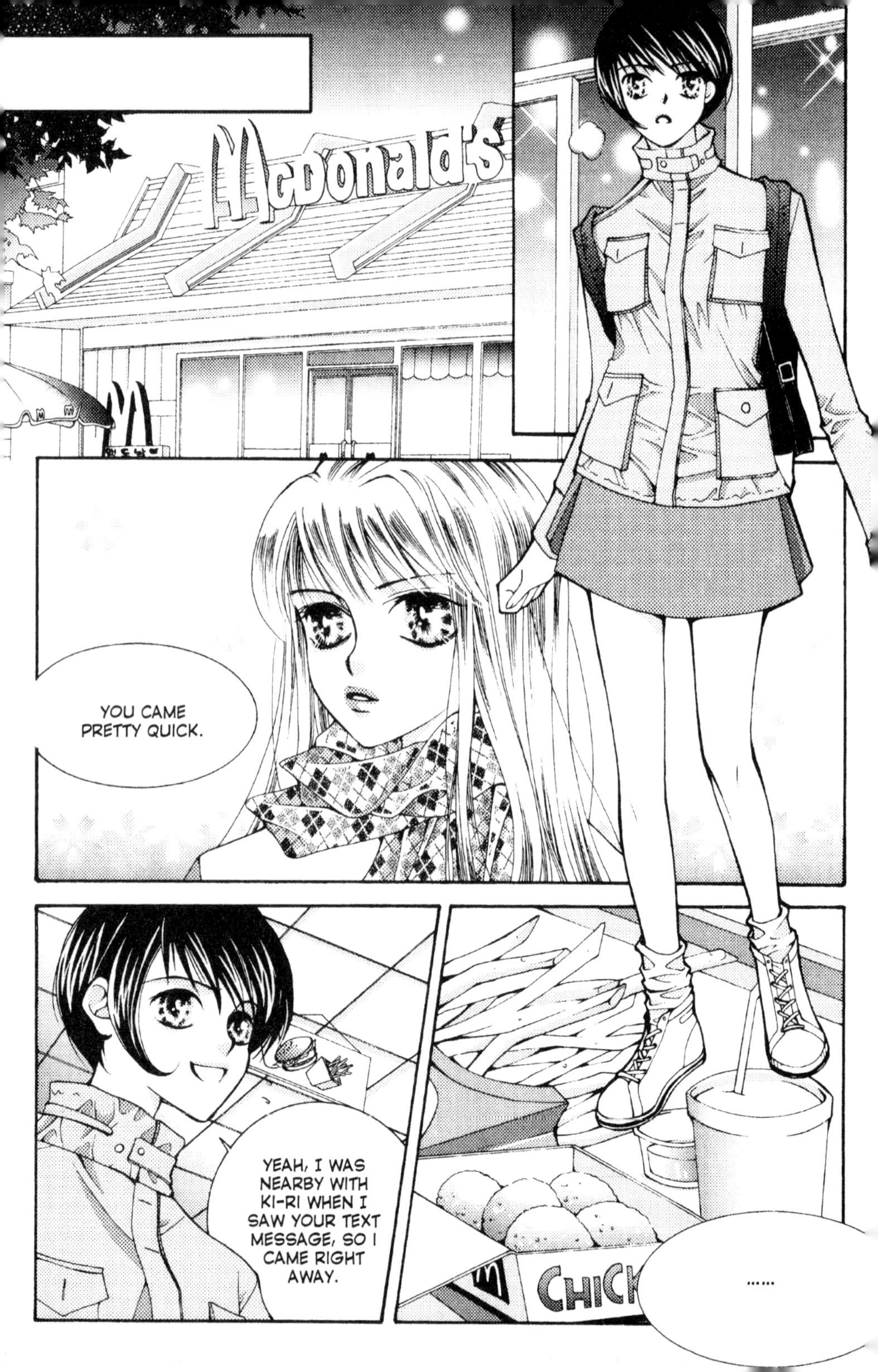
McDONALD'S
YOU CAME PRETTY QUICK.
YEAH, I WAS NEARBY WITH KI-RI WHEN I SAW YOUR TEXT MESSAGE, SO I CAME RIGHT AWAY.
CHICK
......

I'M SORRY--.

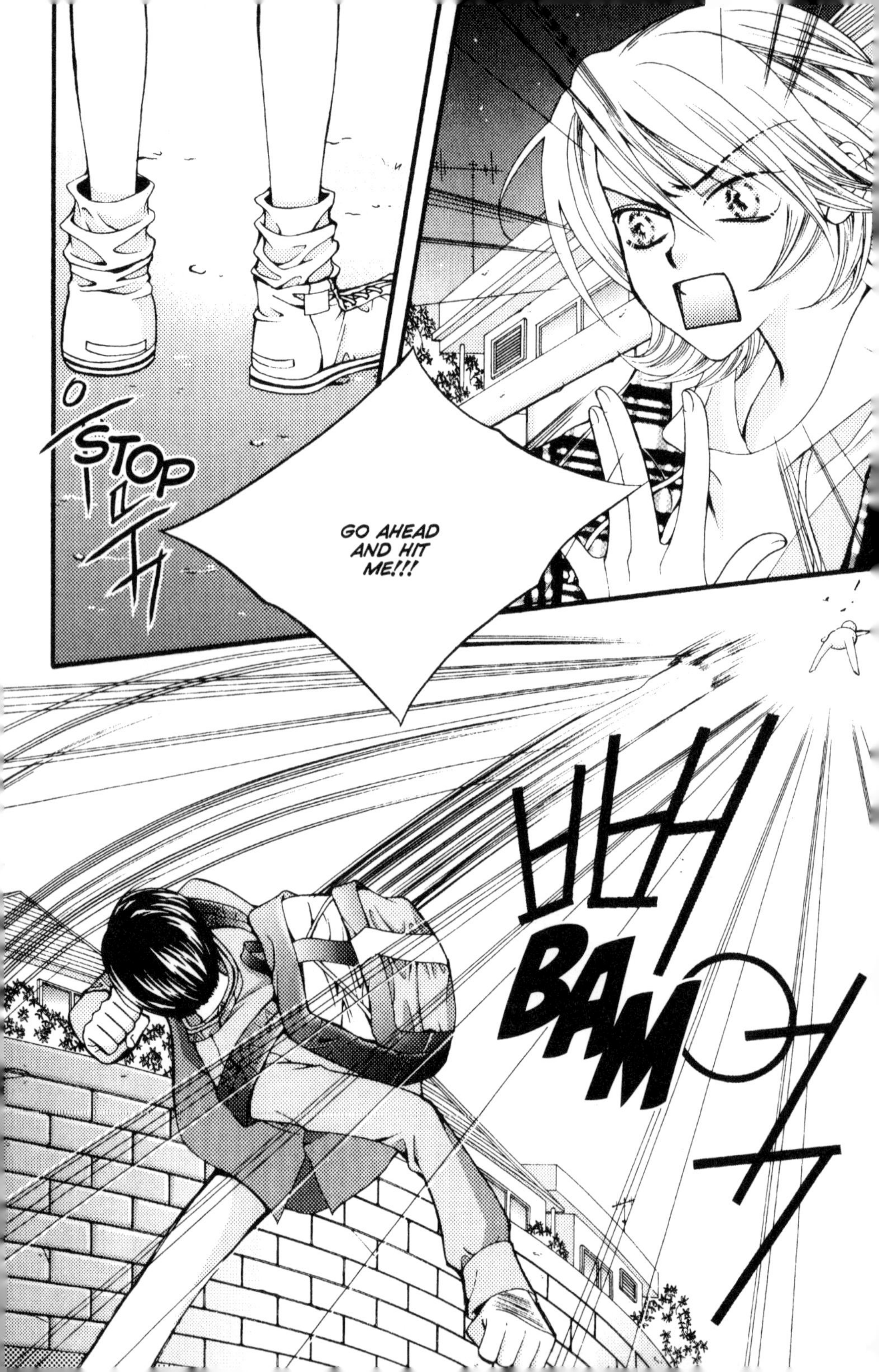
STOP
GO AHEAD AND HIT ME!!!
BAM

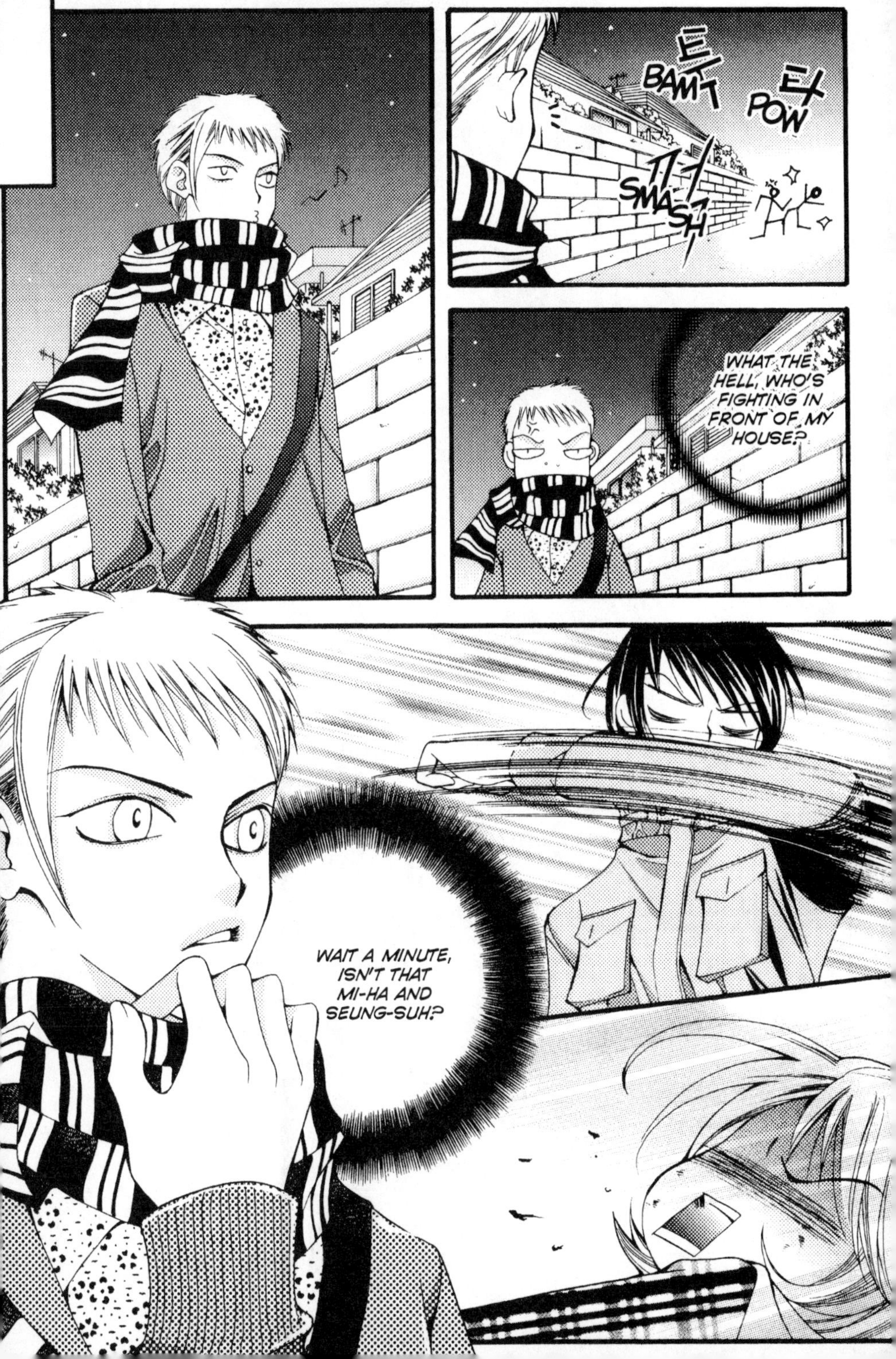
BAM
POW
SMASH
WHAT THE HELL, WHO'S FIGHTING IN FRONT OF MY HOUSE?
WAIT A MINUTE, ISN'T THAT MI-HA AND SEUNG-SUH?

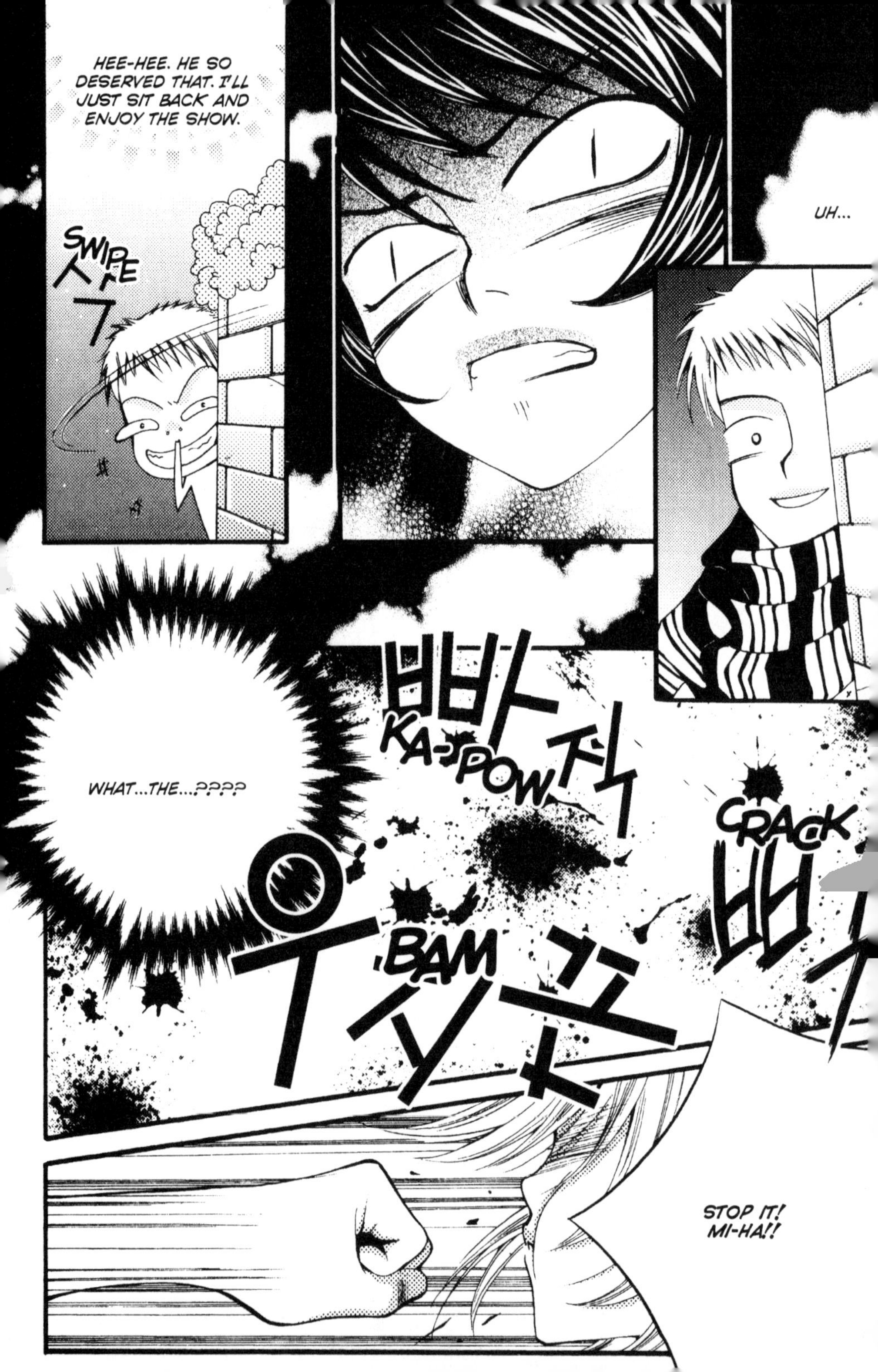
HEE-HEE. HE SO DESERVED THAT. I'LL JUST SIT BACK AND ENJOY THE SHOW.
SWIPE
UH...
WHAT...THE...????
KA-POW
BAM
CRACK
STOP IT! MI-HA!!

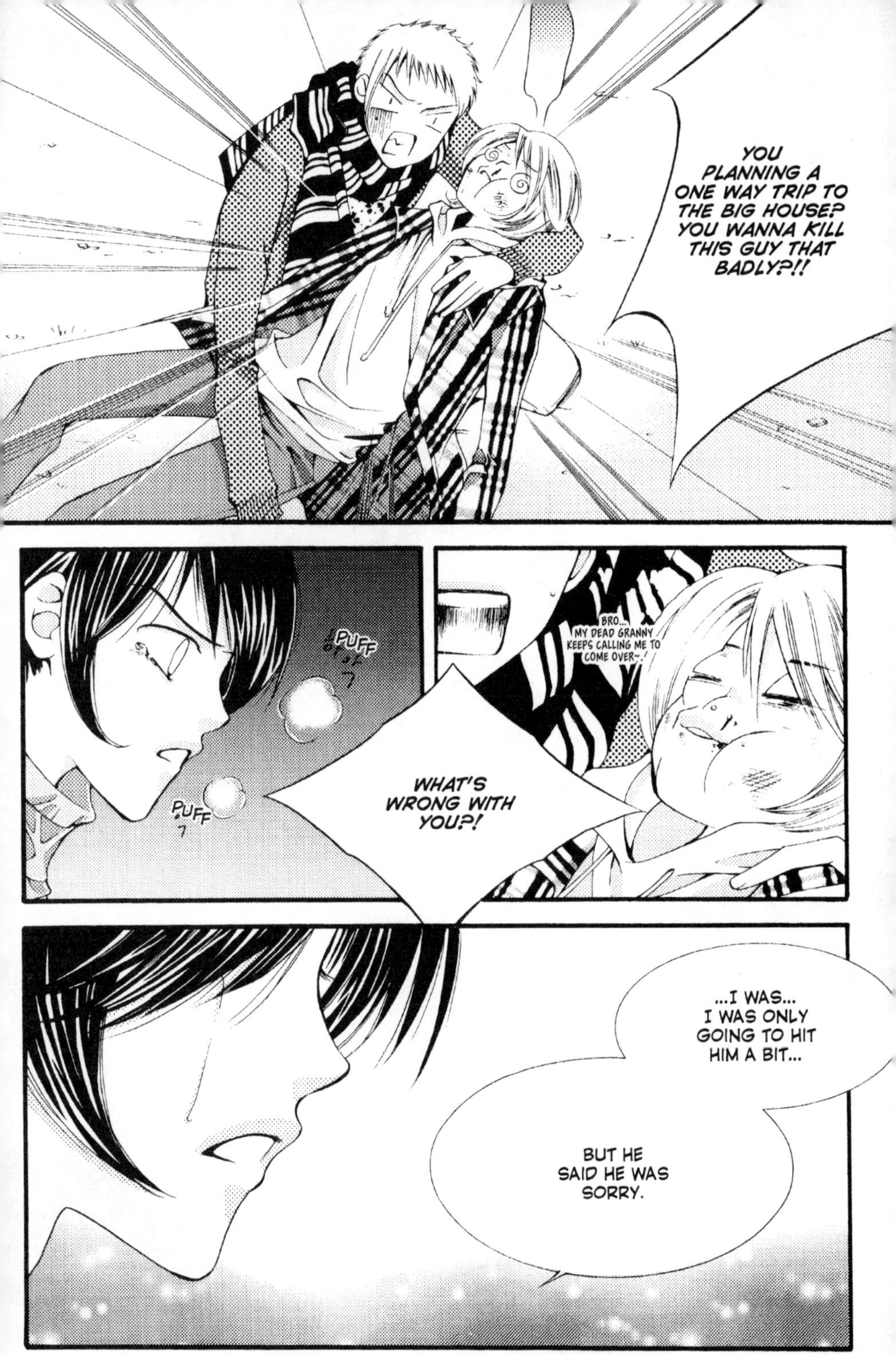
YOU PLANNING A ONE WAY TRIP TO THE BIG HOUSE? YOU WANNA KILL THIS GUY THAT BADLY?!!
PUFF
PUFF
WHAT'S WRONG WITH YOU?!
BRO... MY DEAD GRANNY KEEPS CALLING ME TO COME OVER~.
...I WAS... I WAS ONLY GOING TO HIT HIM A BIT...
BUT HE SAID HE WAS SORRY.

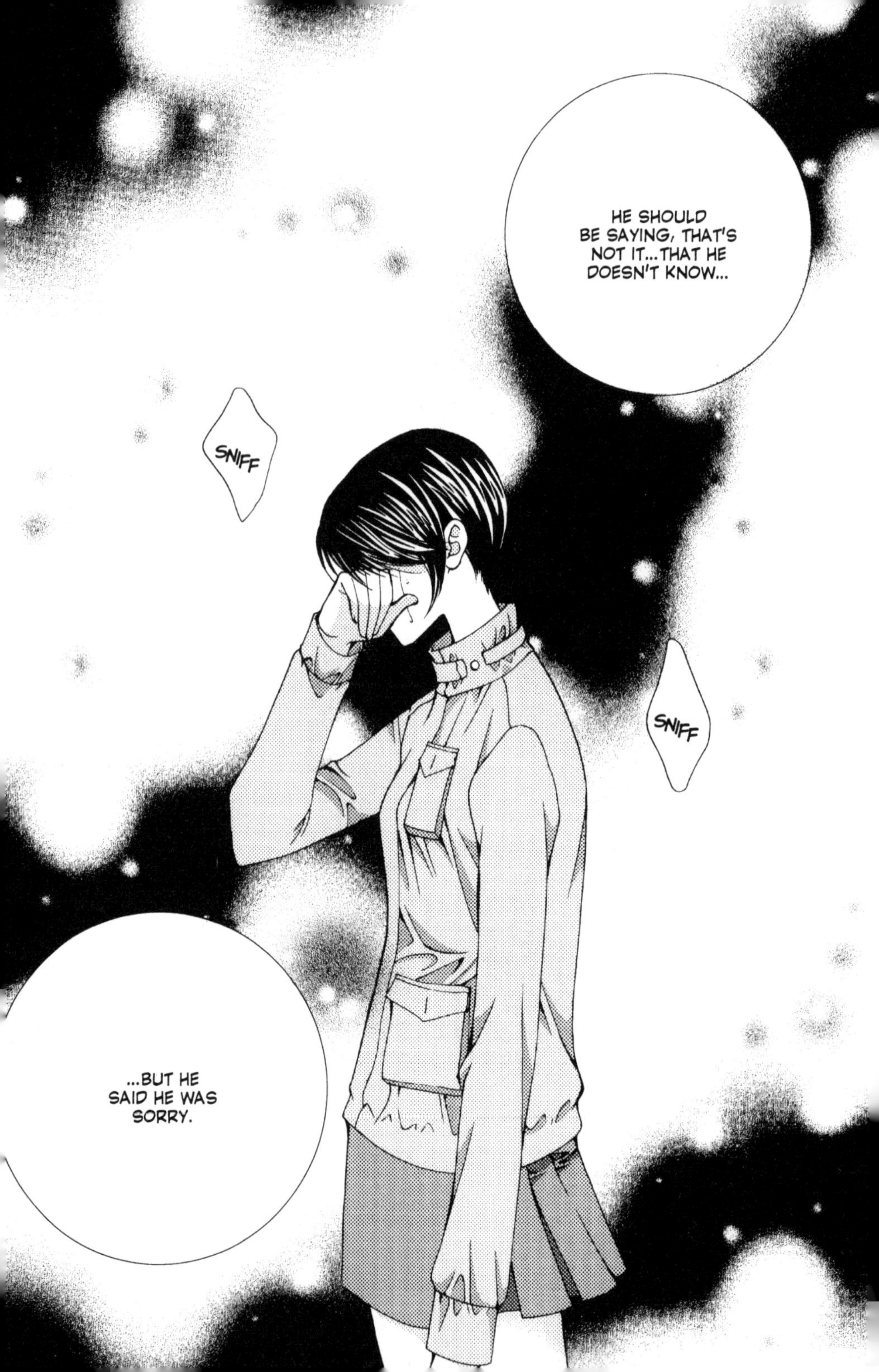
HE SHOULD BE SAYING, THAT'S NOT IT...THAT HE DOESN'T KNOW...
SNIFF
SNIFF
...BUT HE SAID HE WAS SORRY.

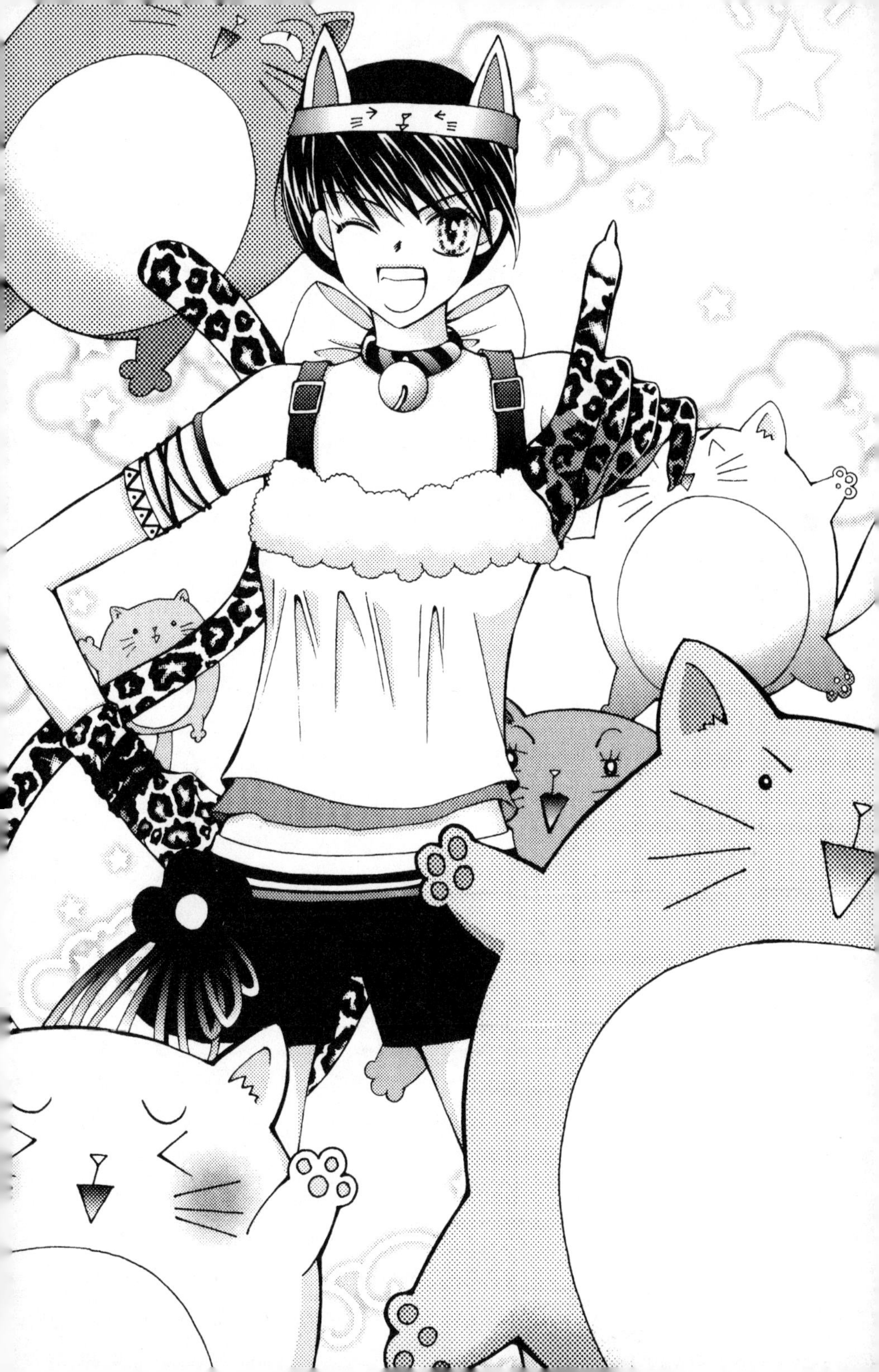

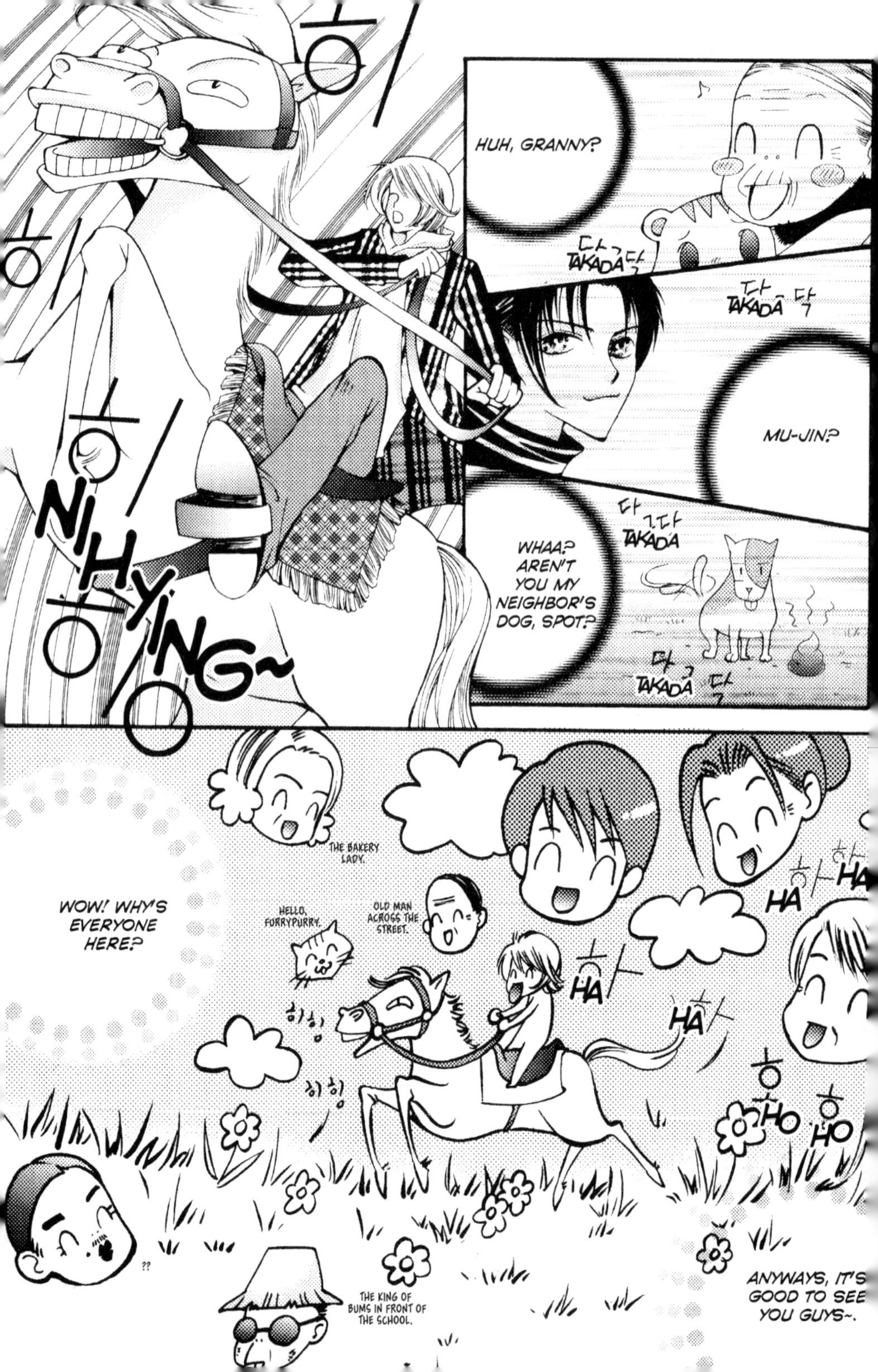

NIHYING~
HUH, GRANNY?
TAKADA
TAKADA
MU-JIN?
TAKADA
WHAA? AREN'T YOU MY NEIGHBOR'S DOG, SPOT?
TAKADA
THE BAKERY LADY.
WOW! WHY'S EVERYONE HERE?
HELLO, FURRYPURRY.
OLD MAN ACROSS THE STREET.
HA HA
HA
HA
HO HO
??
THE KING OF BUMS IN FRONT OF THE SCHOOL.
ANYWAYS, IT'S GOOD TO SEE YOU GUYS~.

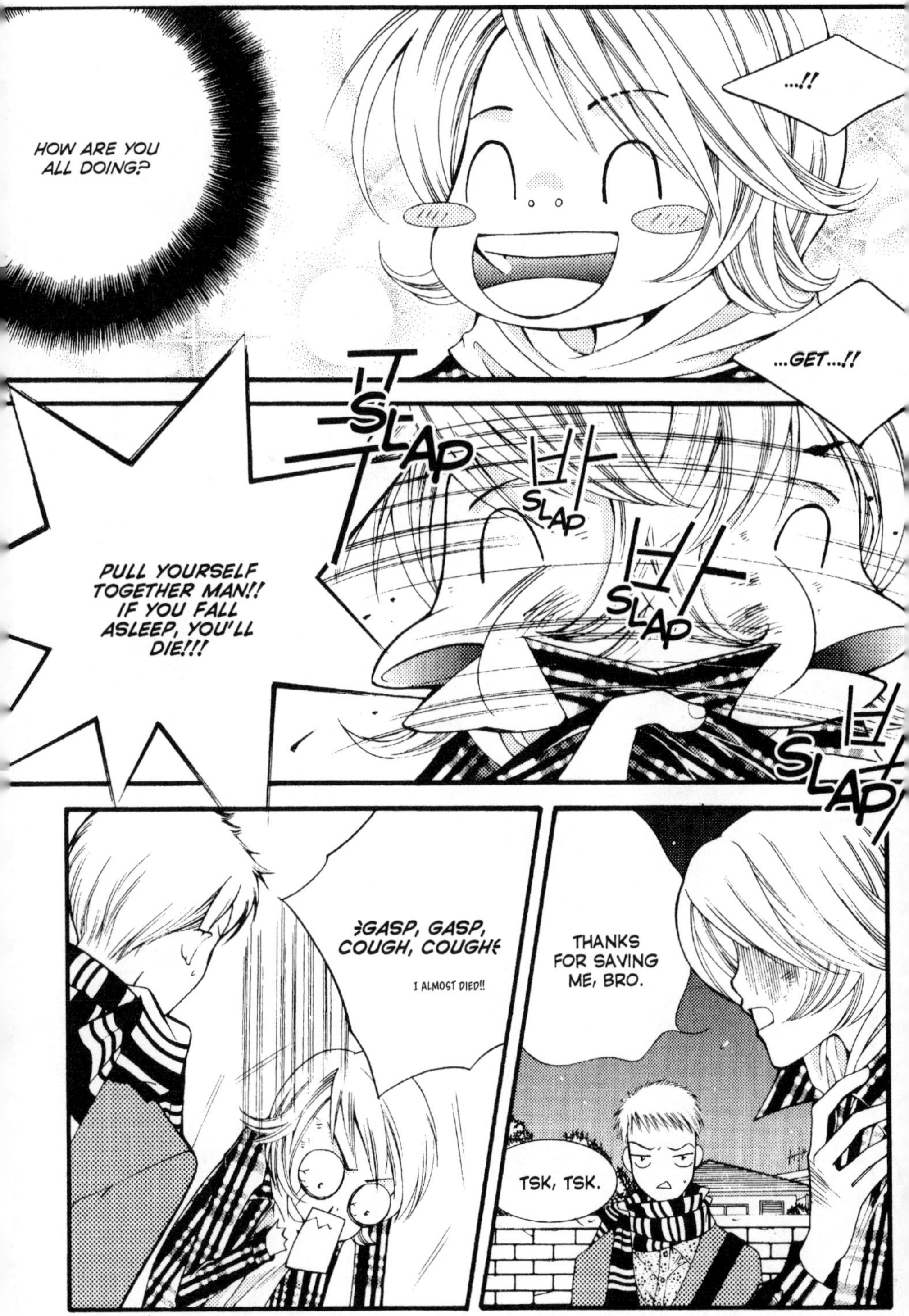
HOW ARE YOU ALL DOING?
...!!
...GET...!!
PULL YOURSELF TOGETHER MAN!! IF YOU FALL ASLEEP, YOU'LL DIE!!!
SLAP
SLAP
SLAP
SLAP
GASP, GASP, COUGH, COUGH
I ALMOST DIED!!
THANKS FOR SAVING ME, BRO.
TSK, TSK.

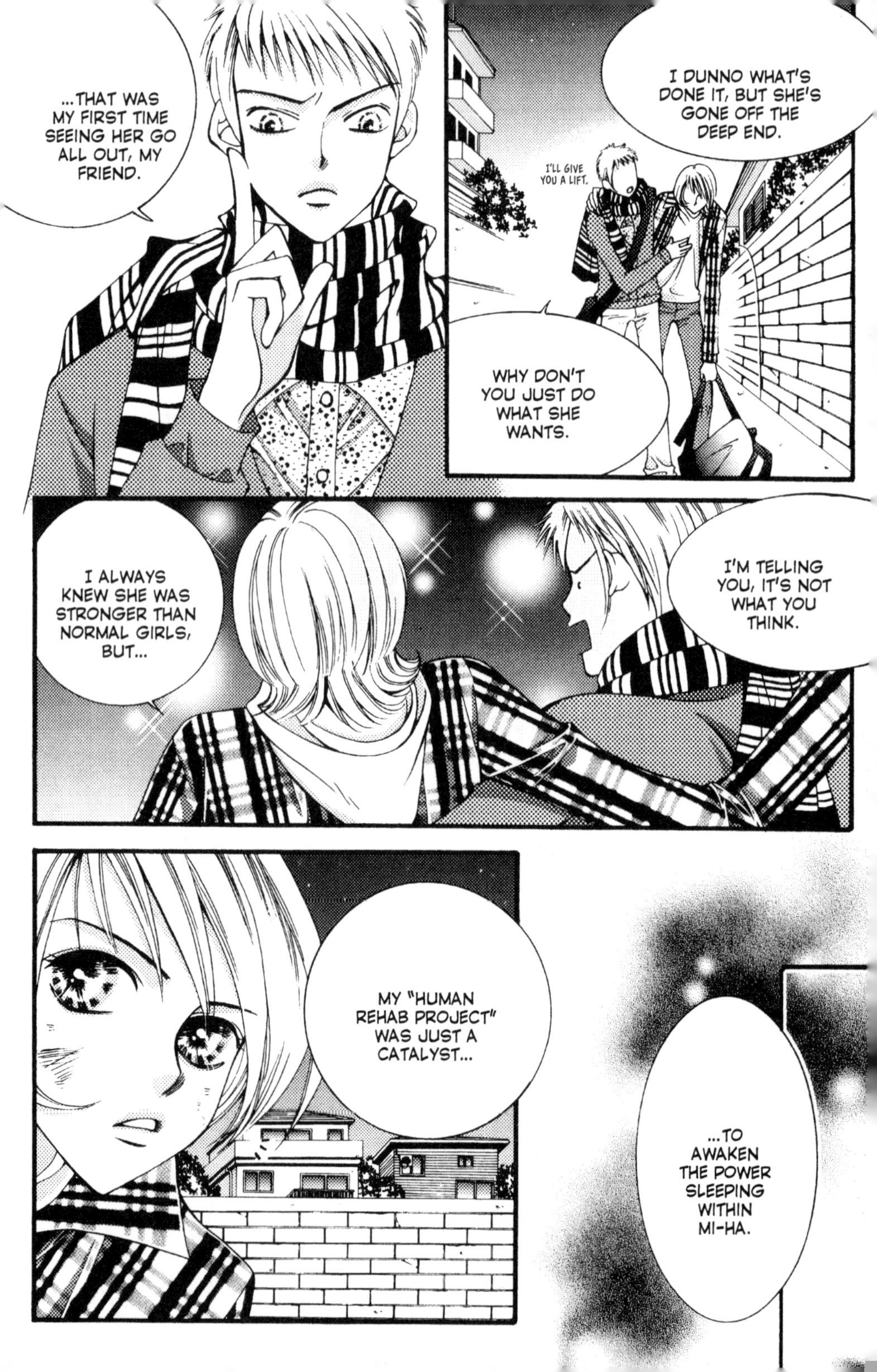
...THAT WAS MY FIRST TIME SEEING HER GO ALL OUT, MY FRIEND.
I DUNNO WHAT'S DONE IT, BUT SHE'S GONE OFF THE DEEP END.
I'LL GIVE YOU A LIFT.
WHY DON'T YOU JUST DO WHAT SHE WANTS.
I ALWAYS KNEW SHE WAS STRONGER THAN NORMAL GIRLS, BUT...
I'M TELLING YOU, IT'S NOT WHAT YOU THINK.
MY "HUMAN REHAB PROJECT" WAS JUST A CATALYST...
...TO AWAKEN THE POWER SLEEPING WITHIN MI-HA.

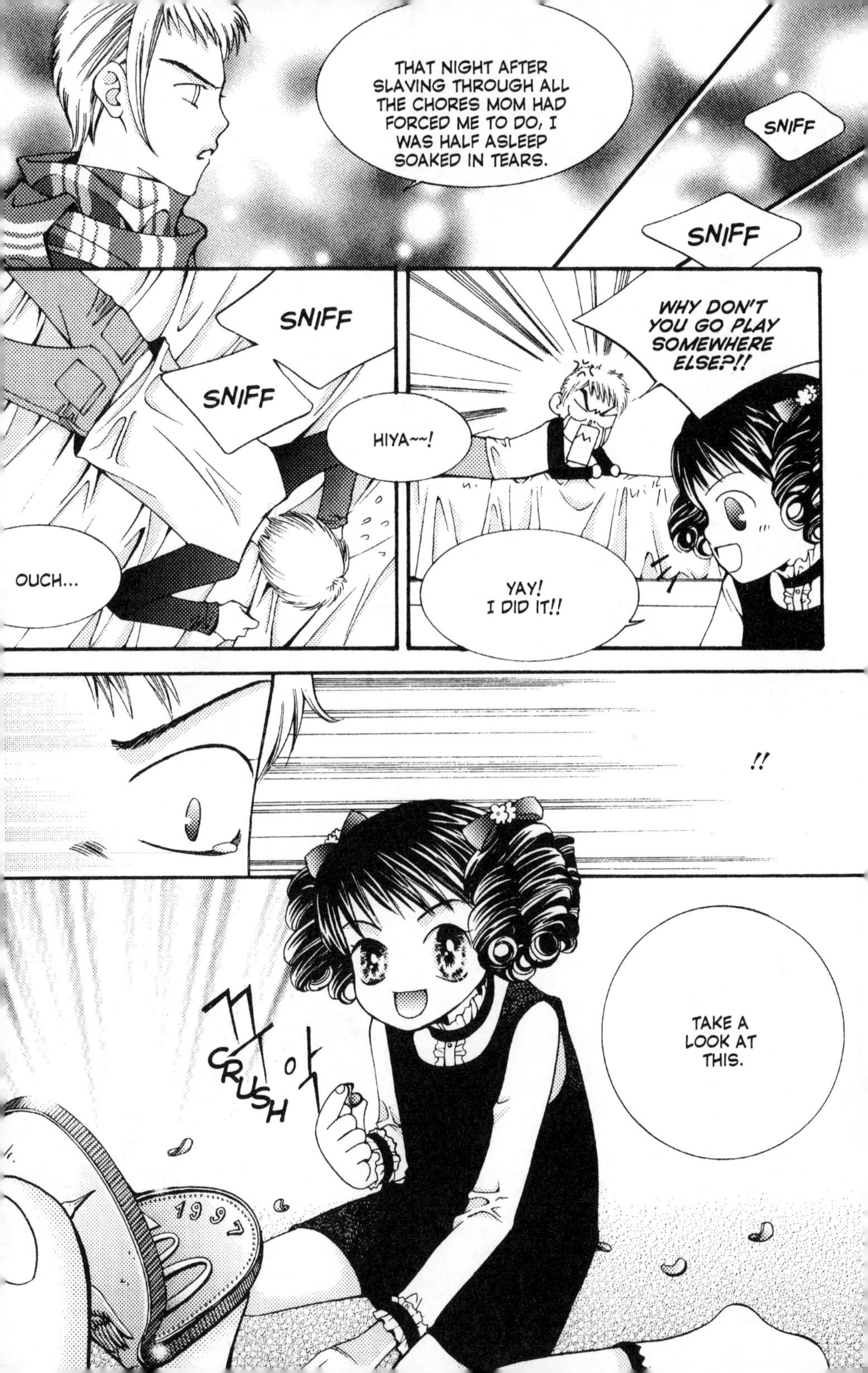
THAT NIGHT AFTER SLAVING THROUGH ALL THE CHORES MOM HAD FORCED ME TO DO, I WAS HALF ASLEEP SOAKED IN TEARS.
SNIFF
SNIFF
SNIFF
SNIFF
HIYA~~!
OUCH...
WHY DON'T YOU GO PLAY SOMEWHERE ELSE?!!
YAY! I DID IT!!
!!
CRUSH
TAKE A LOOK AT THIS.

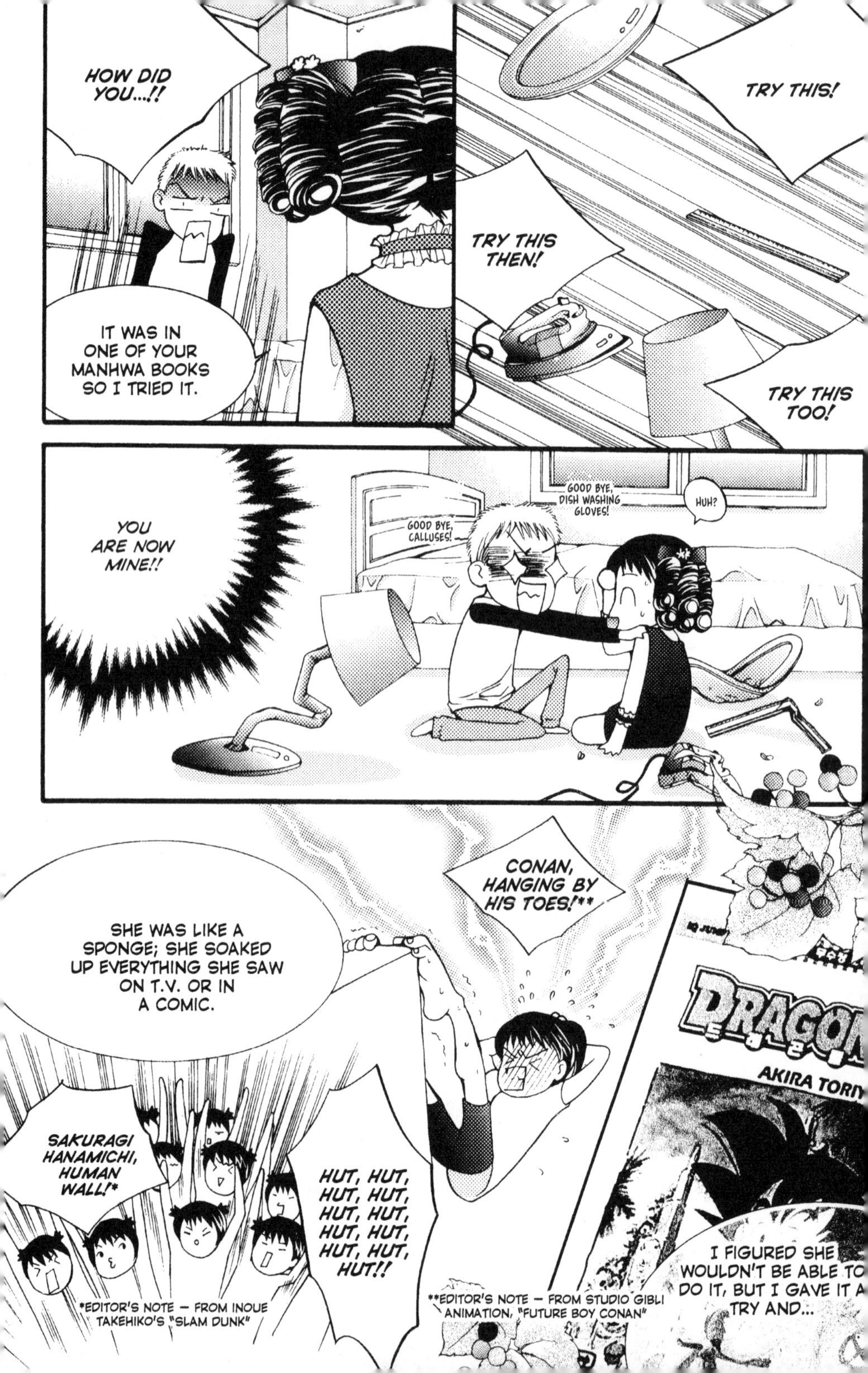
HOW DID YOU...!!
IT WAS IN ONE OF YOUR MANHWA BOOKS SO I TRIED IT.
TRY THIS!
TRY THIS THEN!
TRY THIS TOO!
YOU ARE NOW MINE!!
GOOD BYE, CALLUSES!
GOOD BYE, DISH WASHING GLOVES!
HUH?
SHE WAS LIKE A SPONGE; SHE SOAKED UP EVERYTHING SHE SAW ON T.V. OR IN A COMIC.
CONAN, HANGING BY HIS TOES!**
SAKURAGI HANAMICHI, HUMAN WALL!*
HUT, HUT, HUT, HUT, HUT, HUT, HUT, HUT, HUT, HUT, HUT!!
*EDITOR'S NOTE — FROM INOUE TAKEHIKO'S "SLAM DUNK"
**EDITOR'S NOTE — FROM STUDIO GIBLI ANIMATION, "FUTURE BOY CONAN"
I FIGURED SHE WOULDN'T BE ABLE TO DO IT, BUT I GAVE IT A TRY AND...

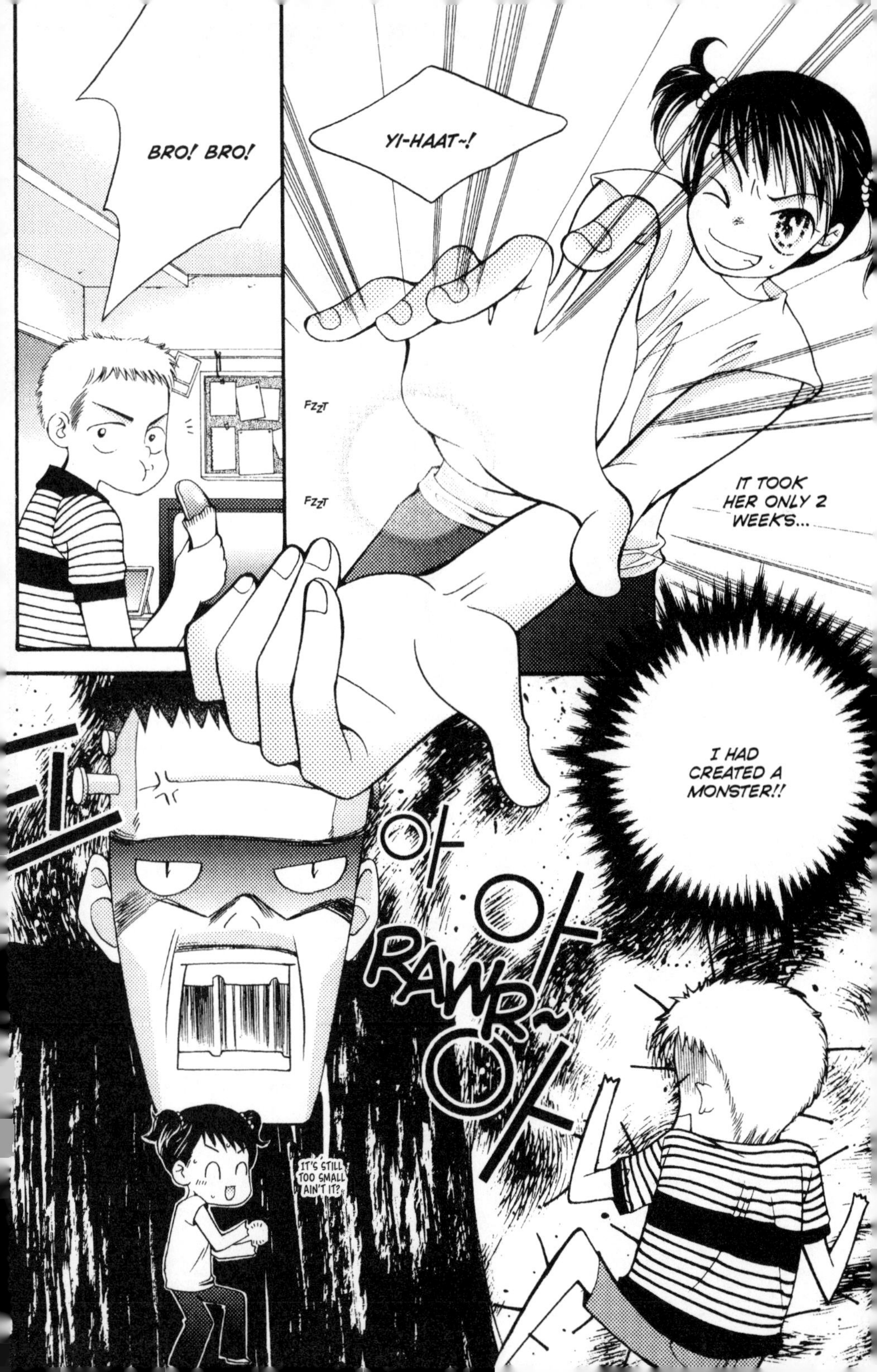
BRO! BRO!
YI-HAAT~!
FZZT
FZZT
IT TOOK HER ONLY 2 WEEKS...
I HAD CREATED A MONSTER!!
RAWR~
IT'S STILL TOO SMALL AIN'T IT?

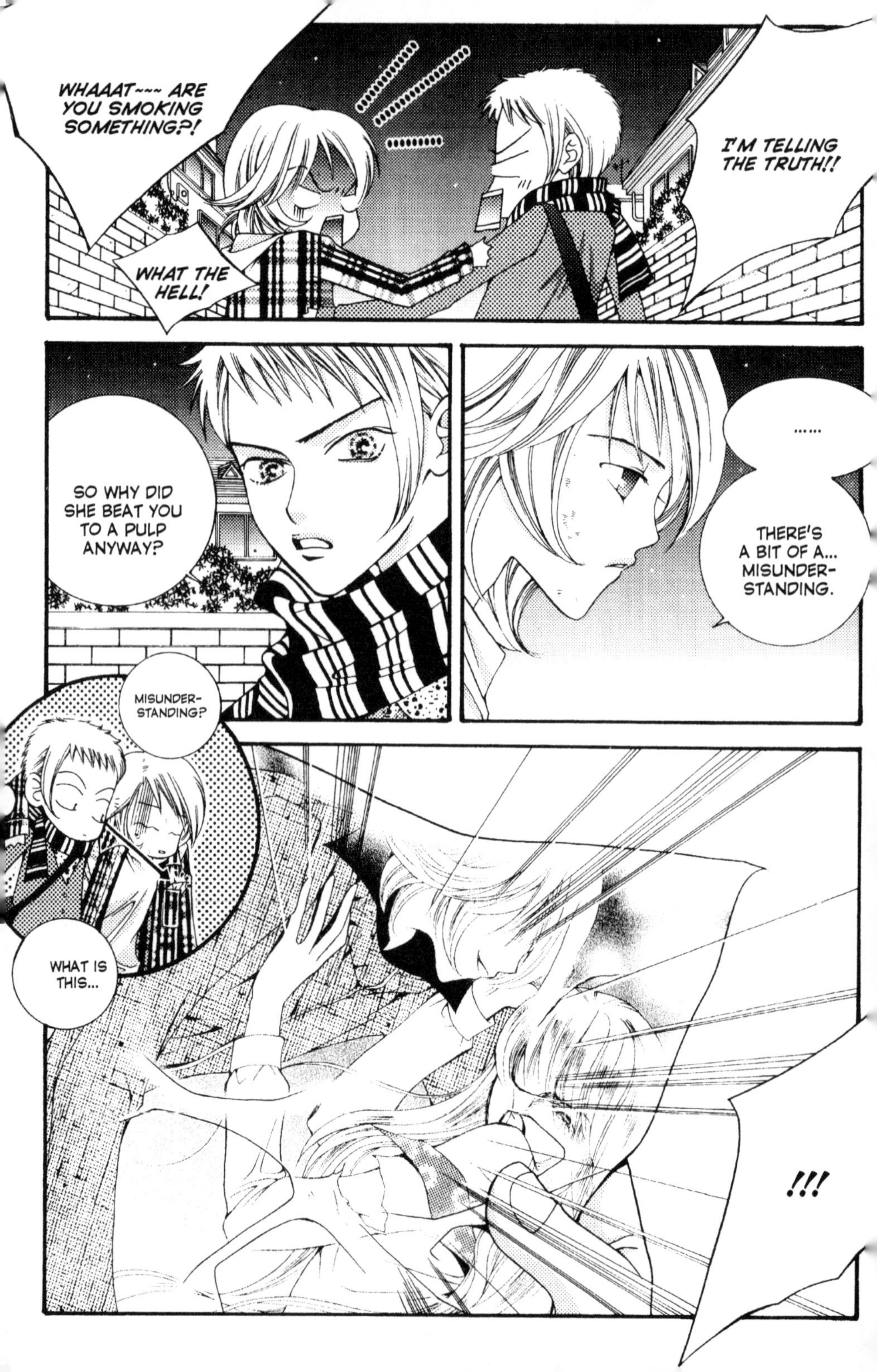
WHAAAT~~~ ARE YOU SMOKING SOMETHING?!
WHAT THE HELL!
I'M TELLING THE TRUTH!!
SO WHY DID SHE BEAT YOU TO A PULP ANYWAY?
……
THERE'S A BIT OF A... MISUNDER-STANDING.
MISUNDER-STANDING?
WHAT IS THIS...
!!!

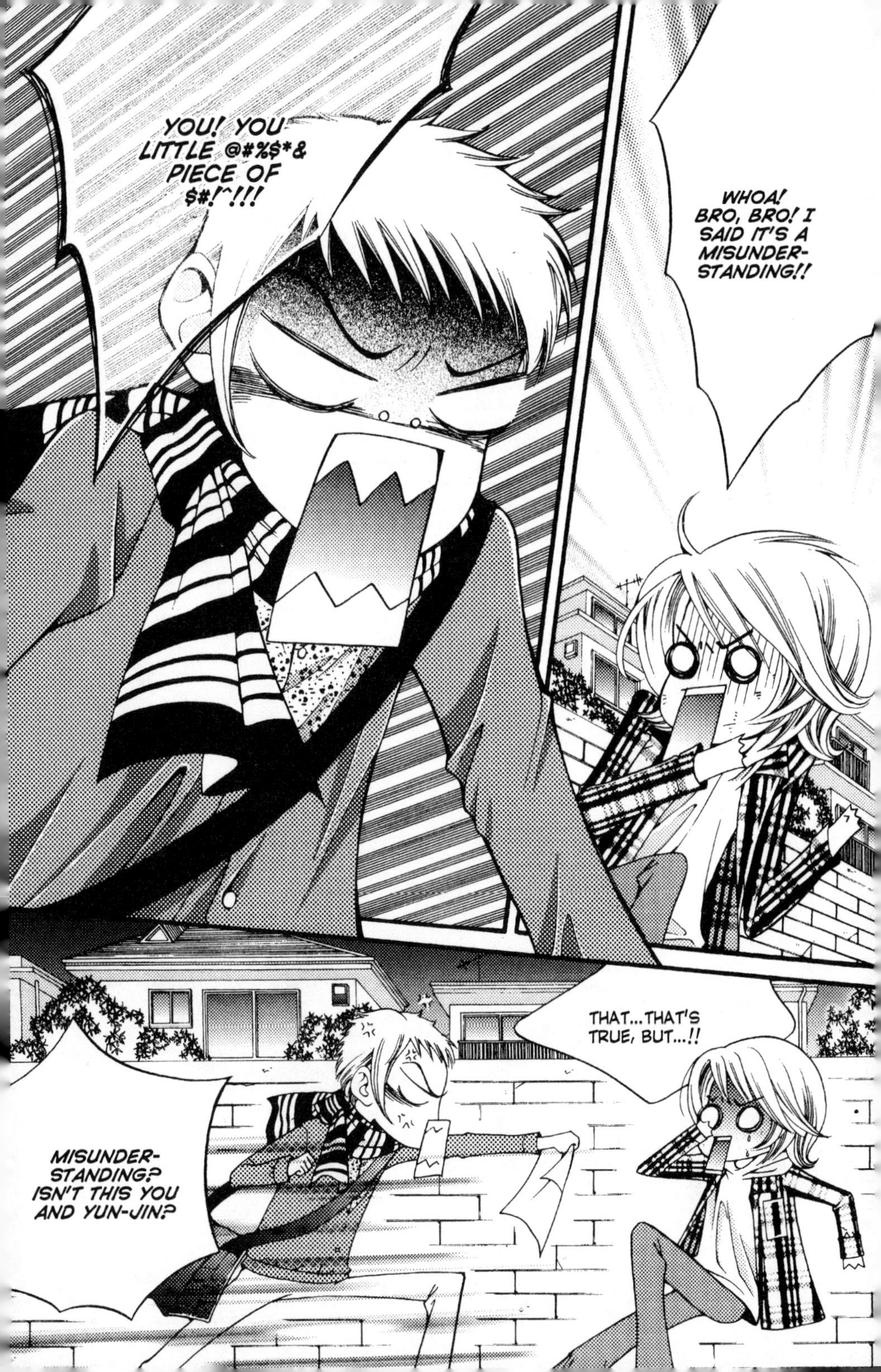
YOU! YOU LITTLE @#%$*& PIECE OF $#!^!!!
WHOA! BRO, BRO! I SAID IT'S A MISUNDER-STANDING!!
MISUNDER-STANDING? ISN'T THIS YOU AND YUN-JIN?
THAT...THAT'S TRUE, BUT...!!

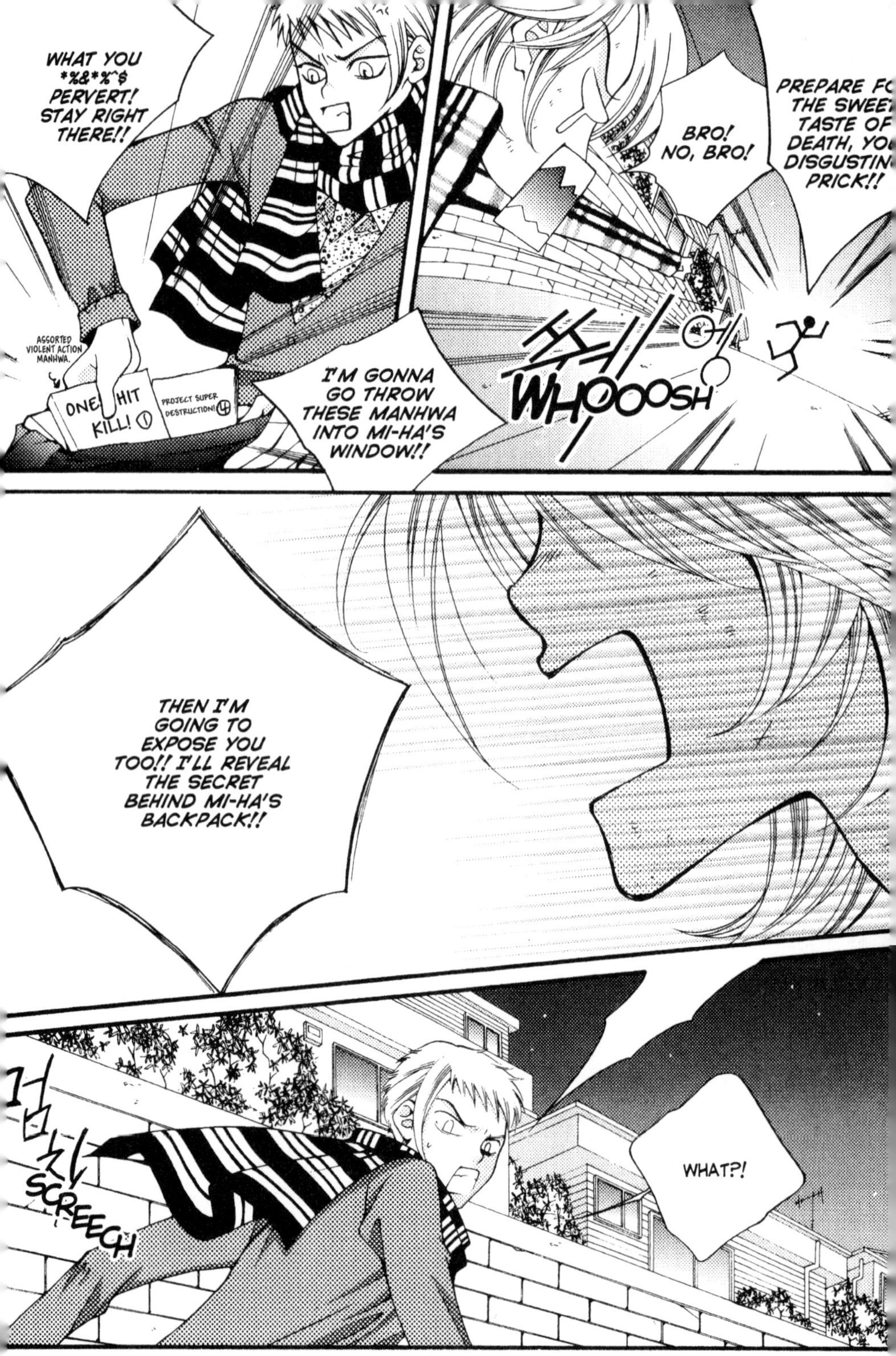
WHAT YOU *%&*%^$ PERVERT! STAY RIGHT THERE!!
ASSORTED VIOLENT ACTION MANHWA.
ONE HIT KILL! 1
PROJECT SUPER DESTRUCTION! 4
I'M GONNA GO THROW THESE MANHWA INTO MI-HA'S WINDOW!!
BRO! NO, BRO!
PREPARE FO THE SWEE TASTE OF DEATH, YO DISGUSTIN PRICK!!
WHOOOSH
THEN I'M GOING TO EXPOSE YOU TOO!! I'LL REVEAL THE SECRET BEHIND MI-HA'S BACKPACK!!
SCREEECH
WHAT?!

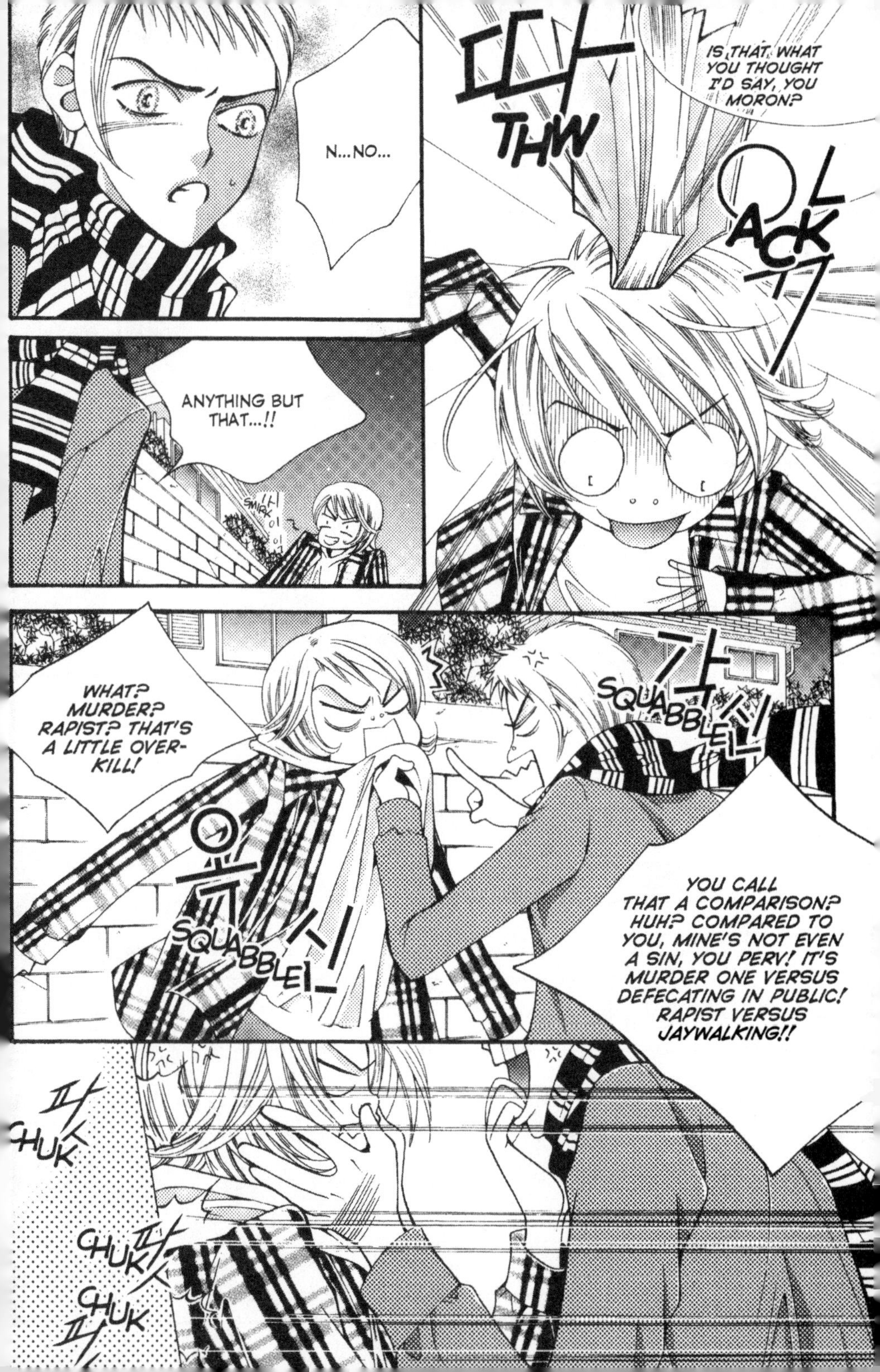
N...NO...
ANYTHING BUT THAT...!!
SMIRK
IS THAT WHAT YOU THOUGHT I'D SAY, YOU MORON?
THW
ACK
WHAT? MURDER? RAPIST? THAT'S A LITTLE OVER-KILL!
SQUABBLE!
SQUABBLE!
YOU CALL THAT A COMPARISON? HUH? COMPARED TO YOU, MINE'S NOT EVEN A SIN, YOU PERV! IT'S MURDER ONE VERSUS DEFECATING IN PUBLIC! RAPIST VERSUS JAYWALKING!!
CHUK
CHUK
CHUK

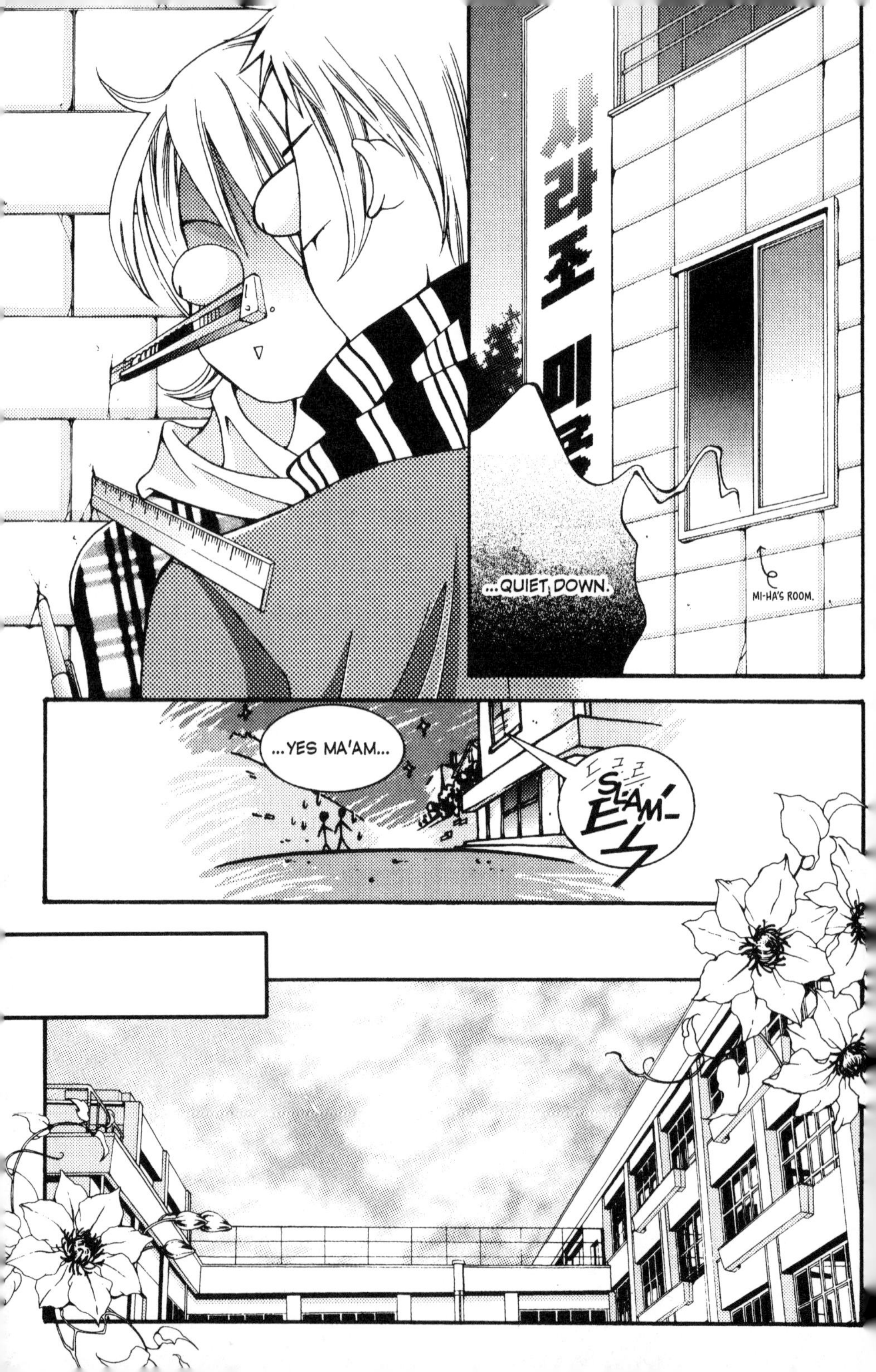
사라조 미
...QUIET DOWN.
MI-HA'S ROOM.
...YES MA'AM...
SLAM

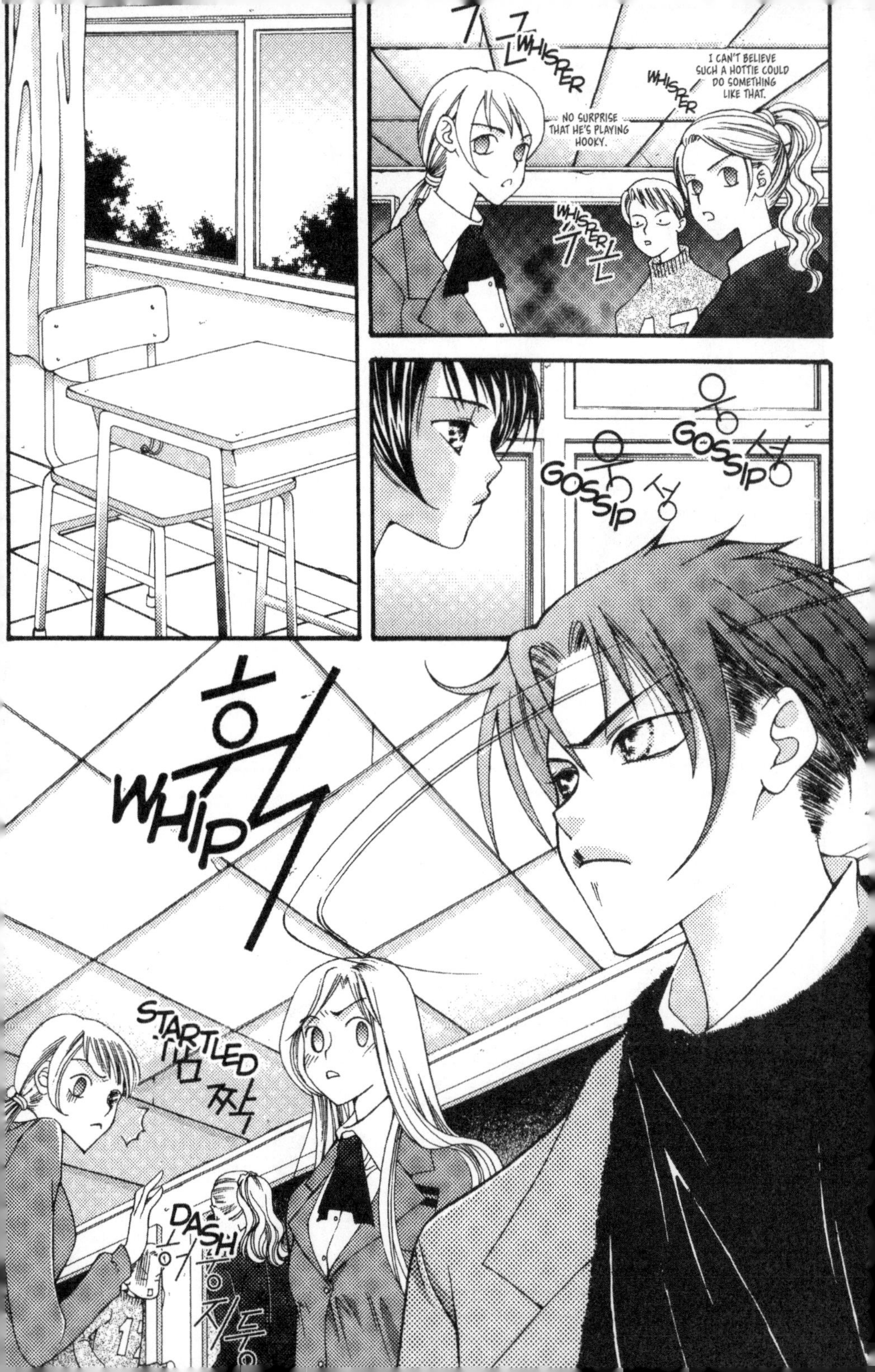
WHISPER
NO SURPRISE THAT HE'S PLAYING HOOKY.
WHISPER
I CAN'T BELIEVE SUCH A HOTTIE COULD DO SOMETHING LIKE THAT.
WHISPER
GOSSIP
GOSSIP
WHIP
STARTLED
DASH

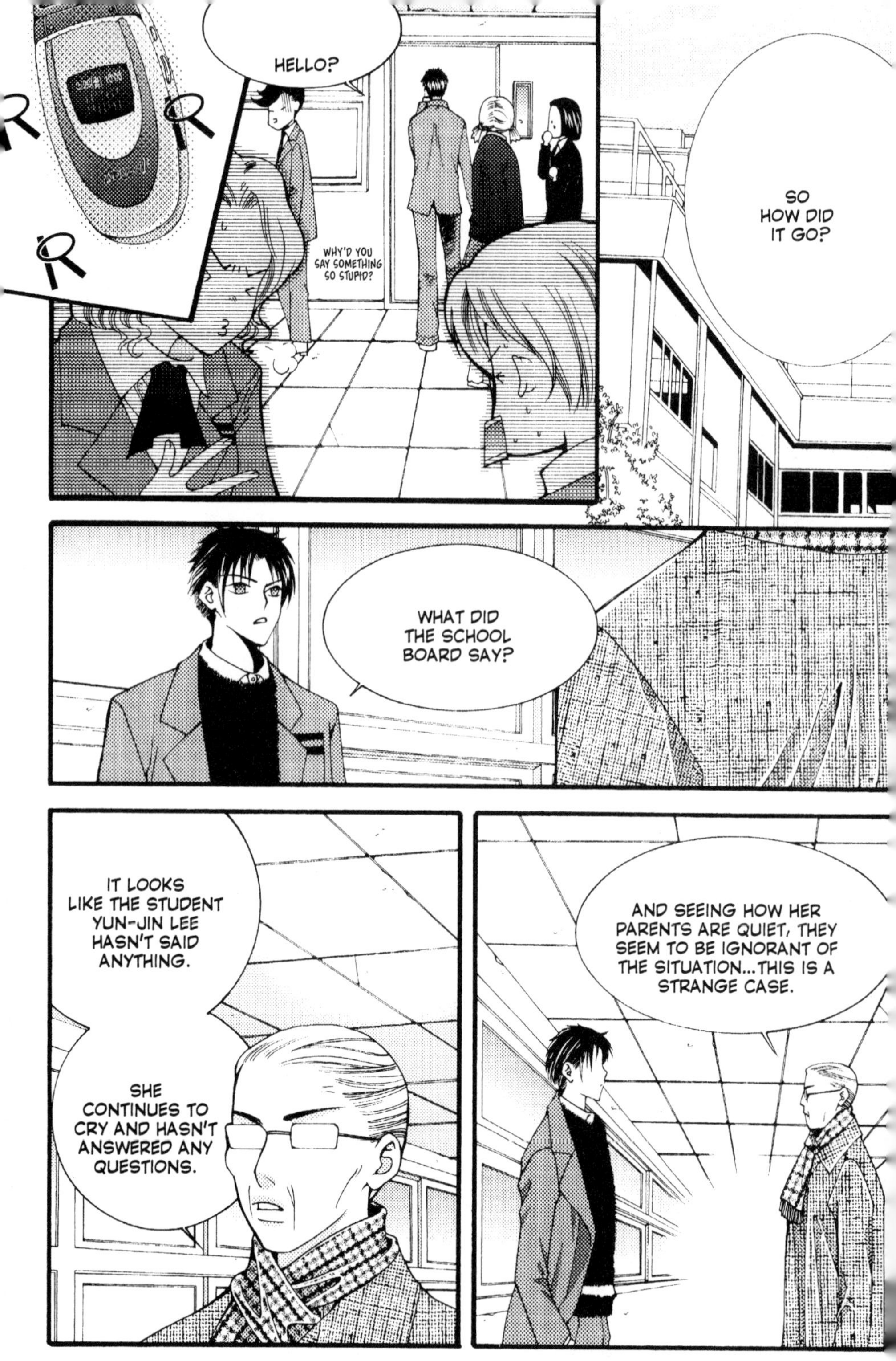
R R R
HELLO?
WHY'D YOU SAY SOMETHING SO STUPID?
SO HOW DID IT GO?
WHAT DID THE SCHOOL BOARD SAY?
IT LOOKS LIKE THE STUDENT YUN-JIN LEE HASN'T SAID ANYTHING.
SHE CONTINUES TO CRY AND HASN'T ANSWERED ANY QUESTIONS.
AND SEEING HOW HER PARENTS ARE QUIET, THEY SEEM TO BE IGNORANT OF THE SITUATION...THIS IS A STRANGE CASE.

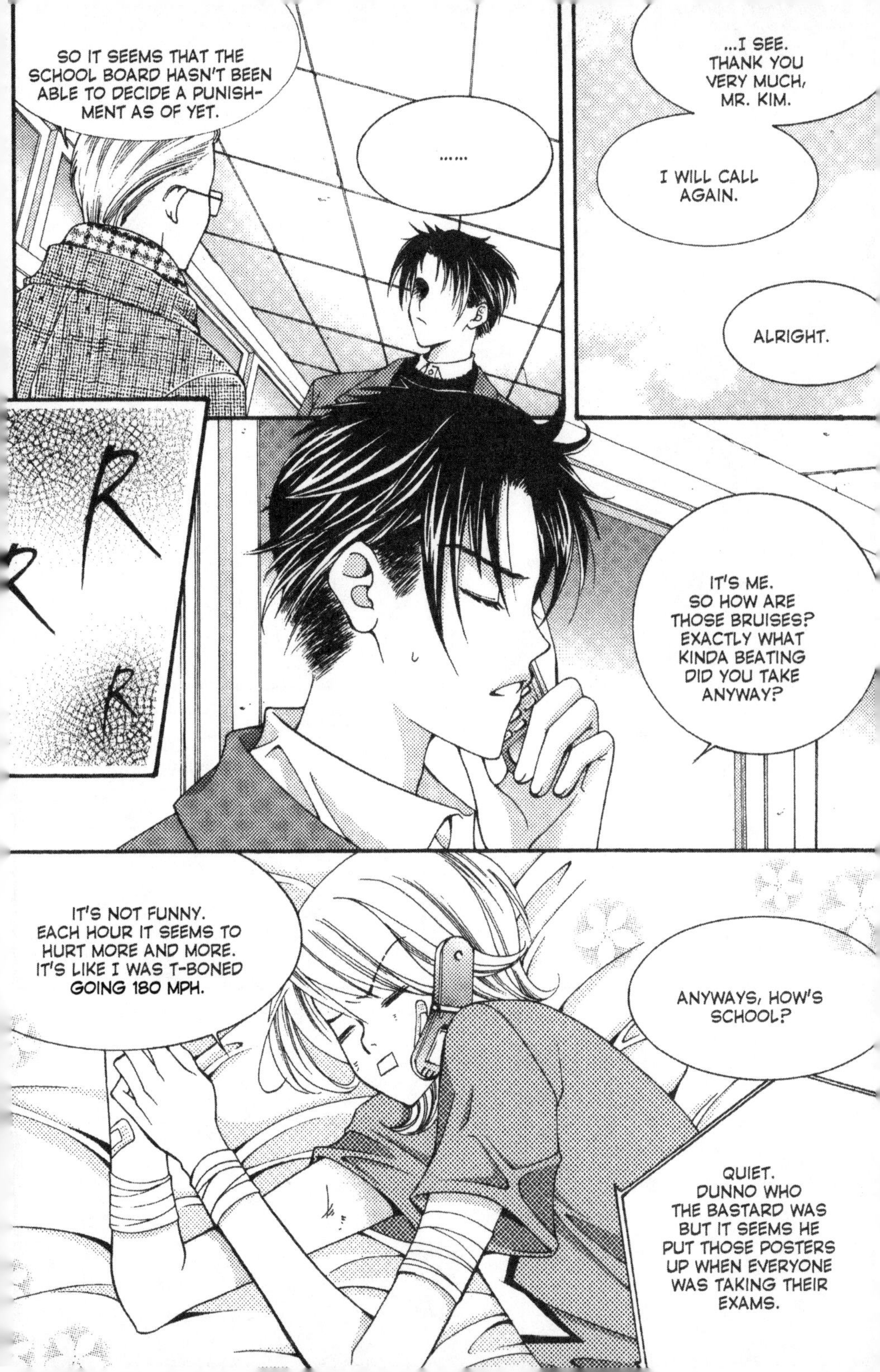
SO IT SEEMS THAT THE SCHOOL BOARD HASN'T BEEN ABLE TO DECIDE A PUNISHMENT AS OF YET.
......
...I SEE. THANK YOU VERY MUCH, MR. KIM.
I WILL CALL AGAIN.
ALRIGHT.
RRRR
IT'S ME. SO HOW ARE THOSE BRUISES? EXACTLY WHAT KINDA BEATING DID YOU TAKE ANYWAY?
IT'S NOT FUNNY. EACH HOUR IT SEEMS TO HURT MORE AND MORE. IT'S LIKE I WAS T-BONED GOING 180 MPH.
ANYWAYS, HOW'S SCHOOL?
QUIET. DUNNO WHO THE BASTARD WAS BUT IT SEEMS HE PUT THOSE POSTERS UP WHEN EVERYONE WAS TAKING THEIR EXAMS.

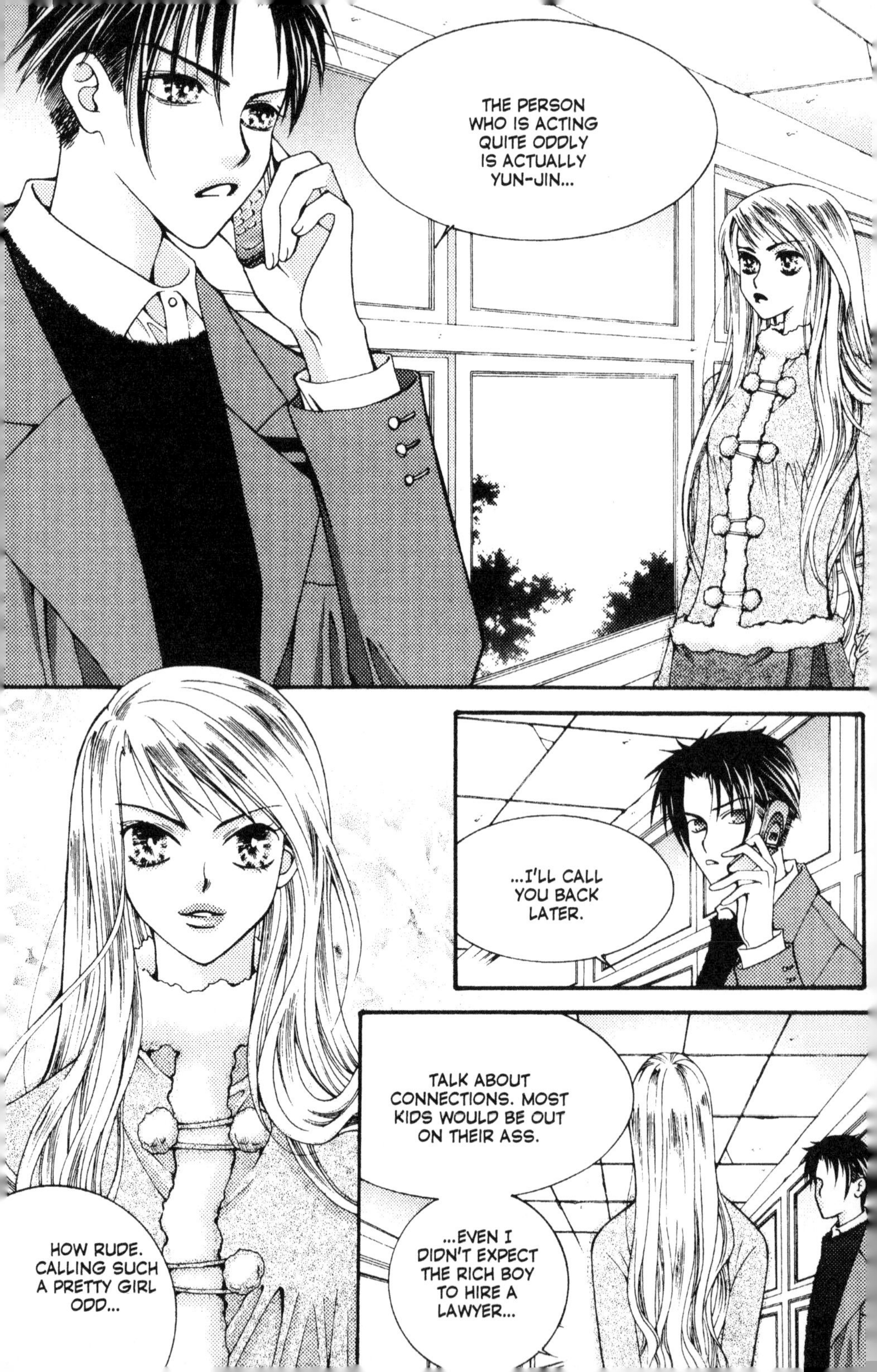
THE PERSON WHO IS ACTING QUITE ODDLY IS ACTUALLY YUN-JIN...
HOW RUDE. CALLING SUCH A PRETTY GIRL ODD...
...I'LL CALL YOU BACK LATER.
TALK ABOUT CONNECTIONS. MOST KIDS WOULD BE OUT ON THEIR ASS.
...EVEN I DIDN'T EXPECT THE RICH BOY TO HIRE A LAWYER...

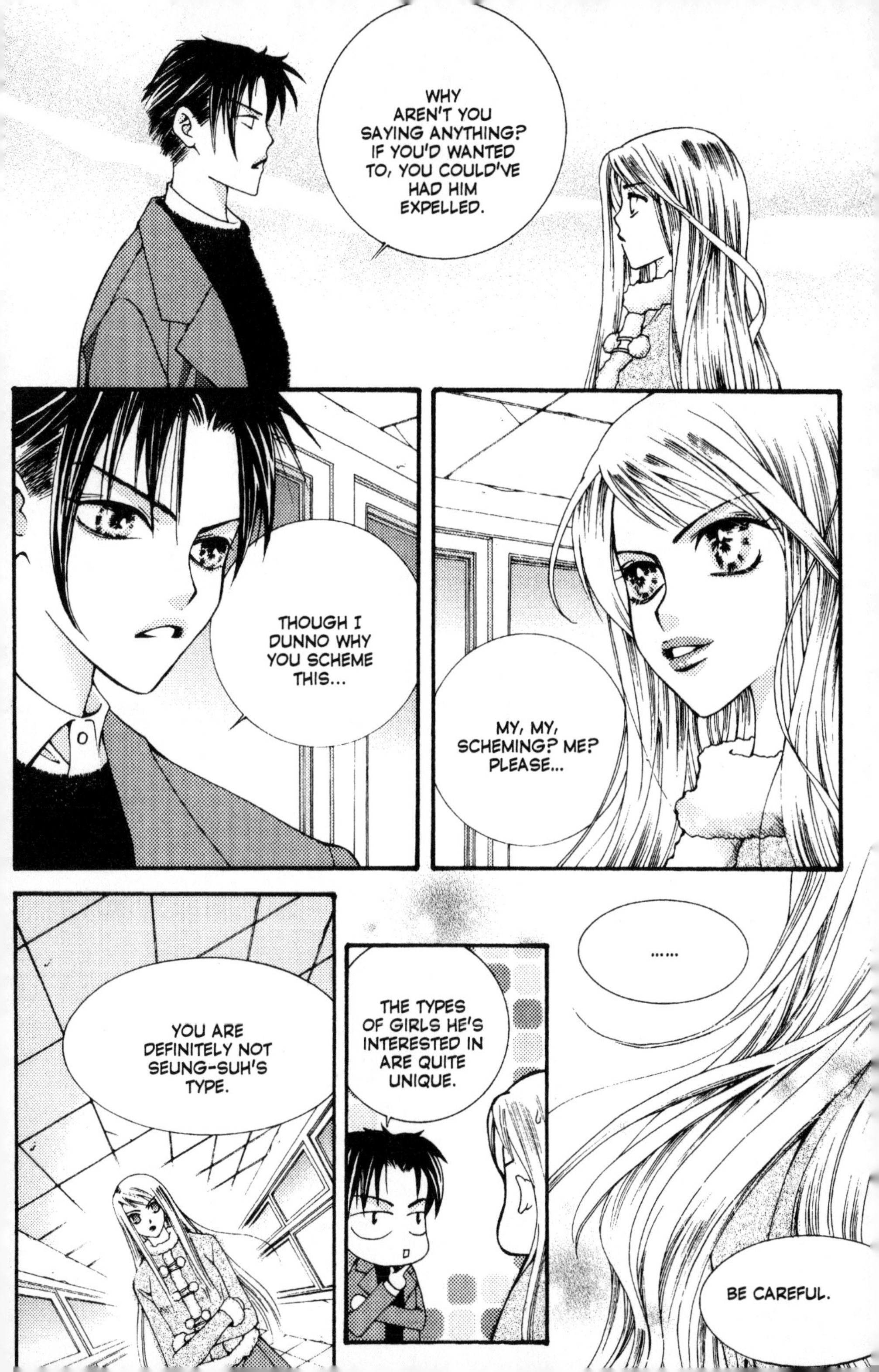
WHY AREN'T YOU SAYING ANYTHING? IF YOU'D WANTED TO, YOU COULD'VE HAD HIM EXPELLED.
THOUGH I DUNNO WHY YOU SCHEME THIS...
MY, MY, SCHEMING? ME? PLEASE...
YOU ARE DEFINITELY NOT SEUNG-SUH'S TYPE.
THE TYPES OF GIRLS HE'S INTERESTED IN ARE QUITE UNIQUE.
......
BE CAREFUL.

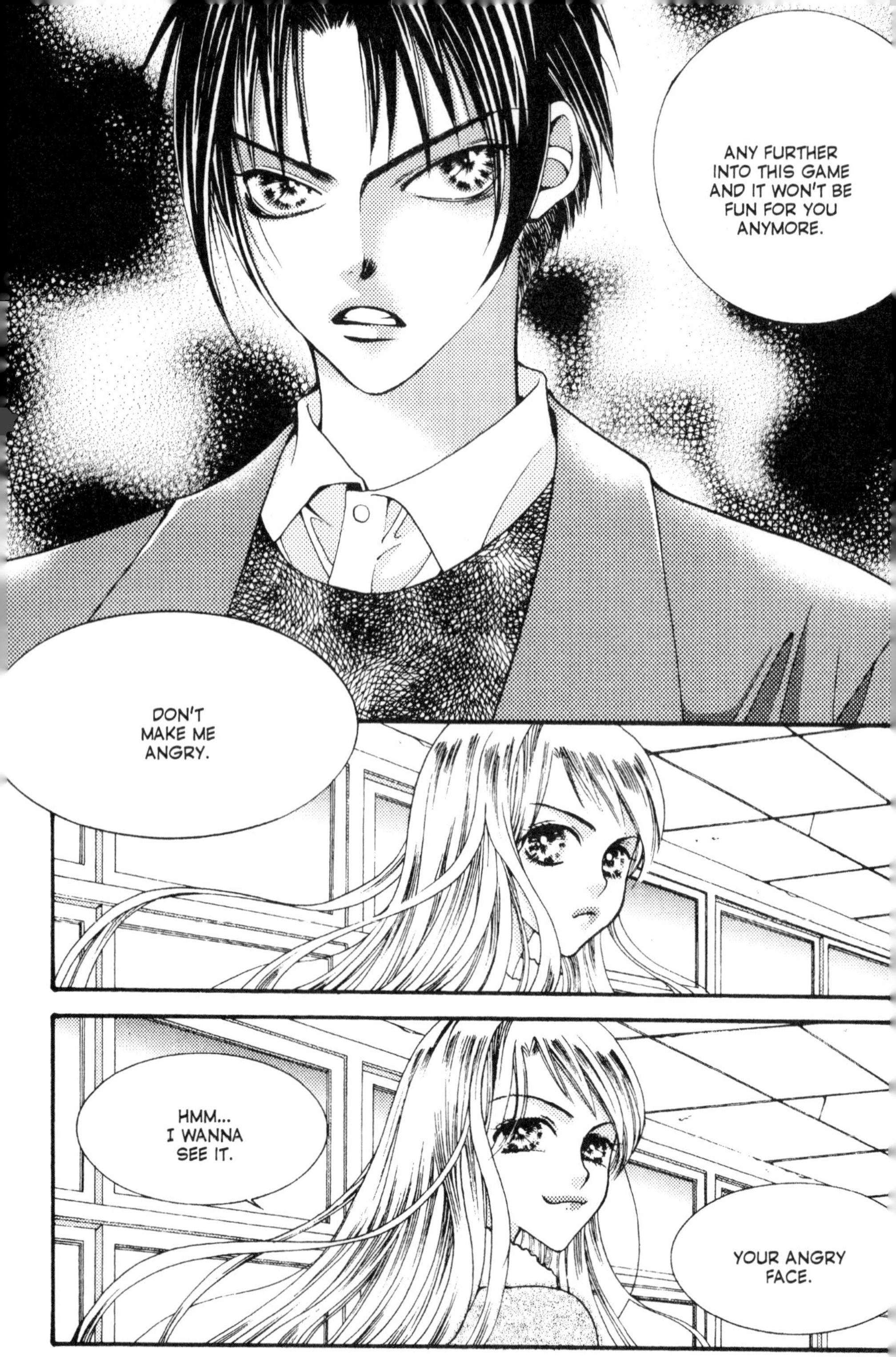
ANY FURTHER INTO THIS GAME AND IT WON'T BE FUN FOR YOU ANYMORE.
DON'T MAKE ME ANGRY.
HMM... I WANNA SEE IT.
YOUR ANGRY FACE.

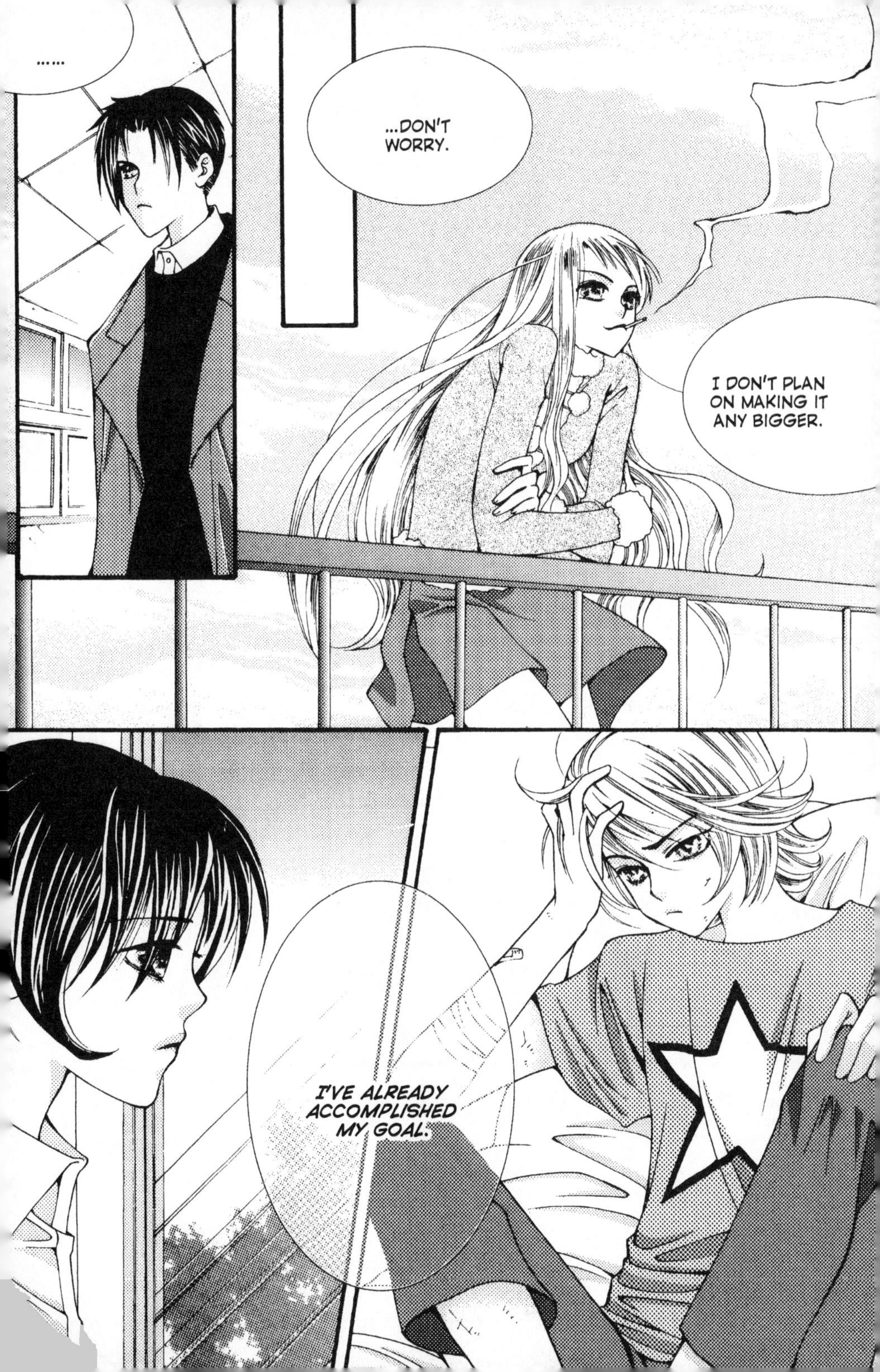
......
...DON'T WORRY.
I DON'T PLAN ON MAKING IT ANY BIGGER.
I'VE ALREADY ACCOMPLISHED MY GOAL.

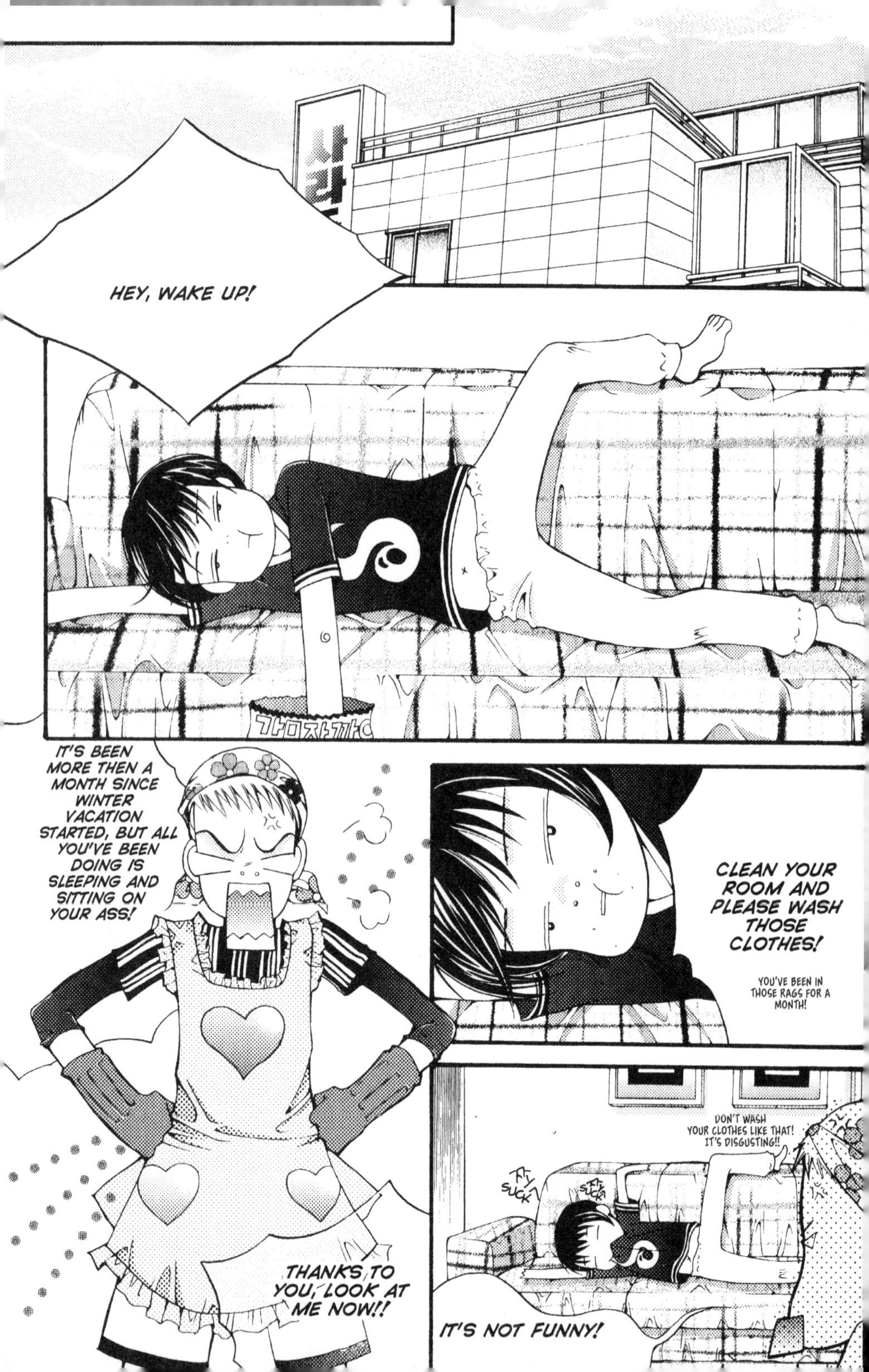

HEY, WAKE UP!
IT'S BEEN MORE THEN A MONTH SINCE WINTER VACATION STARTED, BUT ALL YOU'VE BEEN DOING IS SLEEPING AND SITTING ON YOUR ASS!
THANKS TO YOU, LOOK AT ME NOW!!
CLEAN YOUR ROOM AND PLEASE WASH THOSE CLOTHES!
YOU'VE BEEN IN THOSE RAGS FOR A MONTH!
DON'T WASH YOUR CLOTHES LIKE THAT! IT'S DISGUSTING!!
SUCK
SUCK
IT'S NOT FUNNY!

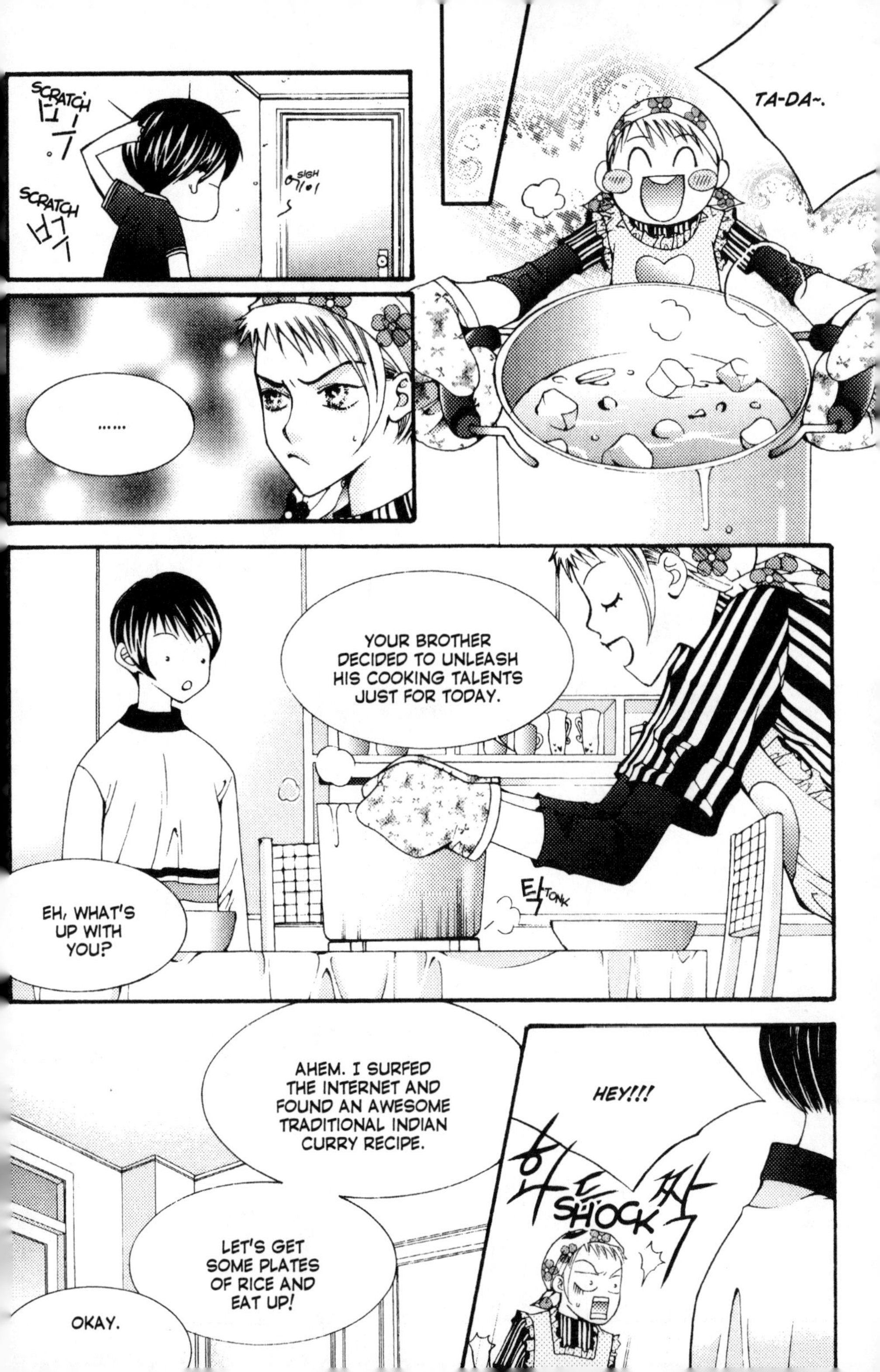
SCRATCH
SCRATCH
SIGH
......
TA-DA~.
YOUR BROTHER DECIDED TO UNLEASH HIS COOKING TALENTS JUST FOR TODAY.
EH, WHAT'S UP WITH YOU?
TONK
AHEM. I SURFED THE INTERNET AND FOUND AN AWESOME TRADITIONAL INDIAN CURRY RECIPE.
LET'S GET SOME PLATES OF RICE AND EAT UP!
OKAY.
HEY!!!
SHOCK

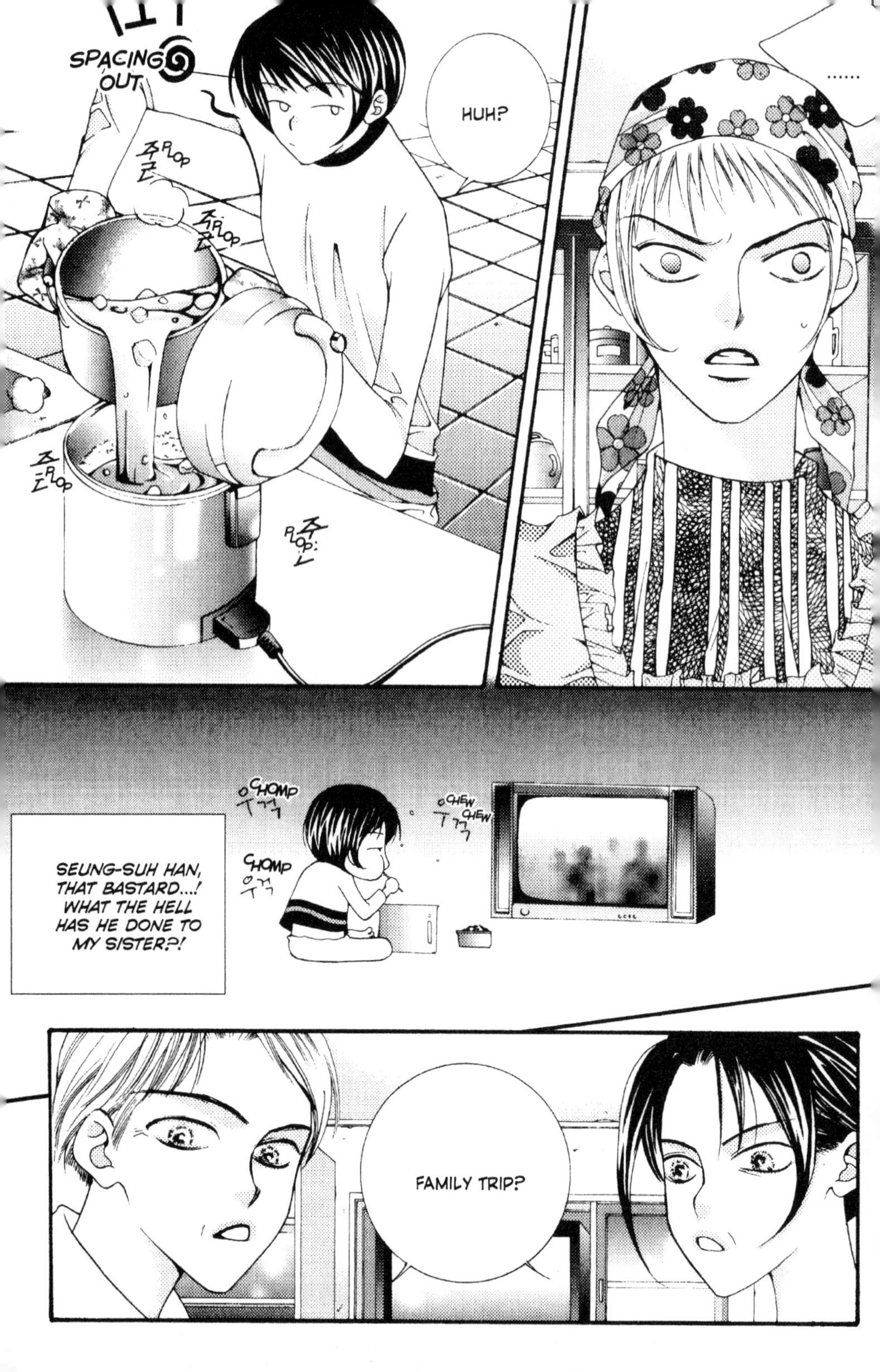
SPACING OUT
PLOP
PLOP
PLOP
PLOP
HUH?
......
CHOMP
CHEW CHEW
CHOMP
SEUNG-SUH HAN, THAT BASTARD...! WHAT THE HELL HAS HE DONE TO MY SISTER?!
FAMILY TRIP?

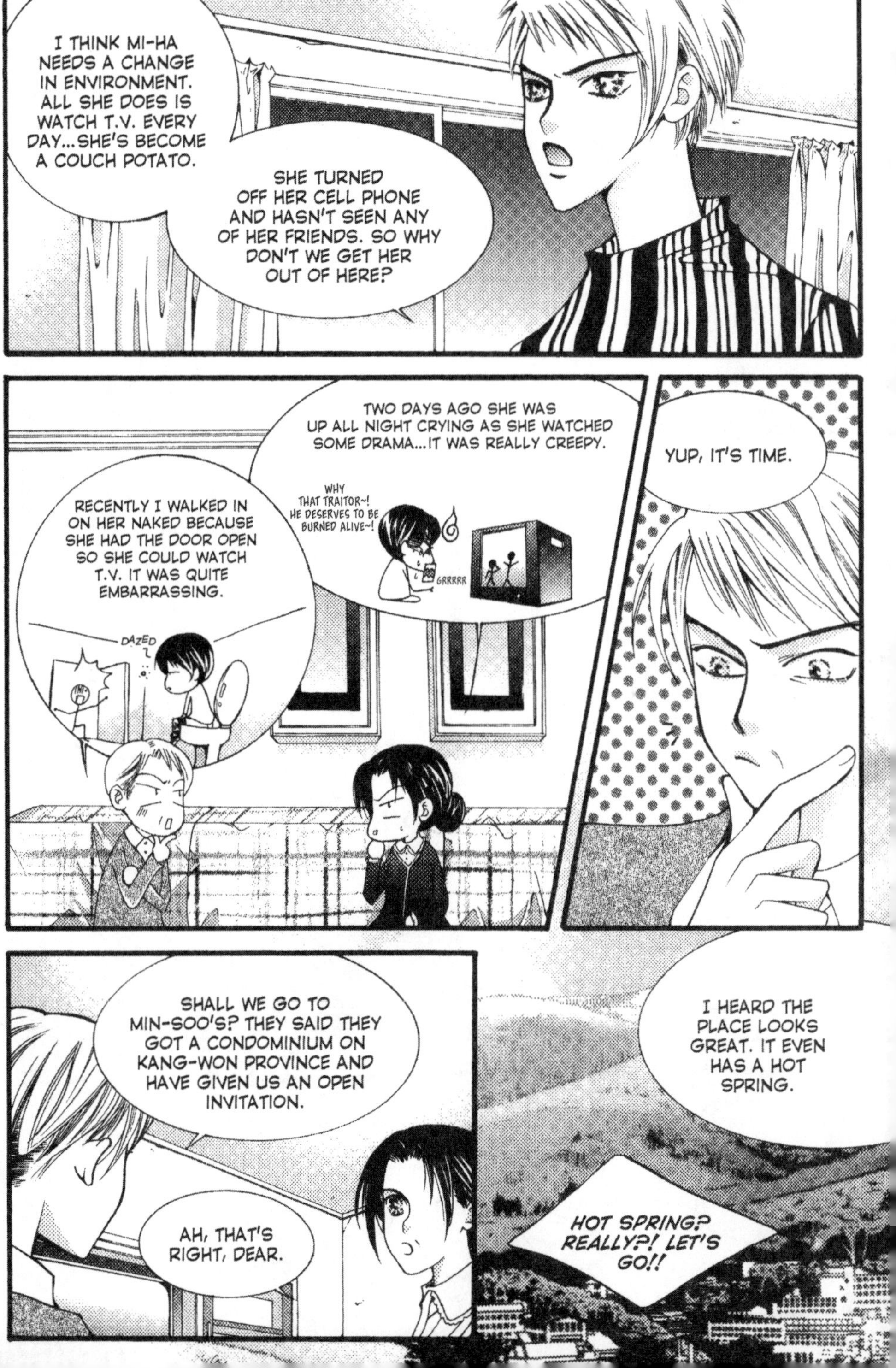
I THINK MI-HA NEEDS A CHANGE IN ENVIRONMENT. ALL SHE DOES IS WATCH T.V. EVERY DAY...SHE'S BECOME A COUCH POTATO.
SHE TURNED OFF HER CELL PHONE AND HASN'T SEEN ANY OF HER FRIENDS. SO WHY DON'T WE GET HER OUT OF HERE?
RECENTLY I WALKED IN ON HER NAKED BECAUSE SHE HAD THE DOOR OPEN SO SHE COULD WATCH T.V. IT WAS QUITE EMBARRASSING.
DAZED
TWO DAYS AGO SHE WAS UP ALL NIGHT CRYING AS SHE WATCHED SOME DRAMA...IT WAS REALLY CREEPY.
WHY THAT TRAITOR~! HE DESERVES TO BE BURNED ALIVE~!
GRRRRR
YUP, IT'S TIME.
SHALL WE GO TO MIN-SOO'S? THEY SAID THEY GOT A CONDOMINIUM ON KANG-WON PROVINCE AND HAVE GIVEN US AN OPEN INVITATION.
AH, THAT'S RIGHT, DEAR.
I HEARD THE PLACE LOOKS GREAT. IT EVEN HAS A HOT SPRING.
HOT SPRING? REALLY?! LET'S GO!!

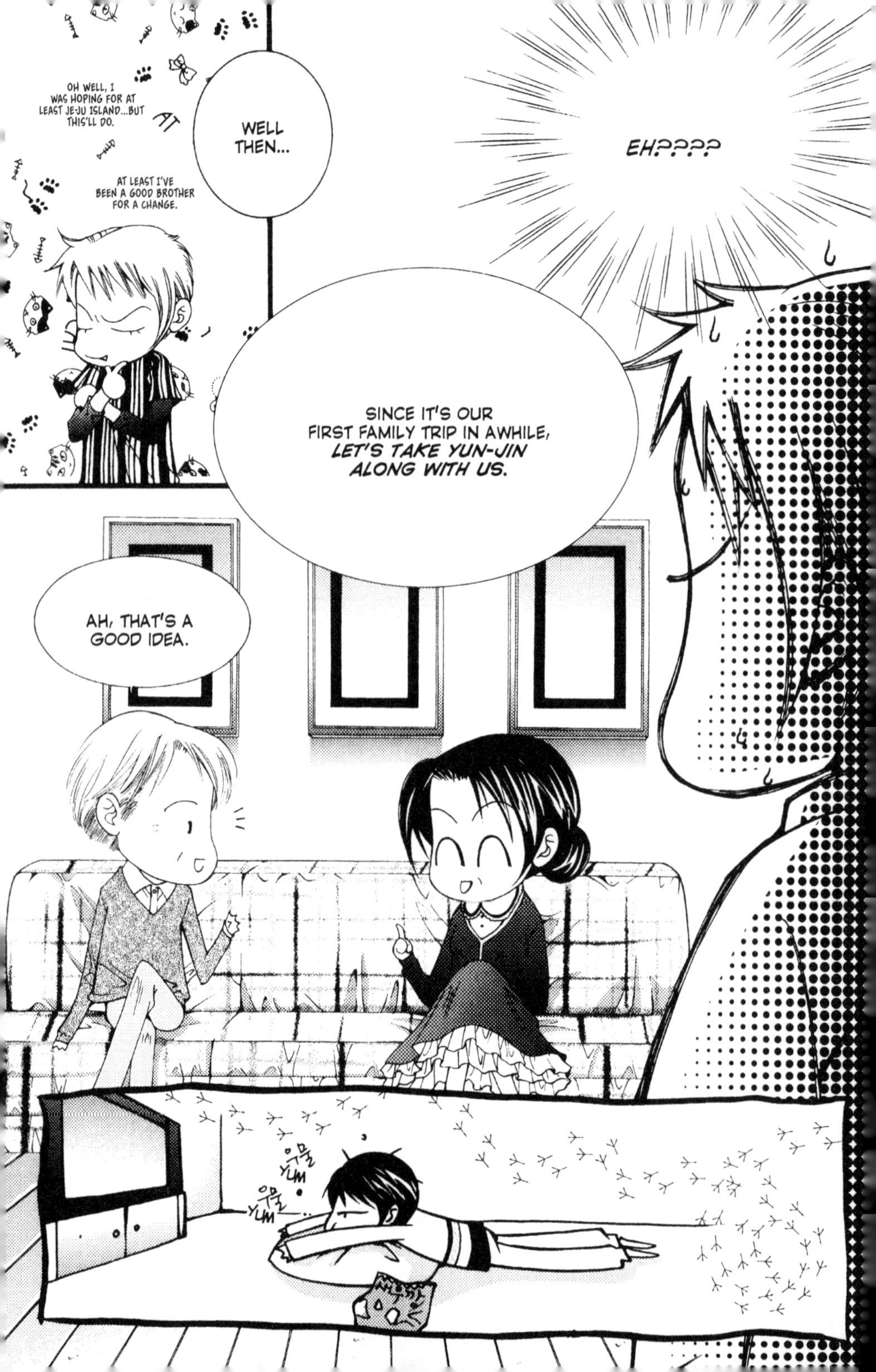
OH WELL, I WAS HOPING FOR AT LEAST JE-JU ISLAND...BUT THIS'LL DO.
AT LEAST I'VE BEEN A GOOD BROTHER FOR A CHANGE.
WELL THEN...
EH????
SINCE IT'S OUR FIRST FAMILY TRIP IN AWHILE, LET'S TAKE YUN-JIN ALONG WITH US.
AH, THAT'S A GOOD IDEA.
YUM
YUM

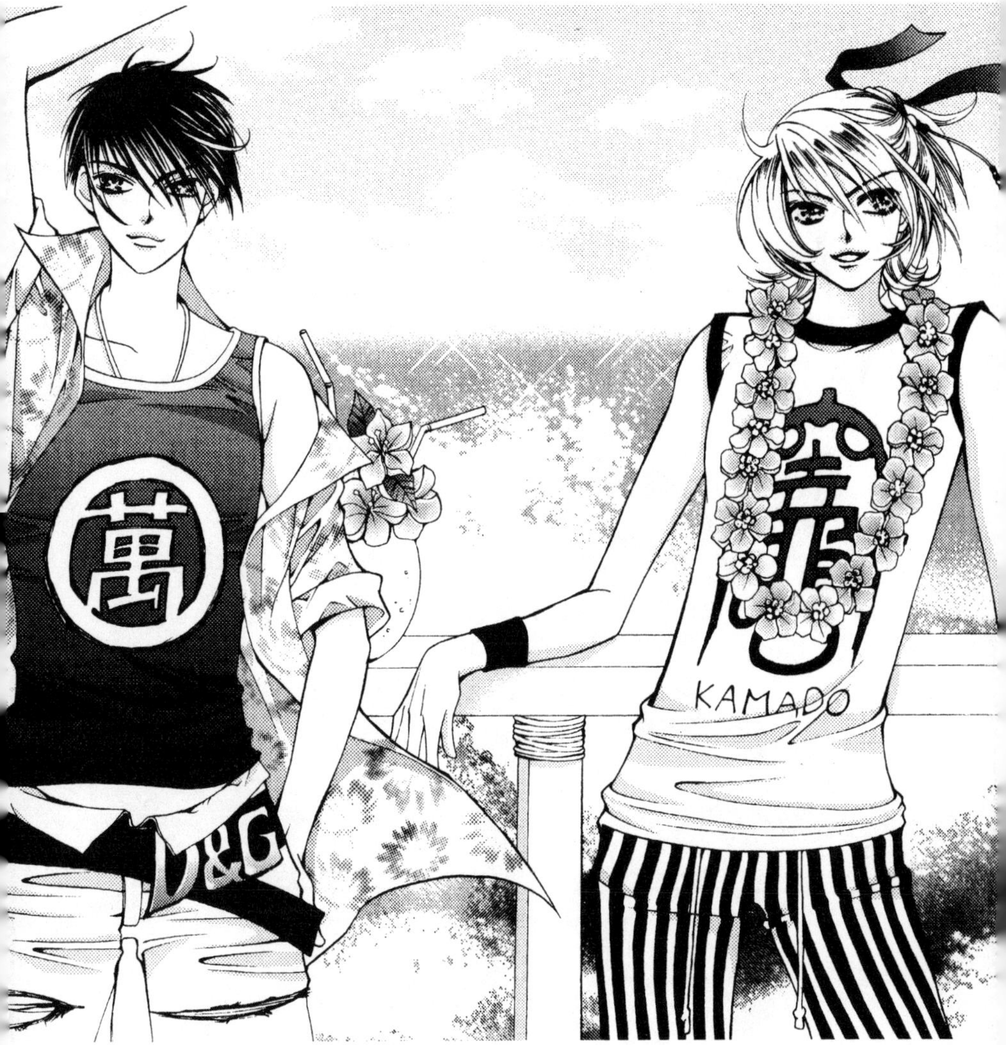
萬
D&G
KAMADO

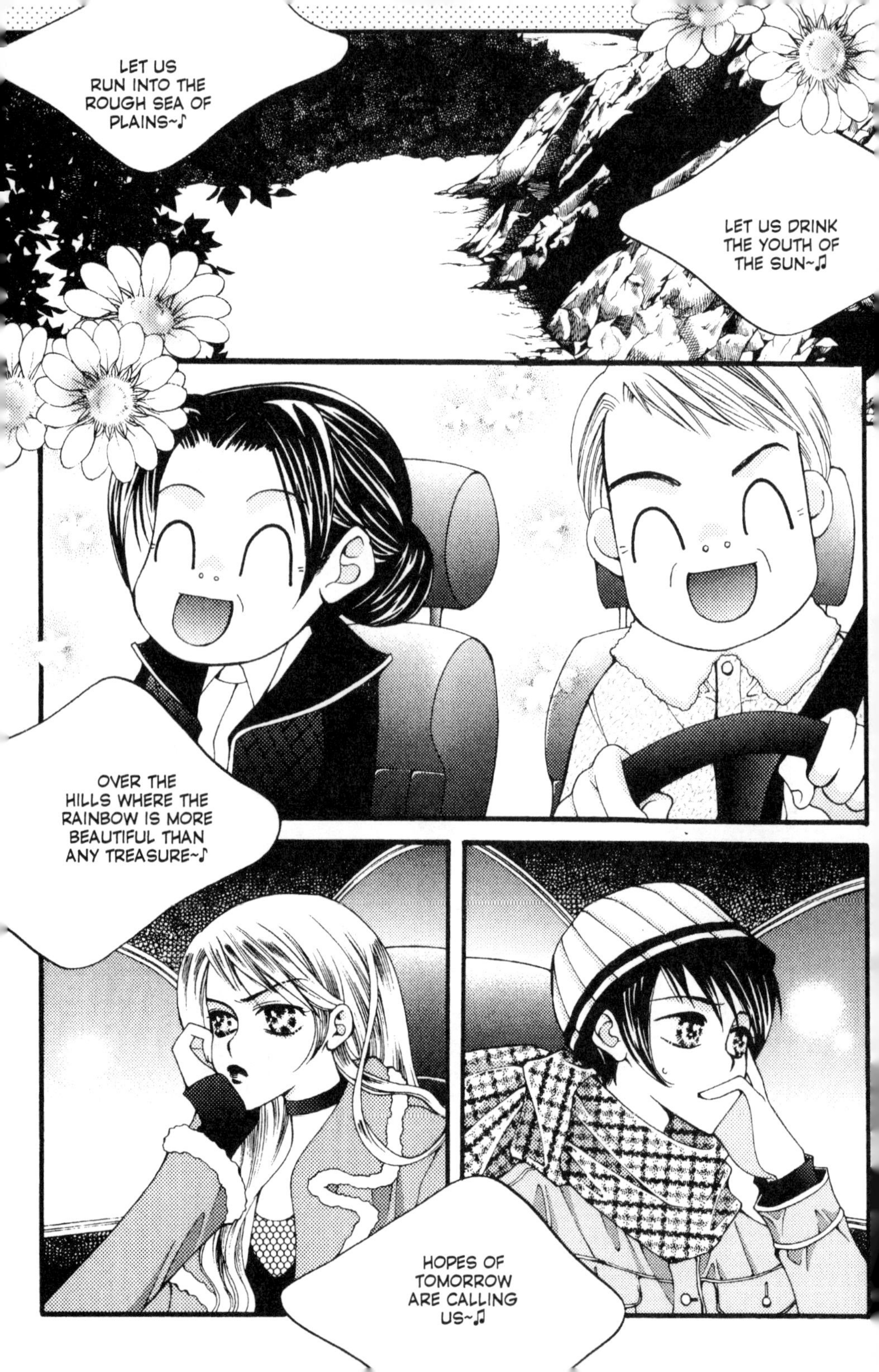
LET US RUN INTO THE ROUGH SEA OF PLAINS~♪
LET US DRINK THE YOUTH OF THE SUN~♫
OVER THE HILLS WHERE THE RAINBOW IS MORE BEAUTIFUL THAN ANY TREASURE~♪
HOPES OF TOMORROW ARE CALLING US~♫

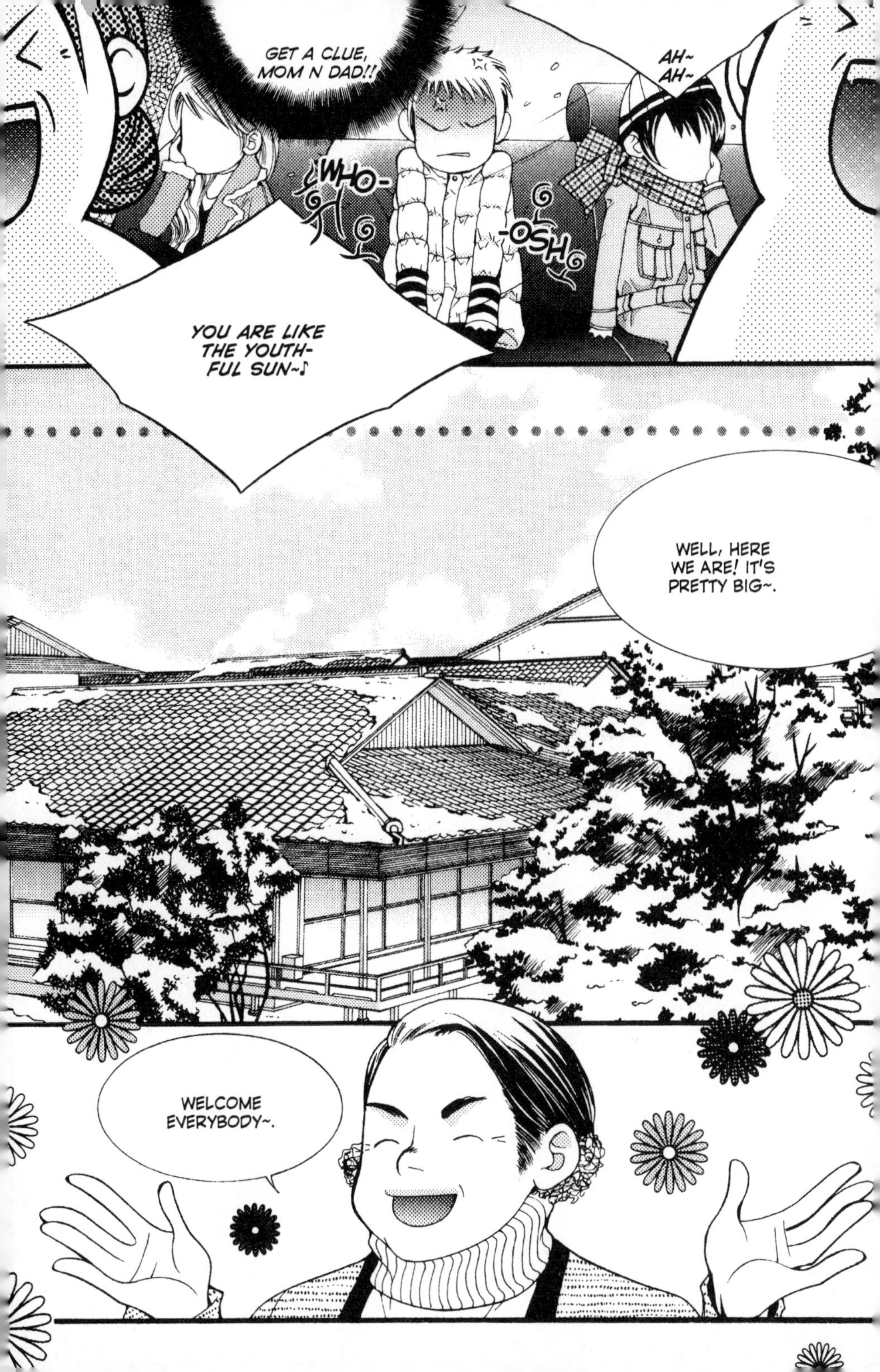
GET A CLUE, MOM N DAD!!
AH~ AH~
WHO-OSH
YOU ARE LIKE THE YOUTHFUL SUN~♪
WELL, HERE WE ARE! IT'S PRETTY BIG~.
WELCOME EVERYBODY~.

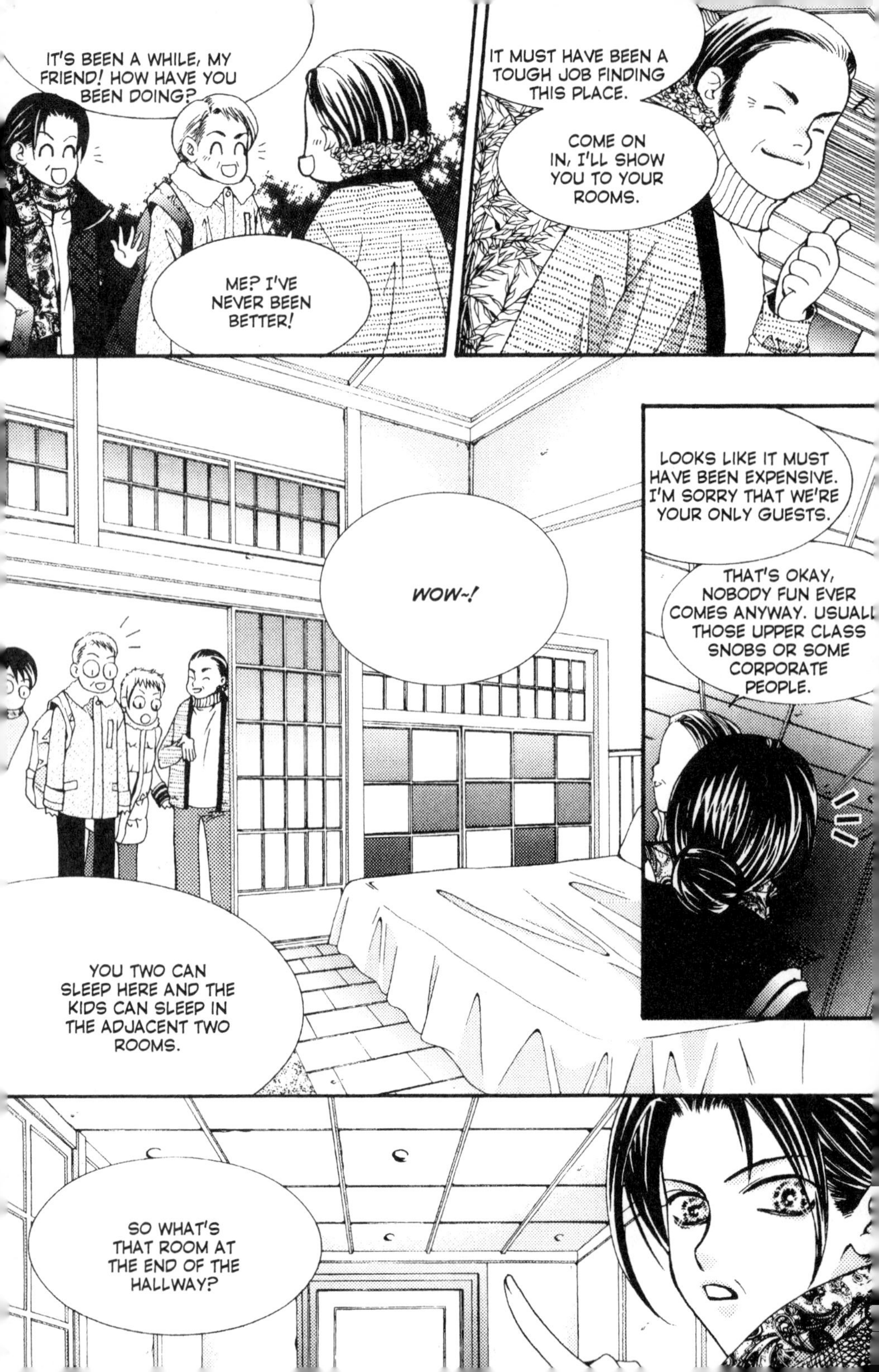
IT'S BEEN A WHILE, MY FRIEND! HOW HAVE YOU BEEN DOING?
ME? I'VE NEVER BEEN BETTER!
IT MUST HAVE BEEN A TOUGH JOB FINDING THIS PLACE.
COME ON IN, I'LL SHOW YOU TO YOUR ROOMS.
WOW~!
YOU TWO CAN SLEEP HERE AND THE KIDS CAN SLEEP IN THE ADJACENT TWO ROOMS.
LOOKS LIKE IT MUST HAVE BEEN EXPENSIVE. I'M SORRY THAT WE'RE YOUR ONLY GUESTS.
THAT'S OKAY, NOBODY FUN EVER COMES ANYWAY. USUALL THOSE UPPER CLASS SNOBS OR SOME CORPORATE PEOPLE.
SO WHAT'S THAT ROOM AT THE END OF THE HALLWAY?

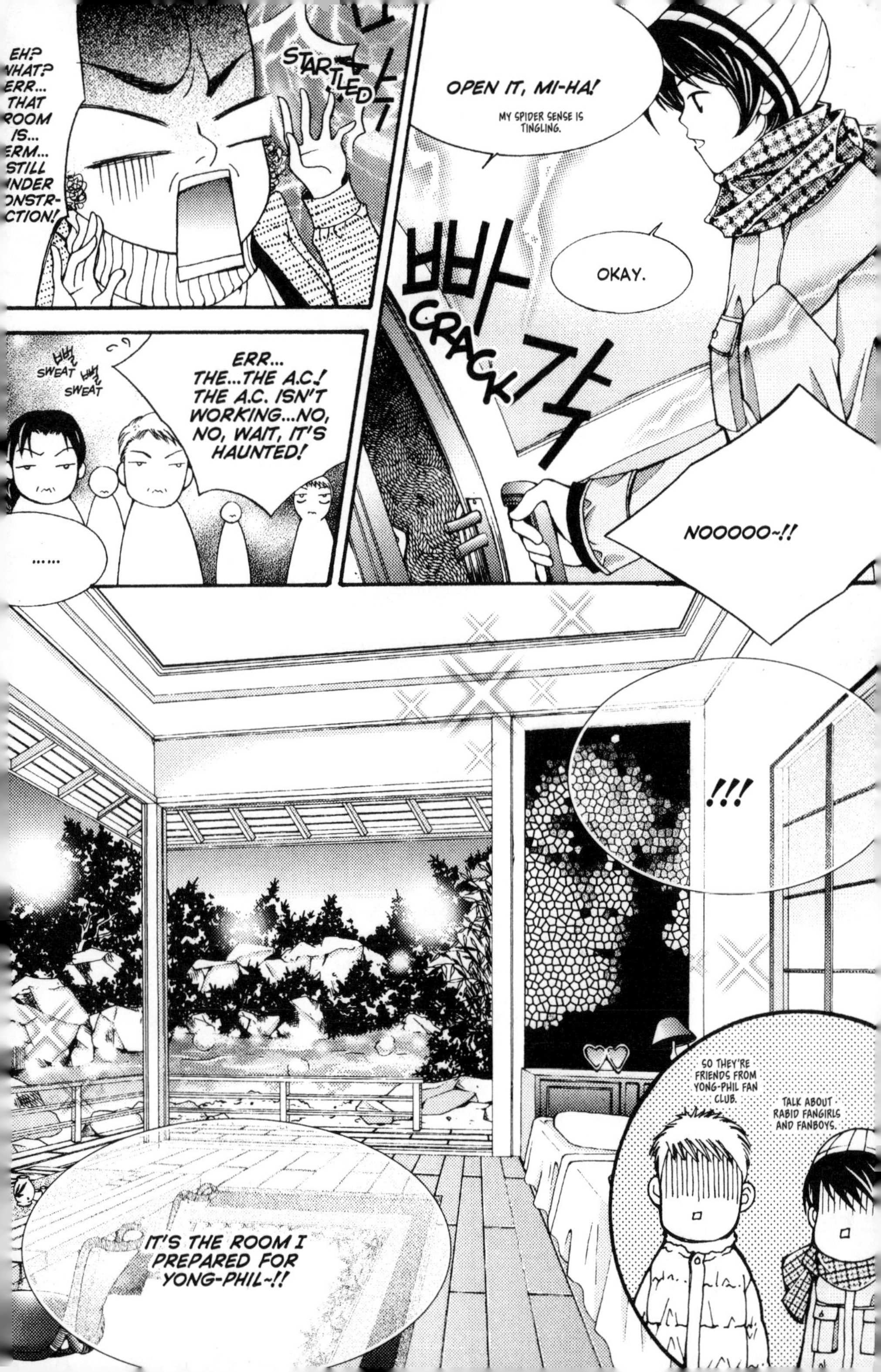
EH? NHAT? ERR... THAT ROOM IS... ERM... STILL NDER ONSTR- CTION!
STARTLED
OPEN IT, MI-HA!
MY SPIDER SENSE IS TINGLING.
OKAY.
CRACK
SWEAT SWEAT
ERR... THE...THE A.C.! THE A.C. ISN'T WORKING...NO, NO, WAIT, IT'S HAUNTED!
......
NOOOOO~!!
!!!
IT'S THE ROOM I PREPARED FOR YONG-PHIL~!!
SO THEY'RE FRIENDS FROM YONG-PHIL FAN CLUB.
TALK ABOUT RABID FANGIRLS AND FANBOYS.

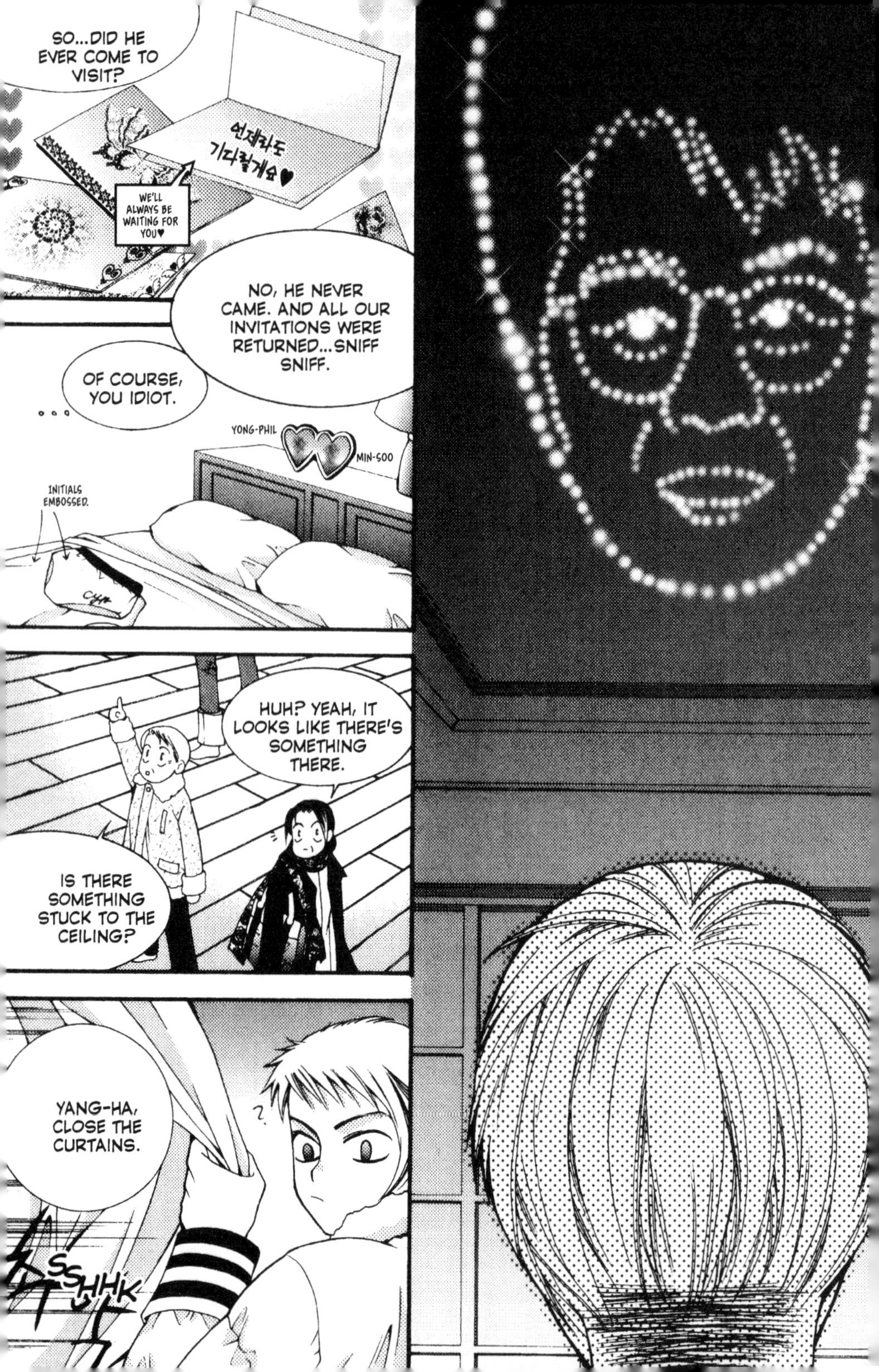

SO...DID HE EVER COME TO VISIT?
언제라도 기다릴게요♥
WE'LL ALWAYS BE WAITING FOR YOU♥
NO, HE NEVER CAME. AND ALL OUR INVITATIONS WERE RETURNED...SNIFF SNIFF.
OF COURSE, YOU IDIOT.
...
YONG-PHIL
MIN-SOO
INITIALS EMBOSSED.
IS THERE SOMETHING STUCK TO THE CEILING?
HUH? YEAH, IT LOOKS LIKE THERE'S SOMETHING THERE.
YANG-HA, CLOSE THE CURTAINS.
SSHHK

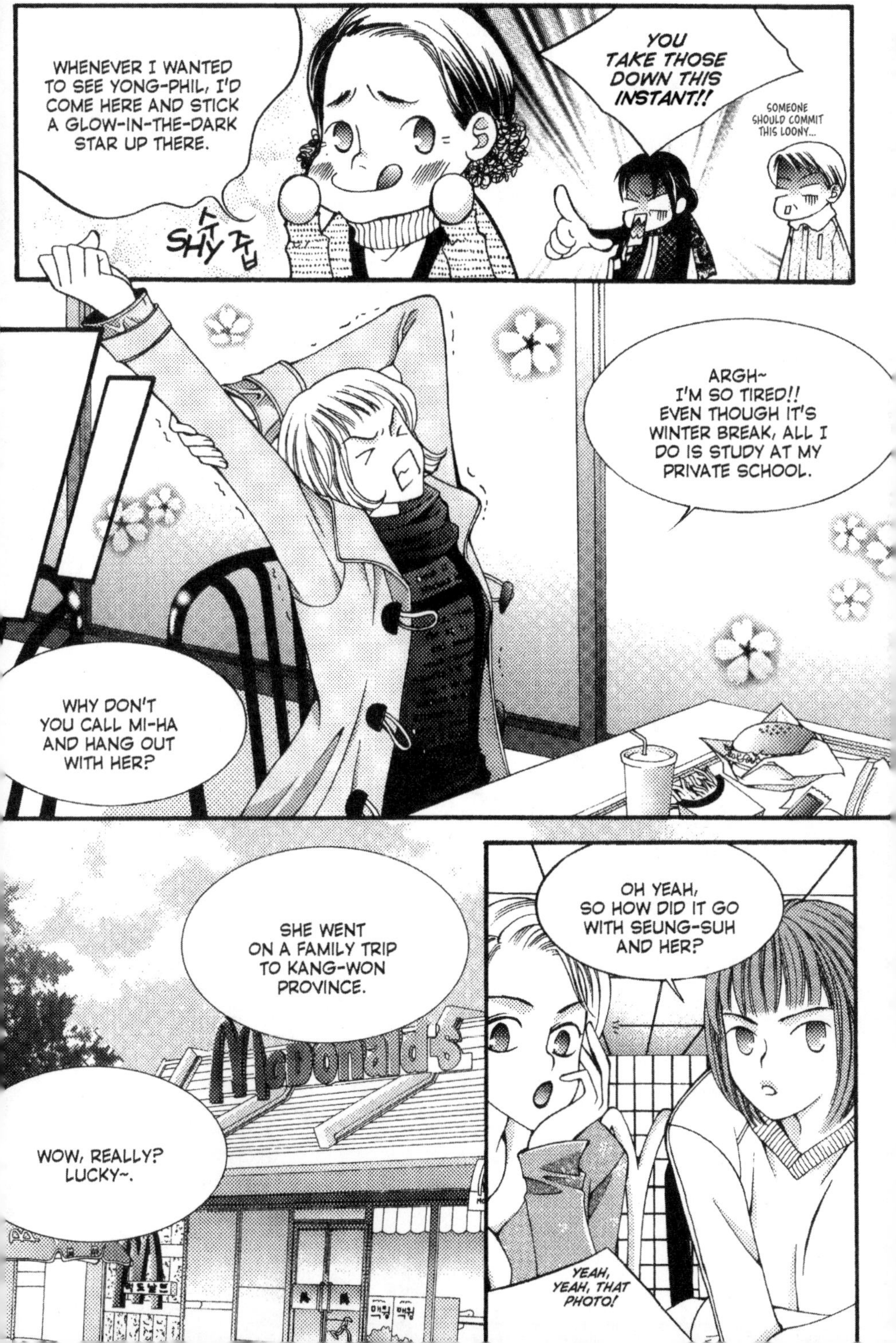
WHENEVER I WANTED TO SEE YONG-PHIL, I'D COME HERE AND STICK A GLOW-IN-THE-DARK STAR UP THERE.
SHY 수줍
YOU TAKE THOSE DOWN THIS INSTANT!!
SOMEONE SHOULD COMMIT THIS LOONY...
ARGH~ I'M SO TIRED!! EVEN THOUGH IT'S WINTER BREAK, ALL I DO IS STUDY AT MY PRIVATE SCHOOL.
WHY DON'T YOU CALL MI-HA AND HANG OUT WITH HER?
SHE WENT ON A FAMILY TRIP TO KANG-WON PROVINCE.
McDonald's
WOW, REALLY? LUCKY~.
OH YEAH, SO HOW DID IT GO WITH SEUNG-SUH AND HER?
YEAH, YEAH, THAT PHOTO!

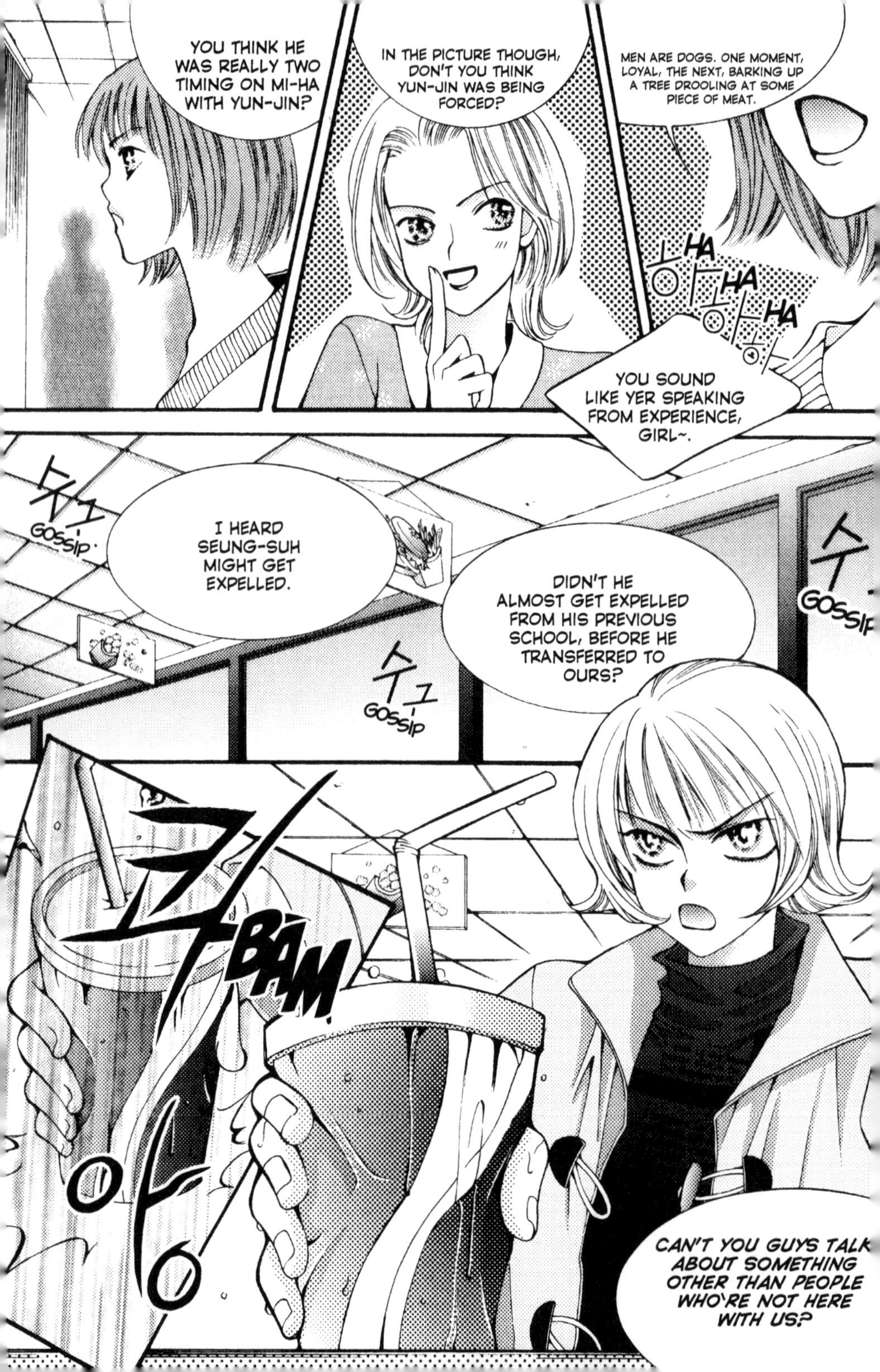
YOU THINK HE WAS REALLY TWO TIMING ON MI-HA WITH YUN-JIN?
IN THE PICTURE THOUGH, DON'T YOU THINK YUN-JIN WAS BEING FORCED?
MEN ARE DOGS. ONE MOMENT, LOYAL, THE NEXT, BARKING UP A TREE DROOLING AT SOME PIECE OF MEAT.
HA HA HA
YOU SOUND LIKE YER SPEAKING FROM EXPERIENCE, GIRL~.
GOSSIP
I HEARD SEUNG-SUH MIGHT GET EXPELLED.
GOSSIP
DIDN'T HE ALMOST GET EXPELLED FROM HIS PREVIOUS SCHOOL, BEFORE HE TRANSFERRED TO OURS?
GOSSIP
BAM
CAN'T YOU GUYS TALK ABOUT SOMETHING OTHER THAN PEOPLE WHO'RE NOT HERE WITH US?

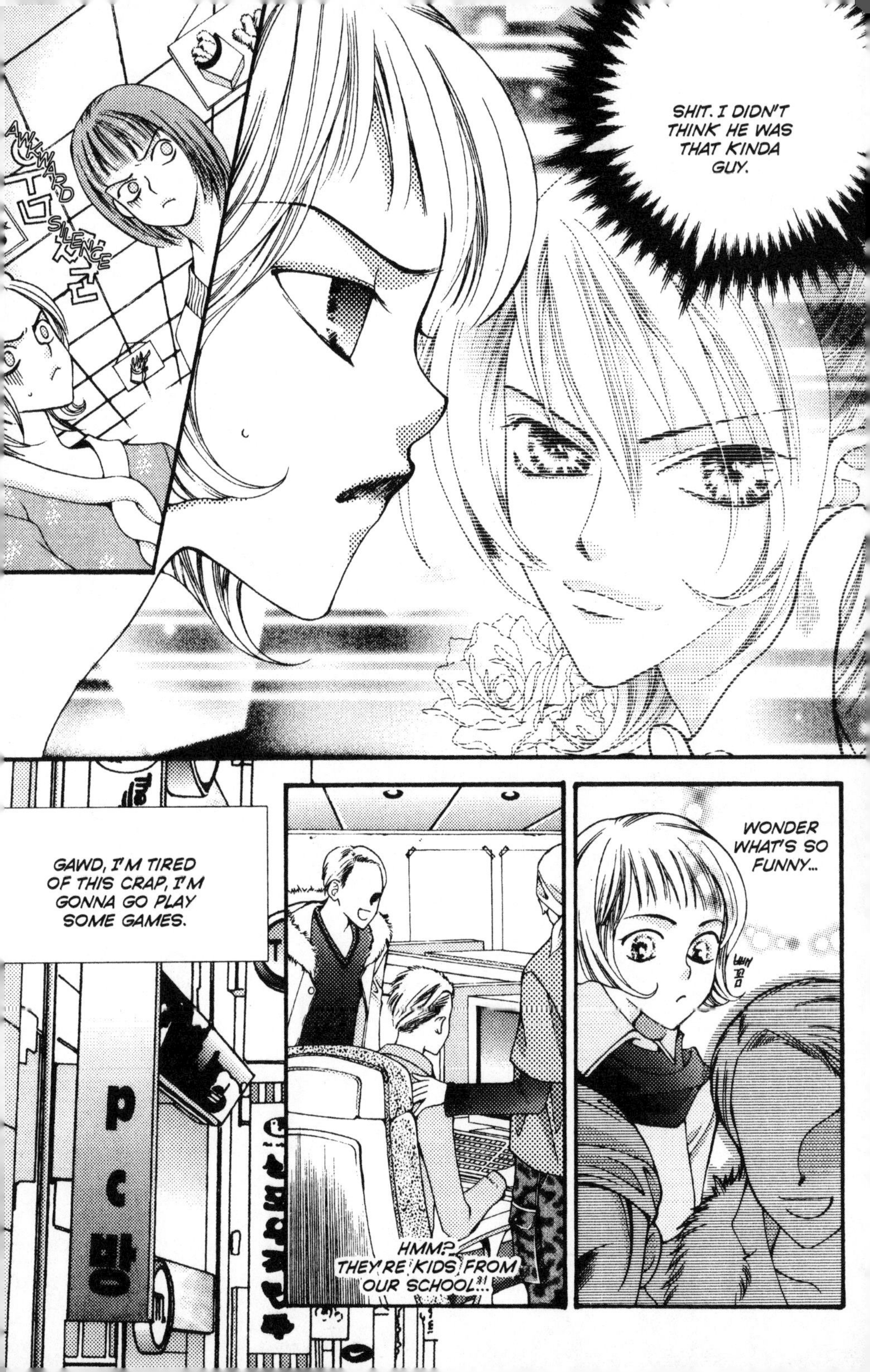
AWKWARD SILENCE
SHIT. I DIDN'T THINK HE WAS THAT KINDA GUY.
GAWD, I'M TIRED OF THIS CRAP, I'M GONNA GO PLAY SOME GAMES.
pc 방
HMM? THEY'RE KIDS FROM OUR SCHOOL...
WONDER WHAT'S SO FUNNY...

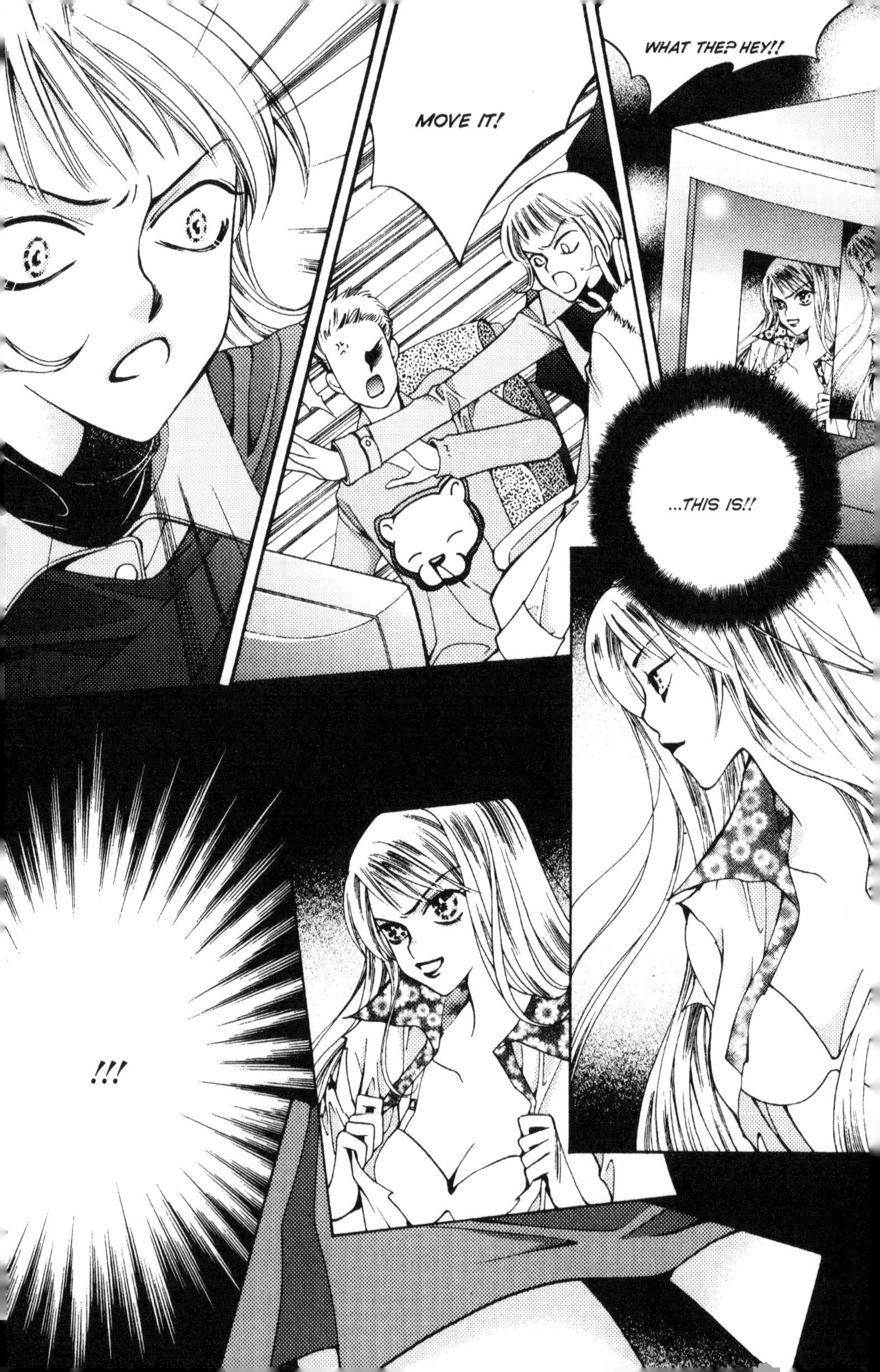
MOVE IT!
WHAT THE? HEY!!
...THIS IS!!
!!!

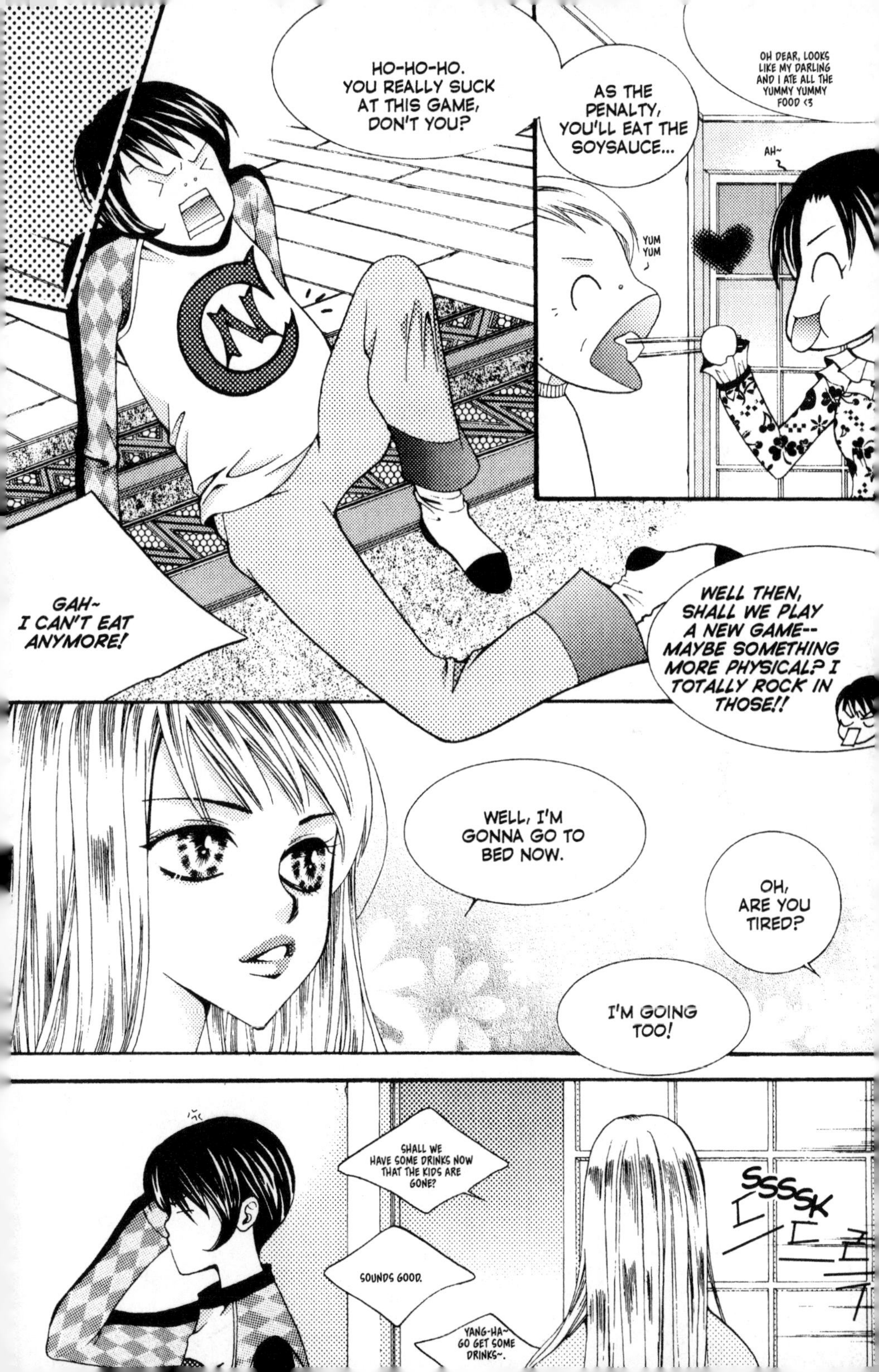
HO-HO-HO. YOU REALLY SUCK AT THIS GAME, DON'T YOU?
AS THE PENALTY, YOU'LL EAT THE SOYSAUCE...
OH DEAR, LOOKS LIKE MY DARLING AND I ATE ALL THE YUMMY YUMMY FOOD <3
AH~
YUM YUM
GAH~ I CAN'T EAT ANYMORE!
WELL THEN, SHALL WE PLAY A NEW GAME-- MAYBE SOMETHING MORE PHYSICAL? I TOTALLY ROCK IN THOSE!!
WELL, I'M GONNA GO TO BED NOW.
OH, ARE YOU TIRED?
I'M GOING TOO!
SHALL WE HAVE SOME DRINKS NOW THAT THE KIDS ARE GONE?
SOUNDS GOOD.
YANG-HA~ GO GET SOME DRINKS~.
SSSSK

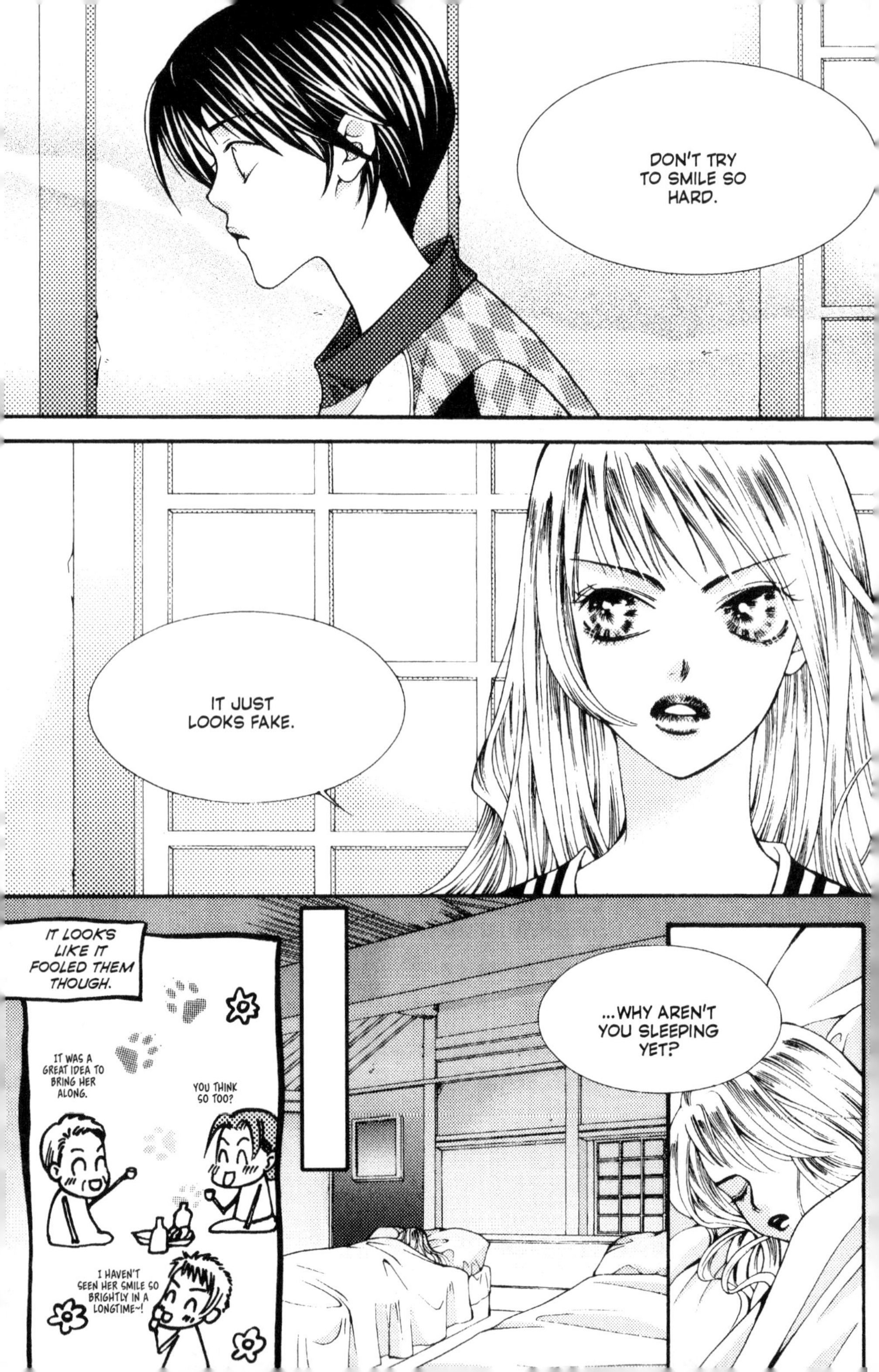
DON'T TRY TO SMILE SO HARD.
IT JUST LOOKS FAKE.
...WHY AREN'T YOU SLEEPING YET?
IT LOOKS LIKE IT FOOLED THEM THOUGH.
IT WAS A GREAT IDEA TO BRING HER ALONG.
YOU THINK SO TOO?
I HAVEN'T SEEN HER SMILE SO BRIGHTLY IN A LONGTIME~!

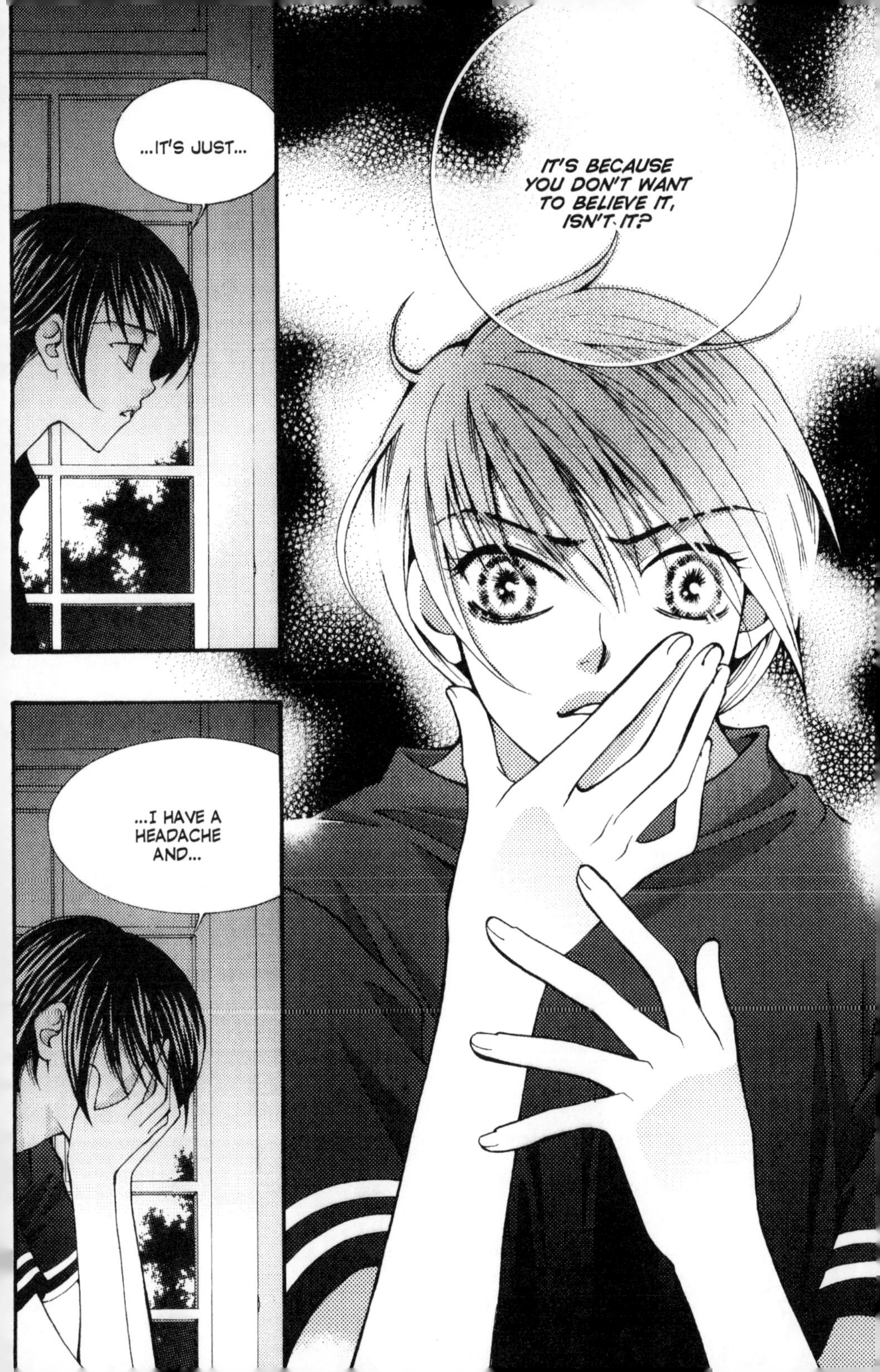
...IT'S JUST...
...I HAVE A HEADACHE AND...
IT'S BECAUSE YOU DON'T WANT TO BELIEVE IT, ISN'T IT?

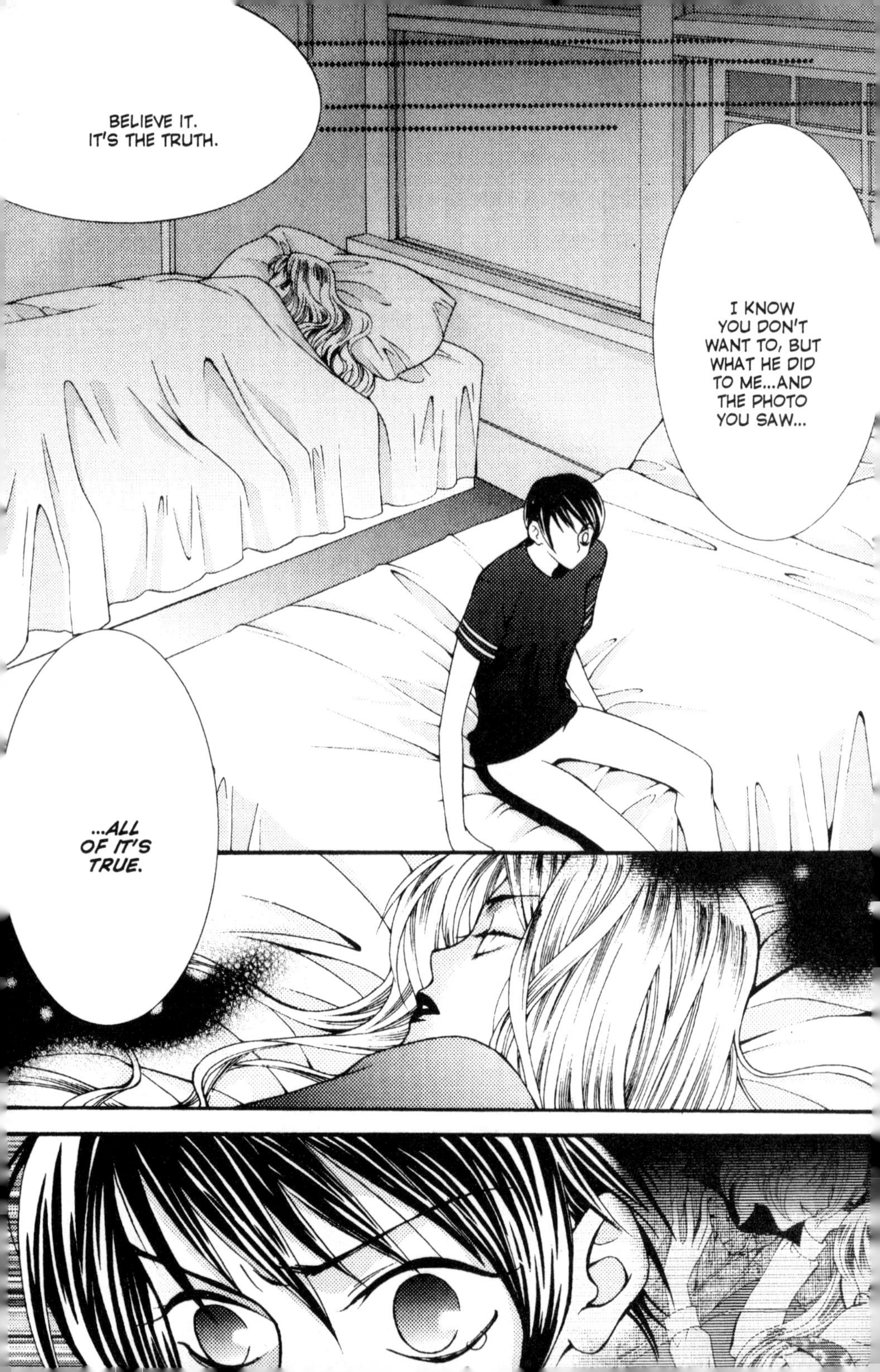
BELIEVE IT. IT'S THE TRUTH.
I KNOW YOU DON'T WANT TO, BUT WHAT HE DID TO ME...AND THE PHOTO YOU SAW...
...ALL OF IT'S TRUE.

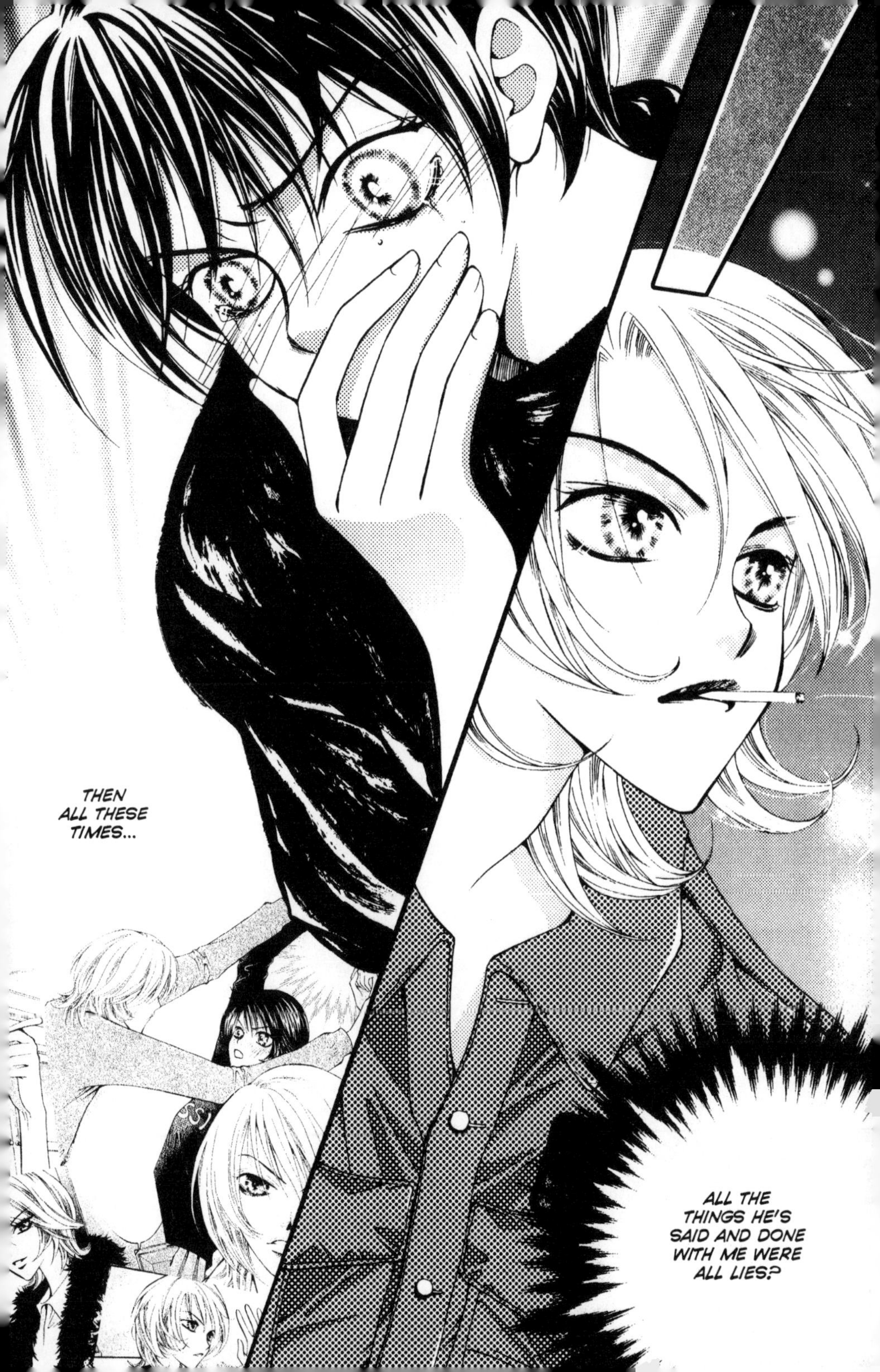
THEN ALL THESE TIMES...
ALL THE THINGS HE'S SAID AND DONE WITH ME WERE ALL LIES?

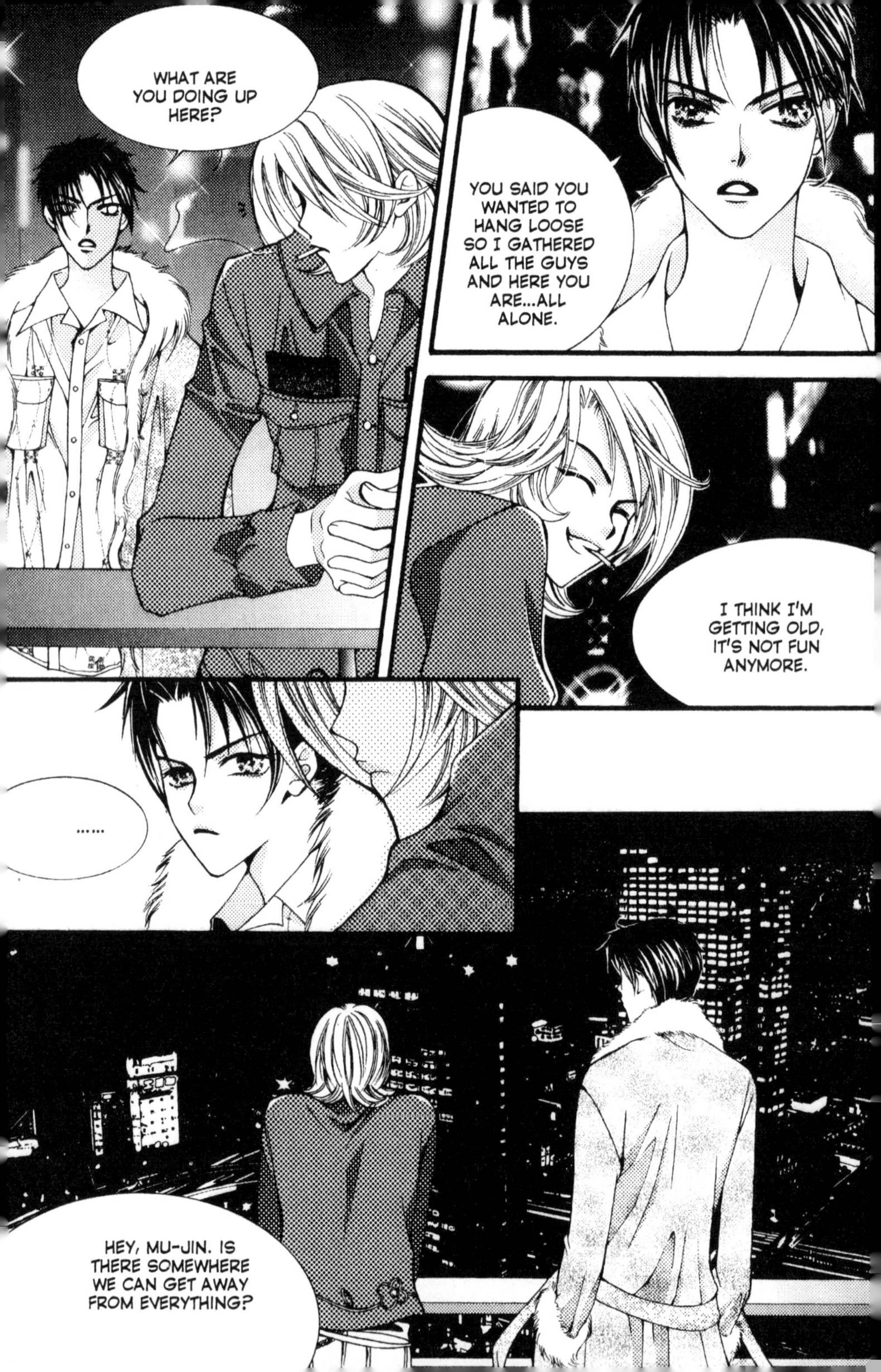
WHAT ARE YOU DOING UP HERE?
YOU SAID YOU WANTED TO HANG LOOSE SO I GATHERED ALL THE GUYS AND HERE YOU ARE...ALL ALONE.
I THINK I'M GETTING OLD, IT'S NOT FUN ANYMORE.
......
HEY, MU-JIN. IS THERE SOMEWHERE WE CAN GET AWAY FROM EVERYTHING?

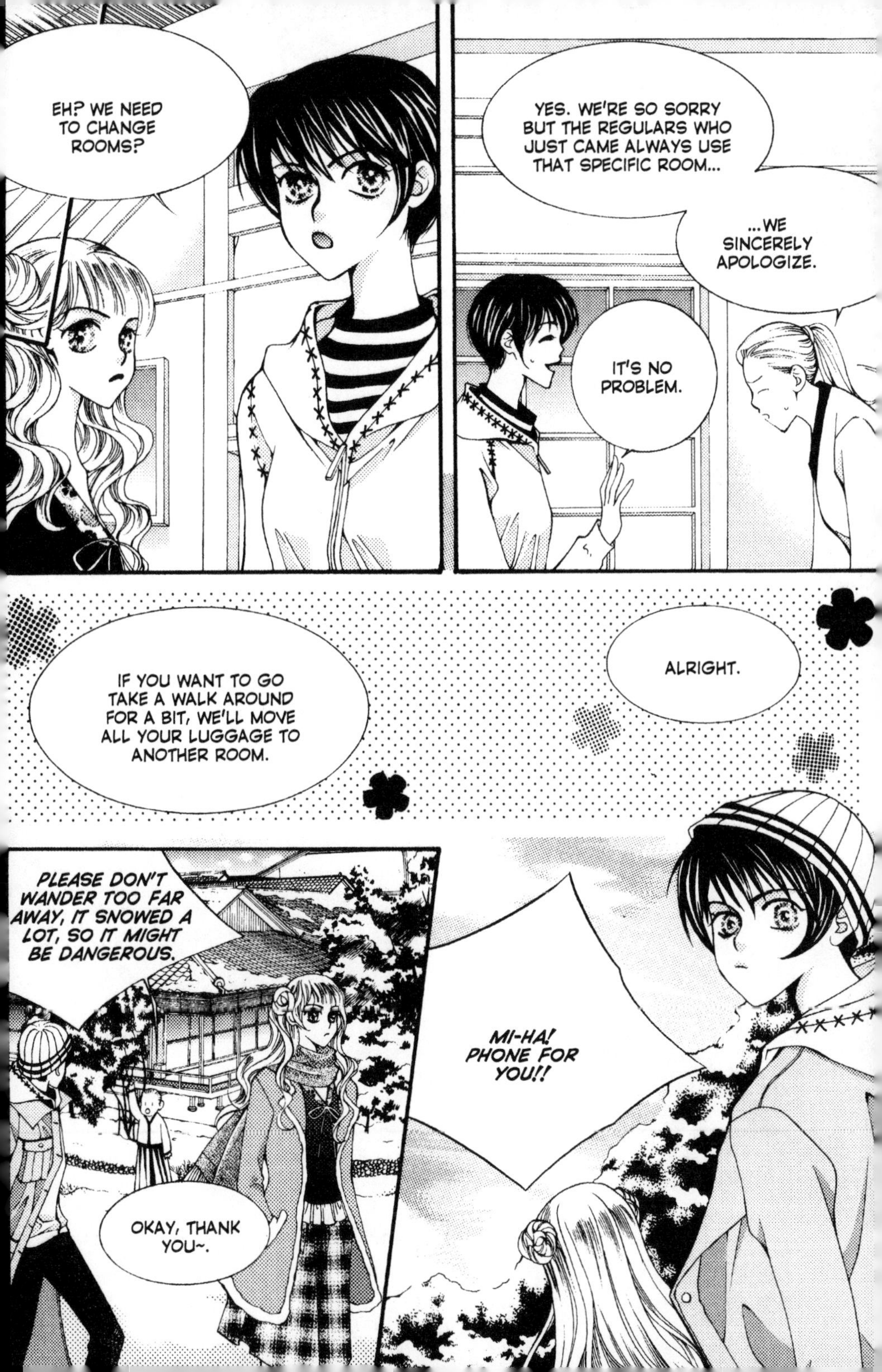
EH? WE NEED TO CHANGE ROOMS?
YES. WE'RE SO SORRY BUT THE REGULARS WHO JUST CAME ALWAYS USE THAT SPECIFIC ROOM...
...WE SINCERELY APOLOGIZE.
IT'S NO PROBLEM.
IF YOU WANT TO GO TAKE A WALK AROUND FOR A BIT, WE'LL MOVE ALL YOUR LUGGAGE TO ANOTHER ROOM.
ALRIGHT.
PLEASE DON'T WANDER TOO FAR AWAY, IT SNOWED A LOT, SO IT MIGHT BE DANGEROUS.
OKAY, THANK YOU~.
MI-HA! PHONE FOR YOU!!

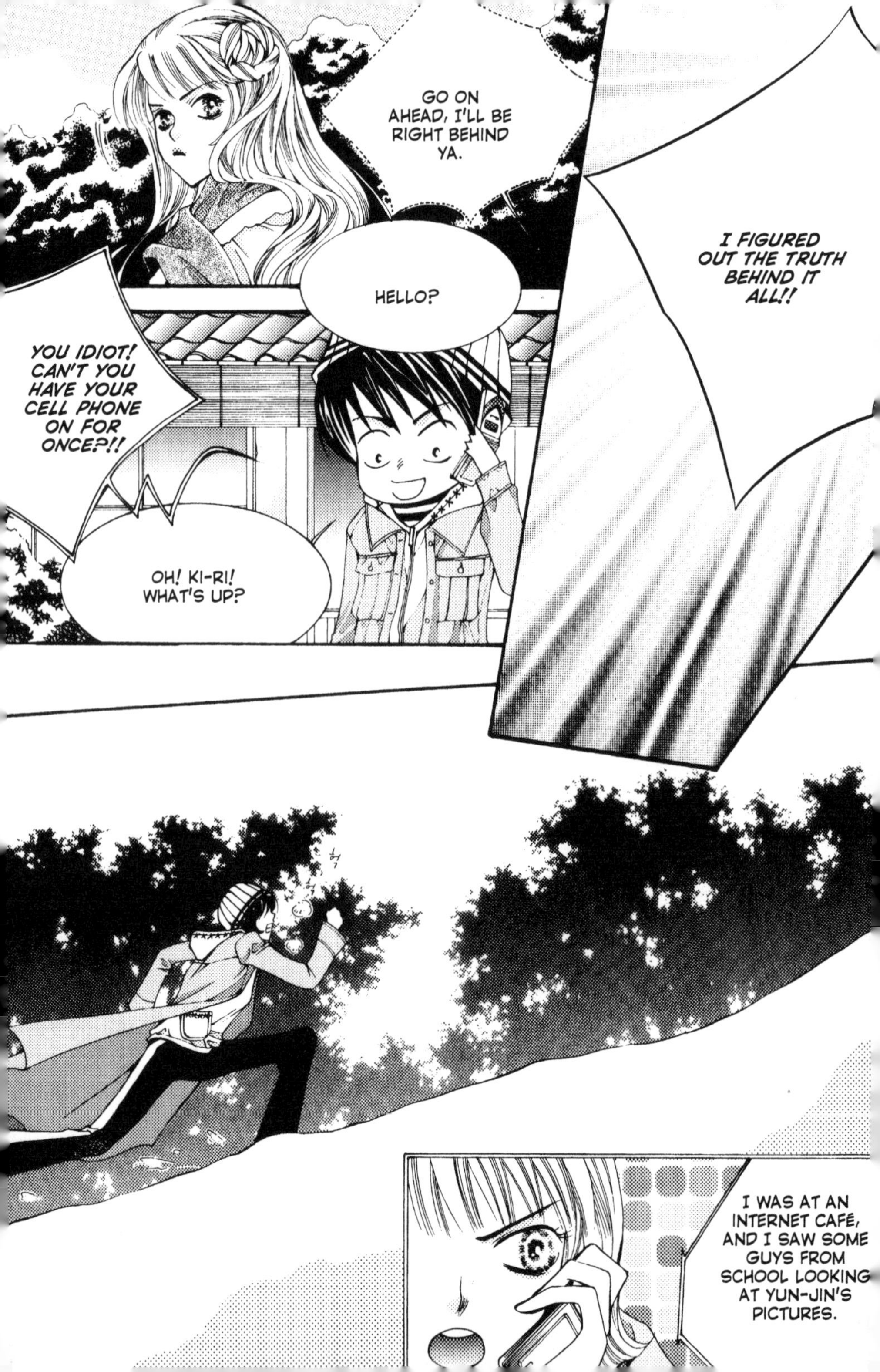
GO ON AHEAD, I'LL BE RIGHT BEHIND YA.
HELLO?
YOU IDIOT! CAN'T YOU HAVE YOUR CELL PHONE ON FOR ONCE?!!
OH! KI-RI! WHAT'S UP?
I FIGURED OUT THE TRUTH BEHIND IT ALL!!
I WAS AT AN INTERNET CAFÉ, AND I SAW SOME GUYS FROM SCHOOL LOOKING AT YUN-JIN'S PICTURES.

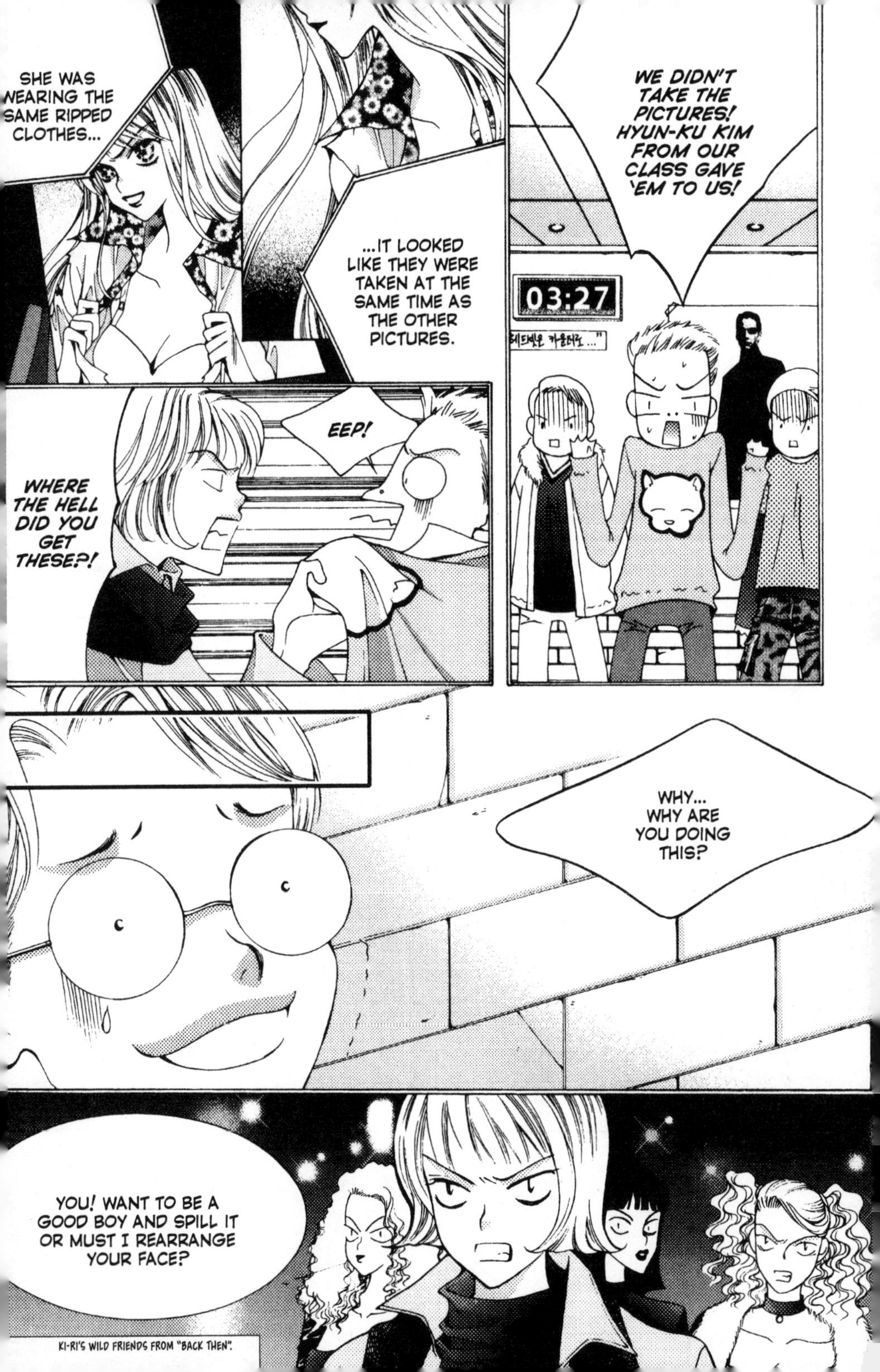
SHE WAS WEARING THE SAME RIPPED CLOTHES...
...IT LOOKED LIKE THEY WERE TAKEN AT THE SAME TIME AS THE OTHER PICTURES.
WHERE THE HELL DID YOU GET THESE?!
EEP!
WE DIDN'T TAKE THE PICTURES! HYUN-KU KIM FROM OUR CLASS GAVE 'EM TO US!
03:27
WHY... WHY ARE YOU DOING THIS?
YOU! WANT TO BE A GOOD BOY AND SPILL IT OR MUST I REARRANGE YOUR FACE?
KI-RI'S WILD FRIENDS FROM "BACK THEN".

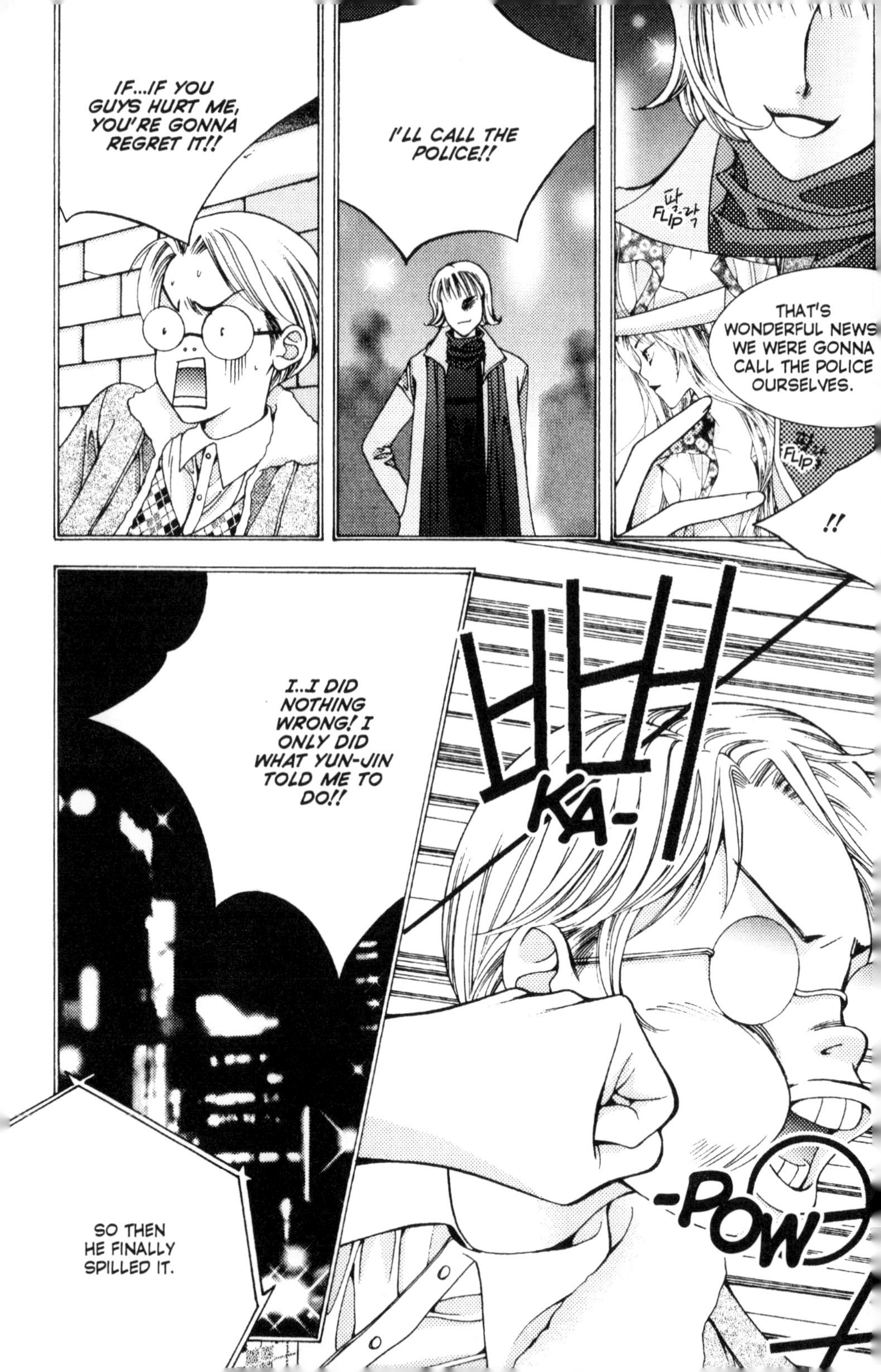
IF...IF YOU GUYS HURT ME, YOU'RE GONNA REGRET IT!!
I'LL CALL THE POLICE!!
FLIP
THAT'S WONDERFUL NEWS WE WERE GONNA CALL THE POLICE OURSELVES.
FLIP
!!
I..I DID NOTHING WRONG! I ONLY DID WHAT YUN-JIN TOLD ME TO DO!!
SO THEN HE FINALLY SPILLED IT.
KA-
-POW

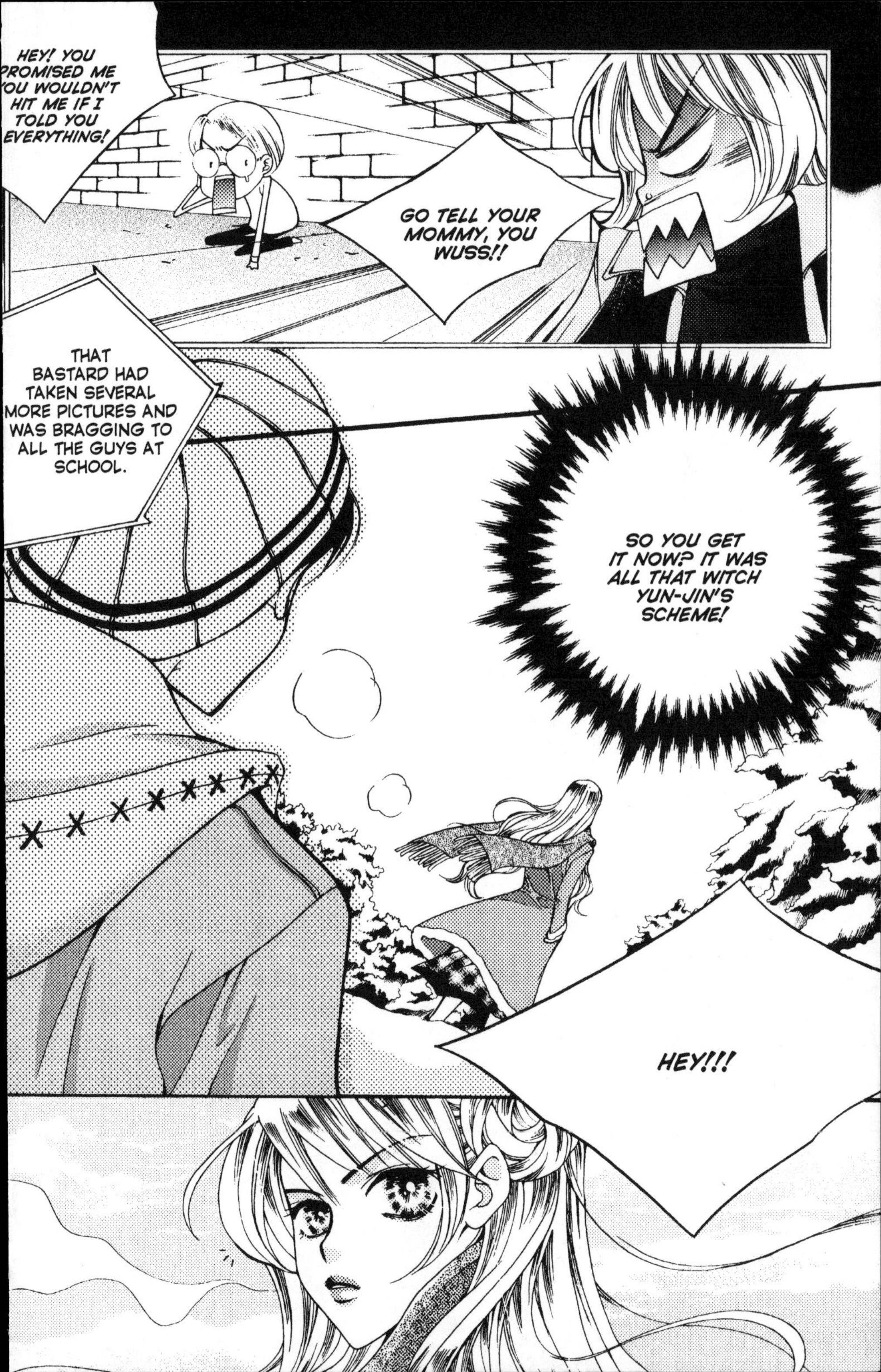
HEY! YOU PROMISED ME YOU WOULDN'T HIT ME IF I TOLD YOU EVERYTHING!
GO TELL YOUR MOMMY, YOU WUSS!!
THAT BASTARD HAD TAKEN SEVERAL MORE PICTURES AND WAS BRAGGING TO ALL THE GUYS AT SCHOOL.
SO YOU GET IT NOW? IT WAS ALL THAT WITCH YUN-JIN'S SCHEME!
HEY!!!

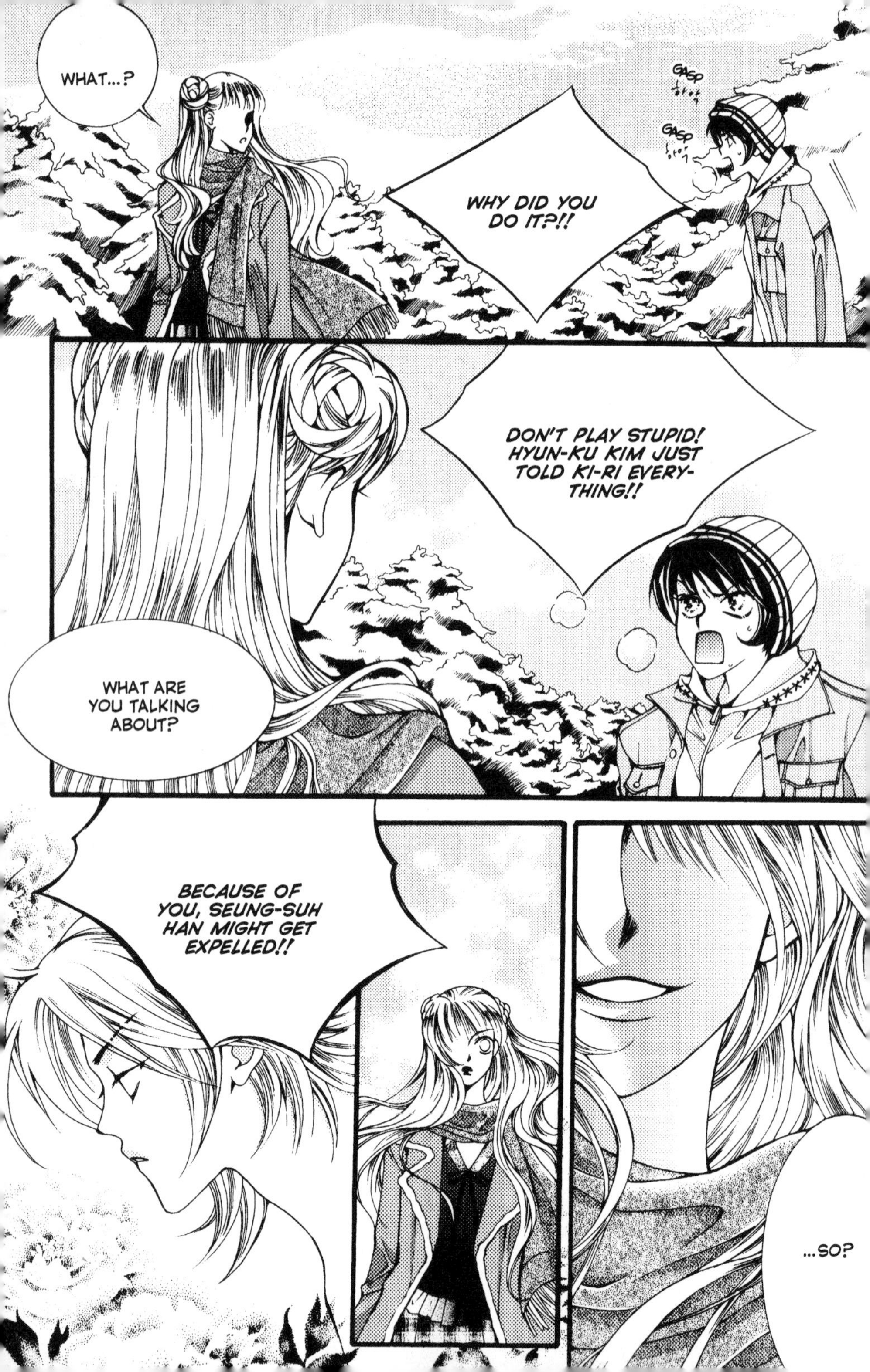
WHAT...?
WHY DID YOU DO IT?!!
GASP
GASP
DON'T PLAY STUPID! HYUN-KU KIM JUST TOLD KI-RI EVERY-THING!!
WHAT ARE YOU TALKING ABOUT?
BECAUSE OF YOU, SEUNG-SUH HAN MIGHT GET EXPELLED!!
...SO?

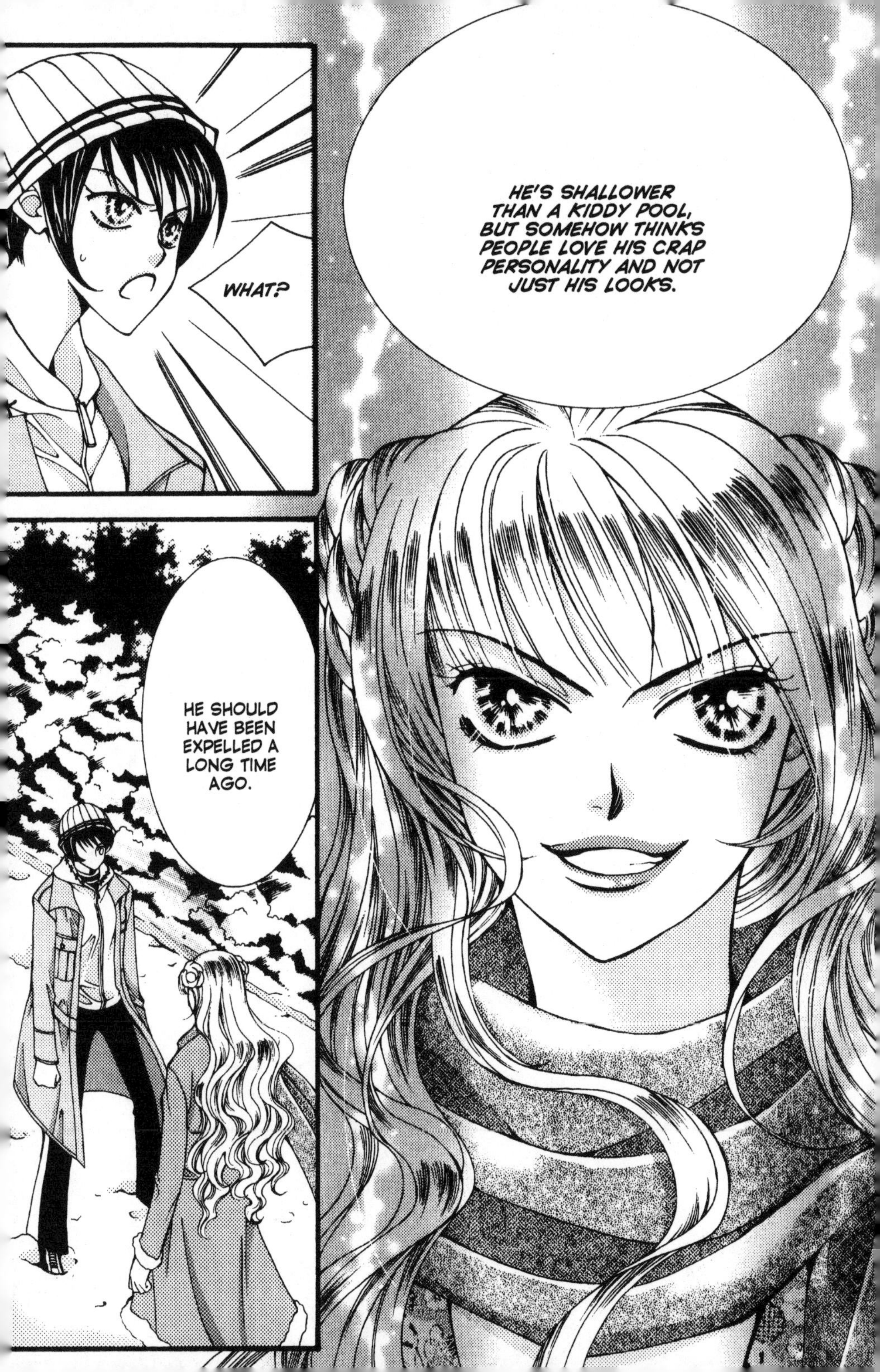
WHAT?
HE SHOULD HAVE BEEN EXPELLED A LONG TIME AGO.
HE'S SHALLOWER THAN A KIDDY POOL, BUT SOMEHOW THINKS PEOPLE LOVE HIS CRAP PERSONALITY AND NOT JUST HIS LOOKS.

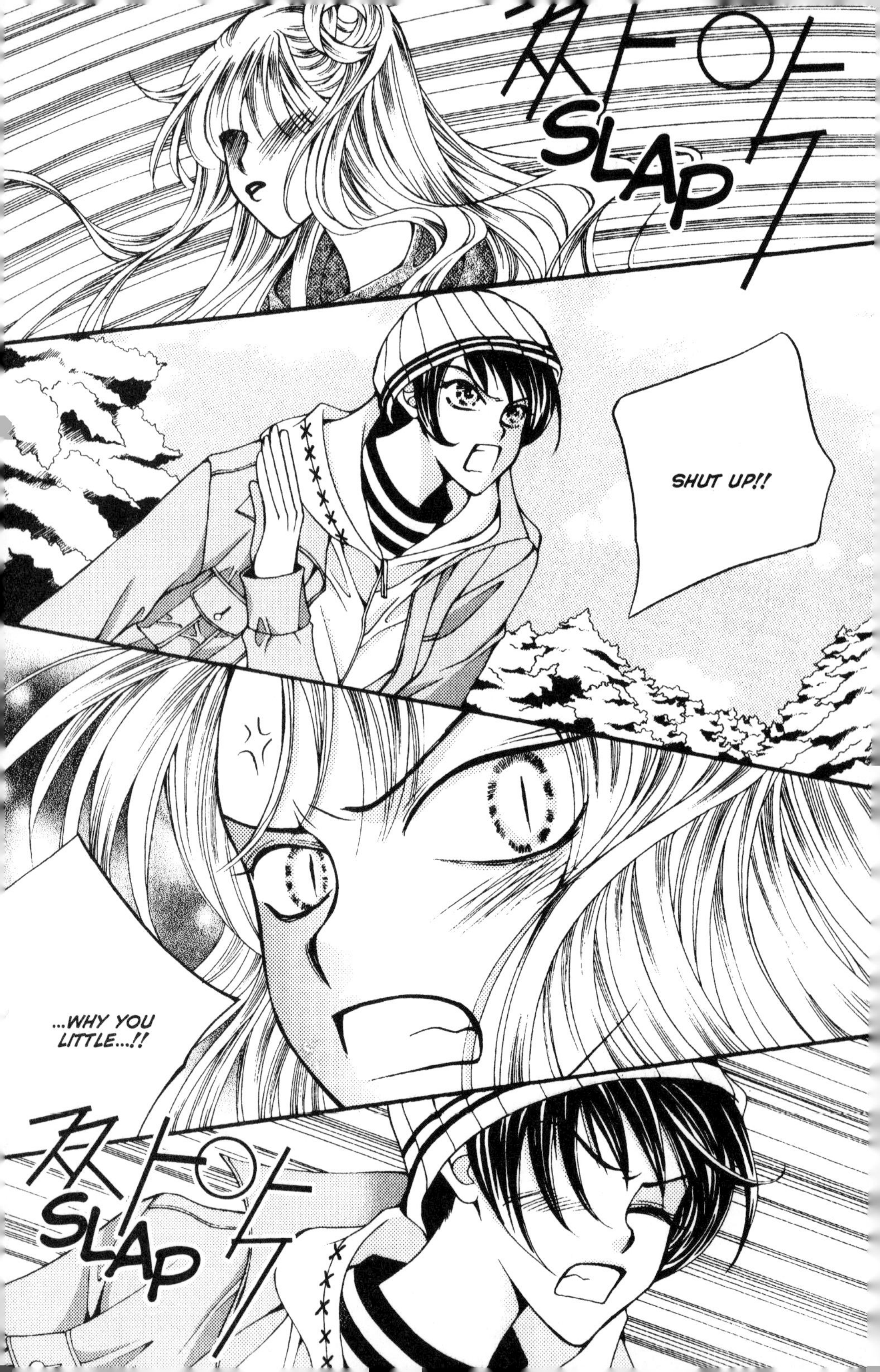
SLAP
SHUT UP!!
...WHY YOU LITTLE...!!
SLAP

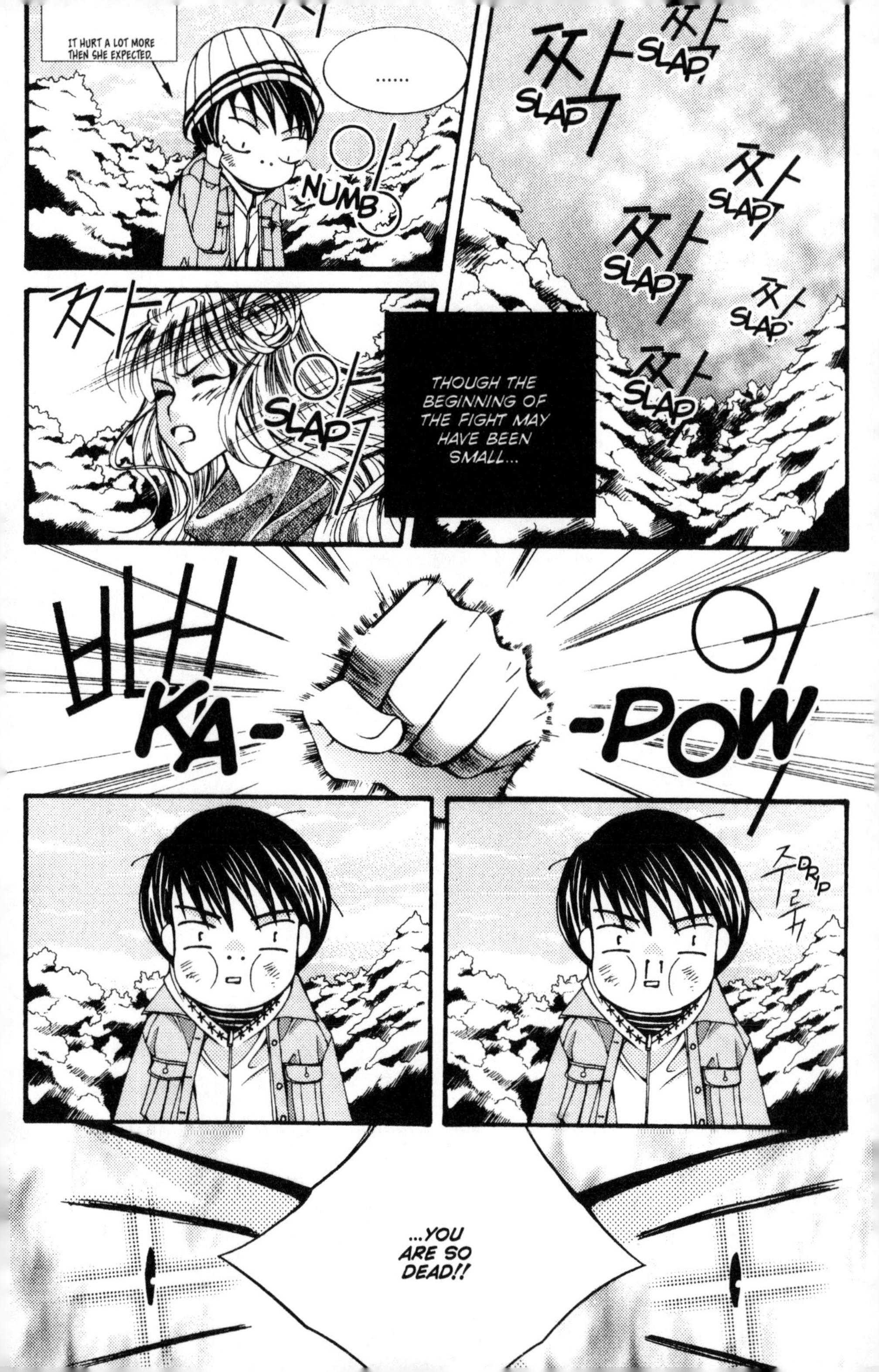
IT HURT A LOT MORE THEN SHE EXPECTED.
......
NUMB
SLAP
SLAP
SLAP
SLAP
SLAP
SLAP
SLAP
THOUGH THE BEGINNING OF THE FIGHT MAY HAVE BEEN SMALL...
KA-
-POW
DRIP
...YOU ARE SO DEAD!!

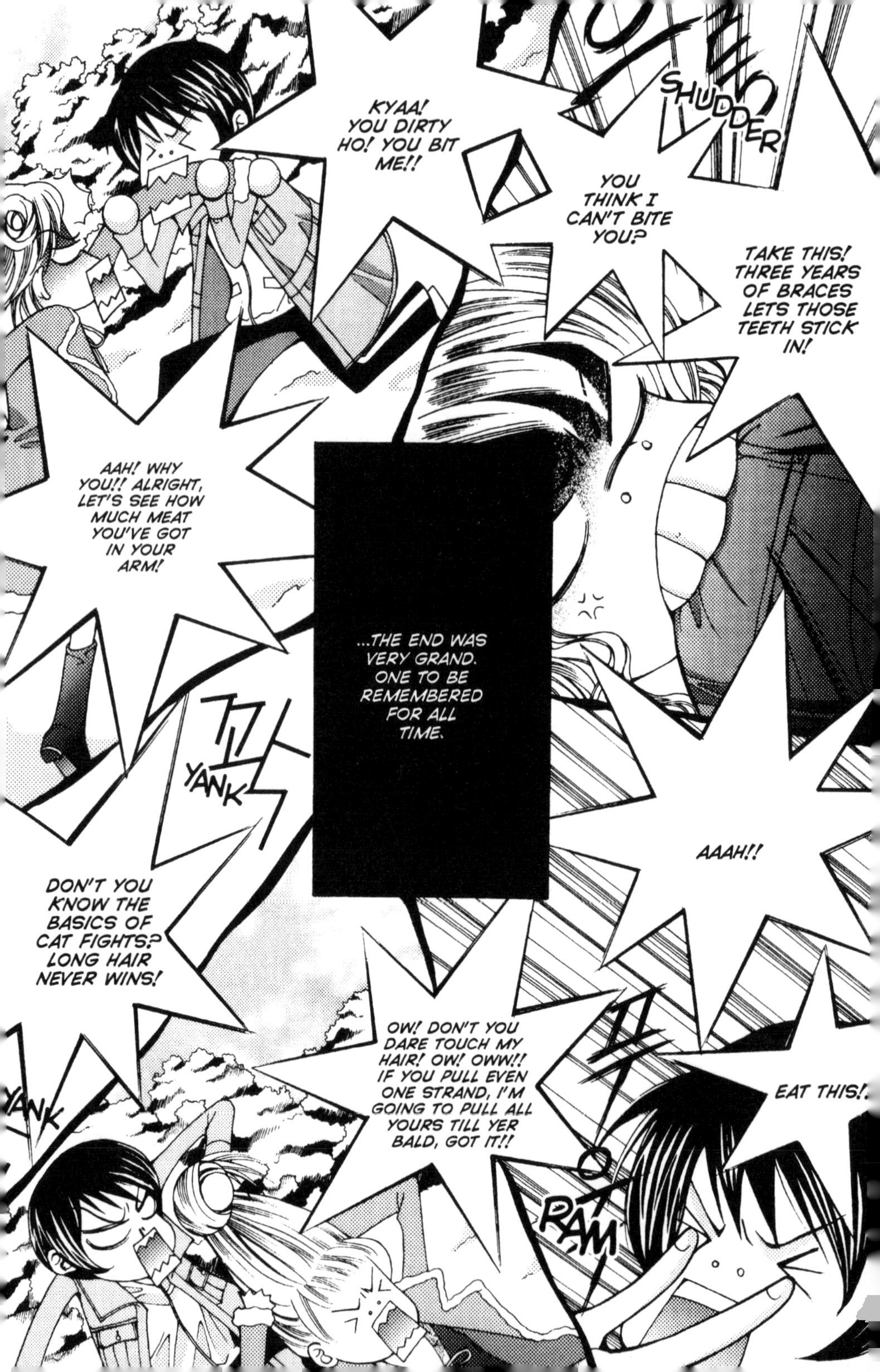
KYAA! YOU DIRTY HO! YOU BIT ME!!
SHUDDER
YOU THINK I CAN'T BITE YOU?
TAKE THIS! THREE YEARS OF BRACES LETS THOSE TEETH STICK IN!
AAH! WHY YOU!! ALRIGHT, LET'S SEE HOW MUCH MEAT YOU'VE GOT IN YOUR ARM!
YANK
...THE END WAS VERY GRAND. ONE TO BE REMEMBERED FOR ALL TIME.
AAAH!!
DON'T YOU KNOW THE BASICS OF CAT FIGHTS? LONG HAIR NEVER WINS!
YANK
OW! DON'T YOU DARE TOUCH MY HAIR! OW! OWW!! IF YOU PULL EVEN ONE STRAND, I'M GOING TO PULL ALL YOURS TILL YER BALD, GOT IT!!
RAM
EAT THIS!.

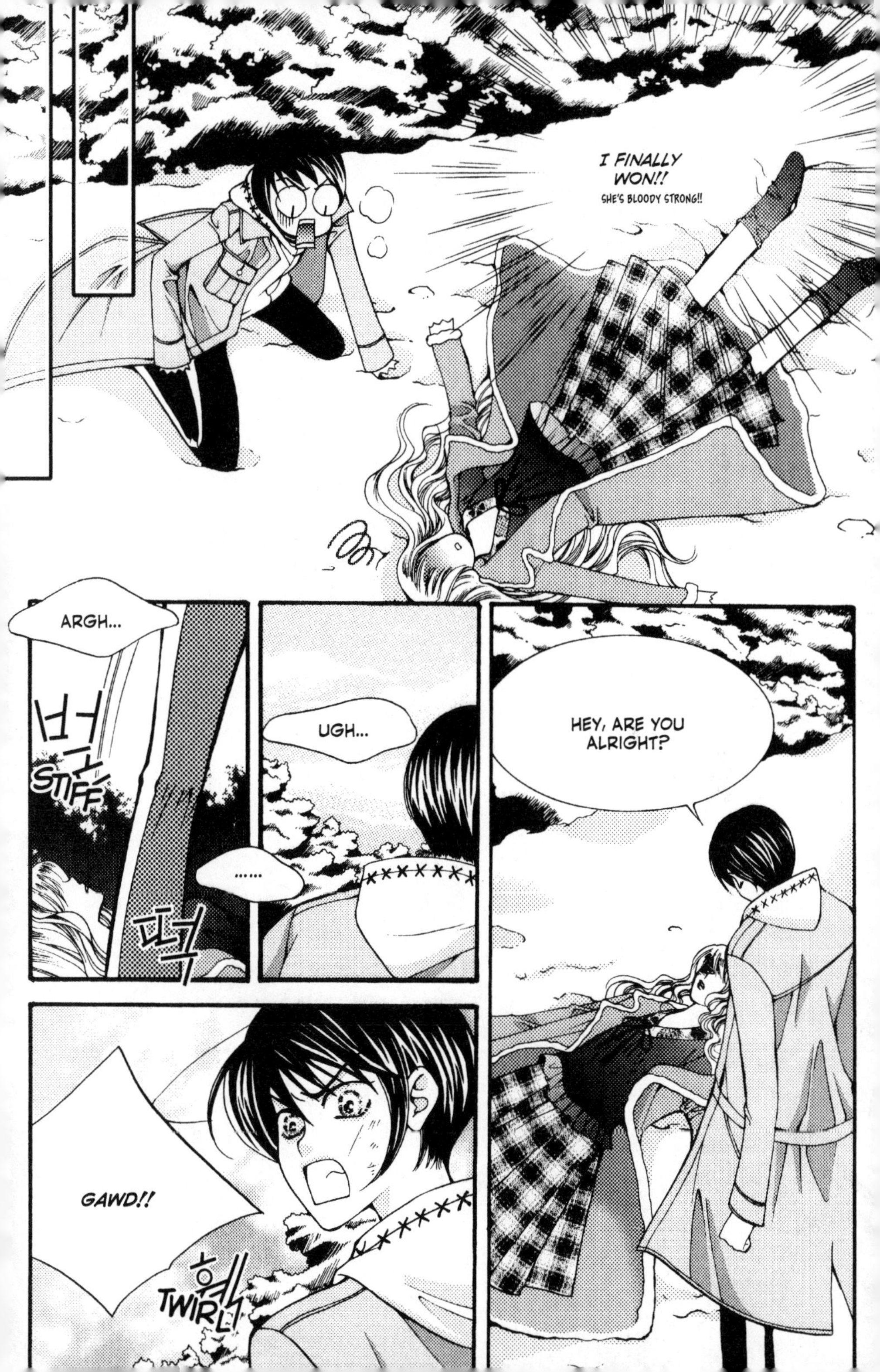
I FINALLY WON!!
SHE'S BLOODY STRONG!!
ARGH...
STIFF
UGH...
......
GAWD!!
TWIRL
HEY, ARE YOU ALRIGHT?

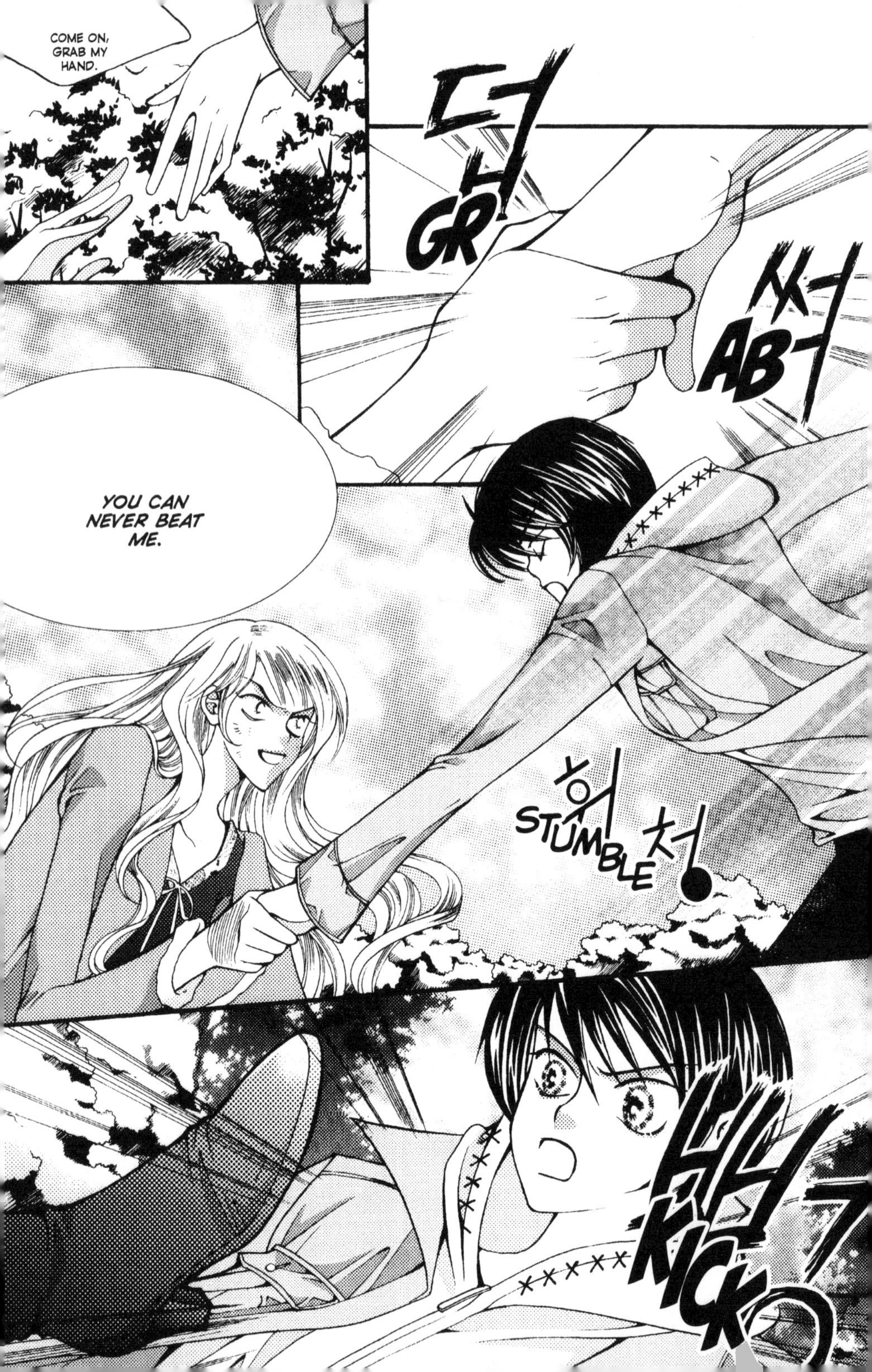
COME ON, GRAB MY HAND.
GRAB
YOU CAN NEVER BEAT ME.
STUMBLE
KICK

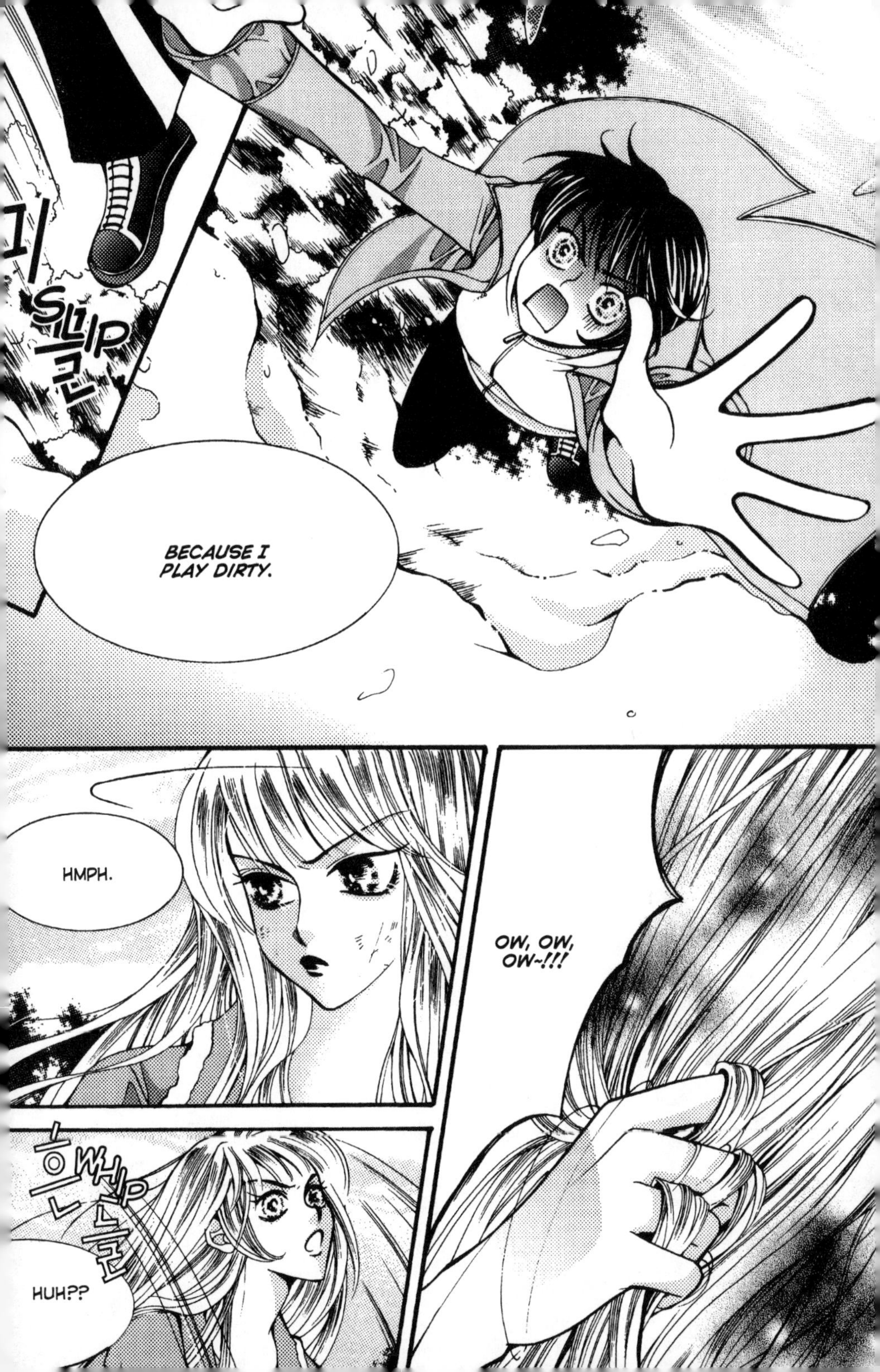
SLIP
BECAUSE I PLAY DIRTY.
HMPH.
WHIP
HUH??
OW, OW, OW~!!!

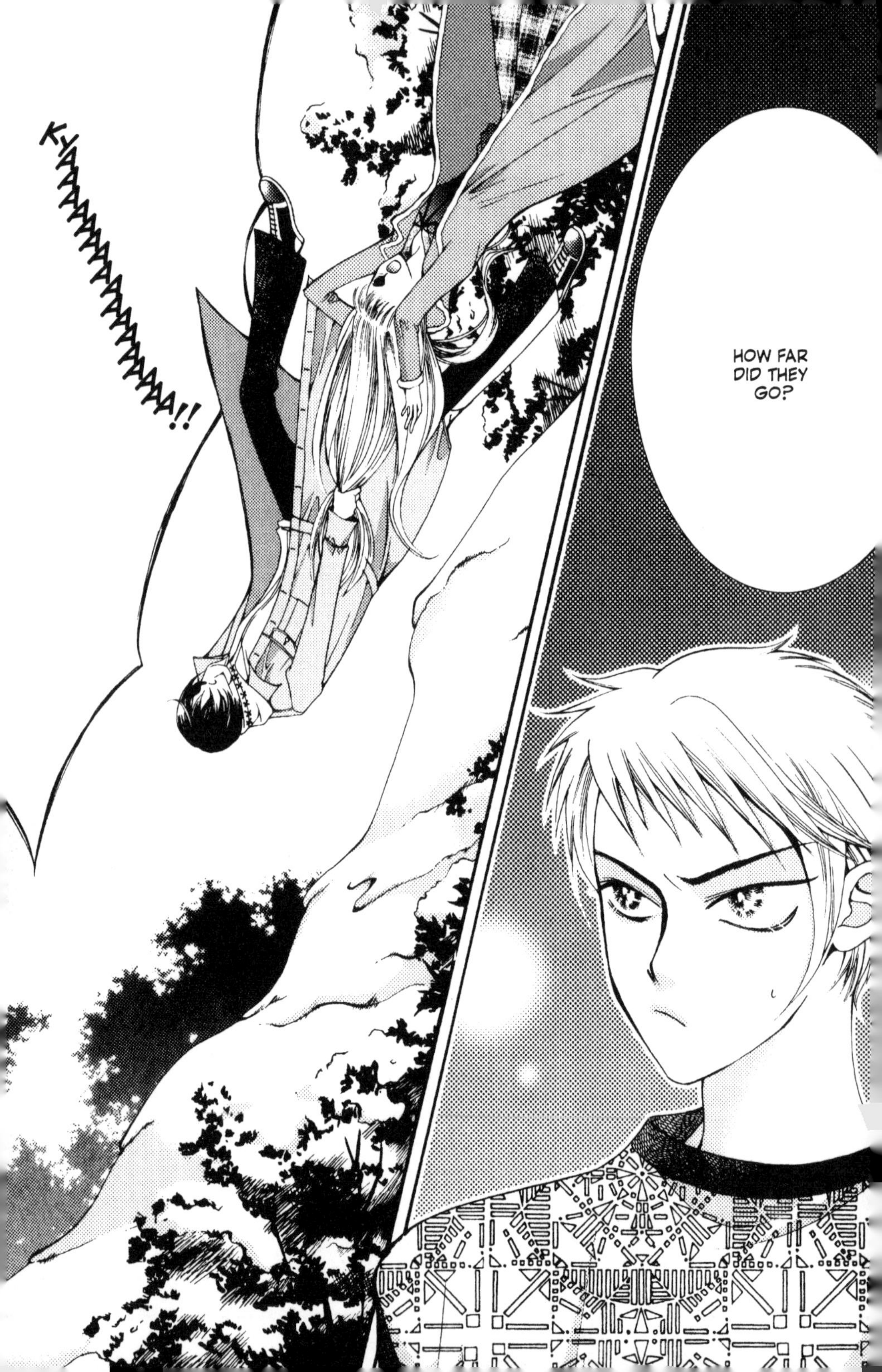
KYAAAAAAAAAAAAAAAA!!
HOW FAR DID THEY GO?

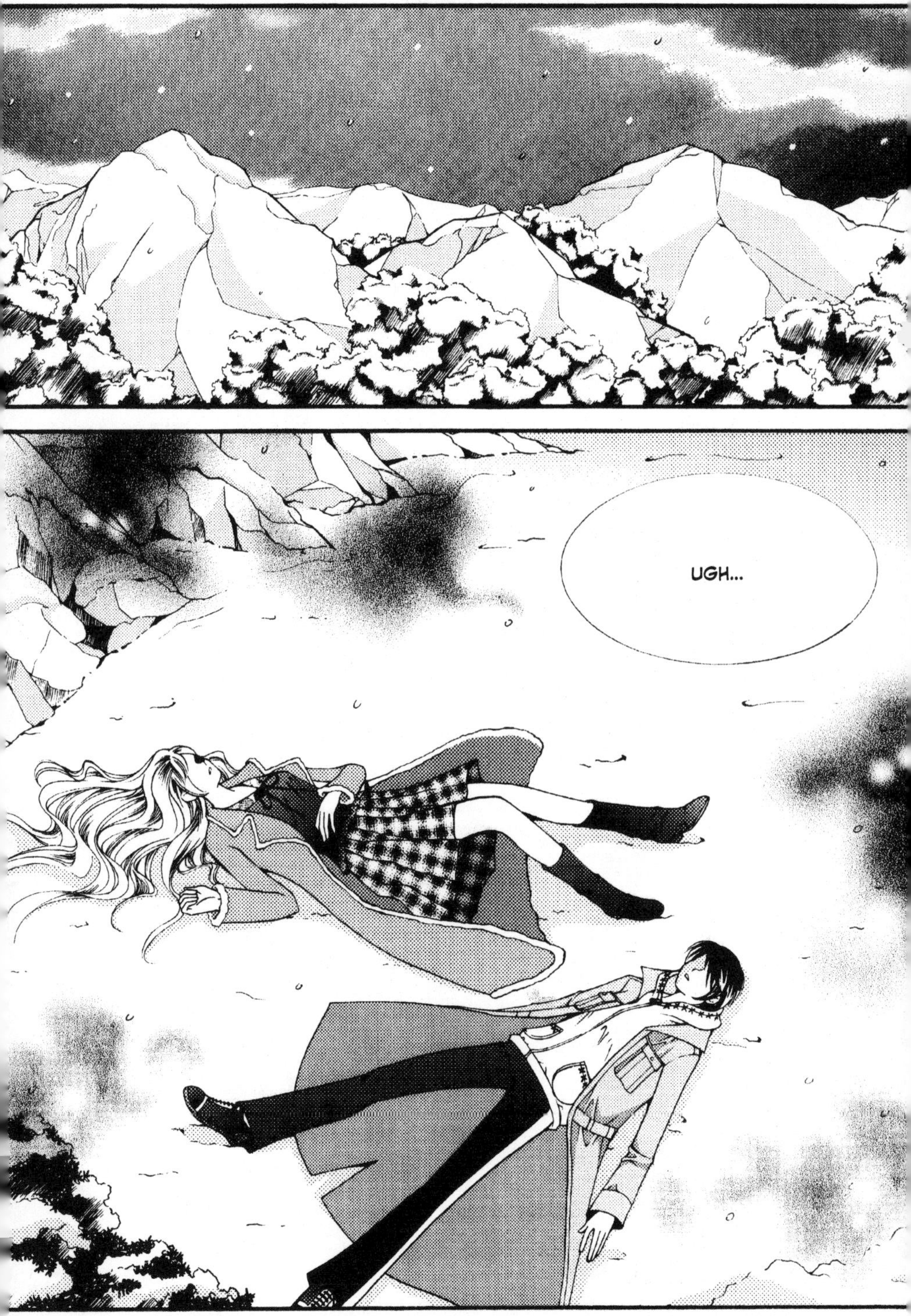
UGH...

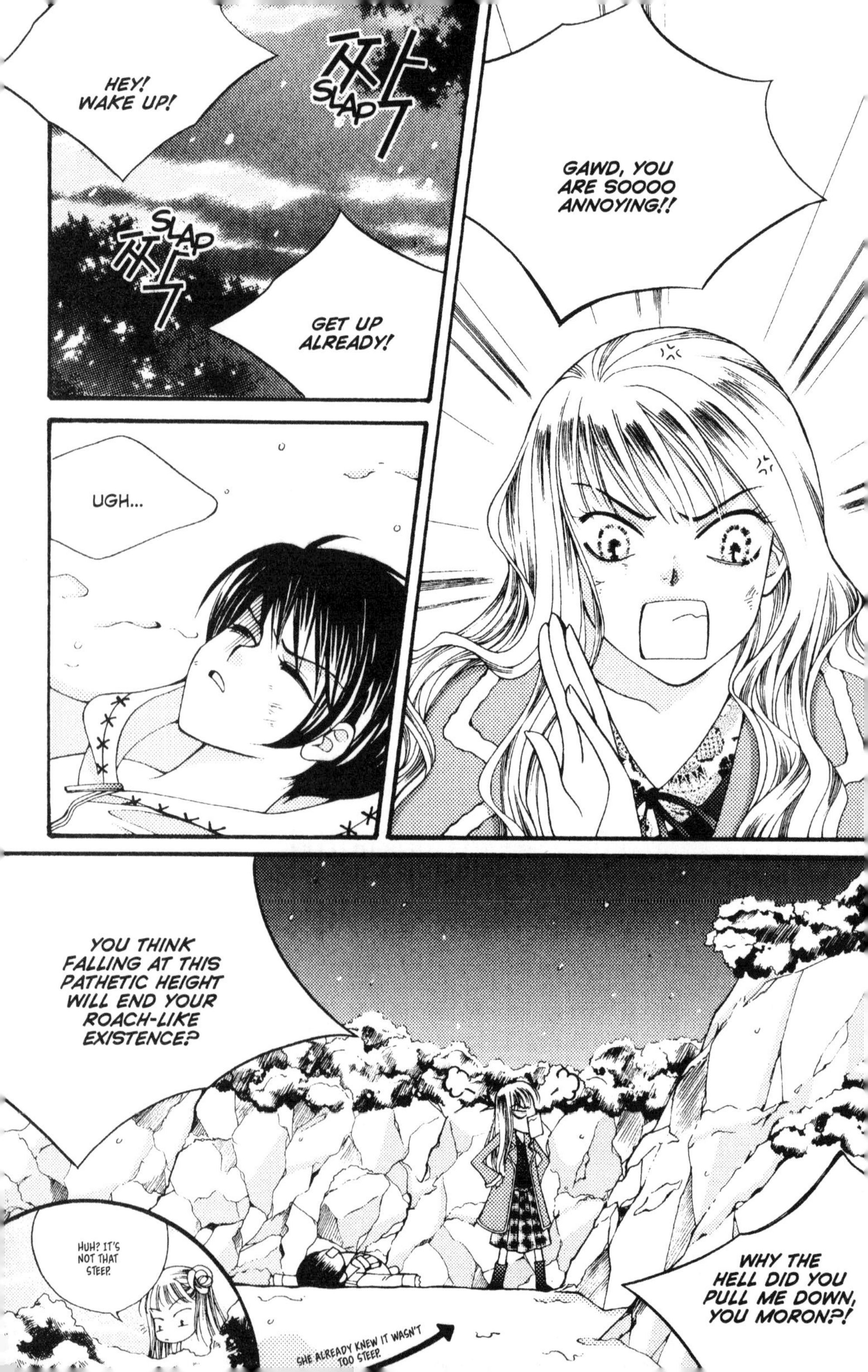
HEY! WAKE UP!
SLAP
SLAP
GET UP ALREADY!
UGH...
GAWD, YOU ARE SOOOO ANNOYING!!
YOU THINK FALLING AT THIS PATHETIC HEIGHT WILL END YOUR ROACH-LIKE EXISTENCE?
HUH? IT'S NOT THAT STEEP.
WHY THE HELL DID YOU PULL ME DOWN, YOU MORON?!
SHE ALREADY KNEW IT WASN'T TOO STEEP.

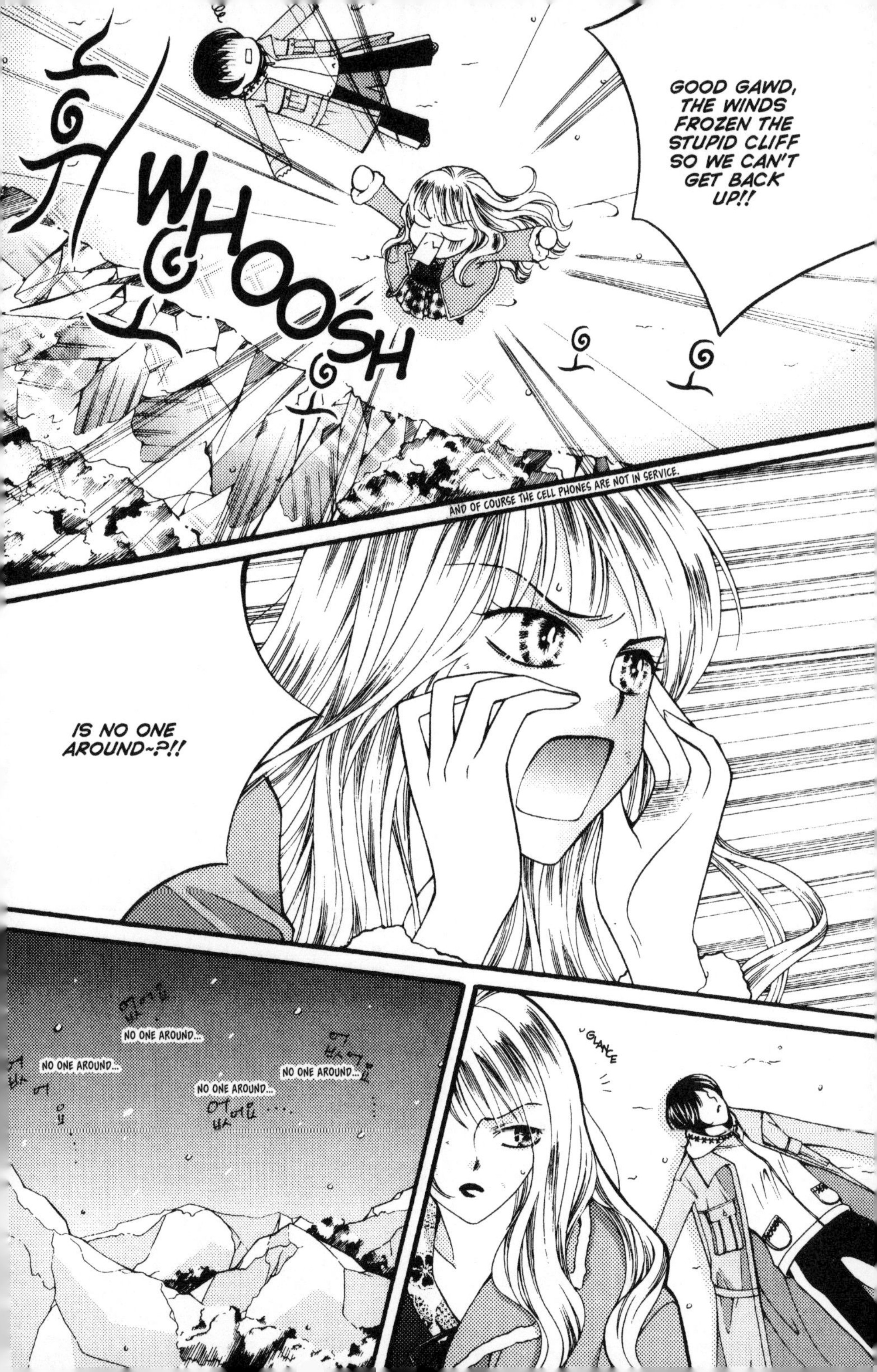
WHOOSH
GOOD GAWD, THE WINDS FROZEN THE STUPID CLIFF SO WE CAN'T GET BACK UP!!
AND OF COURSE THE CELL PHONES ARE NOT IN SERVICE.
IS NO ONE AROUND~?!!
NO ONE AROUND...
NO ONE AROUND...
NO ONE AROUND...
NO ONE AROUND...
GLANCE

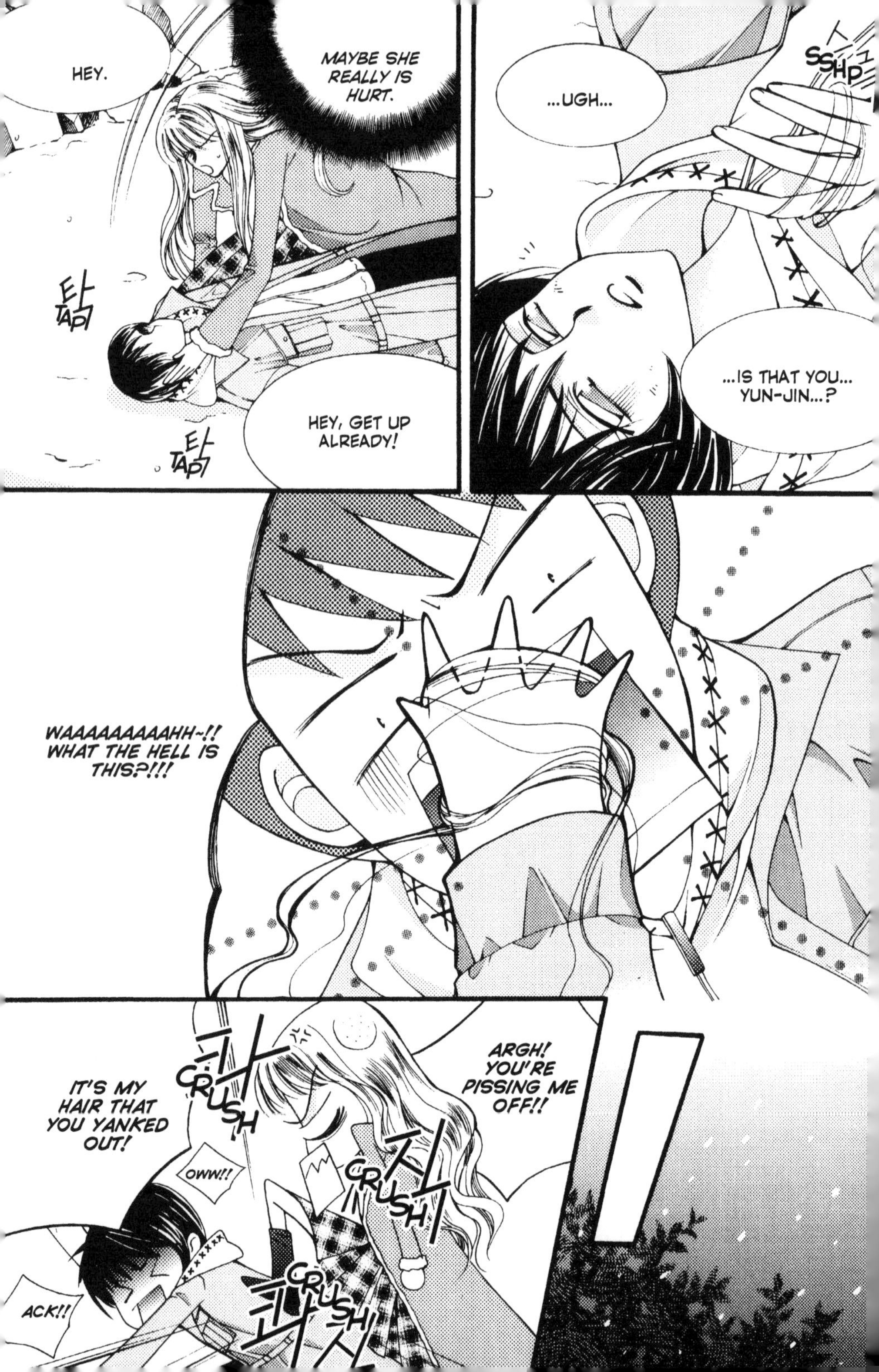
HEY.
MAYBE SHE REALLY IS HURT.
TAP!
TAP!
HEY, GET UP ALREADY!
SSHP
...UGH...
...IS THAT YOU... YUN-JIN...?
WAAAAAAAAAH~!! WHAT THE HELL IS THIS?!!!
IT'S MY HAIR THAT YOU YANKED OUT!
CRUSH
OWW!!
ARGH! YOU'RE PISSING ME OFF!!
CRUSH
ACK!!
CRUSH

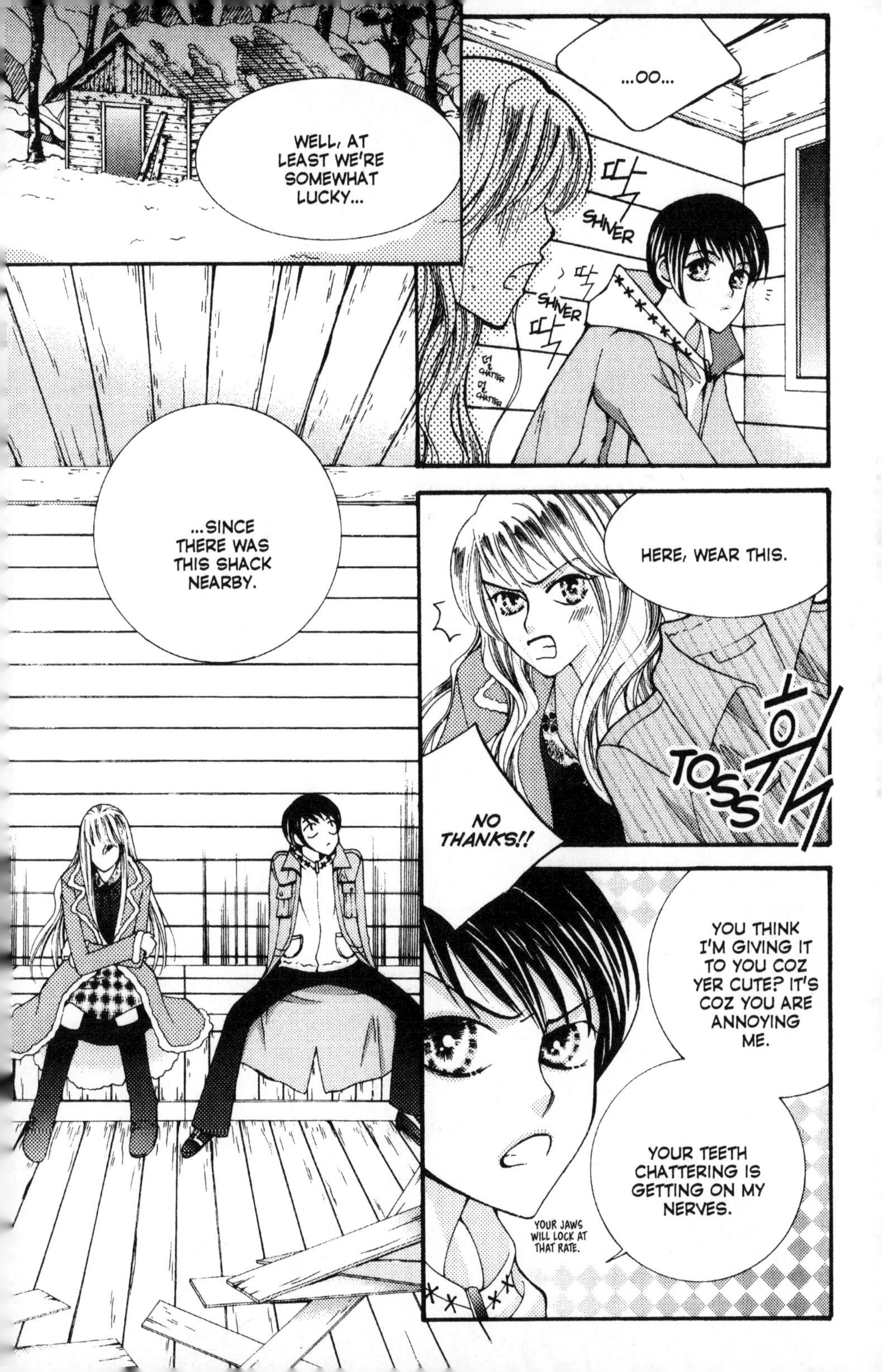
WELL, AT LEAST WE'RE SOMEWHAT LUCKY...
...OO...
SHIVER
SHIVER
CHATTER
CHATTER
...SINCE THERE WAS THIS SHACK NEARBY.
HERE, WEAR THIS.
TOSS
NO THANKS!!
YOU THINK I'M GIVING IT TO YOU COZ YER CUTE? IT'S COZ YOU ARE ANNOYING ME.
YOUR TEETH CHATTERING IS GETTING ON MY NERVES.
YOUR JAWS WILL LOCK AT THAT RATE.

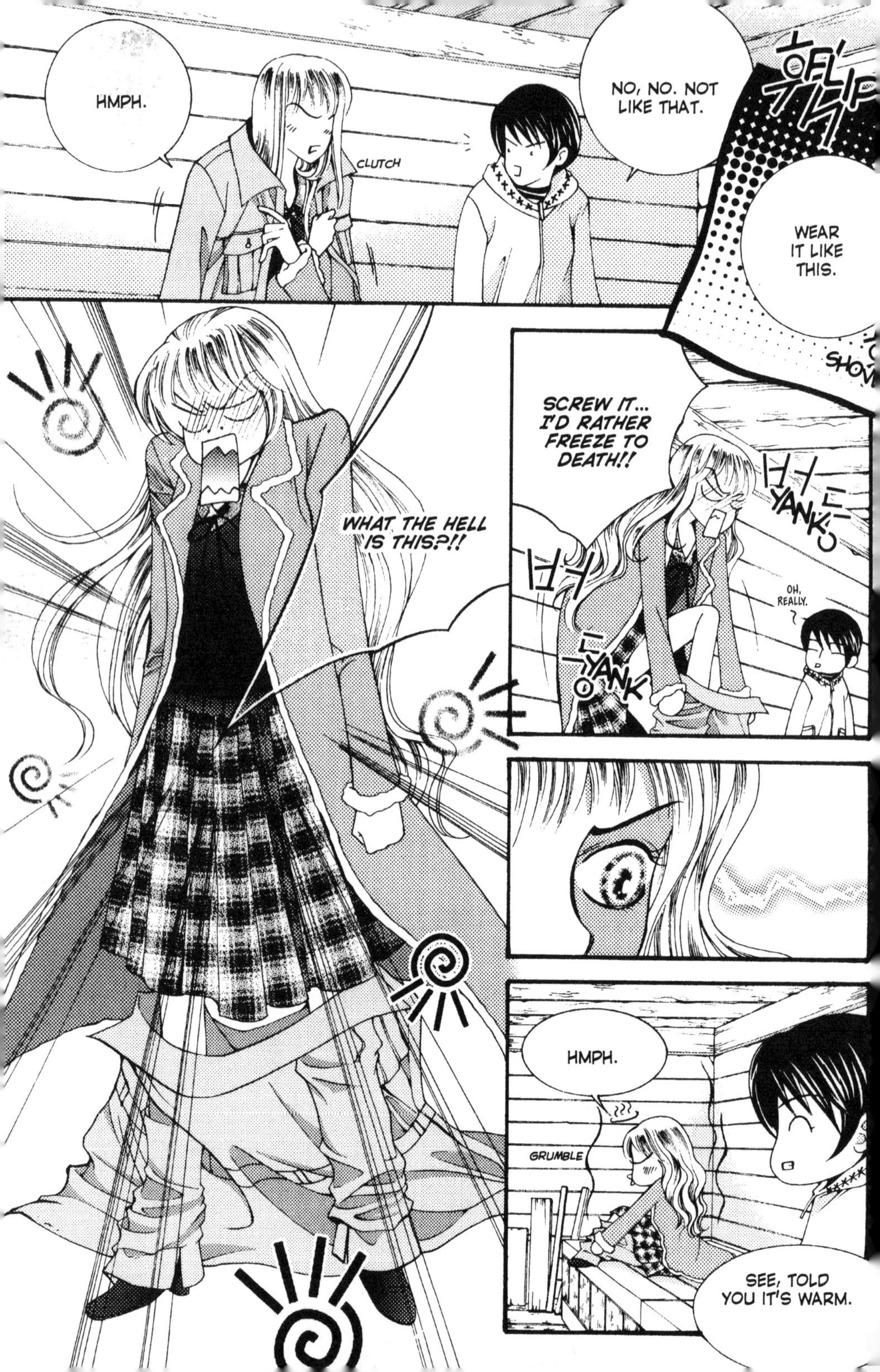
HMPH.
CLUTCH
NO, NO. NOT LIKE THAT.
FLIP
WEAR IT LIKE THIS.
SHOV
WHAT THE HELL IS THIS?!!
SCREW IT... I'D RATHER FREEZE TO DEATH!!
YANK
YANK
OH, REALLY.
HMPH.
GRUMBLE
SEE, TOLD YOU IT'S WARM.

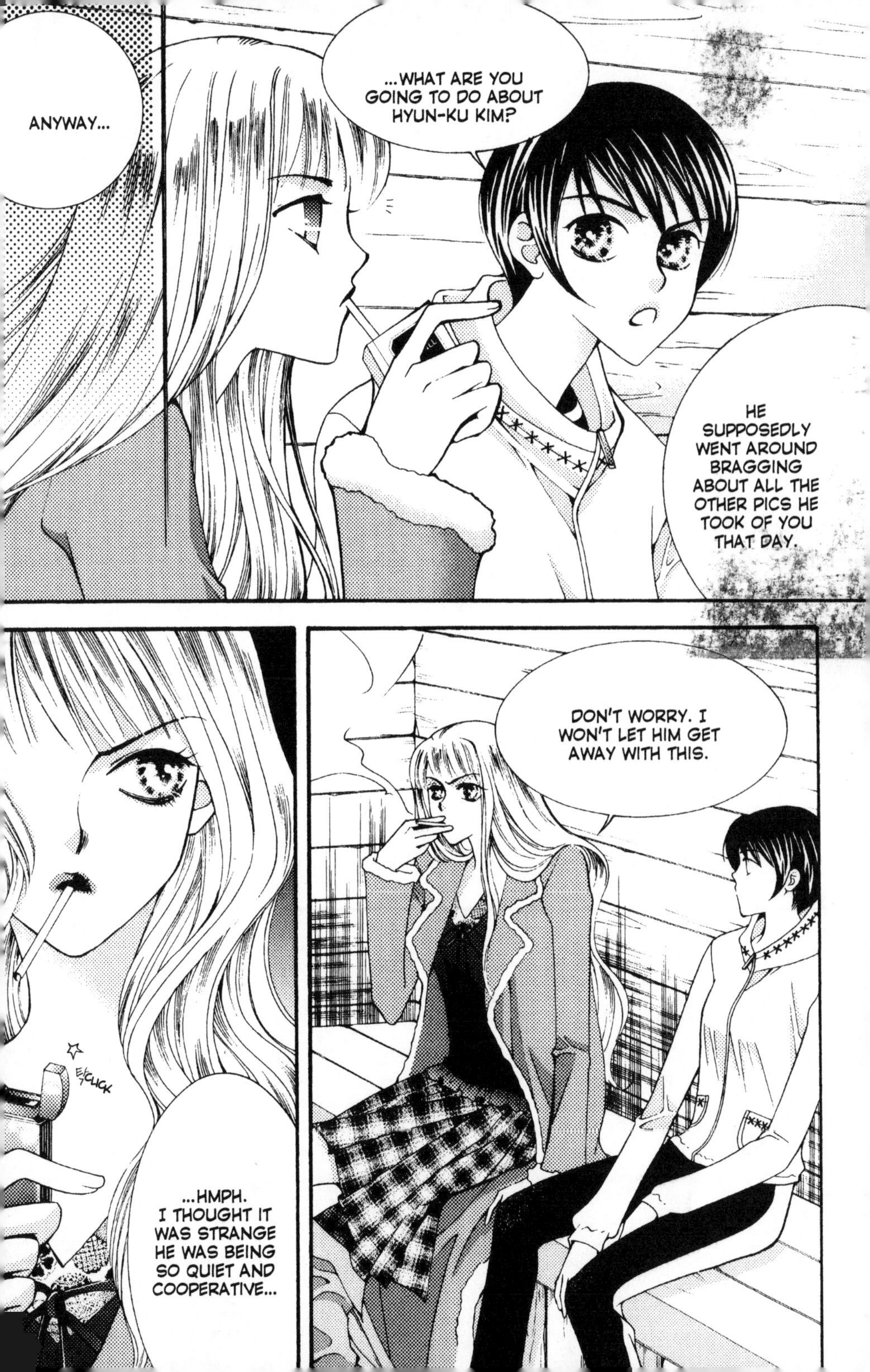
ANYWAY...
...WHAT ARE YOU GOING TO DO ABOUT HYUN-KU KIM?
HE SUPPOSEDLY WENT AROUND BRAGGING ABOUT ALL THE OTHER PICS HE TOOK OF YOU THAT DAY.
CLICK
...HMPH. I THOUGHT IT WAS STRANGE HE WAS BEING SO QUIET AND COOPERATIVE...
DON'T WORRY. I WON'T LET HIM GET AWAY WITH THIS.

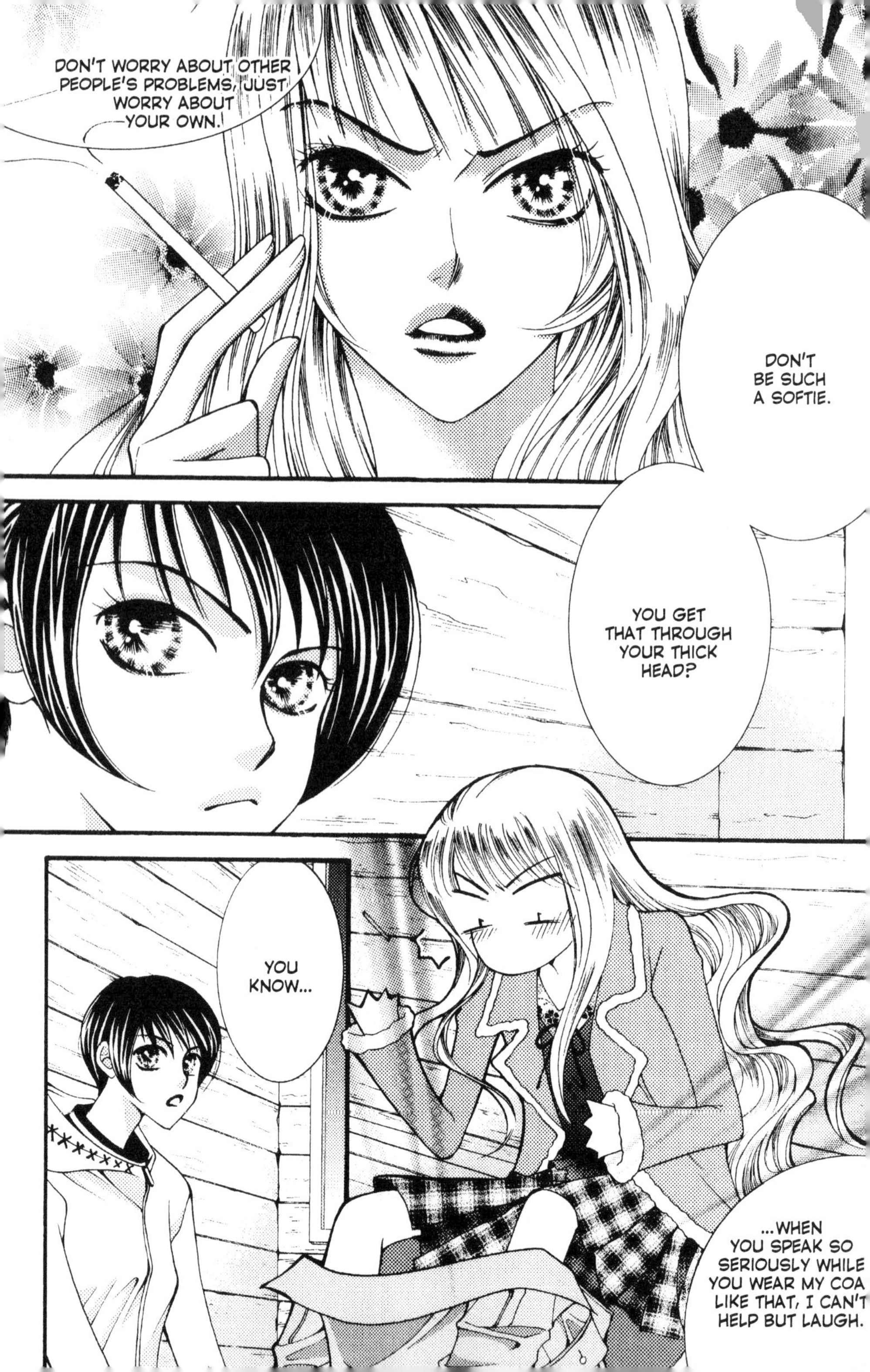
DON'T WORRY ABOUT OTHER PEOPLE'S PROBLEMS, JUST WORRY ABOUT YOUR OWN.
DON'T BE SUCH A SOFTIE.
YOU GET THAT THROUGH YOUR THICK HEAD?
YOU KNOW...
...WHEN YOU SPEAK SO SERIOUSLY WHILE YOU WEAR MY COA LIKE THAT, I CAN'T HELP BUT LAUGH.

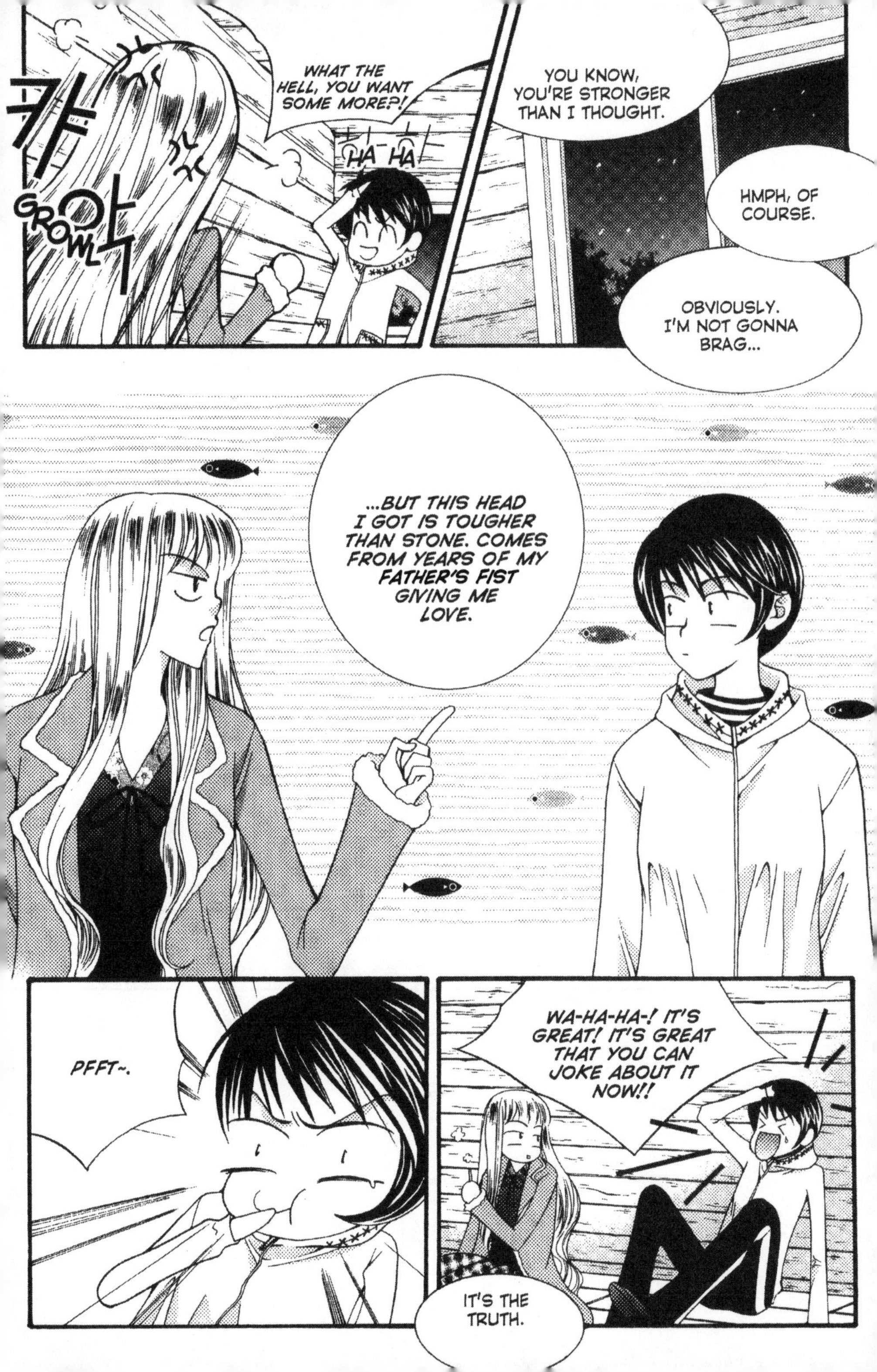
WHAT THE HELL, YOU WANT SOME MORE?!
HA HA
GROWL
YOU KNOW, YOU'RE STRONGER THAN I THOUGHT.
HMPH, OF COURSE.
OBVIOUSLY. I'M NOT GONNA BRAG...
...BUT THIS HEAD I GOT IS TOUGHER THAN STONE. COMES FROM YEARS OF MY FATHER'S FIST GIVING ME LOVE.
PFFT~.
WA-HA-HA-! IT'S GREAT! IT'S GREAT THAT YOU CAN JOKE ABOUT IT NOW!!
IT'S THE TRUTH.

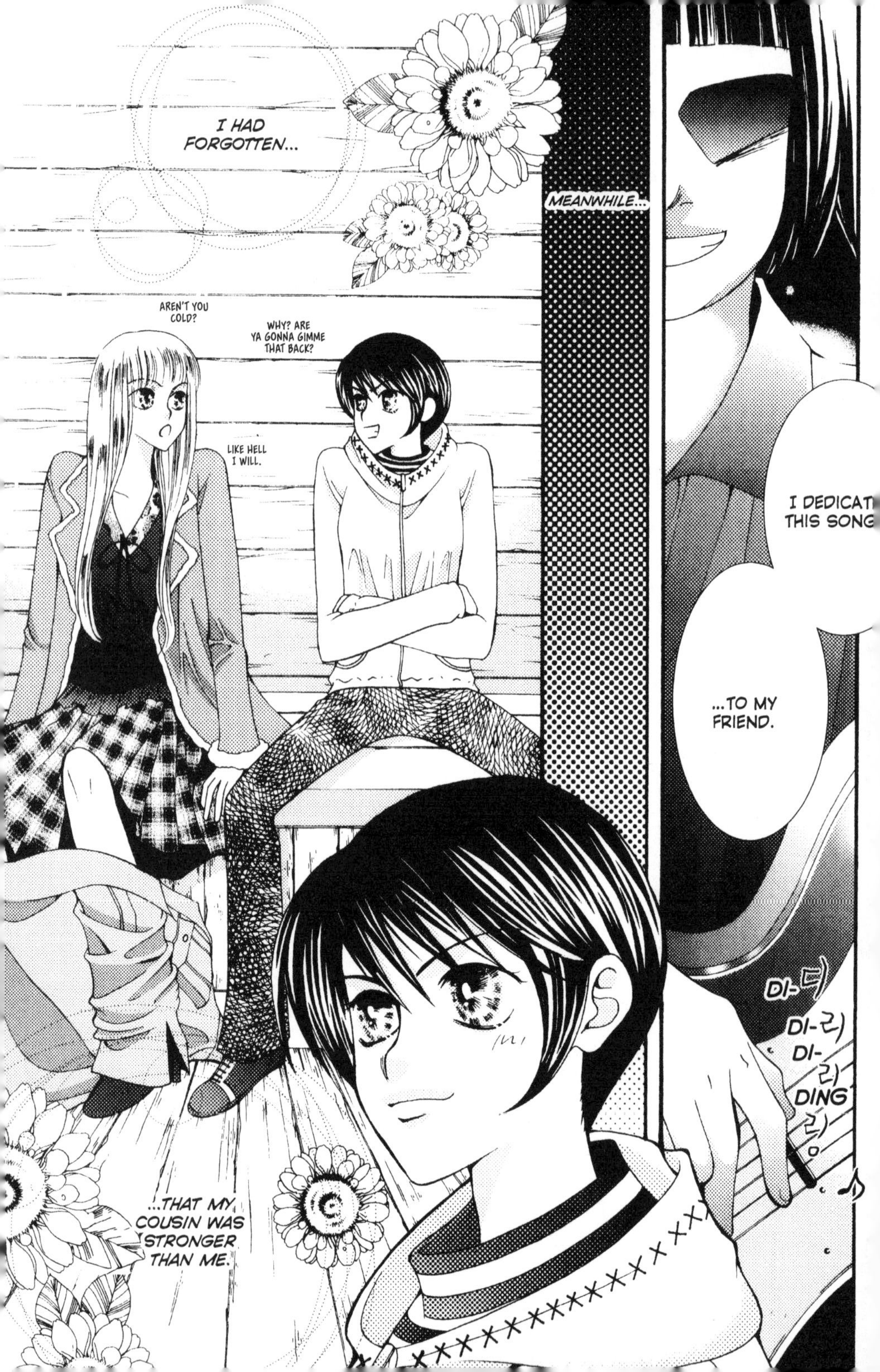
I HAD FORGOTTEN...
AREN'T YOU COLD?
WHY? ARE YA GONNA GIMME THAT BACK?
LIKE HELL I WILL.
...THAT MY COUSIN WAS STRONGER THAN ME.
MEANWHILE...
I DEDICAT THIS SONG
...TO MY FRIEND.
DI-디
DI-리
DI-리
DING 링

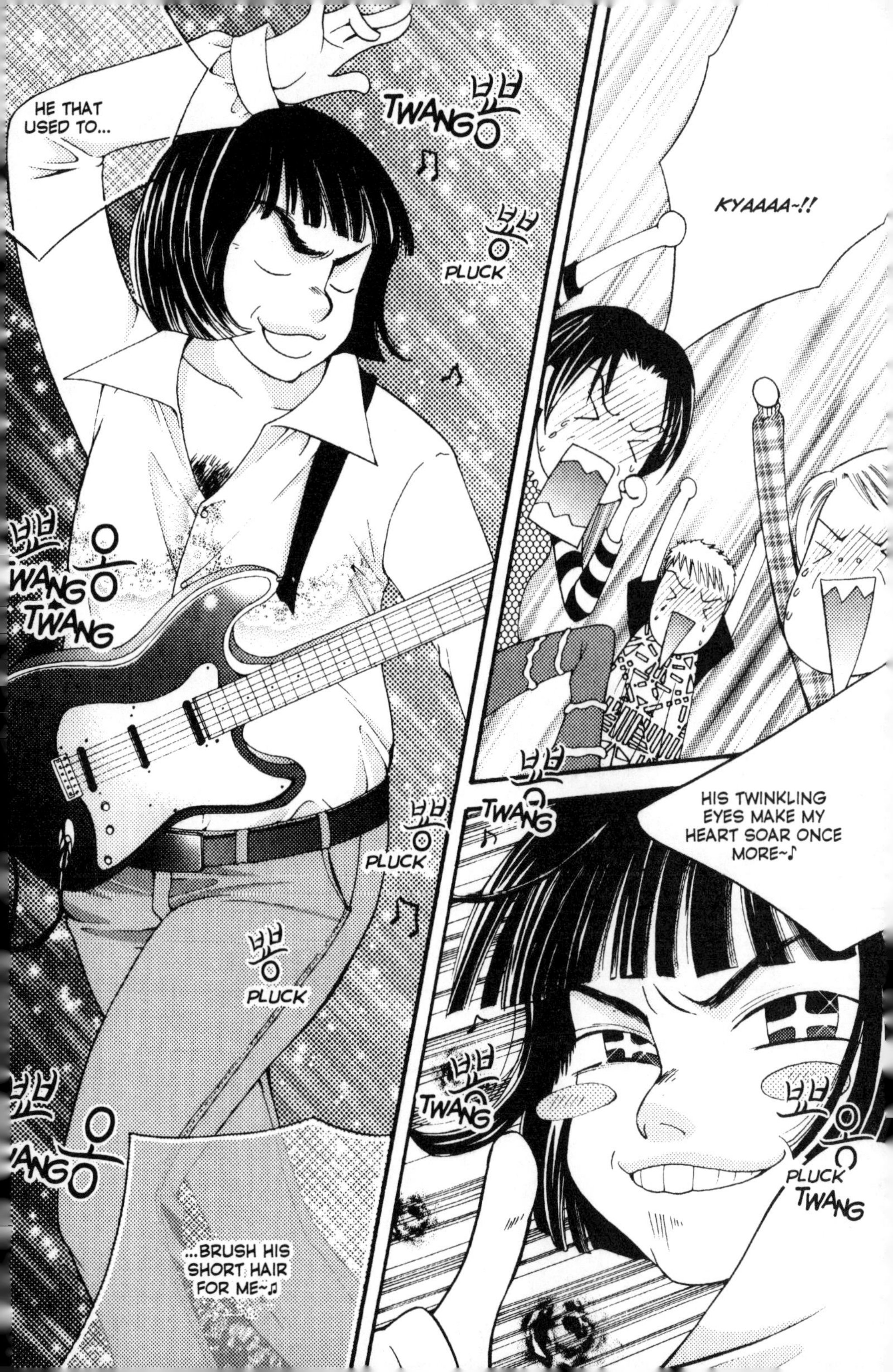
HE THAT USED TO...
TWANG
PLUCK
TWANG TWANG
PLUCK
PLUCK
TWANG
...BRUSH HIS SHORT HAIR FOR ME~♫
KYAAAA~!!
TWANG
HIS TWINKLING EYES MAKE MY HEART SOAR ONCE MORE~♪
TWANG
PLUCK
TWANG

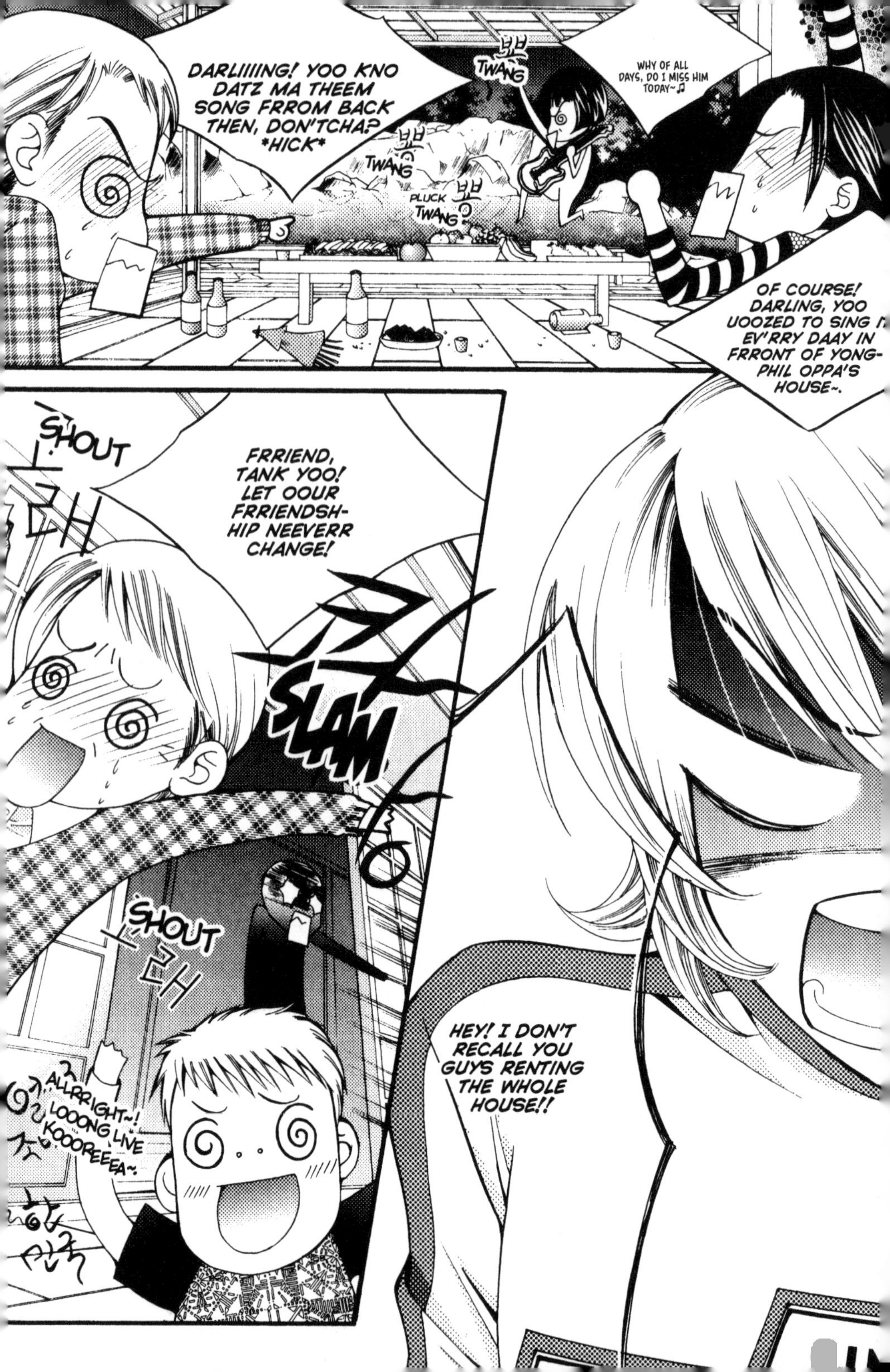
DARLIIIING! YOO KNO DATZ MA THEEM SONG FRROM BACK THEN, DON'TCHA? *HICK*
TWANG
TWANG
PLUCK
TWANG
WHY OF ALL DAYS, DO I MISS HIM TODAY~♫
OF COURSE! DARLING, YOO UOOZED TO SING I EV'RRY DAAY IN FRRONT OF YONG-PHIL OPPA'S HOUSE~.
SHOUT
FRRIEND, TANK YOO! LET OOUR FRRIENDSH-HIP NEEVERR CHANGE!
SLAM
SHOUT
ALLRRIGHT~! LOOOONG LIVE KOOOREEEA~.
HEY! I DON'T RECALL YOU GUYS RENTING THE WHOLE HOUSE!!

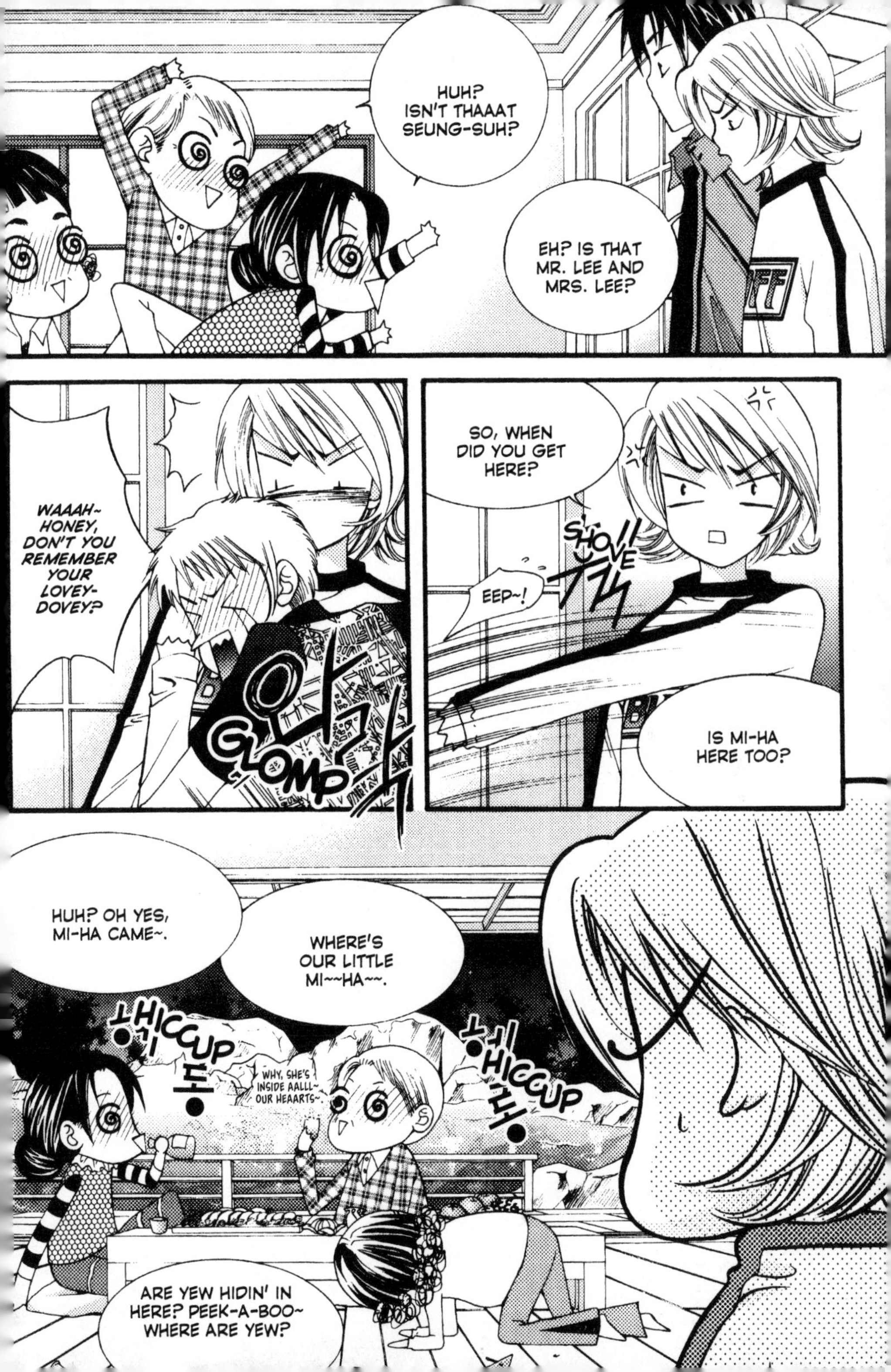
HUH? ISN'T THAAAT SEUNG-SUH?
EH? IS THAT MR. LEE AND MRS. LEE?
WAAAH~ HONEY, DON'T YOU REMEMBER YOUR LOVEY-DOVEY?
GLOMP
SO, WHEN DID YOU GET HERE?
SHOVE
EEP~!
IS MI-HA HERE TOO?
HUH? OH YES, MI-HA CAME~.
WHERE'S OUR LITTLE MI~~HA~~.
HICCUP
WHY, SHE'S INSIDE AALLL~ OUR HEAARTS~.
HICCUP
ARE YEW HIDIN' IN HERE? PEEK-A-BOO~ WHERE ARE YEW?

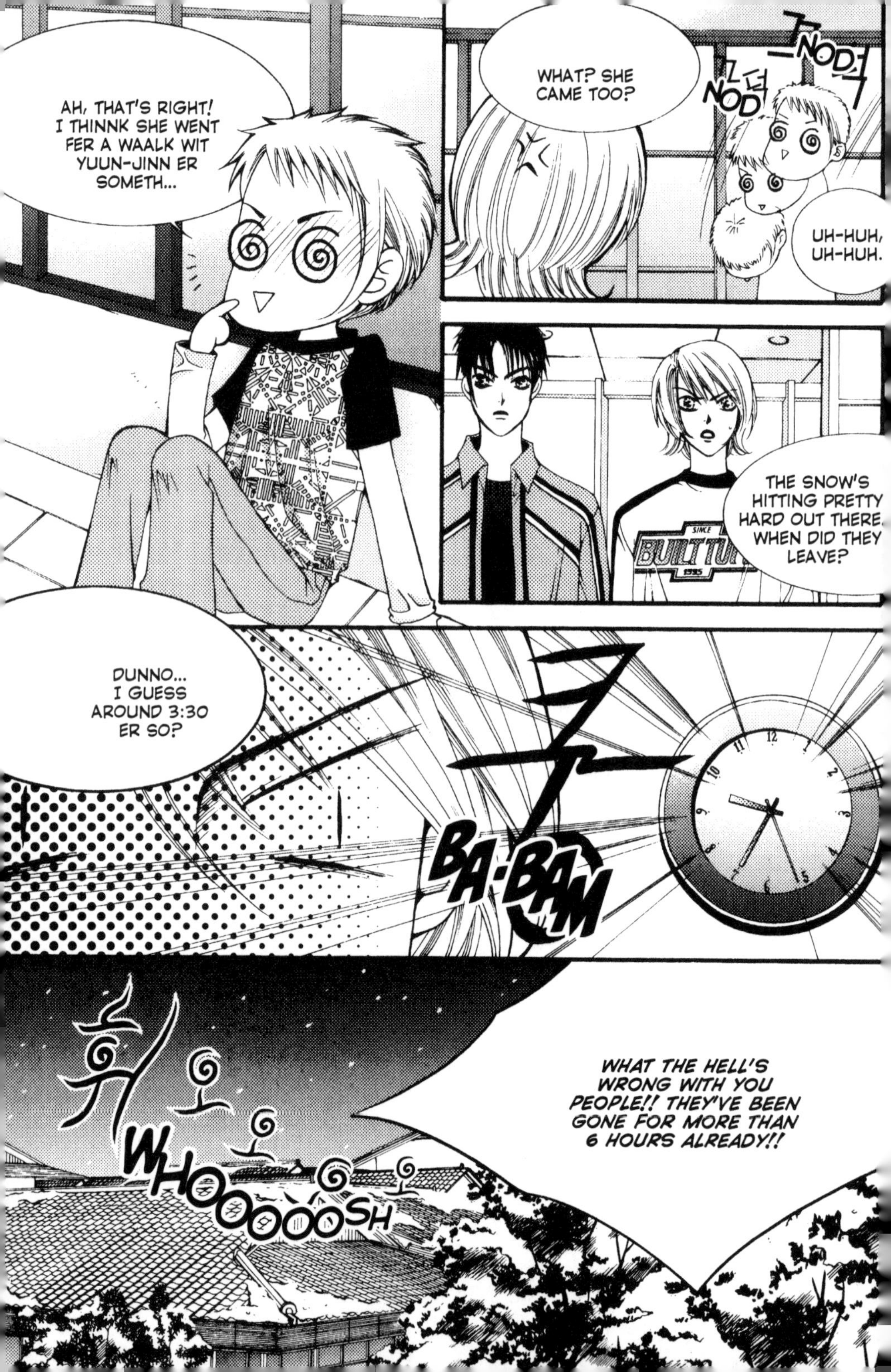
AH, THAT'S RIGHT! I THINNK SHE WENT FER A WAALK WIT YUUN-JINN ER SOMETH...
WHAT? SHE CAME TOO?
NOD NOD
UH-HUH, UH-HUH.
THE SNOW'S HITTING PRETTY HARD OUT THERE. WHEN DID THEY LEAVE?
DUNNO... I GUESS AROUND 3:30 ER SO?
BA-BAM
WHAT THE HELL'S WRONG WITH YOU PEOPLE!! THEY'VE BEEN GONE FOR MORE THAN 6 HOURS ALREADY!!
WHOOOOOOSH

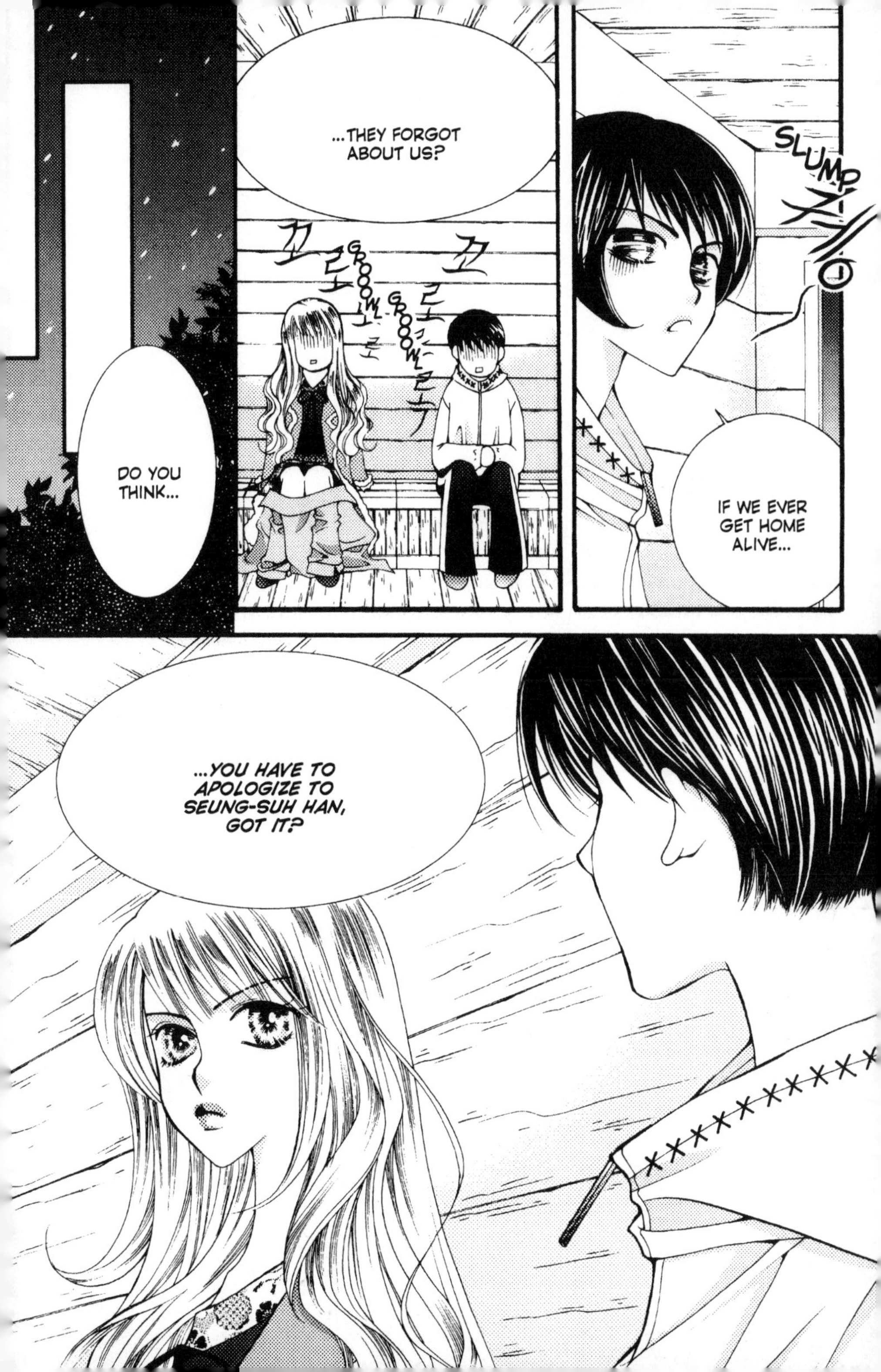
DO YOU THINK...
...THEY FORGOT ABOUT US?
GROOOWL
GROOOWL
SLUMP
IF WE EVER GET HOME ALIVE...
...YOU HAVE TO APOLOGIZE TO SEUNG-SUH HAN, GOT IT?

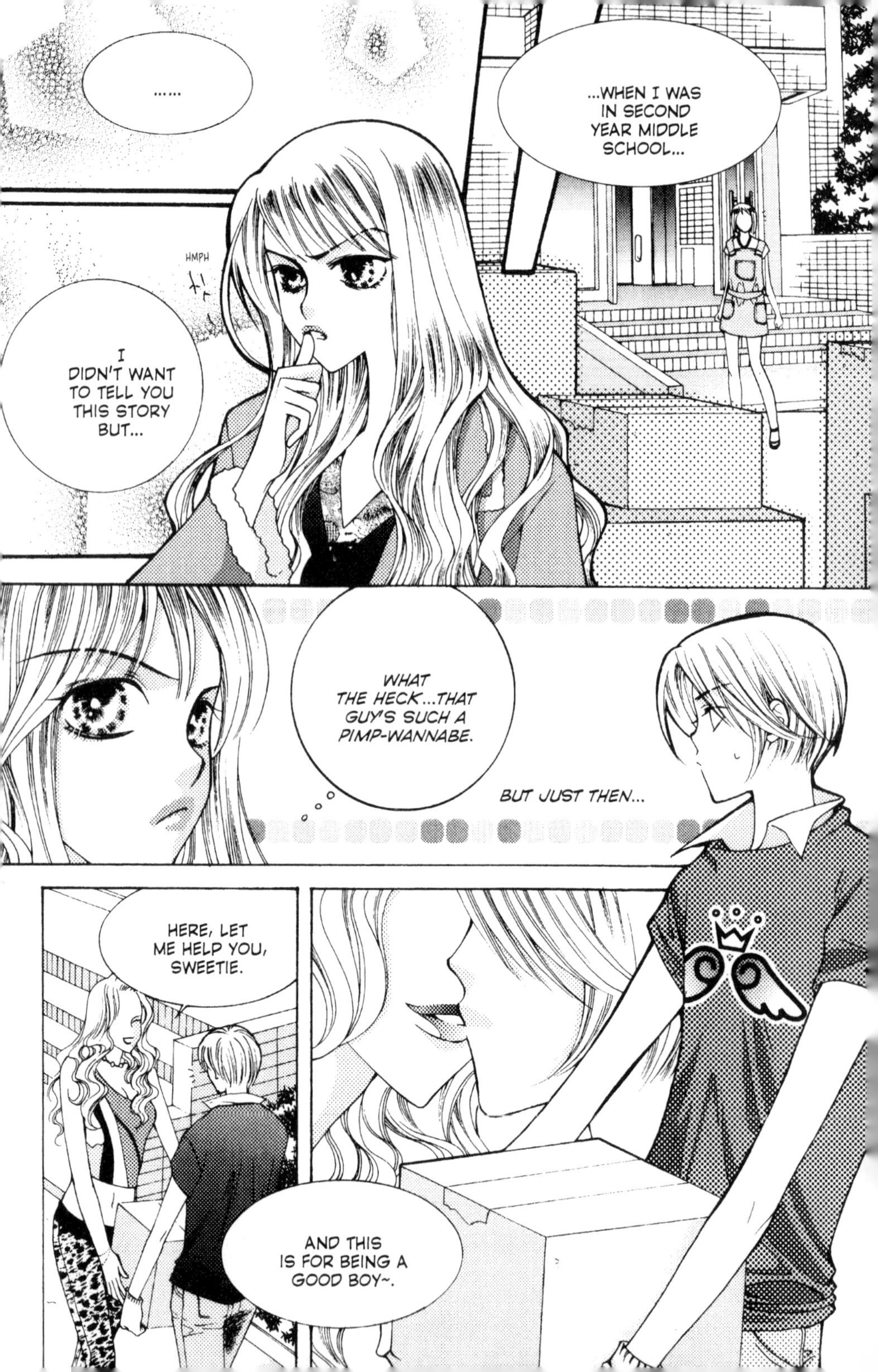
......
HMPH
I DIDN'T WANT TO TELL YOU THIS STORY BUT...
...WHEN I WAS IN SECOND YEAR MIDDLE SCHOOL...
WHAT THE HECK...THAT GUY'S SUCH A PIMP-WANNABE.
BUT JUST THEN...
HERE, LET ME HELP YOU, SWEETIE.
AND THIS IS FOR BEING A GOOD BOY~.

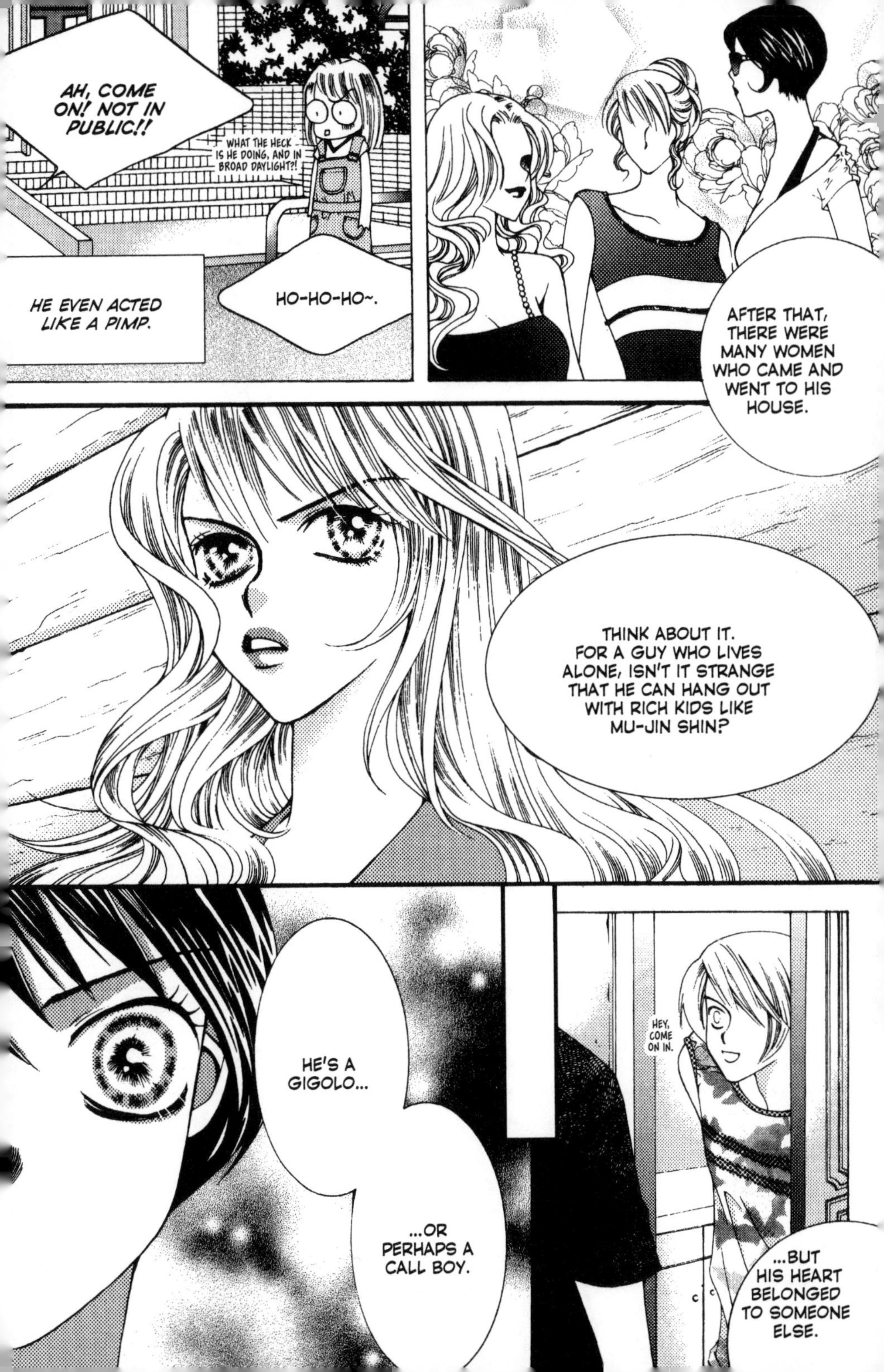
AH, COME ON! NOT IN PUBLIC!!
WHAT THE HECK IS HE DOING, AND IN BROAD DAYLIGHT?!
HE EVEN ACTED LIKE A PIMP.
HO-HO-HO~.
AFTER THAT, THERE WERE MANY WOMEN WHO CAME AND WENT TO HIS HOUSE.
THINK ABOUT IT. FOR A GUY WHO LIVES ALONE, ISN'T IT STRANGE THAT HE CAN HANG OUT WITH RICH KIDS LIKE MU-JIN SHIN?
HE'S A GIGOLO...
...OR PERHAPS A CALL BOY.
HEY, COME ON IN.
...BUT HIS HEART BELONGED TO SOMEONE ELSE.

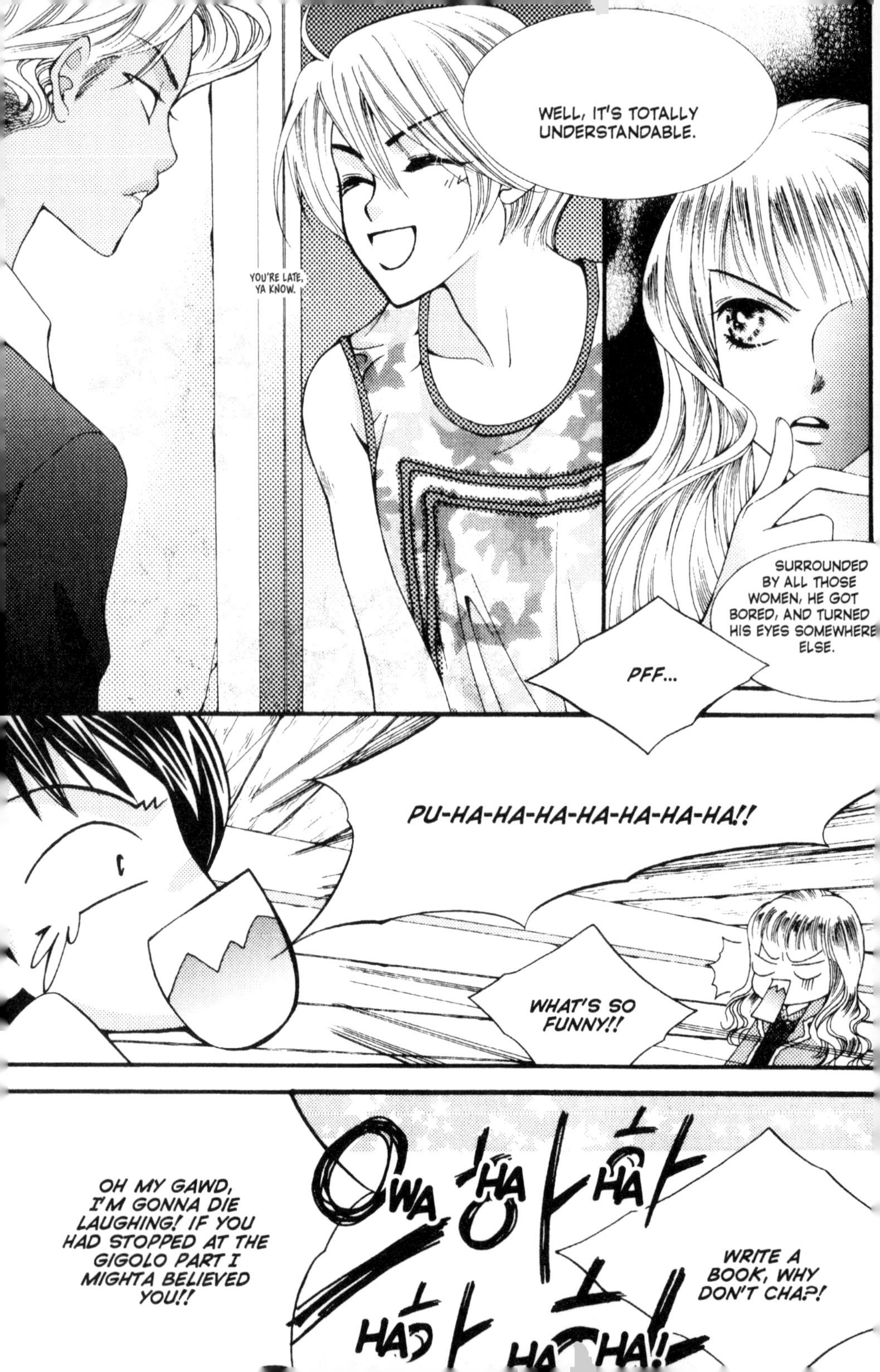
WELL, IT'S TOTALLY UNDERSTANDABLE.
YOU'RE LATE, YA KNOW.
SURROUNDED BY ALL THOSE WOMEN, HE GOT BORED, AND TURNED HIS EYES SOMEWHERE ELSE.
PFF...
PU-HA-HA-HA-HA-HA-HA-HA!!
WHAT'S SO FUNNY!!
OH MY GAWD, I'M GONNA DIE LAUGHING! IF YOU HAD STOPPED AT THE GIGOLO PART I MIGHTA BELIEVED YOU!!
WRITE A BOOK, WHY DON'T CHA?!

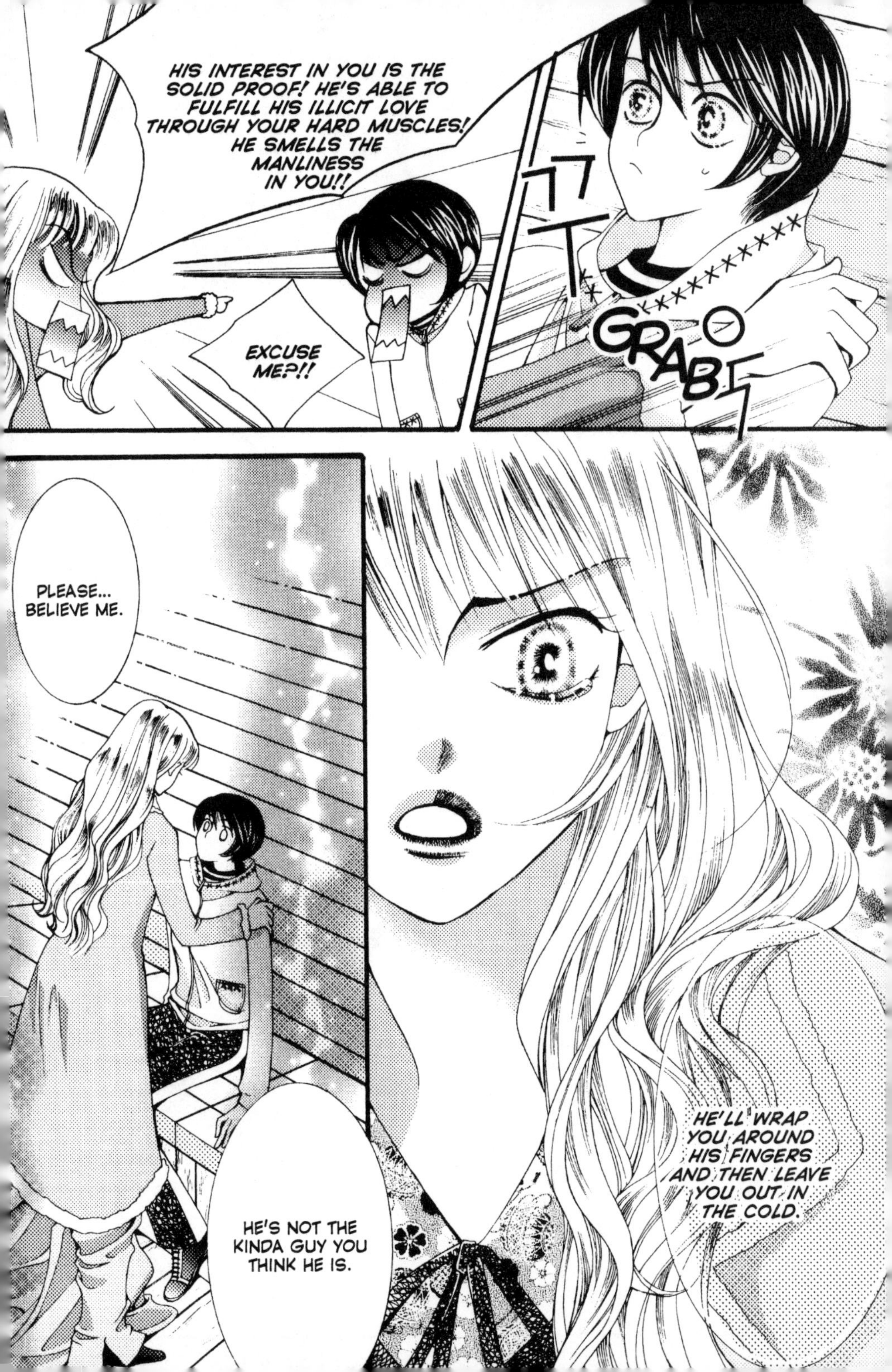
HIS INTEREST IN YOU IS THE SOLID PROOF! HE'S ABLE TO FULFILL HIS ILLICIT LOVE THROUGH YOUR HARD MUSCLES! HE SMELLS THE MANLINESS IN YOU!!
EXCUSE ME?!!
GRAB
PLEASE... BELIEVE ME.
HE'S NOT THE KINDA GUY YOU THINK HE IS.
HE'LL WRAP YOU AROUND HIS FINGERS AND THEN LEAVE YOU OUT IN THE COLD.

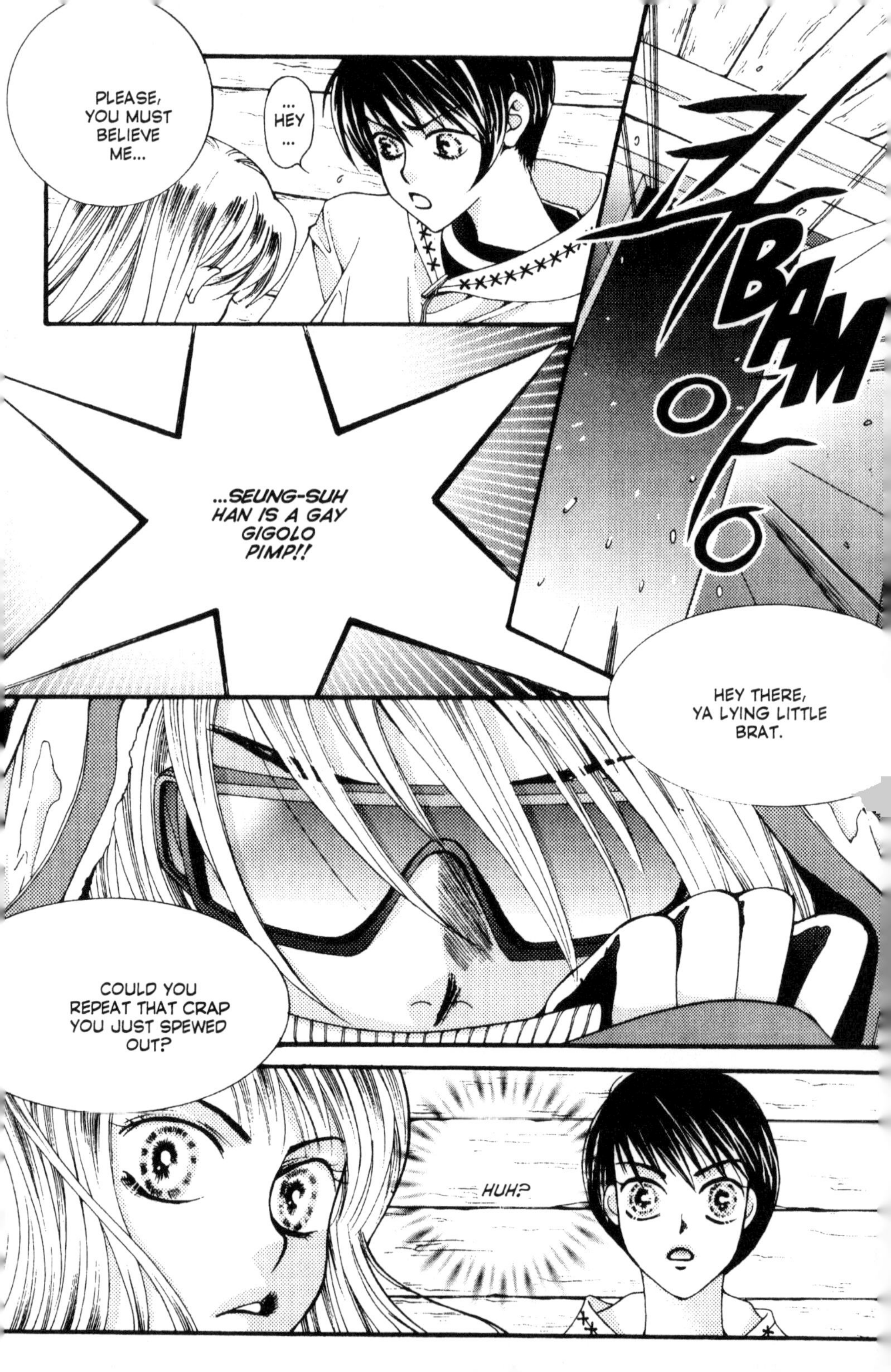
PLEASE, YOU MUST BELIEVE ME...
... HEY ...
BAM
...SEUNG-SUH HAN IS A GAY GIGOLO PIMP!!
HEY THERE, YA LYING LITTLE BRAT.
COULD YOU REPEAT THAT CRAP YOU JUST SPEWED OUT?
HUH?

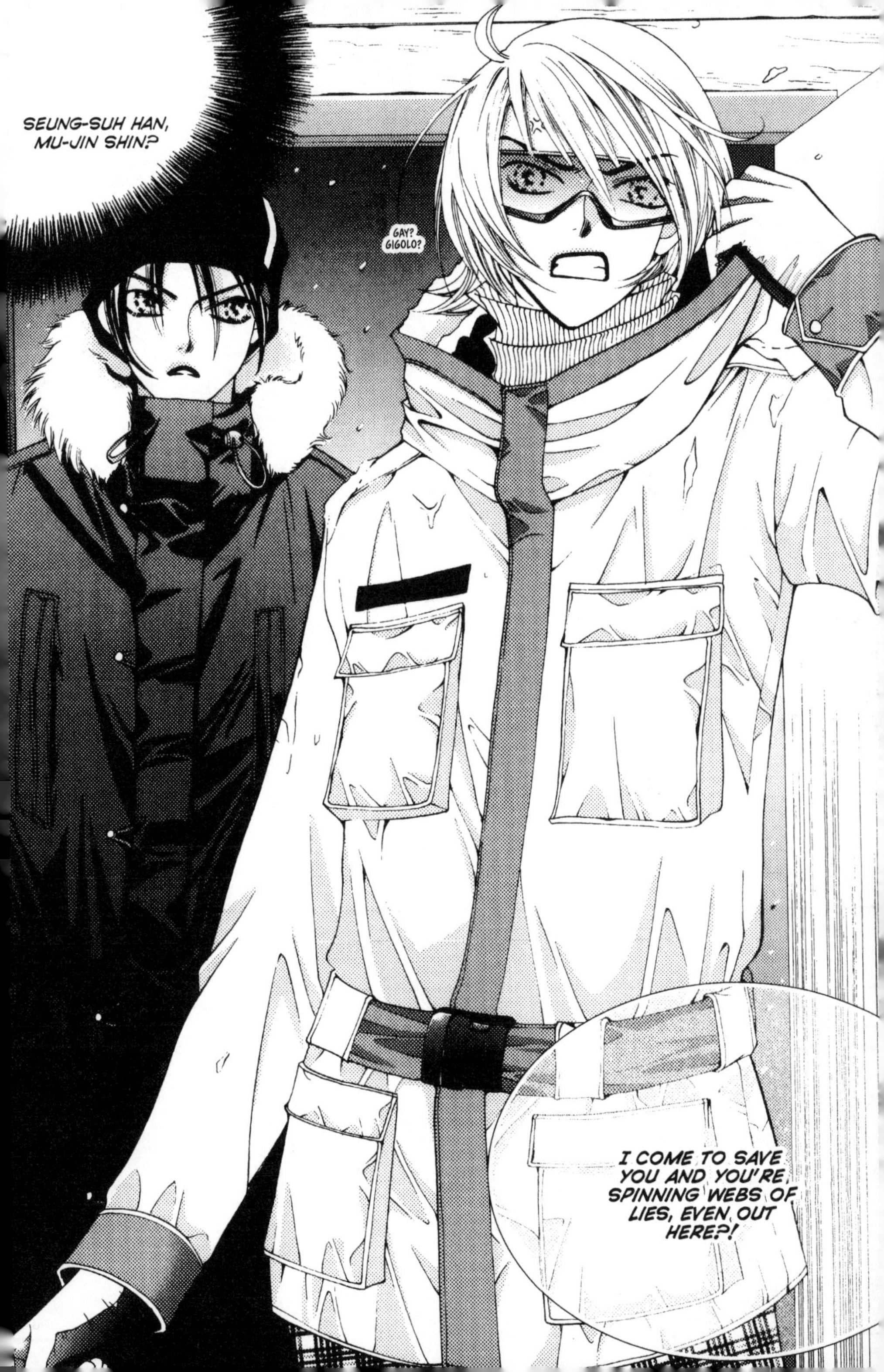
SEUNG-SUH HAN, MU-JIN SHIN?
GAY? GIGOLO?
I COME TO SAVE YOU AND YOU'RE SPINNING WEBS OF LIES, EVEN OUT HERE?!

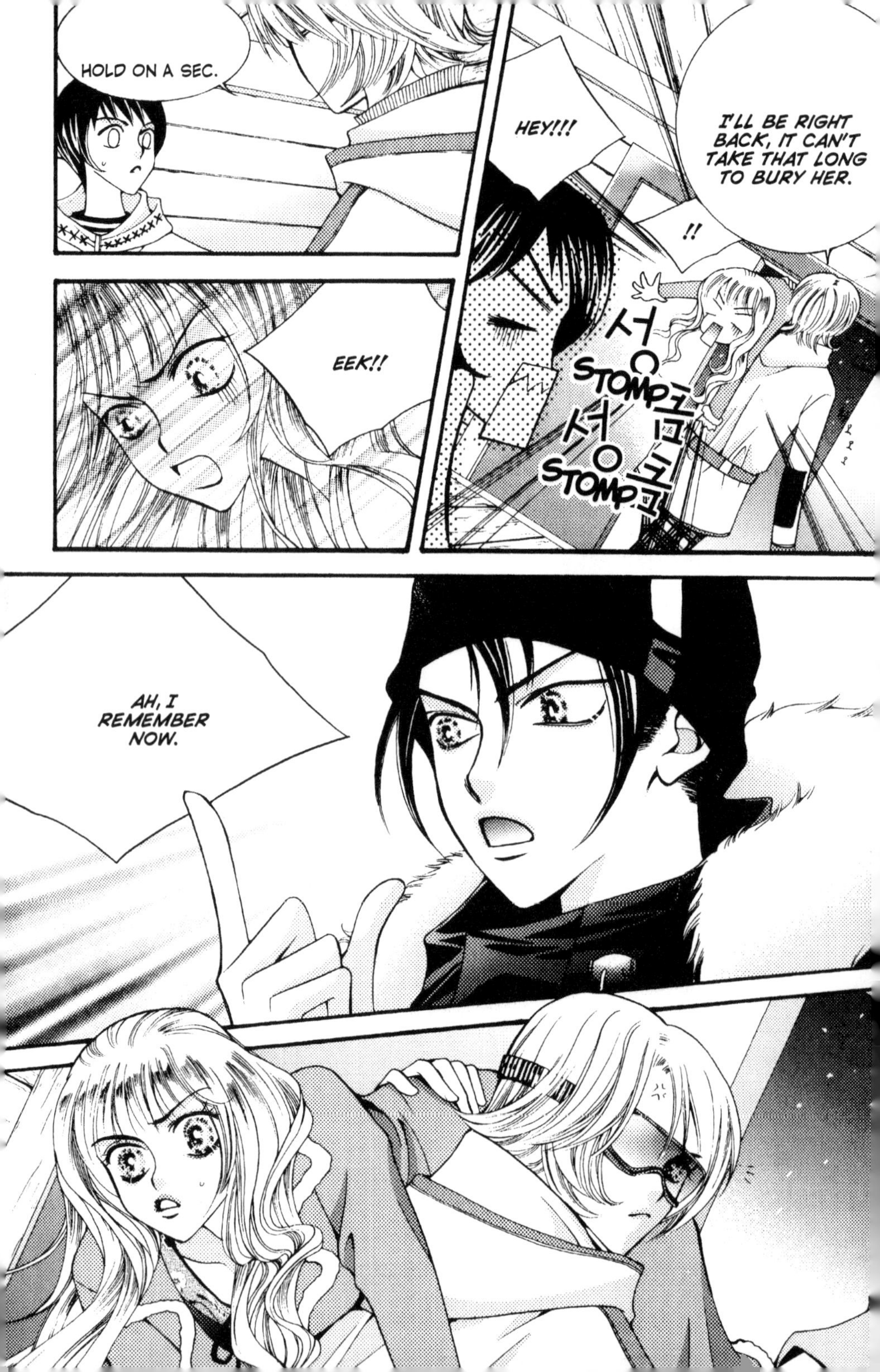
HOLD ON A SEC.
EEK!!
HEY!!!
I'LL BE RIGHT BACK, IT CAN'T TAKE THAT LONG TO BURY HER.
!!
STOMP
STOMP
AH, I REMEMBER NOW.

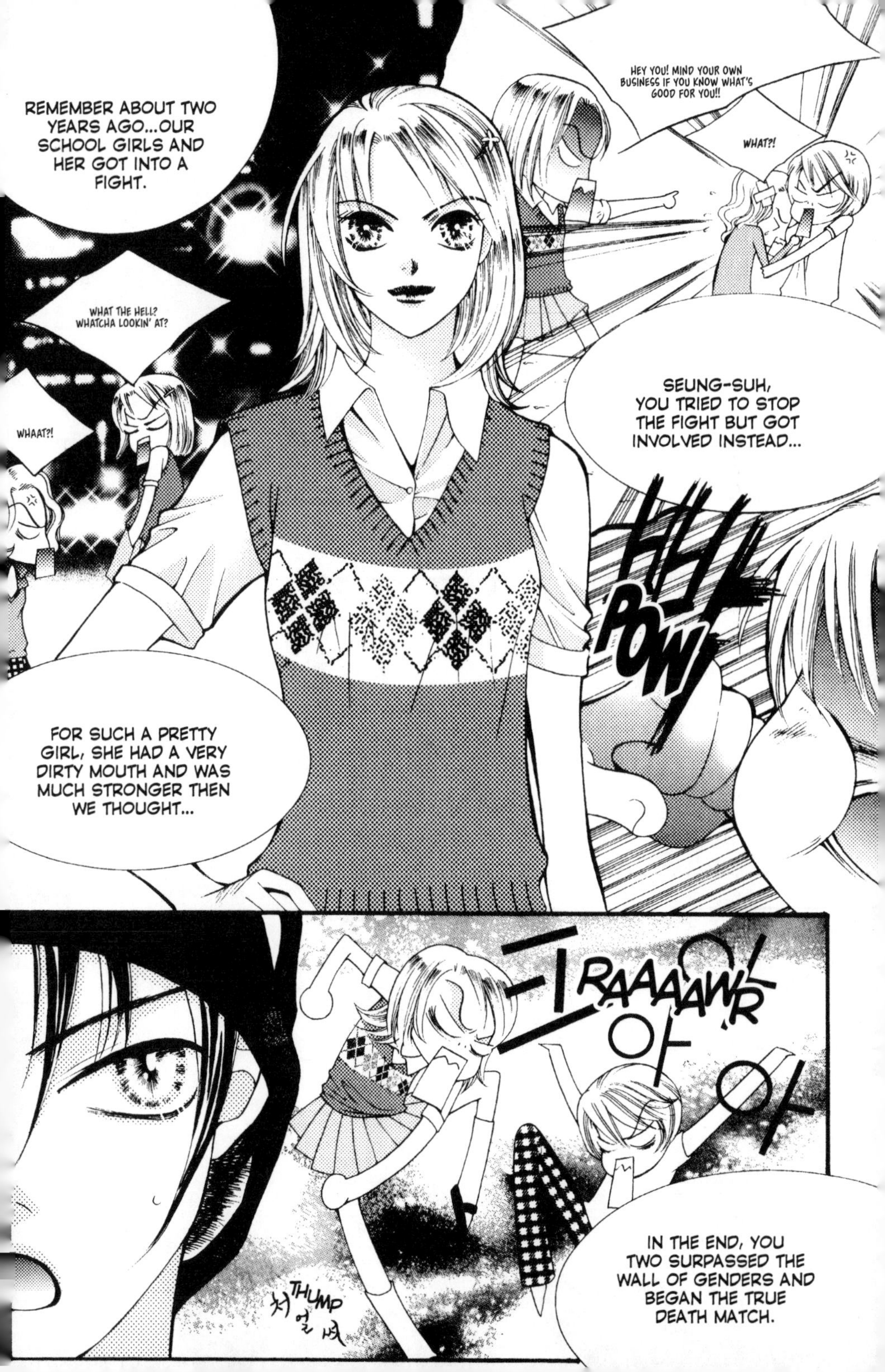
REMEMBER ABOUT TWO YEARS AGO...OUR SCHOOL GIRLS AND HER GOT INTO A FIGHT.
HEY YOU! MIND YOUR OWN BUSINESS IF YOU KNOW WHAT'S GOOD FOR YOU!!
WHAT?!
WHAT THE HELL? WHATCHA LOOKIN' AT?
WHAAT?!
SEUNG-SUH, YOU TRIED TO STOP THE FIGHT BUT GOT INVOLVED INSTEAD...
POW
FOR SUCH A PRETTY GIRL, SHE HAD A VERY DIRTY MOUTH AND WAS MUCH STRONGER THEN WE THOUGHT...
RAAAAWR
THUMP
IN THE END, YOU TWO SURPASSED THE WALL OF GENDERS AND BEGAN THE TRUE DEATH MATCH.

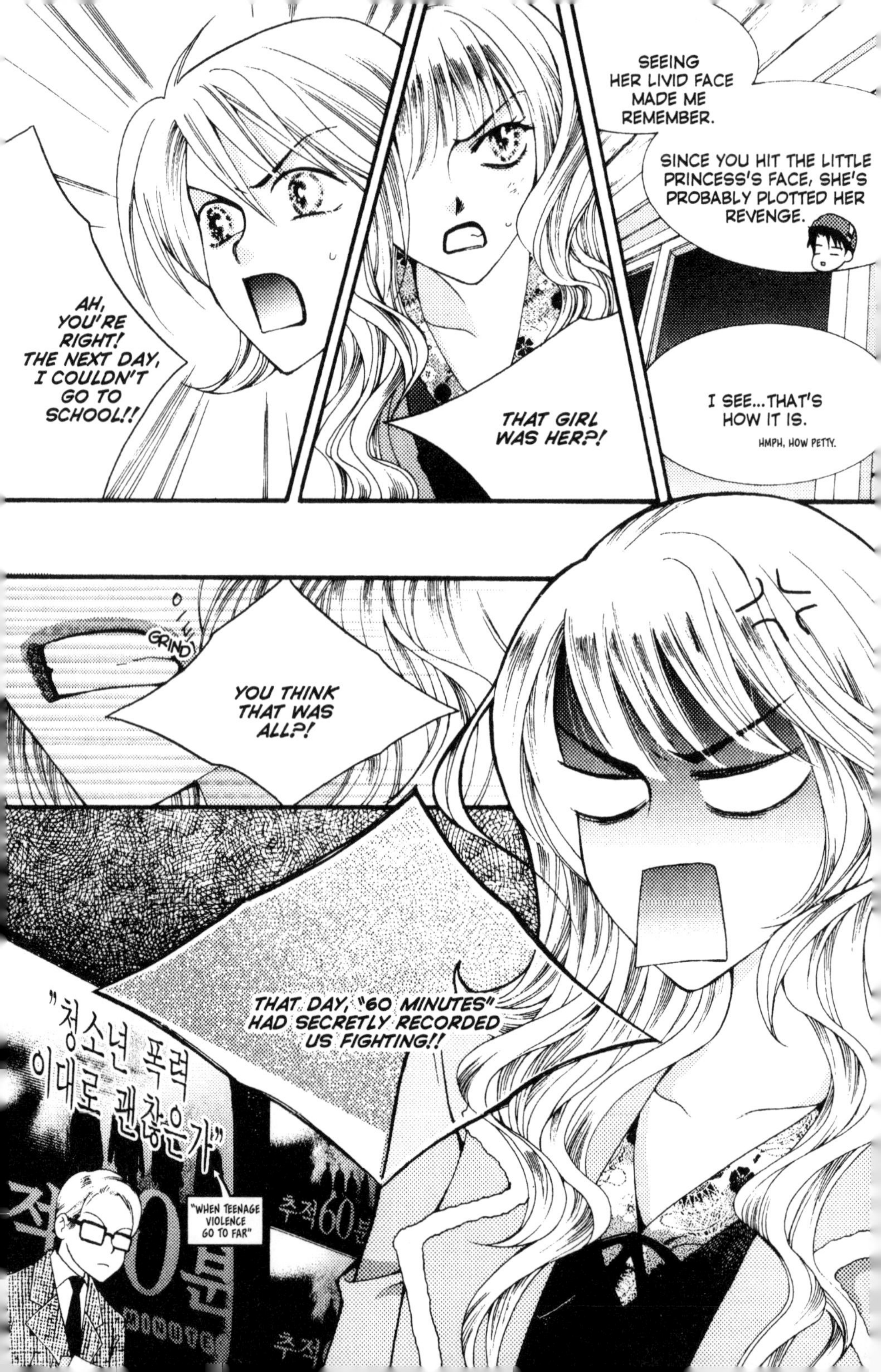
AH, YOU'RE RIGHT! THE NEXT DAY, I COULDN'T GO TO SCHOOL!!
THAT GIRL WAS HER?!
SEEING HER LIVID FACE MADE ME REMEMBER.
SINCE YOU HIT THE LITTLE PRINCESS'S FACE, SHE'S PROBABLY PLOTTED HER REVENGE.
I SEE...THAT'S HOW IT IS.
HMPH, HOW PETTY.
GRIND
YOU THINK THAT WAS ALL?!
THAT DAY, "60 MINUTES" HAD SECRETLY RECORDED US FIGHTING!!
"청소년 폭력 이대로 괜찮은가"
"WHEN TEENAGE VIOLENCE GO TO FAR"

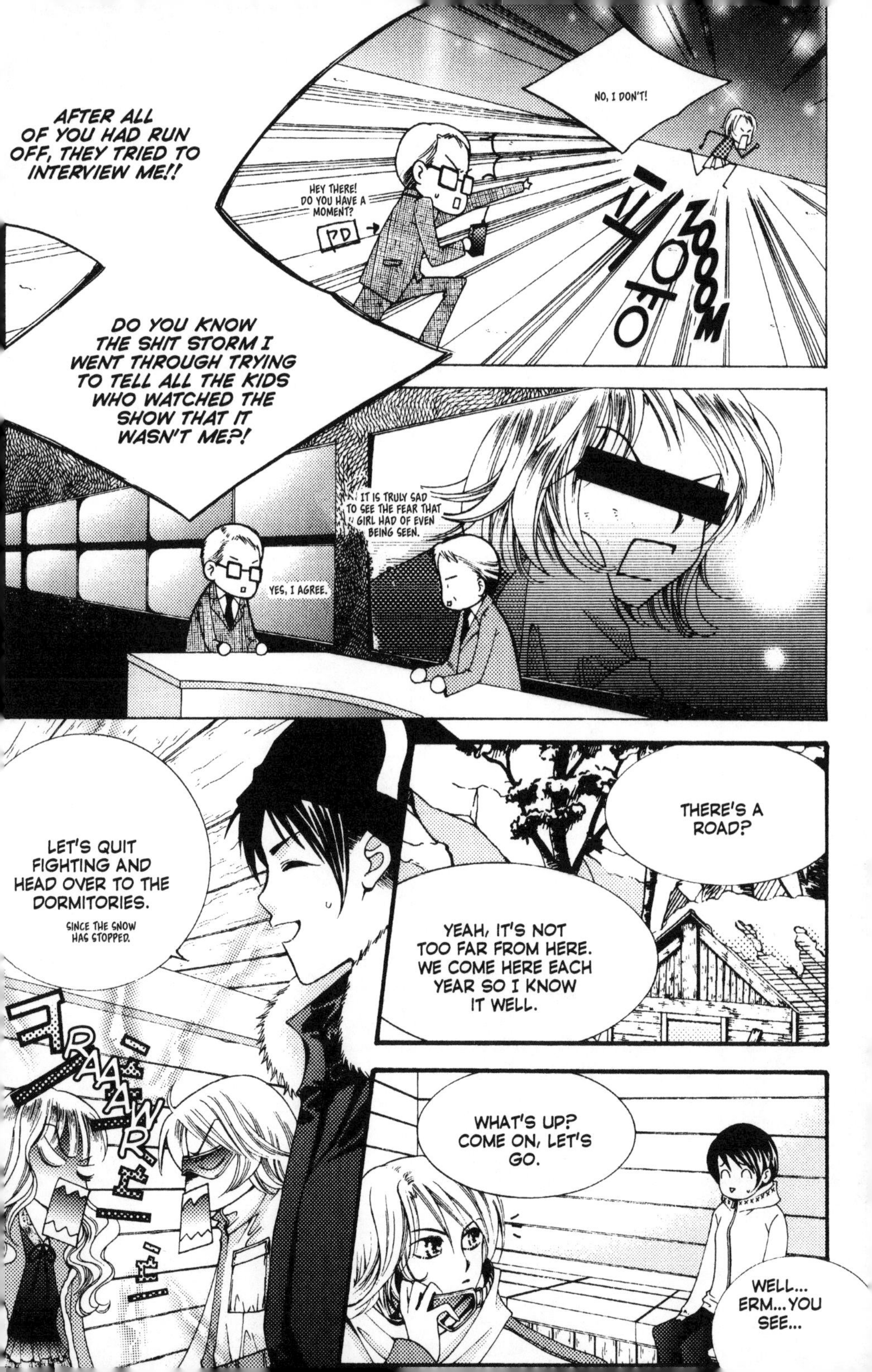
AFTER ALL OF YOU HAD RUN OFF, THEY TRIED TO INTERVIEW ME!!
HEY THERE! DO YOU HAVE A MOMENT?
PD
NO, I DON'T!
ZOOOOM
DO YOU KNOW THE SHIT STORM I WENT THROUGH TRYING TO TELL ALL THE KIDS WHO WATCHED THE SHOW THAT IT WASN'T ME?!
IT IS TRULY SAD TO SEE THE FEAR THAT GIRL HAD OF EVEN BEING SEEN.
YES, I AGREE.
LET'S QUIT FIGHTING AND HEAD OVER TO THE DORMITORIES.
SINCE THE SNOW HAS STOPPED.
RAAAWR
THERE'S A ROAD?
YEAH, IT'S NOT TOO FAR FROM HERE. WE COME HERE EACH YEAR SO I KNOW IT WELL.
WHAT'S UP? COME ON, LET'S GO.
WELL... ERM...YOU SEE...

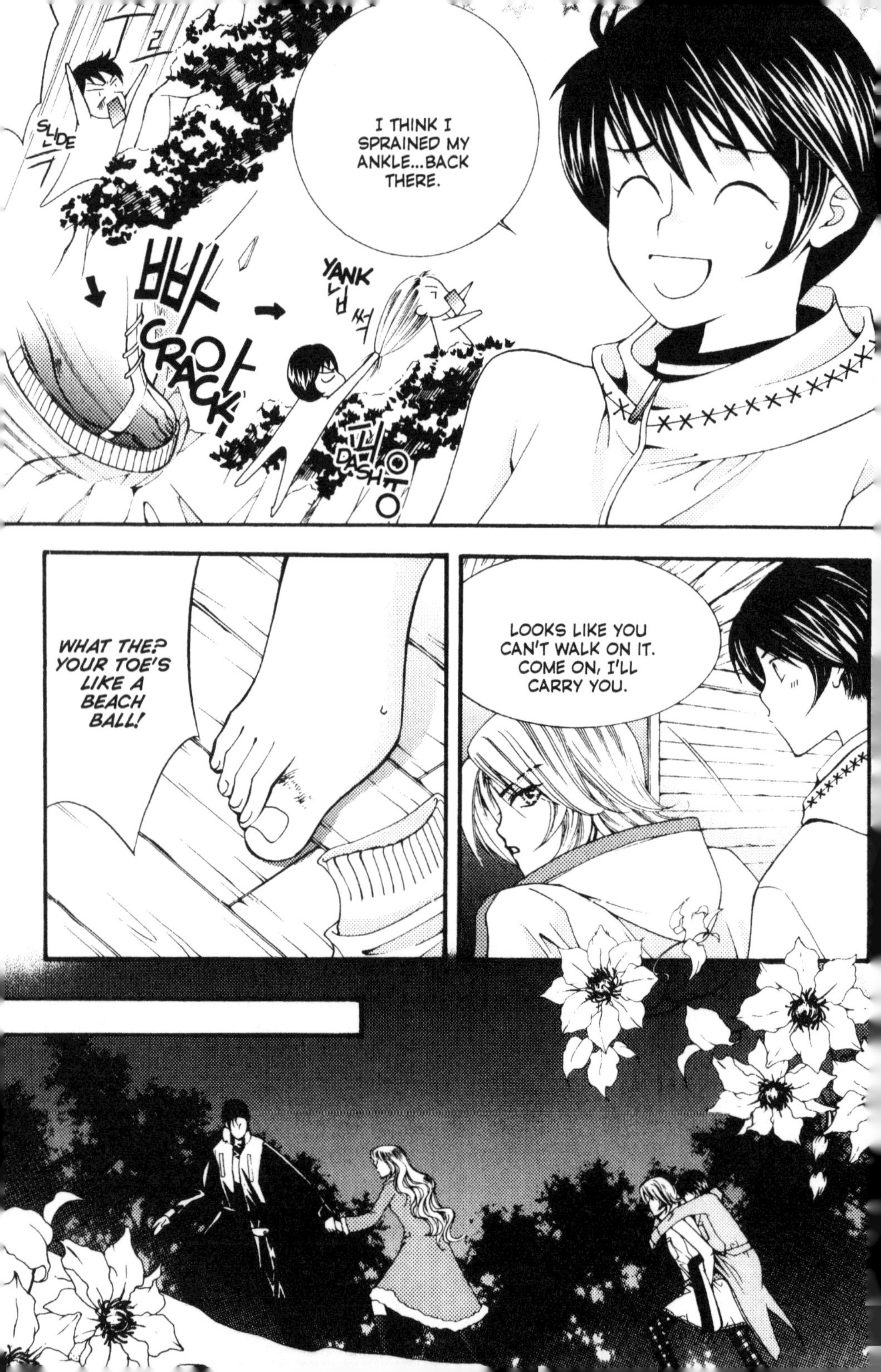
SLIDE
I THINK I SPRAINED MY ANKLE...BACK THERE.
YANK
빡
CRACK!
DASH
WHAT THE? YOUR TOE'S LIKE A BEACH BALL!
LOOKS LIKE YOU CAN'T WALK ON IT. COME ON, I'LL CARRY YOU.

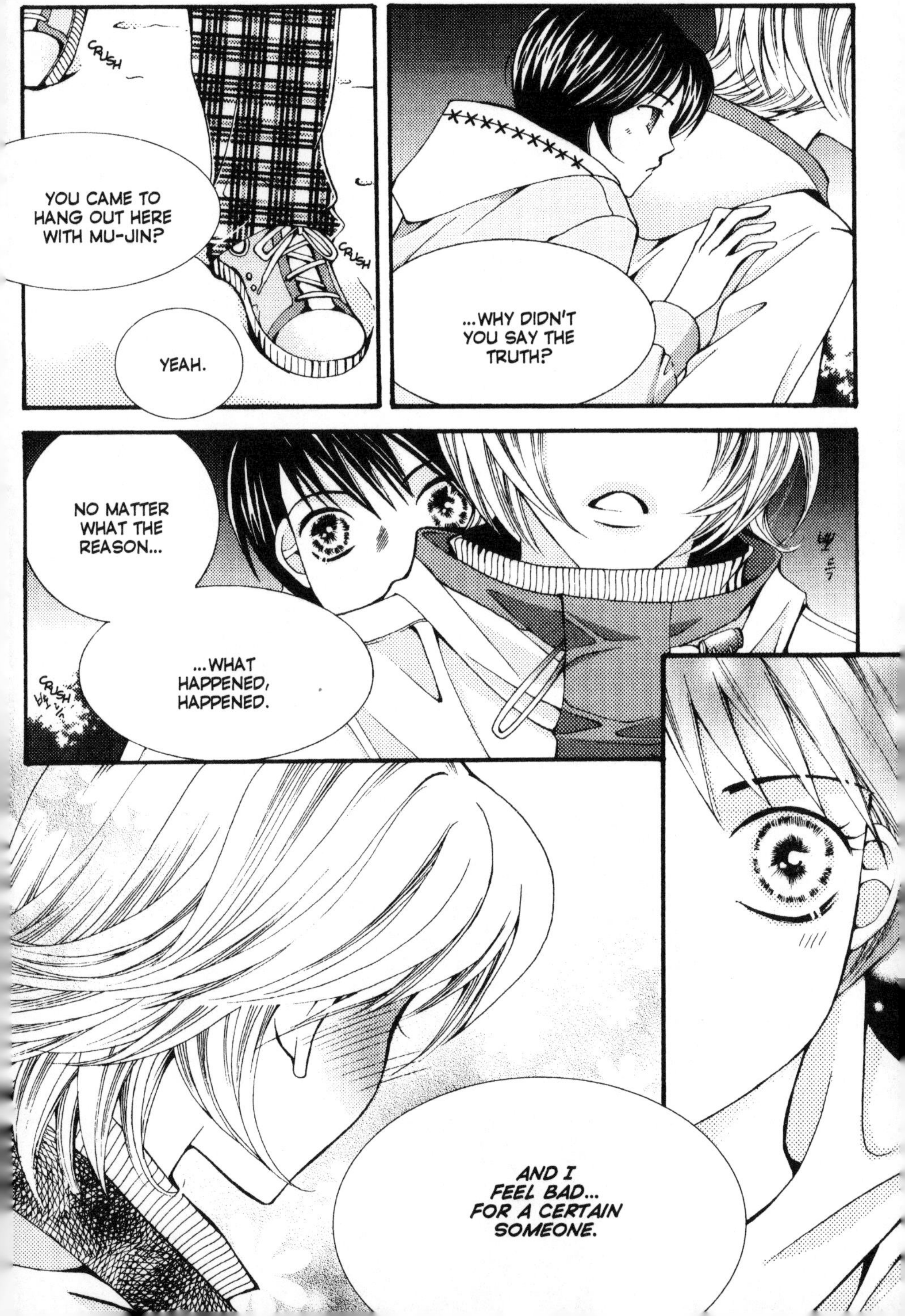
CRUSH
YOU CAME TO HANG OUT HERE WITH MU-JIN?
CRUSH
YEAH.
...WHY DIDN'T YOU SAY THE TRUTH?
NO MATTER WHAT THE REASON...
...WHAT HAPPENED, HAPPENED.
CRUSH
AND I FEEL BAD... FOR A CERTAIN SOMEONE.

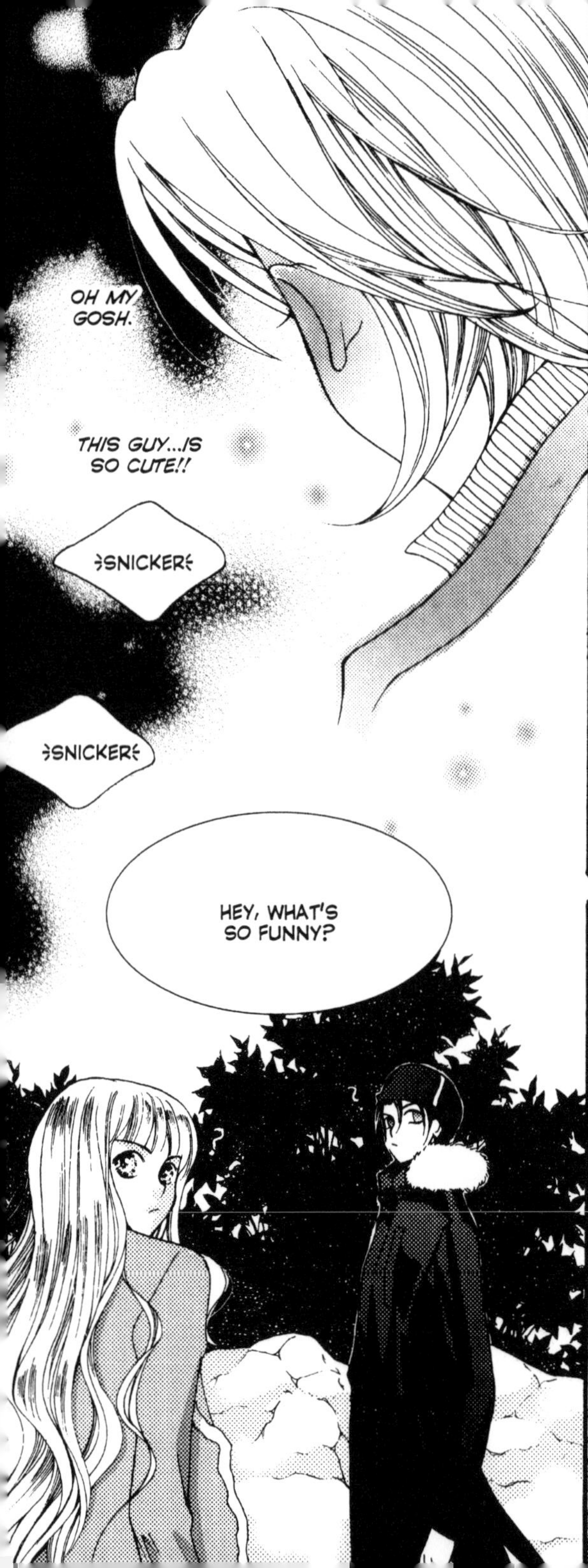
OH MY GOSH.
THIS GUY...IS SO CUTE!!
SNICKER
SNICKER
HEY, WHAT'S SO FUNNY?
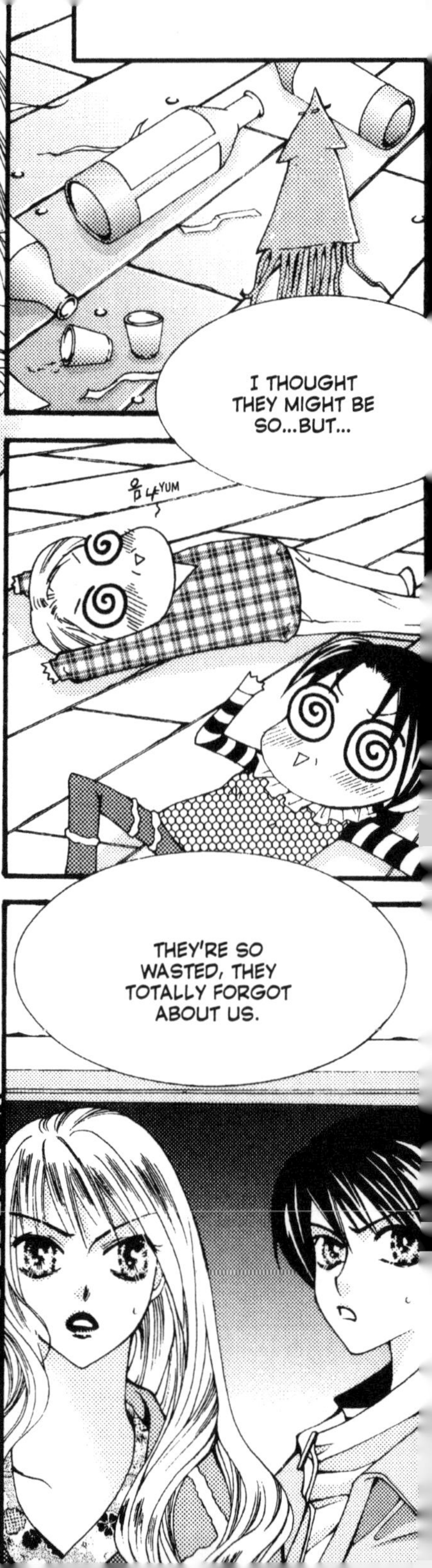
I THOUGHT THEY MIGHT BE SO...BUT...
YUM
THEY'RE SO WASTED, THEY TOTALLY FORGOT ABOUT US.

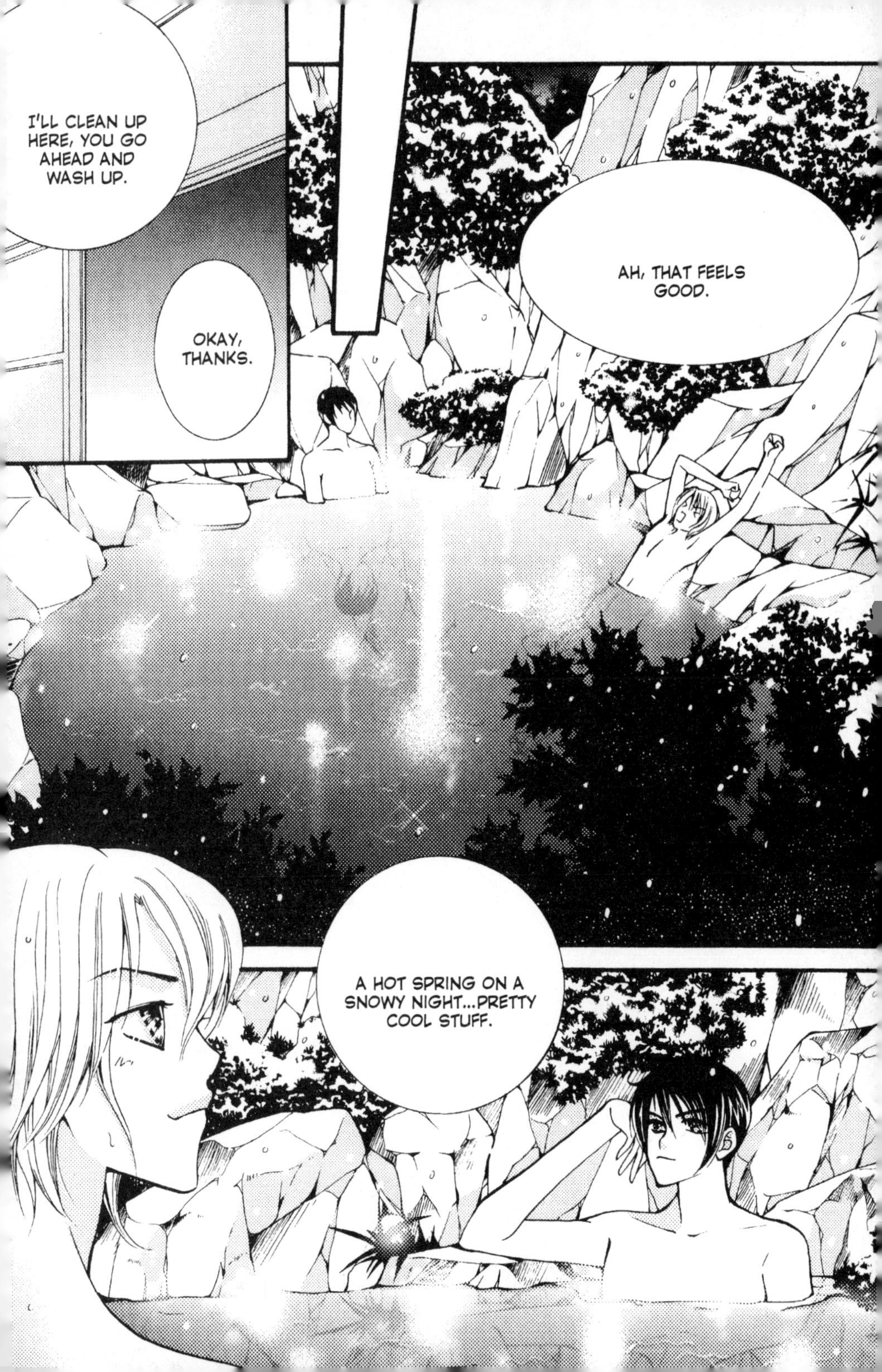
I'LL CLEAN UP HERE, YOU GO AHEAD AND WASH UP.
OKAY, THANKS.
AH, THAT FEELS GOOD.
A HOT SPRING ON A SNOWY NIGHT...PRETTY COOL STUFF.

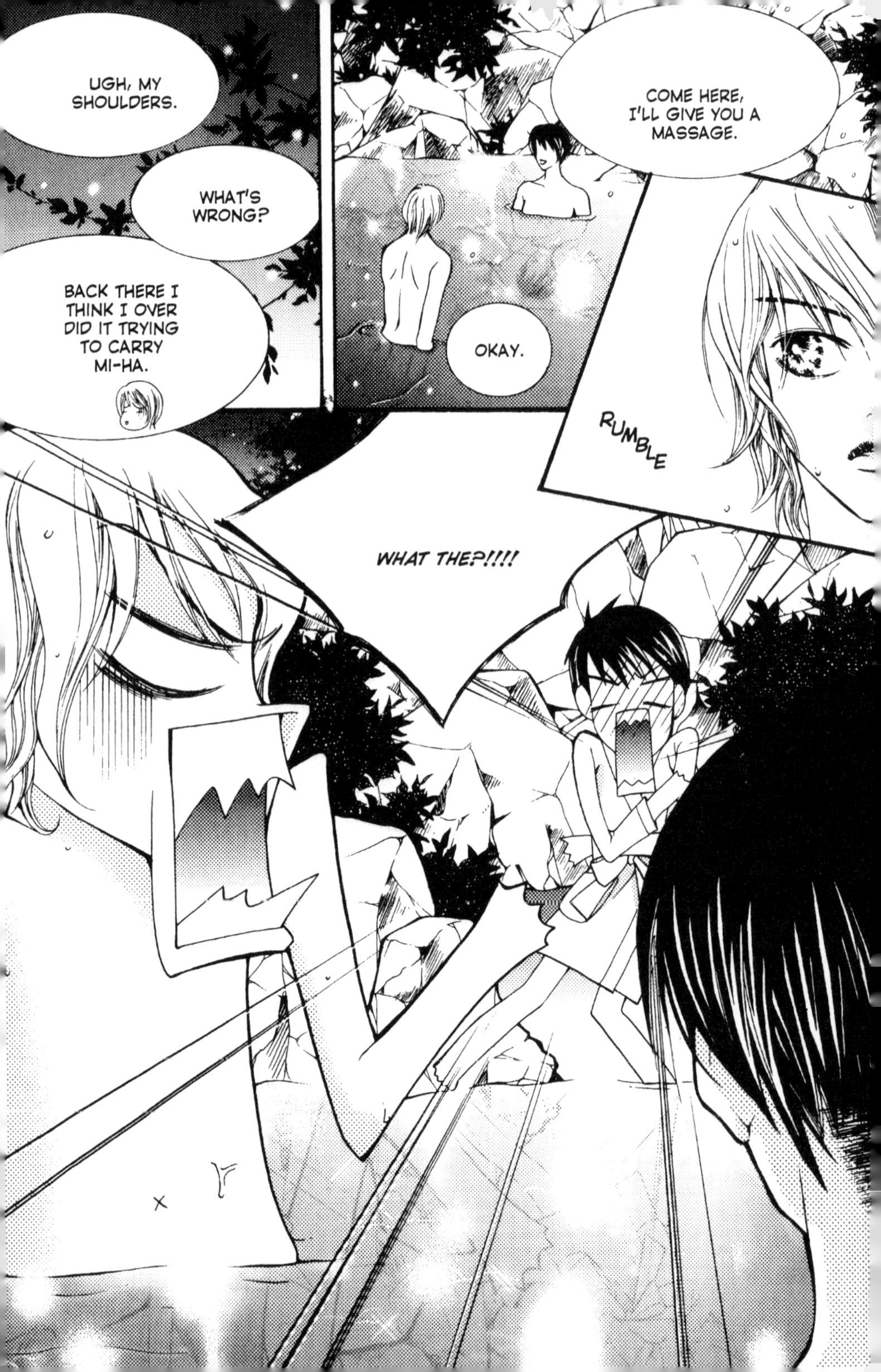
UGH, MY SHOULDERS.
WHAT'S WRONG?
BACK THERE I THINK I OVER DID IT TRYING TO CARRY MI-HA.
OKAY.
COME HERE, I'LL GIVE YOU A MASSAGE.
RUMBLE
WHAT THE?!!!!

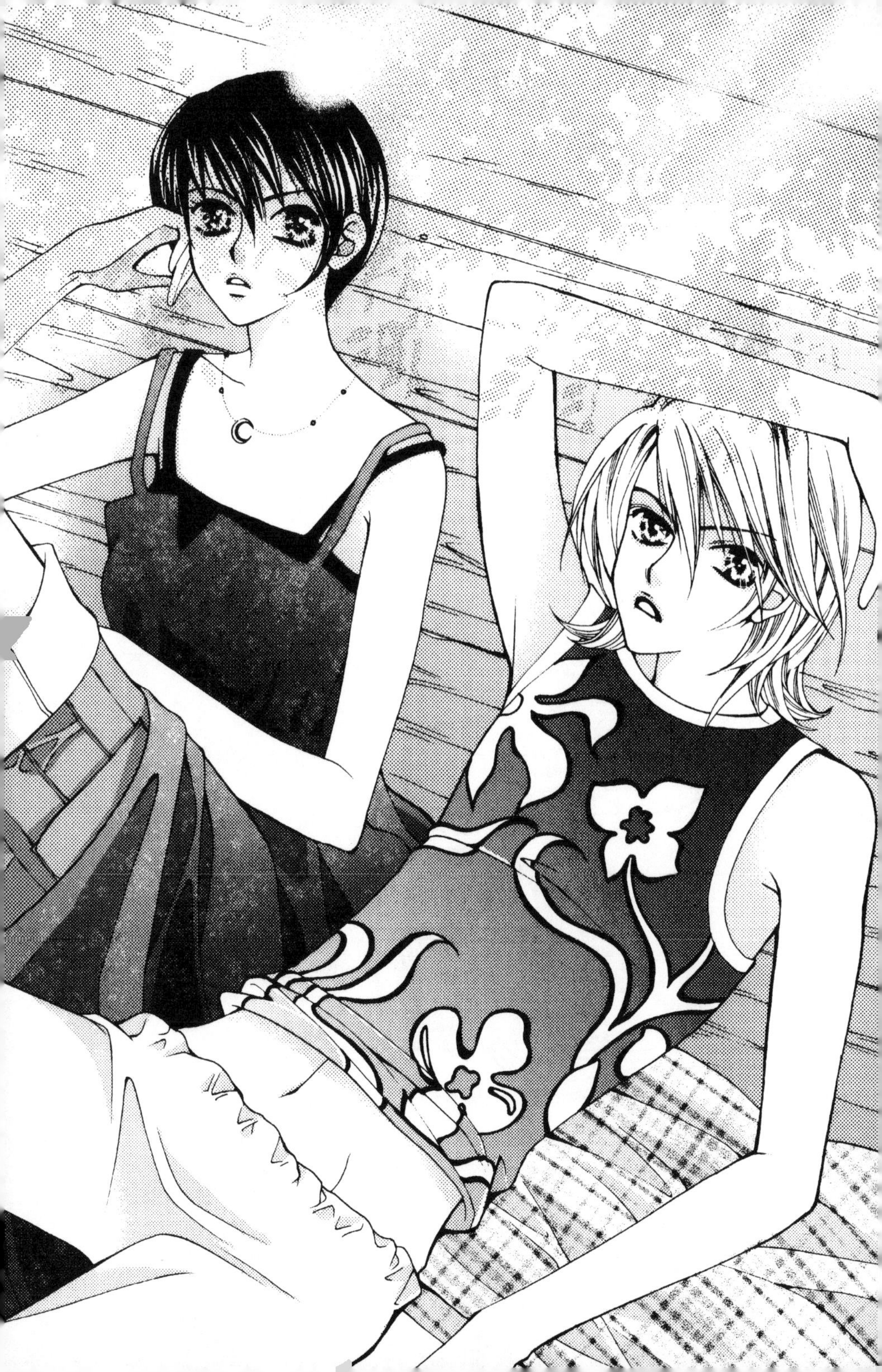

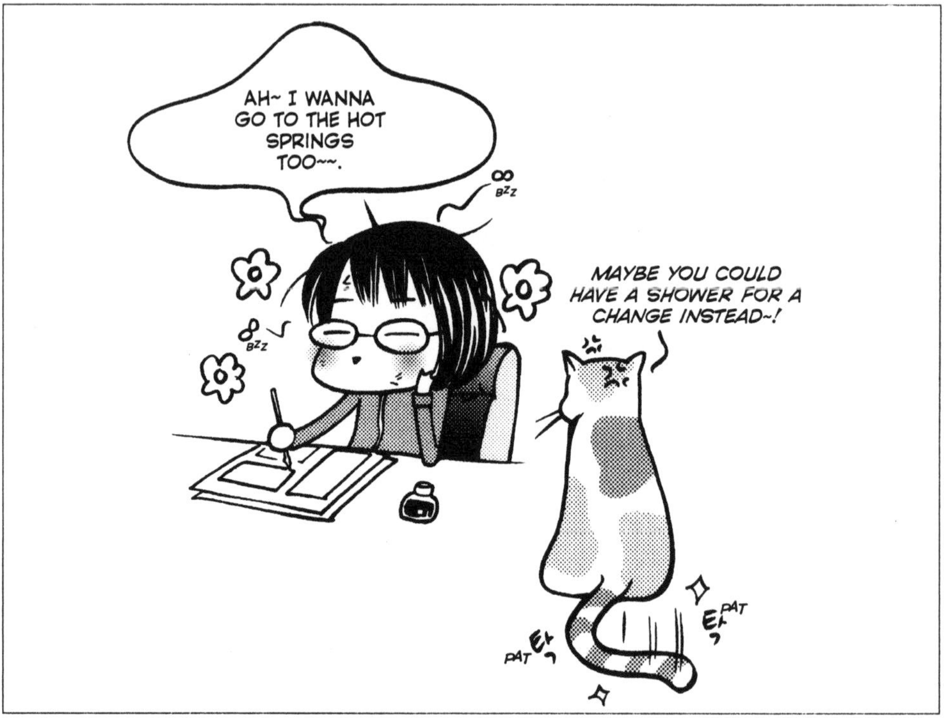
AH~ I WANNA GO TO THE HOT SPRINGS TOO~~.
BZZ
BZZ
MAYBE YOU COULD HAVE A SHOWER FOR A CHANGE INSTEAD~!
PAT
PAT

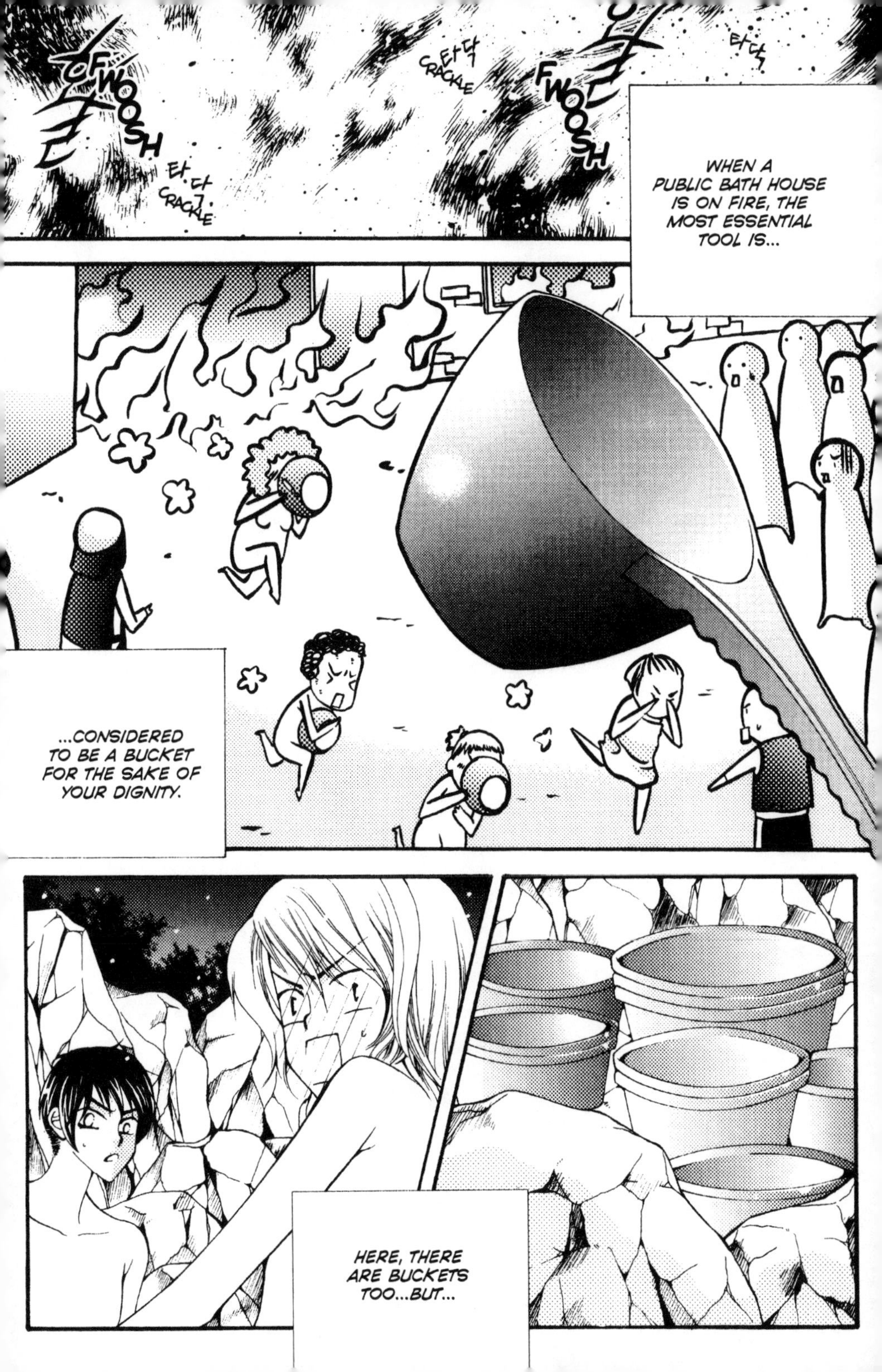
FWOOSH
타닥
CRACKLE
CRACKLE
FWOOSH
타닥
WHEN A PUBLIC BATH HOUSE IS ON FIRE, THE MOST ESSENTIAL TOOL IS...
...CONSIDERED TO BE A BUCKET FOR THE SAKE OF YOUR DIGNITY.
HERE, THERE ARE BUCKETS TOO...BUT...

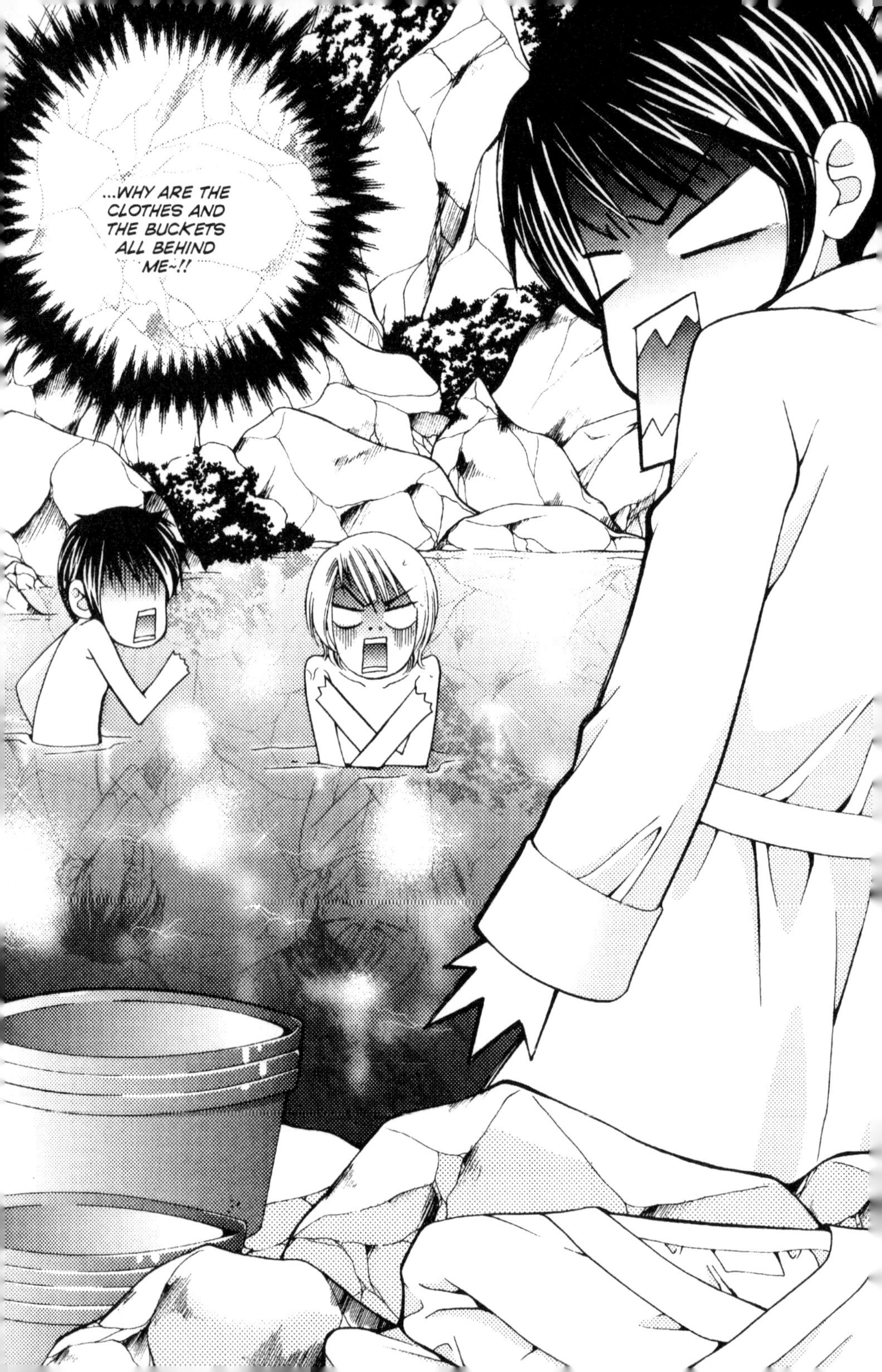
...WHY ARE THE CLOTHES AND THE BUCKETS ALL BEHIND ME~!!

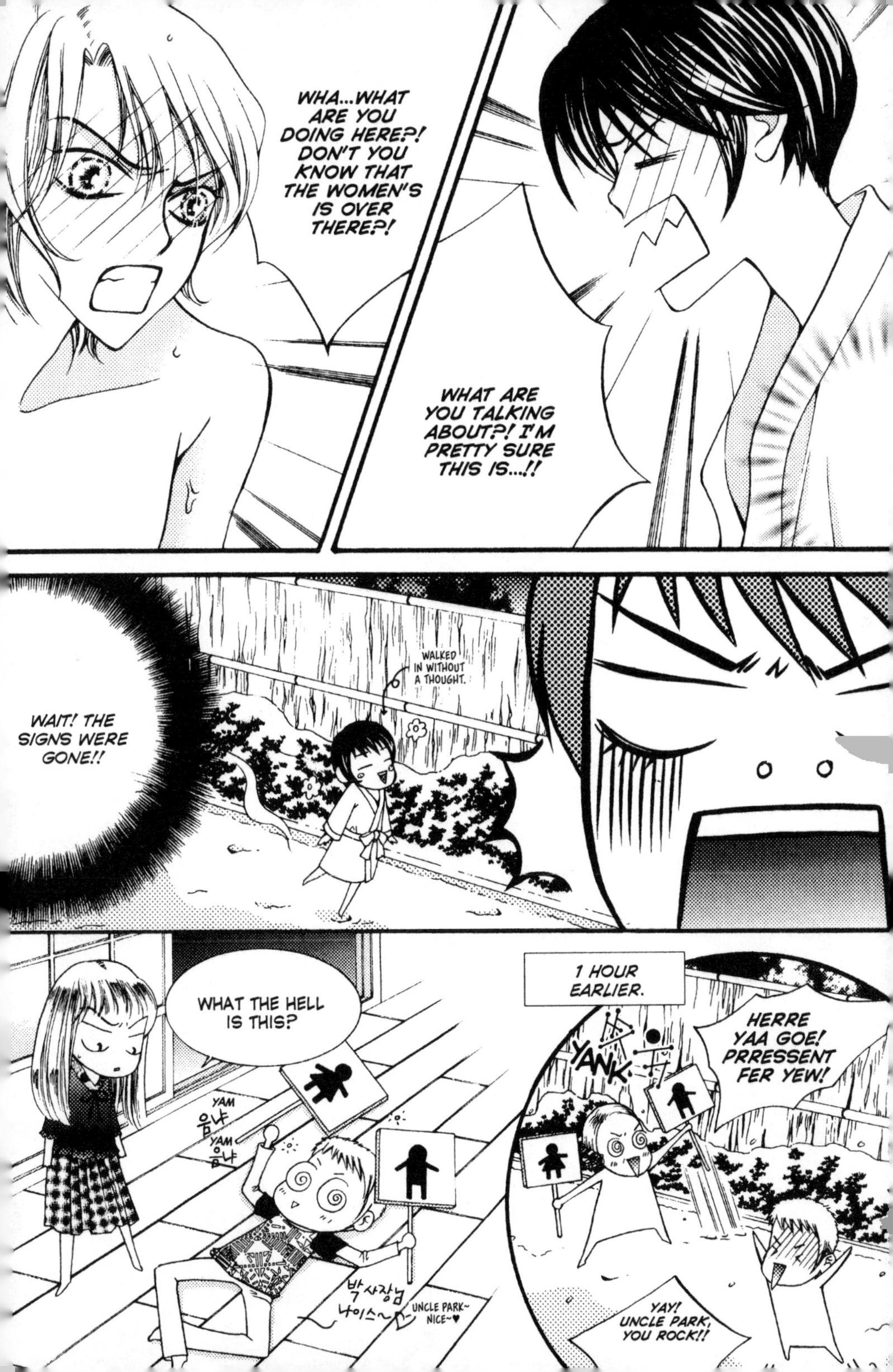
WHA...WHAT ARE YOU DOING HERE?! DON'T YOU KNOW THAT THE WOMEN'S IS OVER THERE?!
WHAT ARE YOU TALKING ABOUT?! I'M PRETTY SURE THIS IS...!!
WAIT! THE SIGNS WERE GONE!!
WALKED IN WITHOUT A THOUGHT.
WHAT THE HELL IS THIS?
YAM
YAM
박사장님 나이스~
UNCLE PARK~ NICE~♥
1 HOUR EARLIER.
HERRE YAA GOE! PRRESSENT FER YEW!
YANK
YAY! UNCLE PARK, YOU ROCK!!

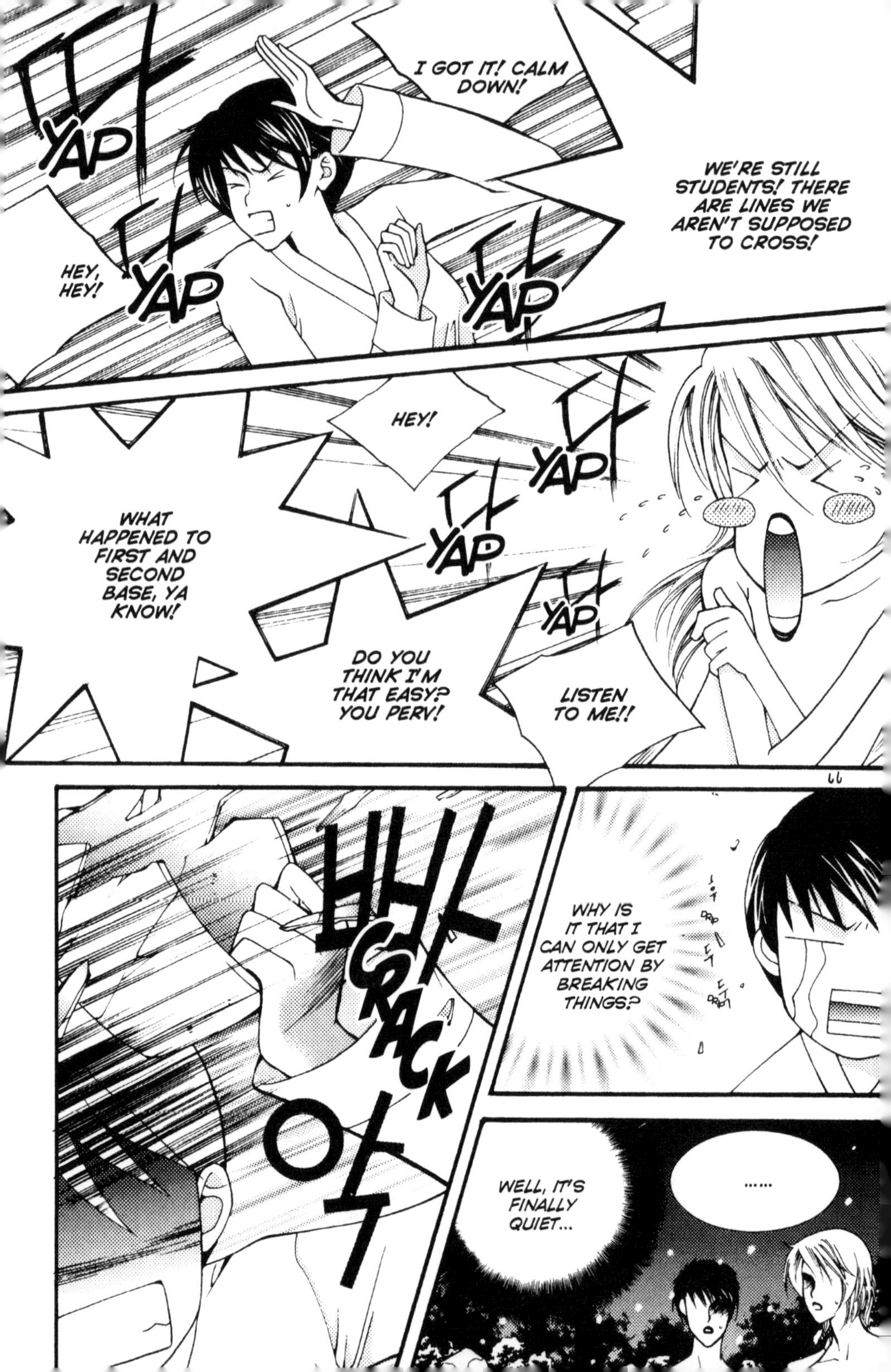
YAP
YAP
HEY, HEY!
I GOT IT! CALM DOWN!
YAP
WE'RE STILL STUDENTS! THERE ARE LINES WE AREN'T SUPPOSED TO CROSS!
WHAT HAPPENED TO FIRST AND SECOND BASE, YA KNOW!
HEY!
YAP
YAP
YAP
DO YOU THINK I'M THAT EASY? YOU PERV!
LISTEN TO ME!!
CRACK
WHY IS IT THAT I CAN ONLY GET ATTENTION BY BREAKING THINGS?
WELL, IT'S FINALLY QUIET...
......

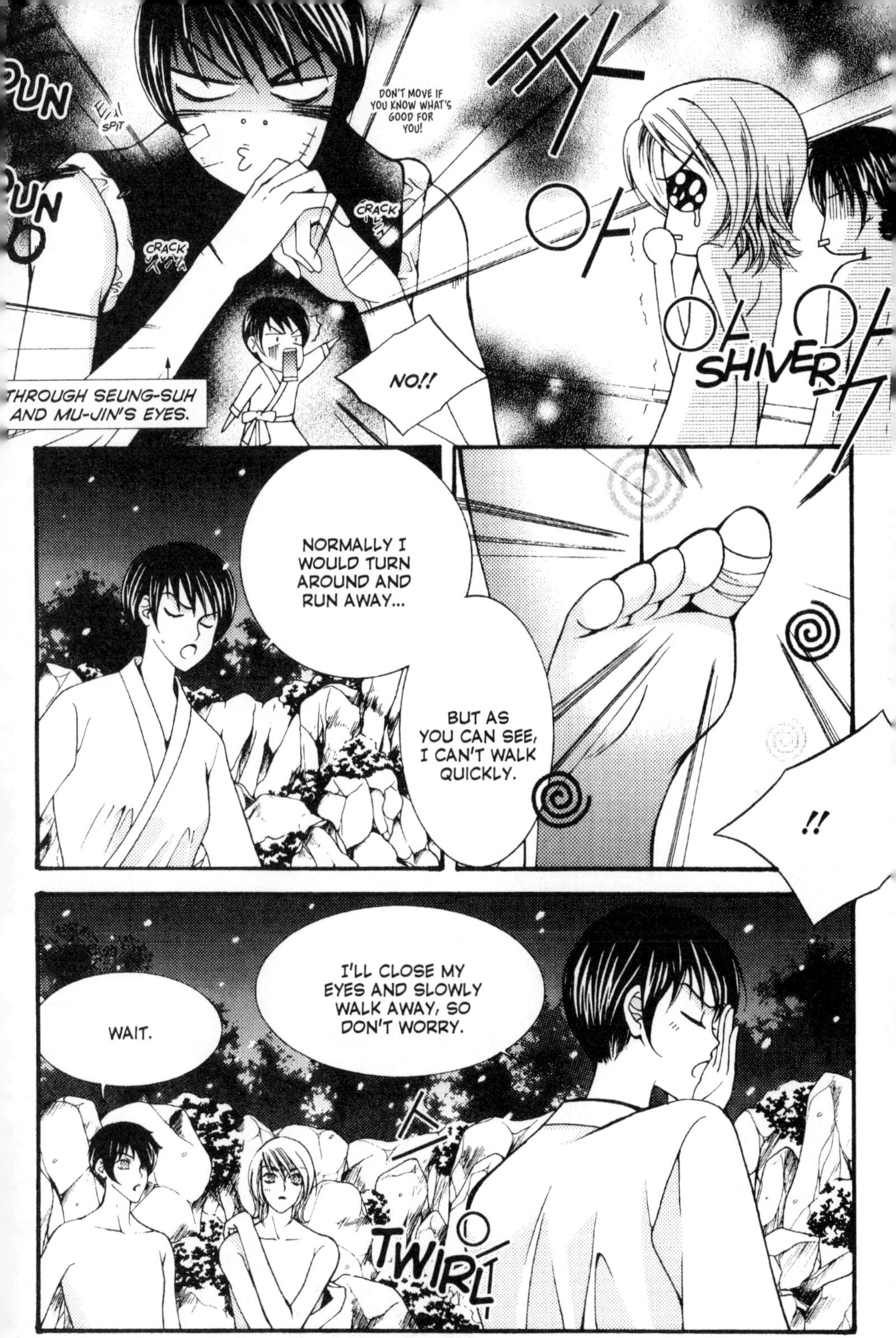

SPIT
DON'T MOVE IF YOU KNOW WHAT'S GOOD FOR YOU!
CRACK
CRACK
THROUGH SEUNG-SUH AND MU-JIN'S EYES.
NO!!
SHIVER
NORMALLY I WOULD TURN AROUND AND RUN AWAY...
BUT AS YOU CAN SEE, I CAN'T WALK QUICKLY.
!!
WAIT.
I'LL CLOSE MY EYES AND SLOWLY WALK AWAY, SO DON'T WORRY.
TWIRL

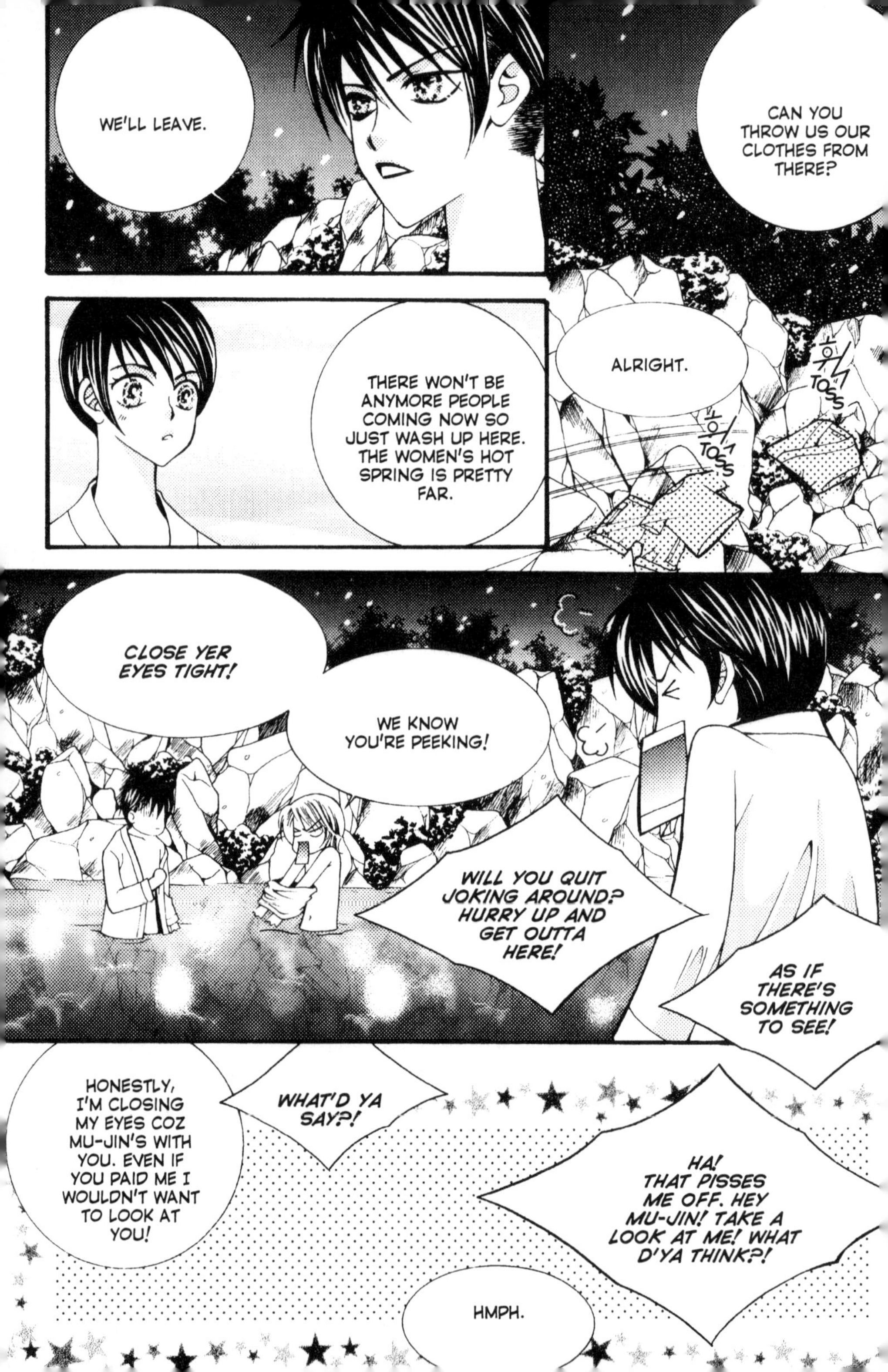
WE'LL LEAVE.
CAN YOU THROW US OUR CLOTHES FROM THERE?
THERE WON'T BE ANYMORE PEOPLE COMING NOW SO JUST WASH UP HERE. THE WOMEN'S HOT SPRING IS PRETTY FAR.
ALRIGHT.
TOSS
TOSS
CLOSE YER EYES TIGHT!
WE KNOW YOU'RE PEEKING!
WILL YOU QUIT JOKING AROUND? HURRY UP AND GET OUTTA HERE!
AS IF THERE'S SOMETHING TO SEE!
HONESTLY, I'M CLOSING MY EYES COZ MU-JIN'S WITH YOU. EVEN IF YOU PAID ME I WOULDN'T WANT TO LOOK AT YOU!
WHAT'D YA SAY?!
HA! THAT PISSES ME OFF. HEY MU-JIN! TAKE A LOOK AT ME! WHAT D'YA THINK?!
HMPH.

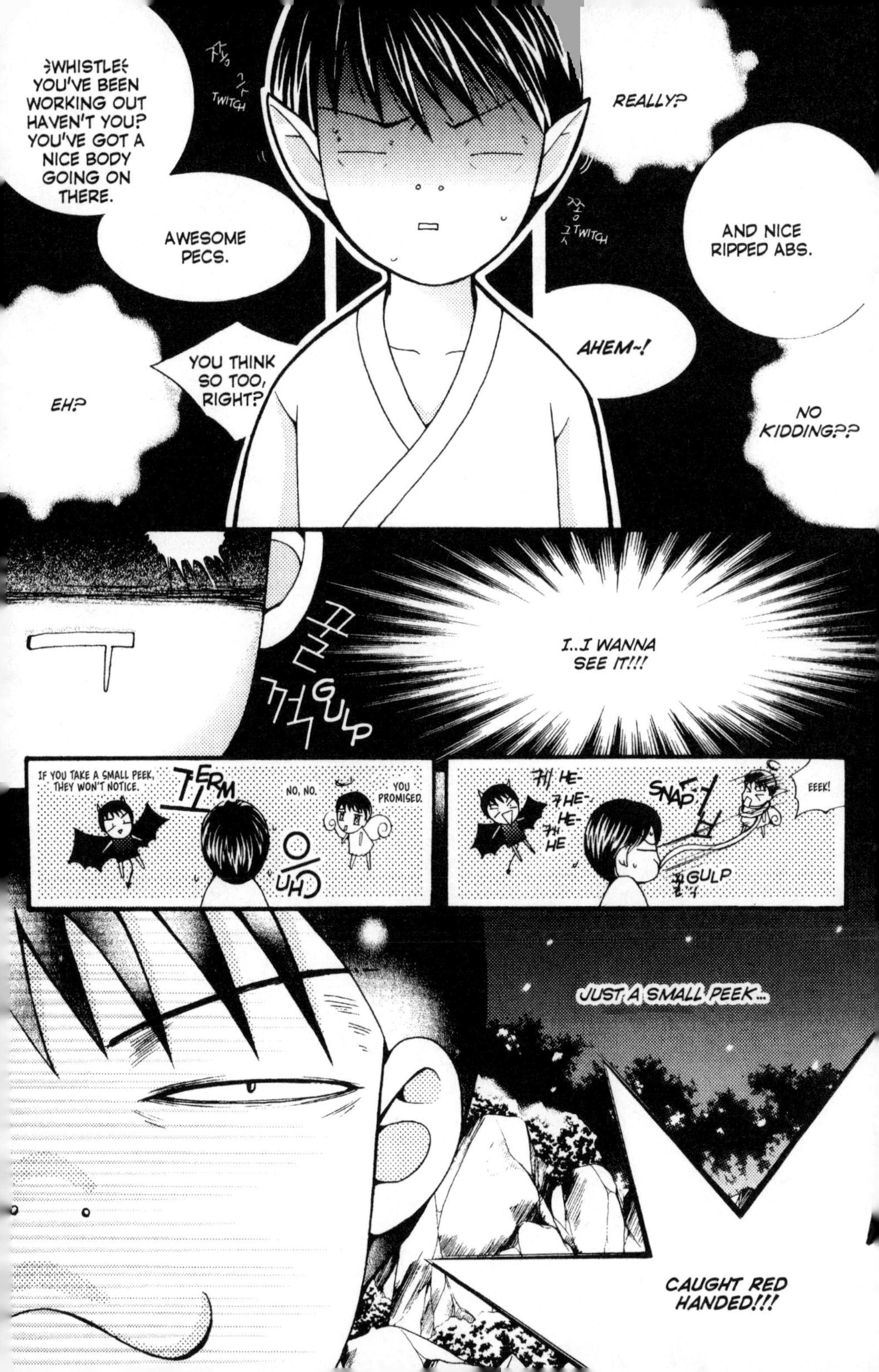

≶WHISTLE≶ YOU'VE BEEN WORKING OUT HAVEN'T YOU? YOU'VE GOT A NICE BODY GOING ON THERE.
TWITCH
AWESOME PECS.
YOU THINK SO TOO, RIGHT?
EH?
TWITCH
REALLY?
AND NICE RIPPED ABS.
AHEM~!
NO KIDDING??
GULP
I..I WANNA SEE IT!!!
IF YOU TAKE A SMALL PEEK, THEY WON'T NOTICE.
ERM
NO, NO.
YOU PROMISED.
UH
HE-HE-HE-HE
SNAP!
EEEK!
GULP
JUST A SMALL PEEK...
CAUGHT RED HANDED!!!

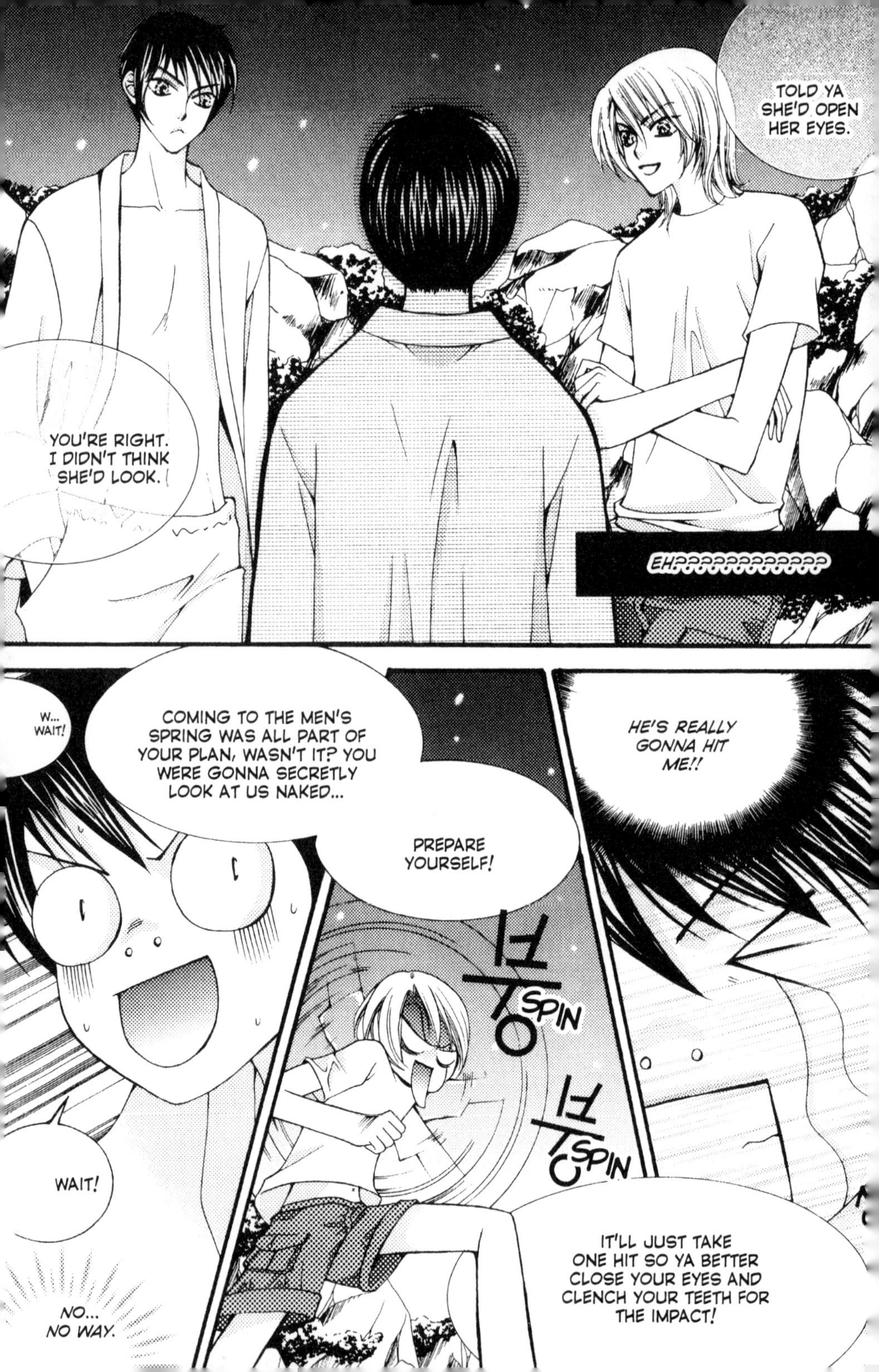

TOLD YA SHE'D OPEN HER EYES.
YOU'RE RIGHT. I DIDN'T THINK SHE'D LOOK.
EH???????????
W... WAIT!
WAIT!
NO... NO WAY.
COMING TO THE MEN'S SPRING WAS ALL PART OF YOUR PLAN, WASN'T IT? YOU WERE GONNA SECRETLY LOOK AT US NAKED...
PREPARE YOURSELF!
SPIN
SPIN
IT'LL JUST TAKE ONE HIT SO YA BETTER CLOSE YOUR EYES AND CLENCH YOUR TEETH FOR THE IMPACT!
HE'S REALLY GONNA HIT ME!!

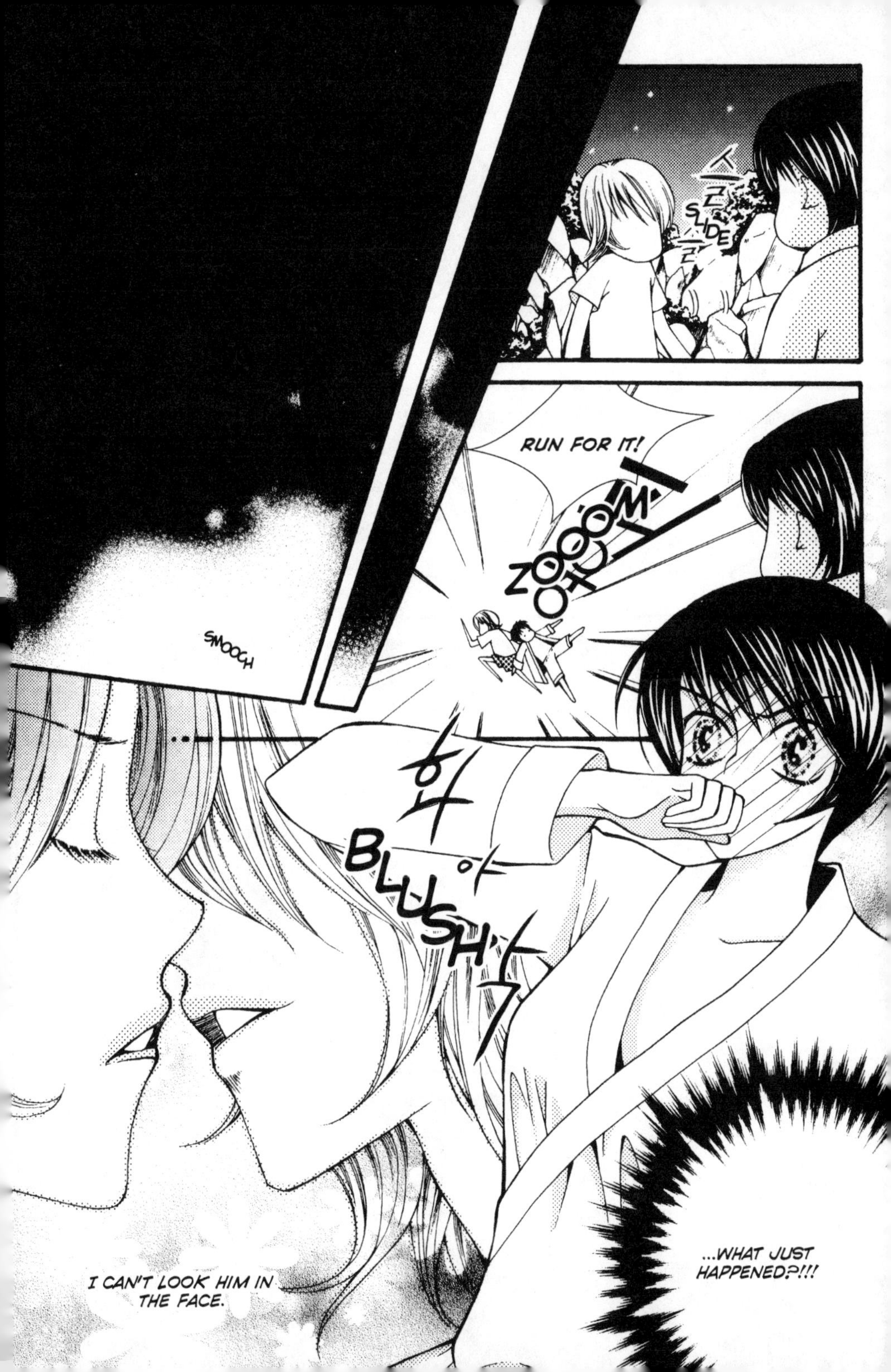
SMOOCH
SLIDE
RUN FOR IT!
ZOOOOM!
BLUSH
I CAN'T LOOK HIM IN THE FACE.
...WHAT JUST HAPPENED?!!!

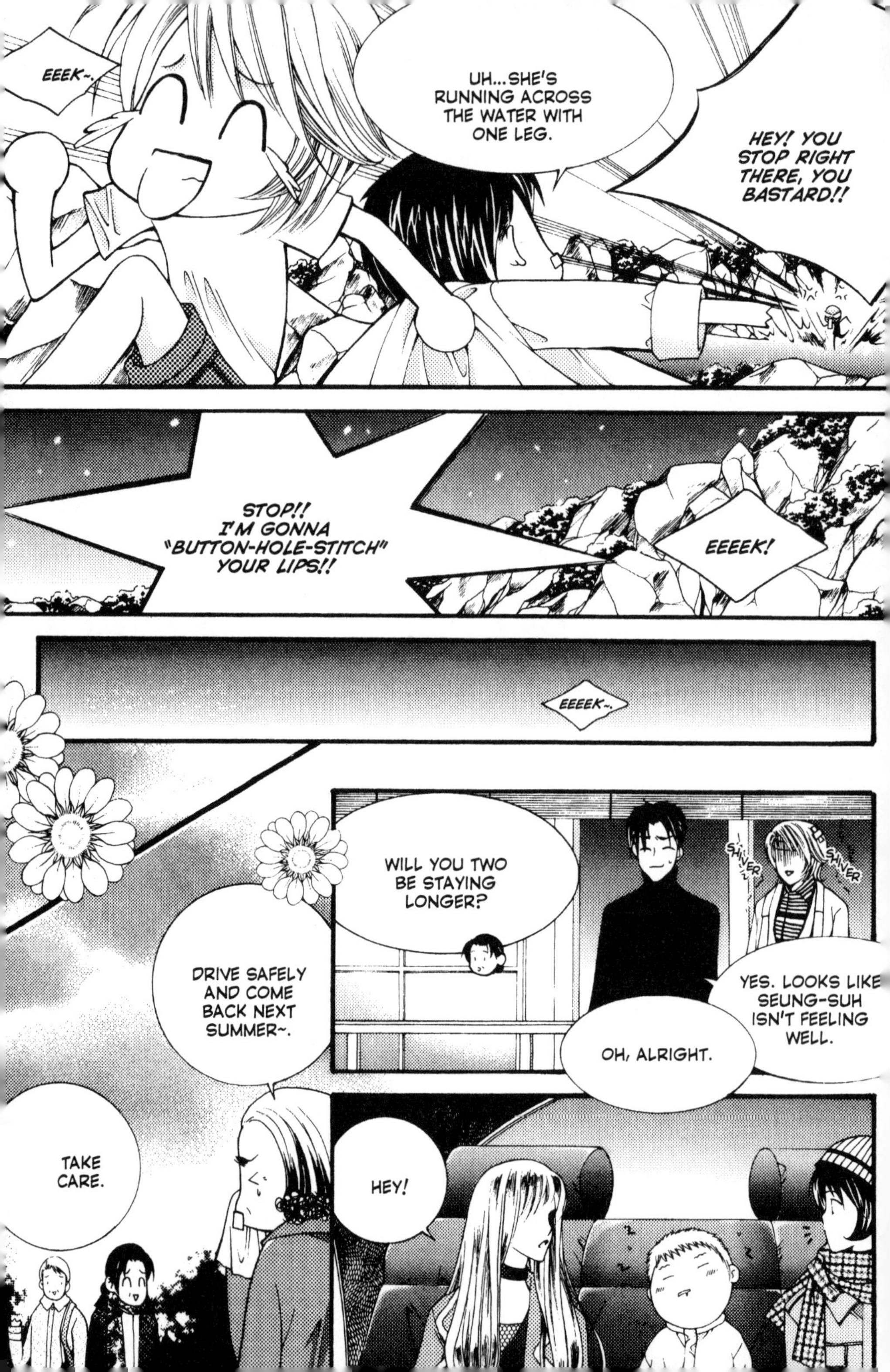
EEEK~.
UH...SHE'S RUNNING ACROSS THE WATER WITH ONE LEG.
HEY! YOU STOP RIGHT THERE, YOU BASTARD!!
STOP!! I'M GONNA "BUTTON-HOLE-STITCH" YOUR LIPS!!
EEEEK!
EEEEK~.
WILL YOU TWO BE STAYING LONGER?
SHIVER
SHIVER
YES. LOOKS LIKE SEUNG-SUH ISN'T FEELING WELL.
OH, ALRIGHT.
DRIVE SAFELY AND COME BACK NEXT SUMMER~.
TAKE CARE.
HEY!

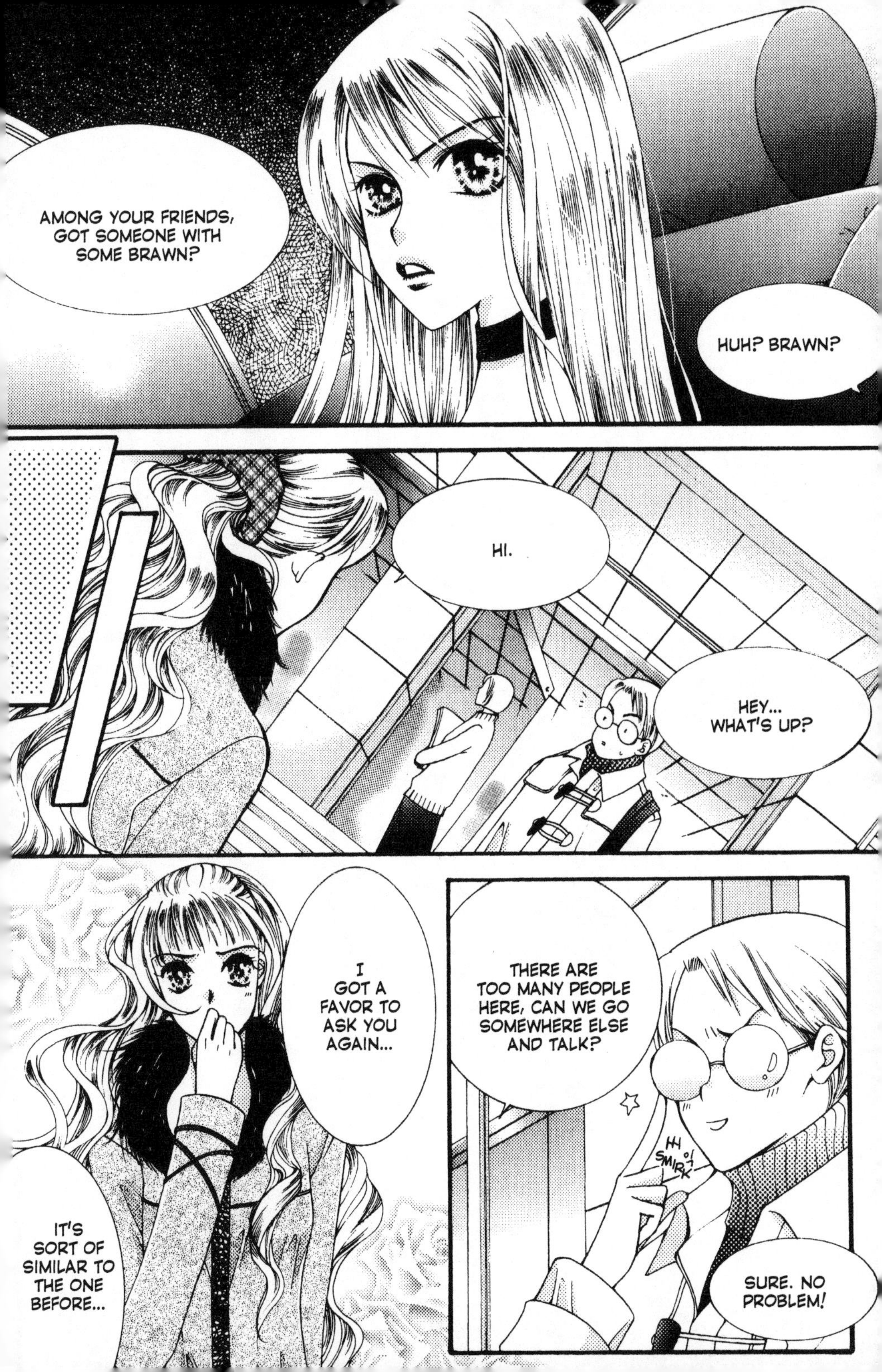
AMONG YOUR FRIENDS, GOT SOMEONE WITH SOME BRAWN?
HUH? BRAWN?
HI.
HEY... WHAT'S UP?
I GOT A FAVOR TO ASK YOU AGAIN...
IT'S SORT OF SIMILAR TO THE ONE BEFORE...
THERE ARE TOO MANY PEOPLE HERE, CAN WE GO SOMEWHERE ELSE AND TALK?
SMIRK
SURE. NO PROBLEM!

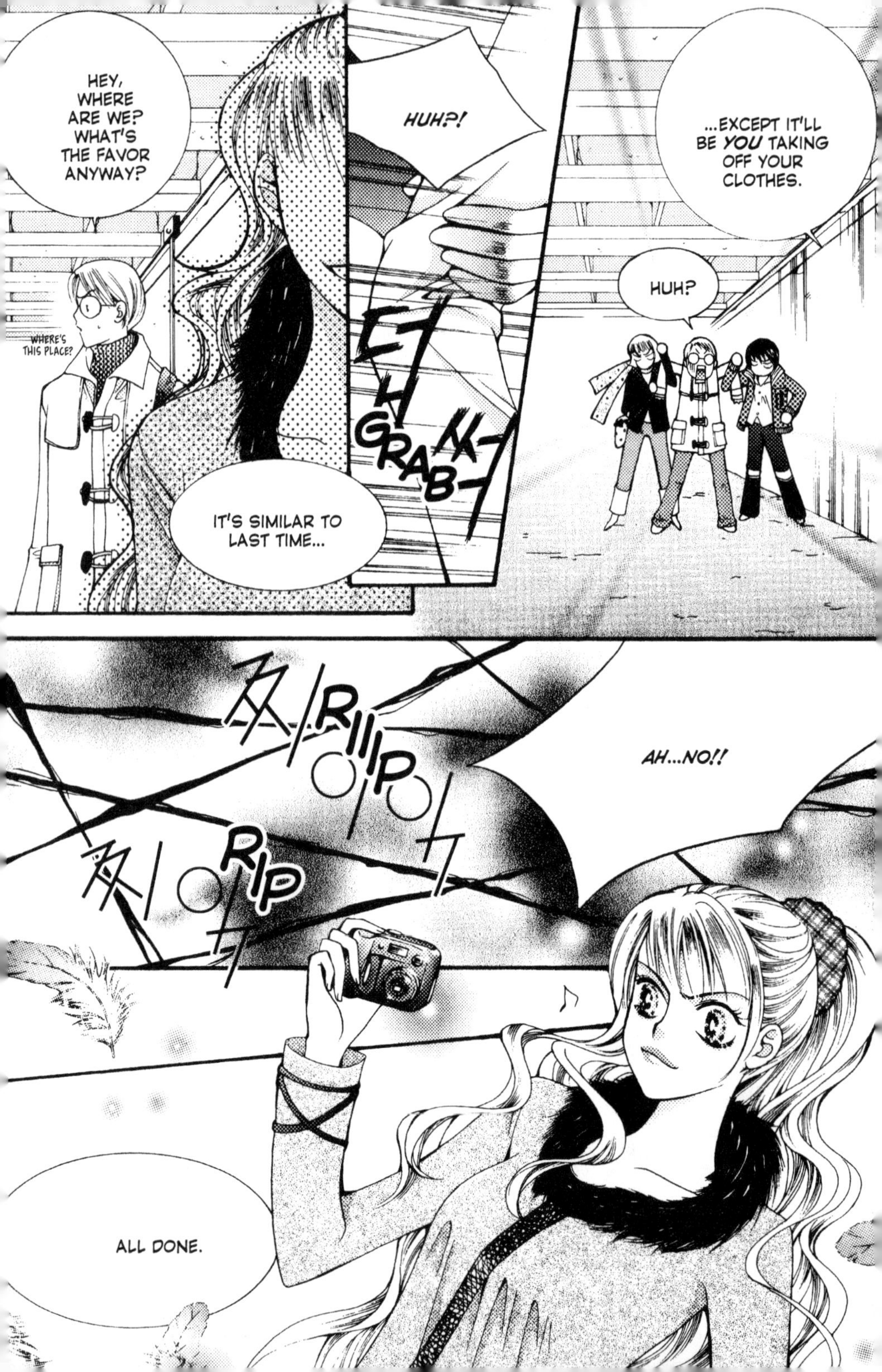
HEY, WHERE ARE WE? WHAT'S THE FAVOR ANYWAY?
WHERE'S THIS PLACE?
IT'S SIMILAR TO LAST TIME...
HUH?!
GRAB
...EXCEPT IT'LL BE YOU TAKING OFF YOUR CLOTHES.
HUH?
RIIIP
RIP
AH...NO!!
ALL DONE.

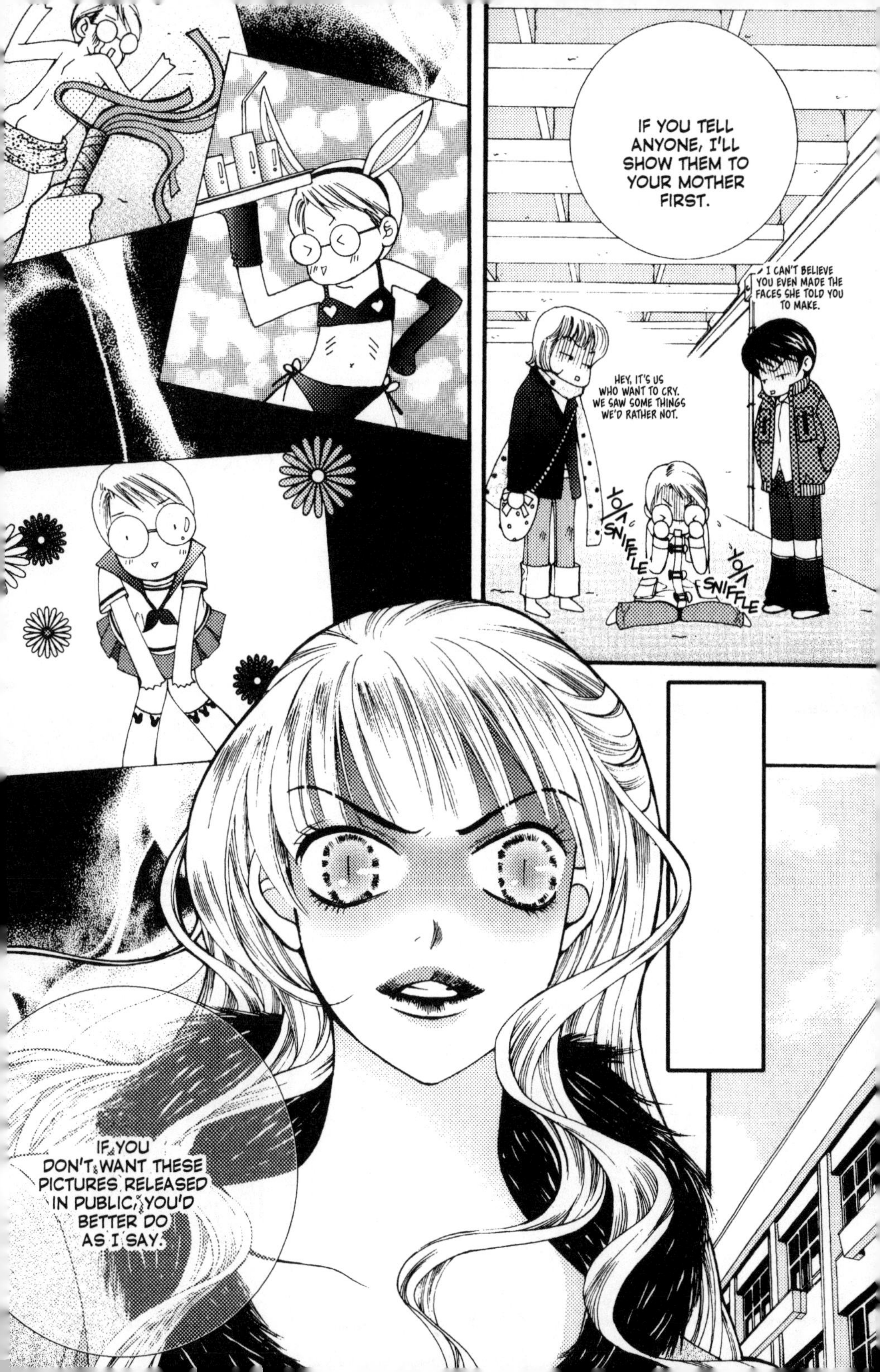
IF YOU TELL ANYONE, I'LL SHOW THEM TO YOUR MOTHER FIRST.
I CAN'T BELIEVE YOU EVEN MADE THE FACES SHE TOLD YOU TO MAKE.
HEY, IT'S US WHO WANT TO CRY. WE SAW SOME THINGS WE'D RATHER NOT.
SNIFFLE
SNIFFLE
IF YOU DON'T WANT THESE PICTURES RELEASED IN PUBLIC, YOU'D BETTER DO AS I SAY.

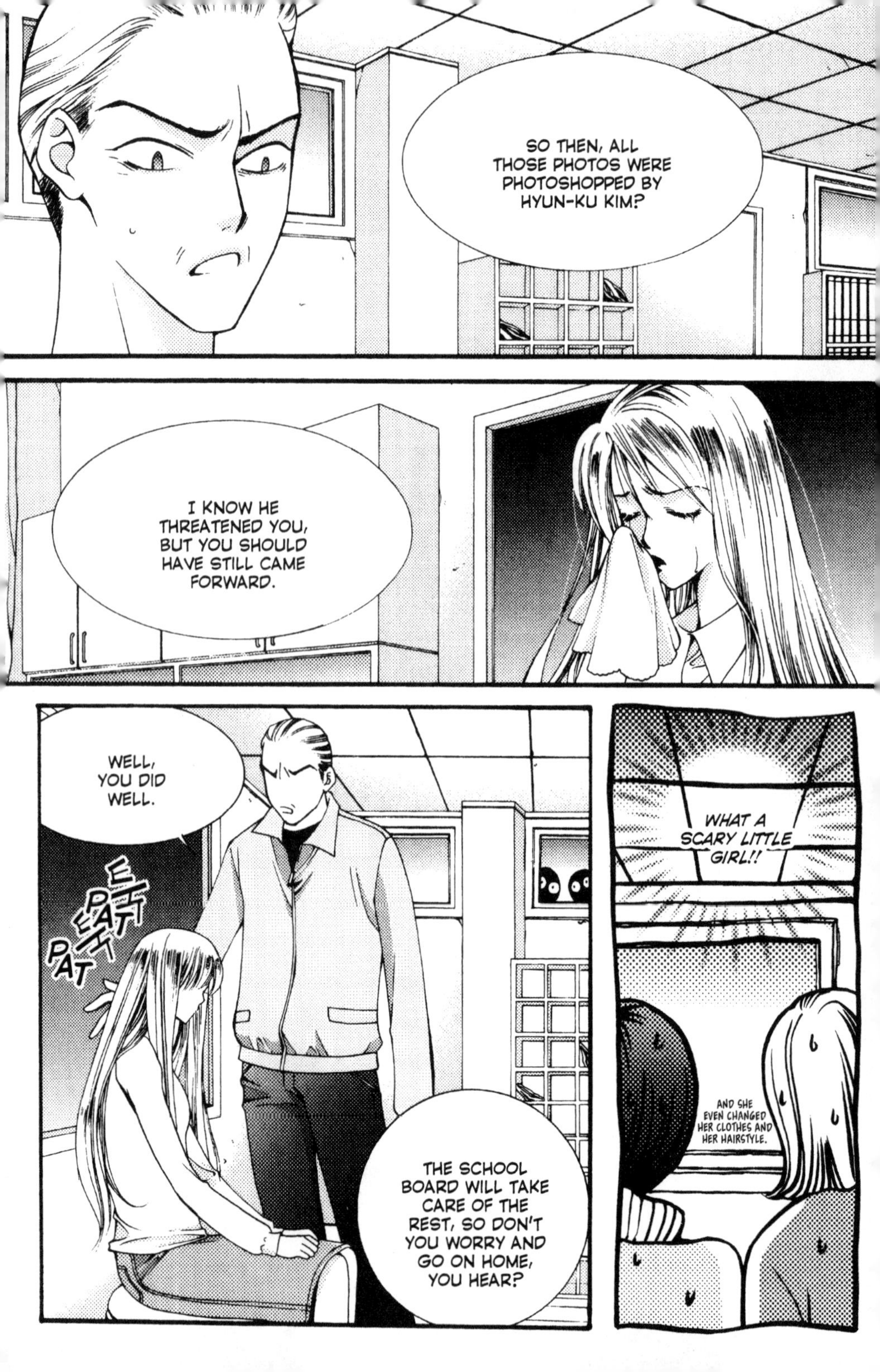
SO THEN, ALL THOSE PHOTOS WERE PHOTOSHOPPED BY HYUN-KU KIM?
I KNOW HE THREATENED YOU, BUT YOU SHOULD HAVE STILL CAME FORWARD.
WELL, YOU DID WELL.
PAT PAT PAT
THE SCHOOL BOARD WILL TAKE CARE OF THE REST, SO DON'T YOU WORRY AND GO ON HOME, YOU HEAR?
WHAT A SCARY LITTLE GIRL!!
AND SHE EVEN CHANGED HER CLOTHES AND HER HAIRSTYLE.

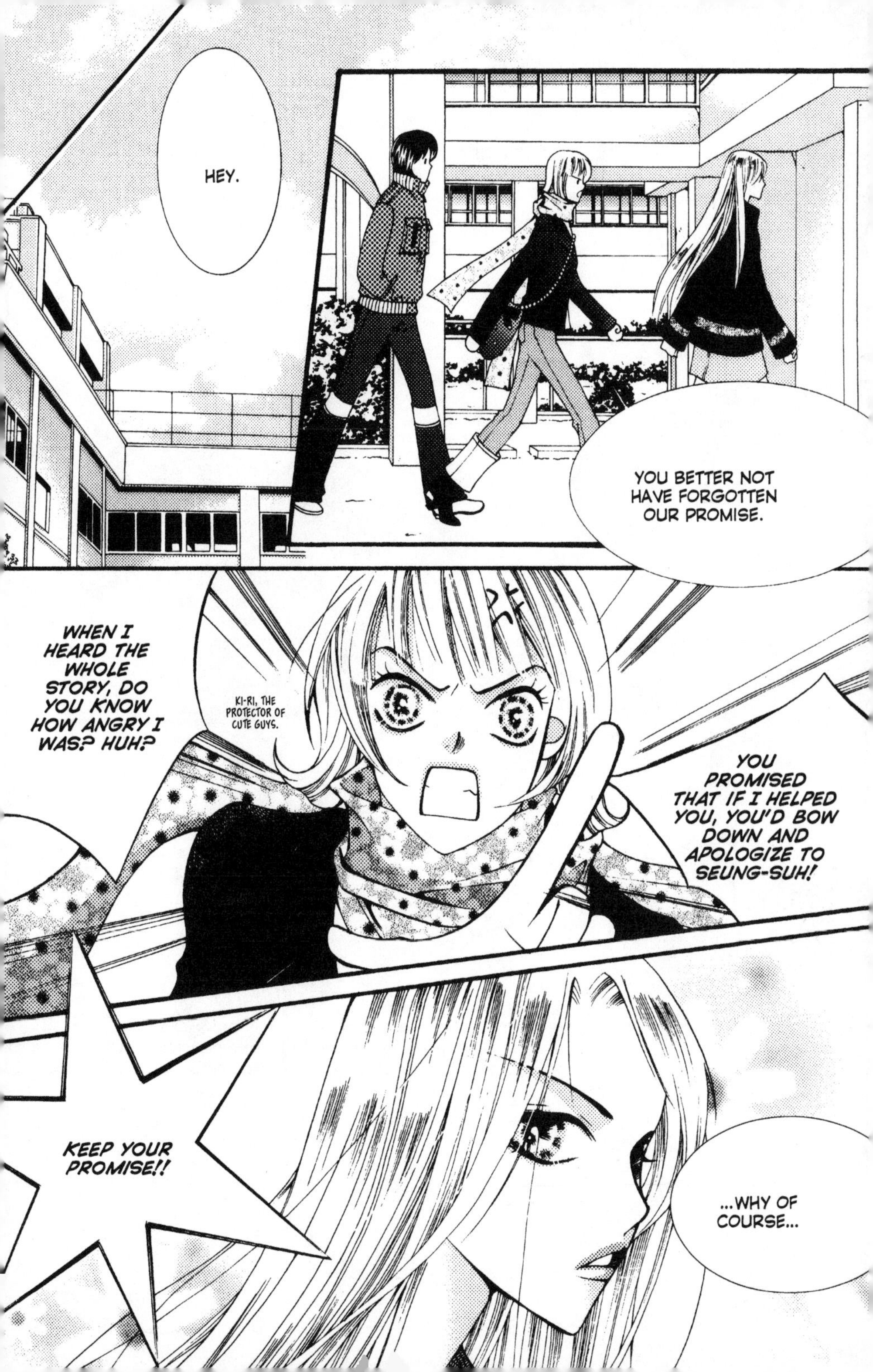
HEY.
YOU BETTER NOT HAVE FORGOTTEN OUR PROMISE.
WHEN I HEARD THE WHOLE STORY, DO YOU KNOW HOW ANGRY I WAS? HUH?
KI-RI, THE PROTECTOR OF CUTE GUYS.
YOU PROMISED THAT IF I HELPED YOU, YOU'D BOW DOWN AND APOLOGIZE TO SEUNG-SUH!
KEEP YOUR PROMISE!!
...WHY OF COURSE...

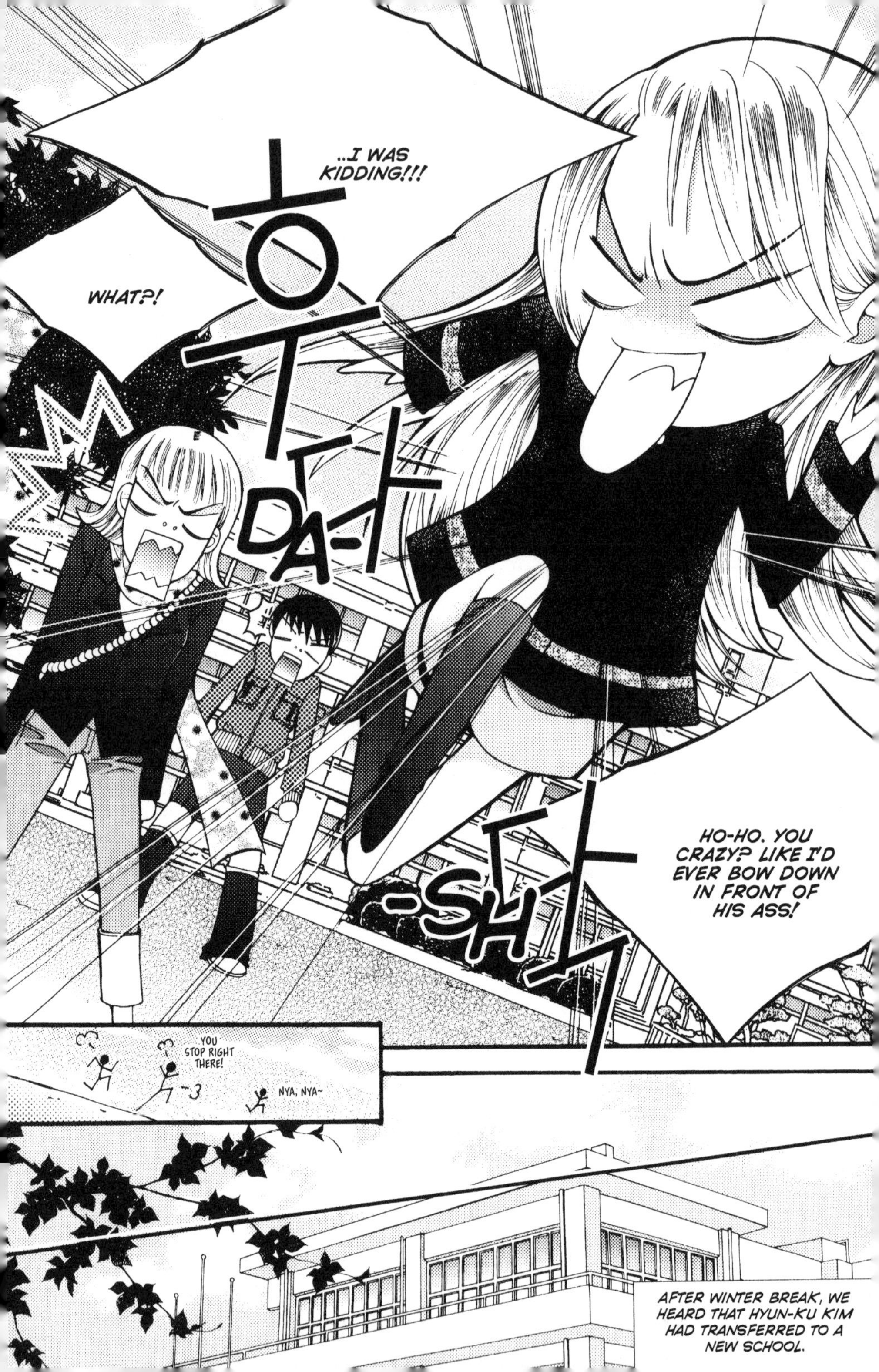
..I WAS KIDDING!!!
WHAT?!
DA-
HO-HO. YOU CRAZY? LIKE I'D EVER BOW DOWN IN FRONT OF HIS ASS!
-SH
YOU STOP RIGHT THERE!
NYA, NYA~
AFTER WINTER BREAK, WE HEARD THAT HYUN-KU KIM HAD TRANSFERRED TO A NEW SCHOOL.

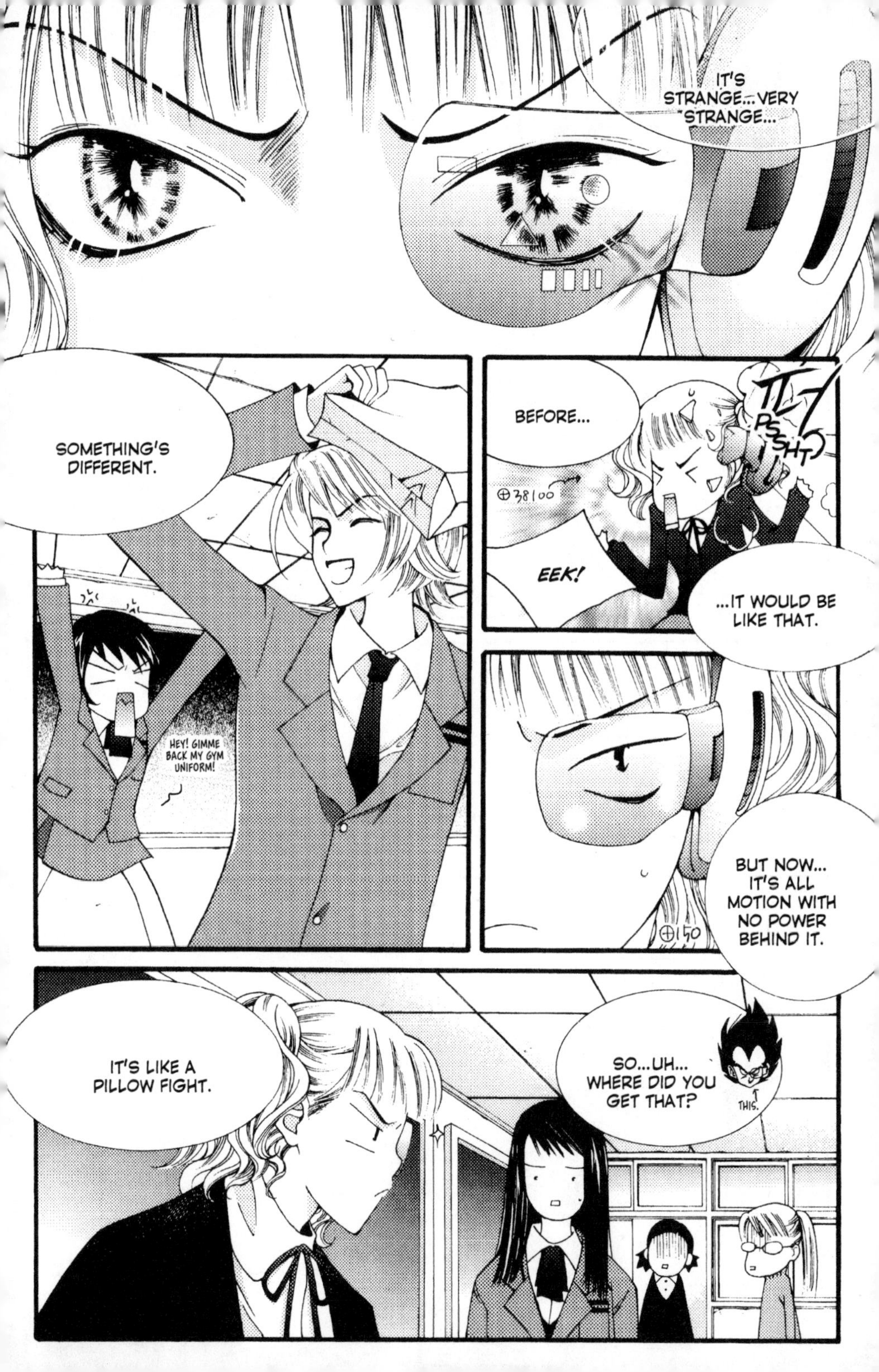
IT'S STRANGE... VERY STRANGE...
SOMETHING'S DIFFERENT.
HEY! GIMME BACK MY GYM UNIFORM!
BEFORE...
⊕38100
PSSHT
EEK!
...IT WOULD BE LIKE THAT.
⊕150
BUT NOW... IT'S ALL MOTION WITH NO POWER BEHIND IT.
IT'S LIKE A PILLOW FIGHT.
SO...UH... WHERE DID YOU GET THAT?
THIS.

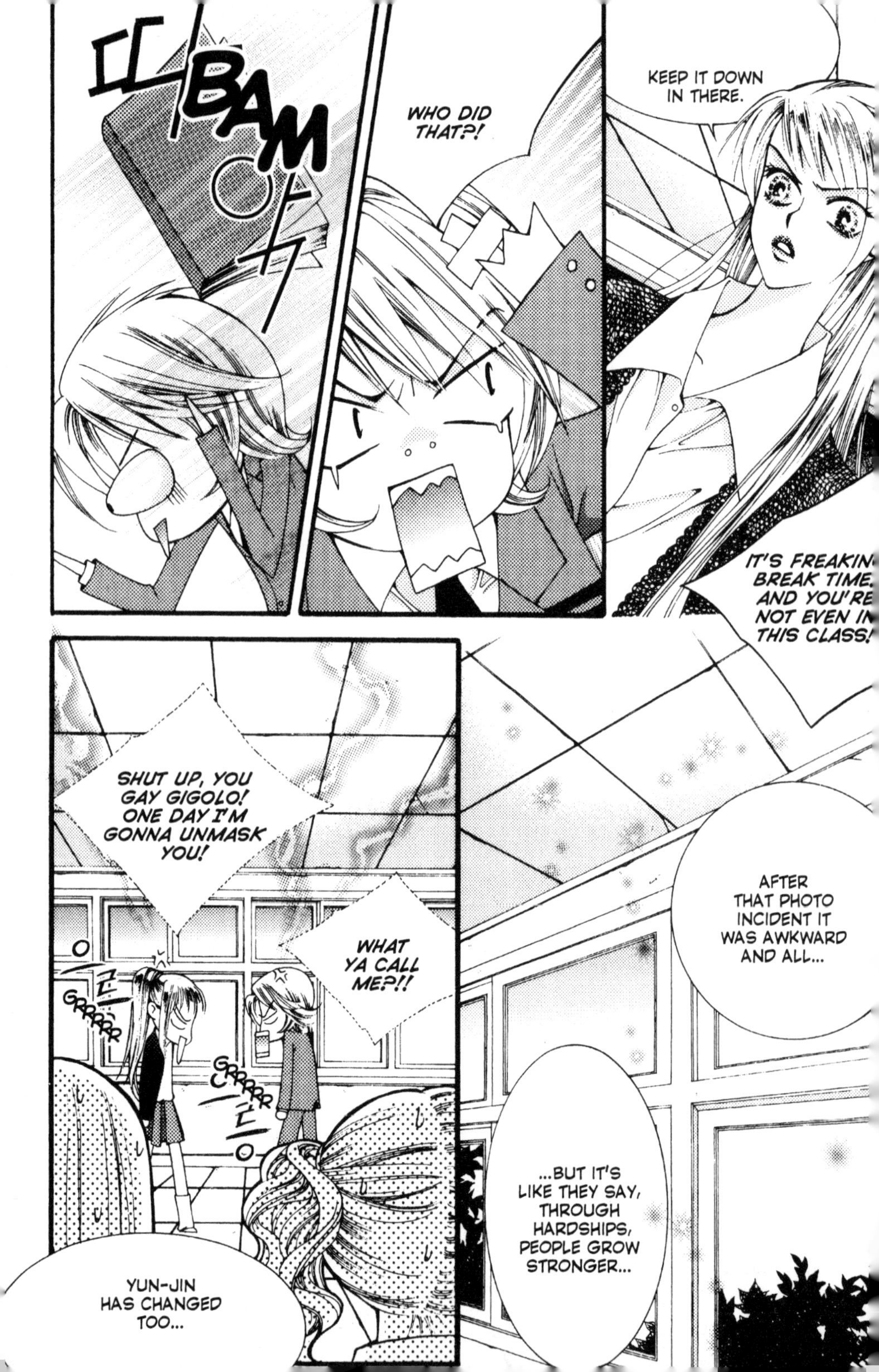
BAM
WHO DID THAT?!
KEEP IT DOWN IN THERE.
IT'S FREAKIN' BREAK TIME. AND YOU'RE NOT EVEN IN THIS CLASS!
SHUT UP, YOU GAY GIGOLO! ONE DAY I'M GONNA UNMASK YOU!
WHAT YA CALL ME?!!
GRRRRRR
GRRRRRR
AFTER THAT PHOTO INCIDENT IT WAS AWKWARD AND ALL...
...BUT IT'S LIKE THEY SAY, THROUGH HARDSHIPS, PEOPLE GROW STRONGER...
YUN-JIN HAS CHANGED TOO...

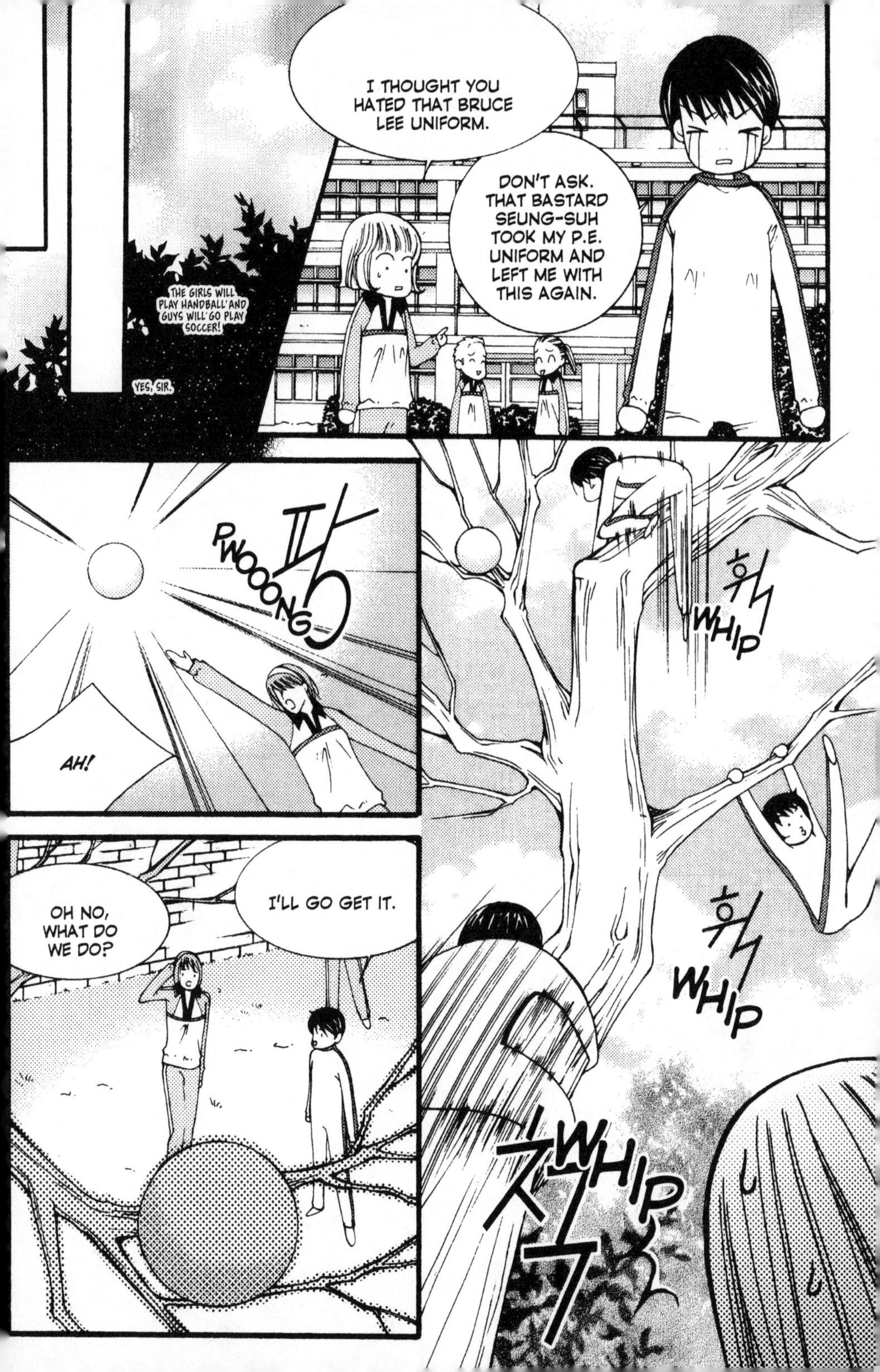
THE GIRLS WILL PLAY HANDBALL AND GUYS WILL GO PLAY SOCCER!
YES, SIR.
I THOUGHT YOU HATED THAT BRUCE LEE UNIFORM.
DON'T ASK. THAT BASTARD SEUNG-SUH TOOK MY P.E. UNIFORM AND LEFT ME WITH THIS AGAIN.
PWOOONG
AH!
OH NO, WHAT DO WE DO?
I'LL GO GET IT.
WHIP
WHIP
WHIP

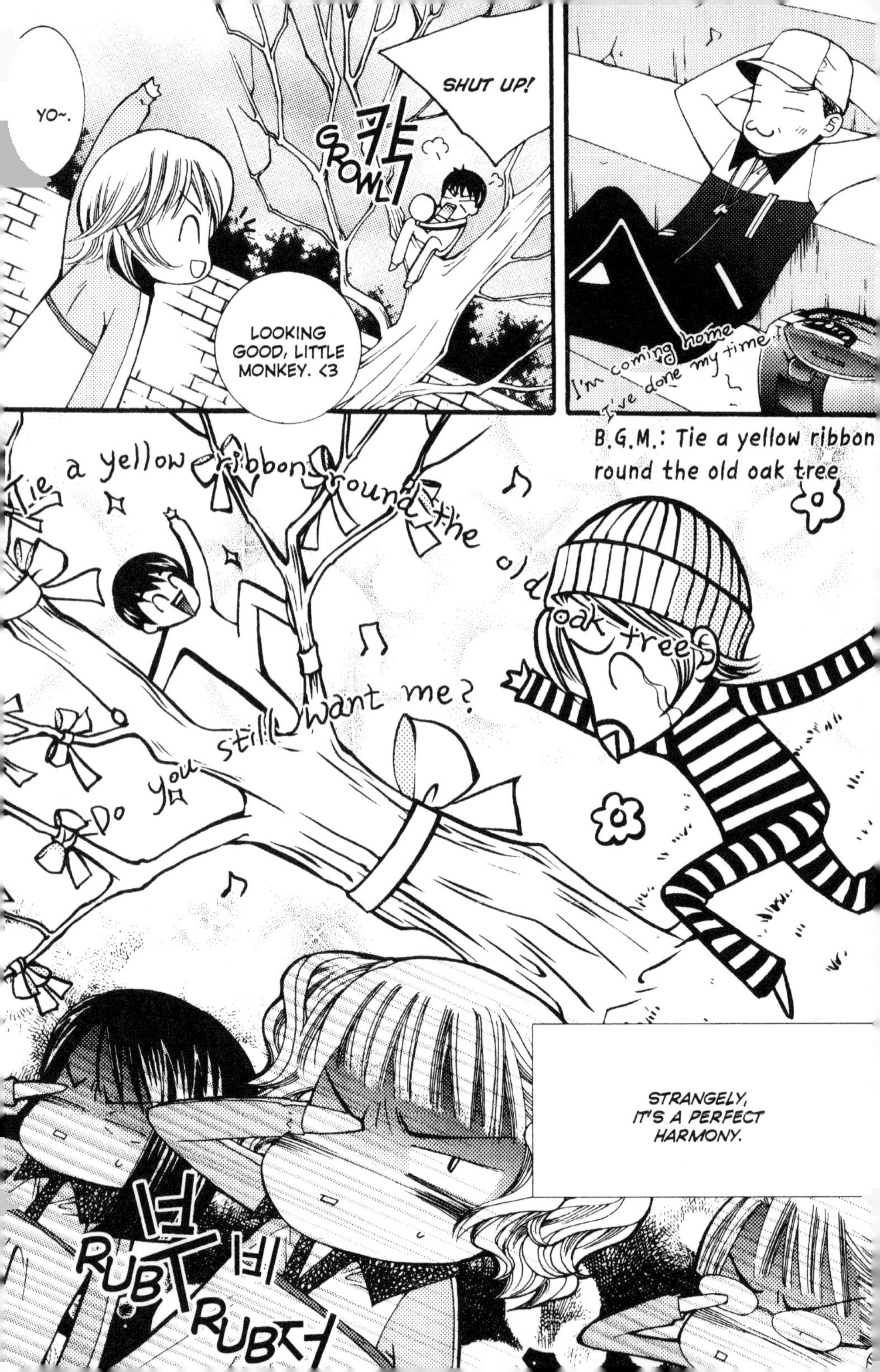
YO~.
SHUT UP!
GROWL
LOOKING GOOD, LITTLE MONKEY. <3
I'm coming home
I've done my time
B.G.M.: Tie a yellow ribbon round the old oak tree
Tie a yellow ribbon round the old oak tree
Do you still want me?
STRANGELY, IT'S A PERFECT HARMONY.
RUB
RUB

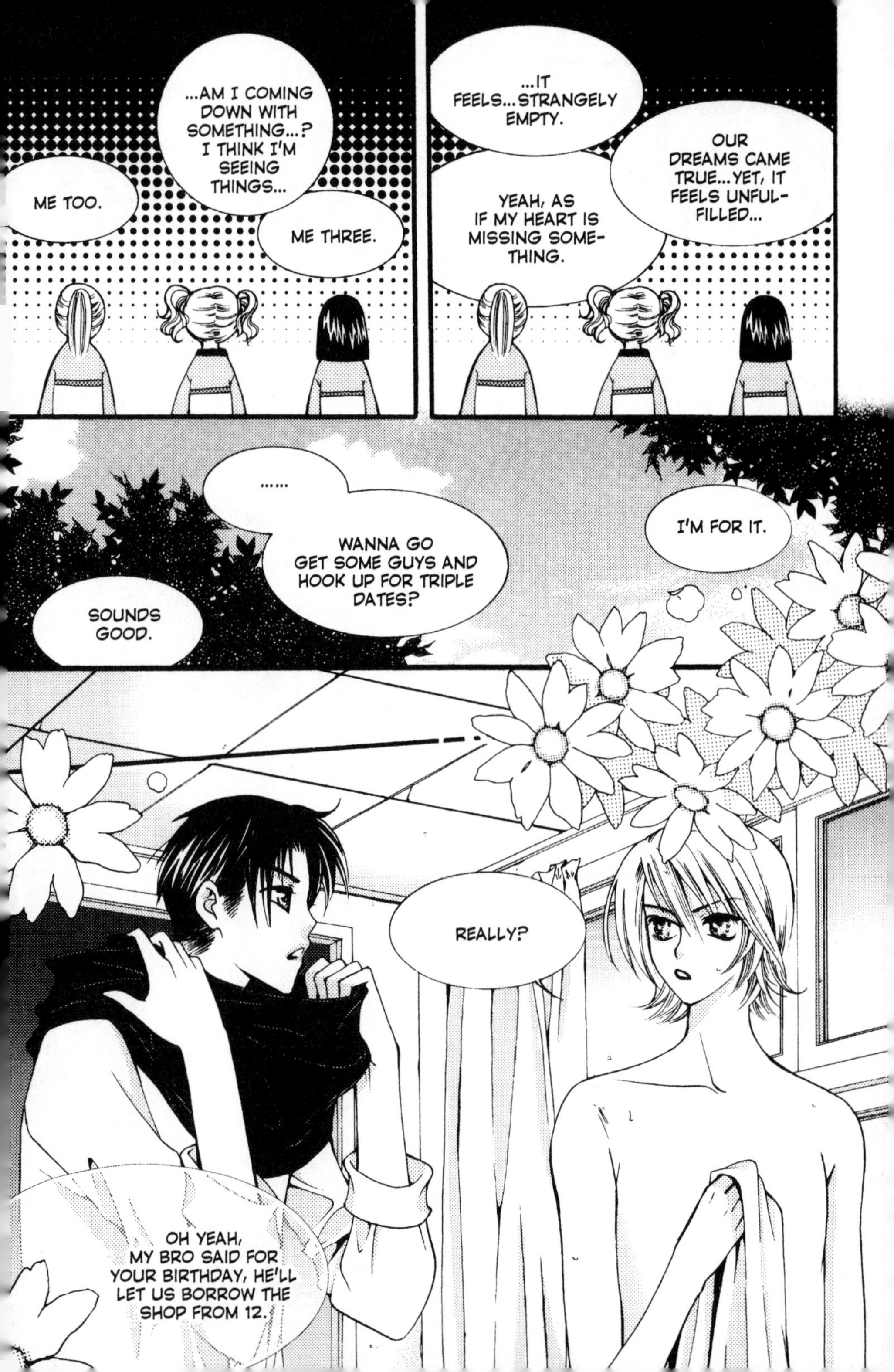
ME TOO.
...AM I COMING DOWN WITH SOMETHING...? I THINK I'M SEEING THINGS...
ME THREE.
...IT FEELS...STRANGELY EMPTY.
YEAH, AS IF MY HEART IS MISSING SOME-THING.
OUR DREAMS CAME TRUE...YET, IT FEELS UNFUL-FILLED...
......
WANNA GO GET SOME GUYS AND HOOK UP FOR TRIPLE DATES?
SOUNDS GOOD.
I'M FOR IT.
REALLY?
OH YEAH, MY BRO SAID FOR YOUR BIRTHDAY, HE'LL LET US BORROW THE SHOP FROM 12.

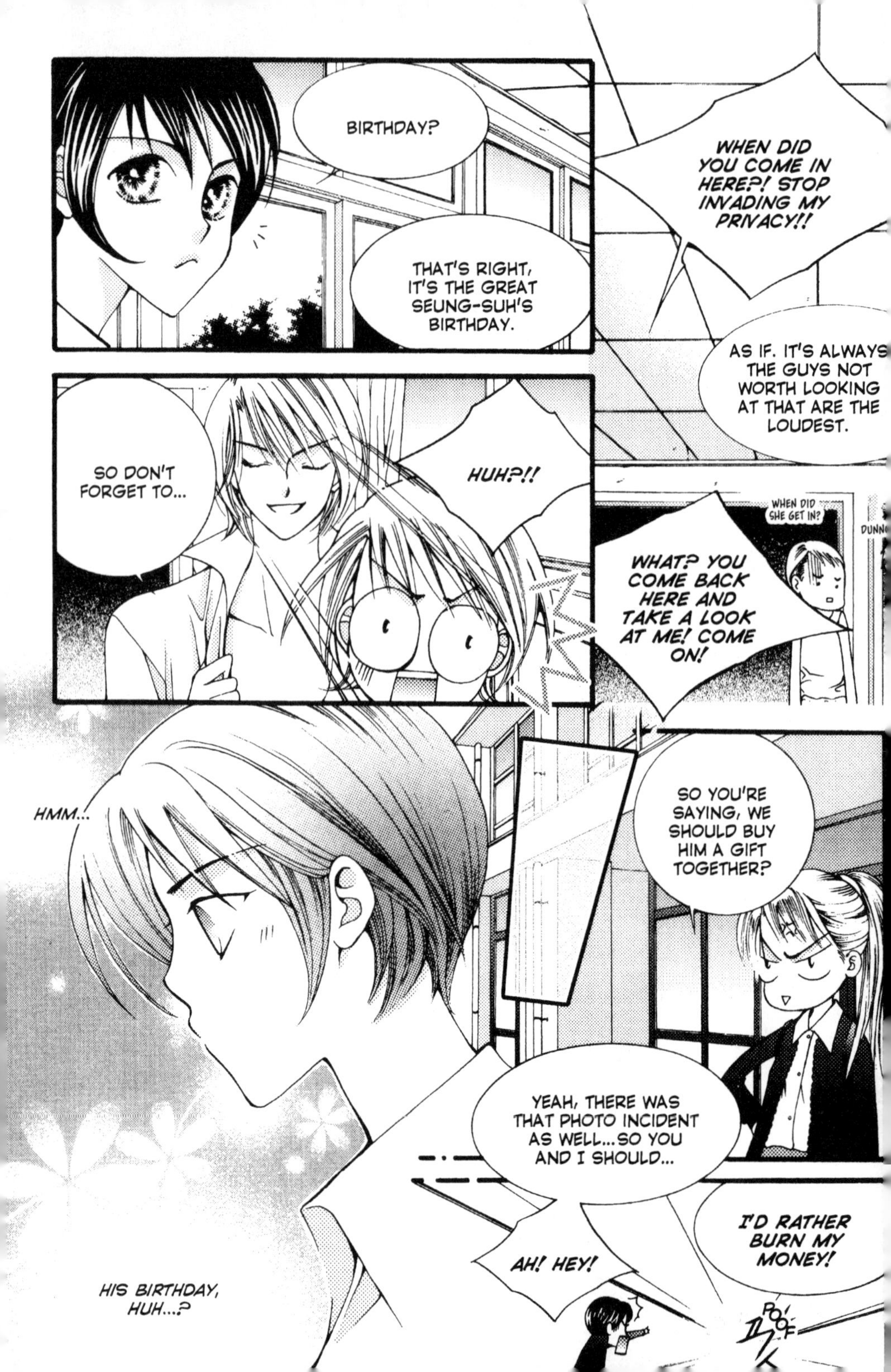

BIRTHDAY?
THAT'S RIGHT, IT'S THE GREAT SEUNG-SUH'S BIRTHDAY.
SO DON'T FORGET TO...
HUH?!!
WHEN DID YOU COME IN HERE?! STOP INVADING MY PRIVACY!!
AS IF. IT'S ALWAYS THE GUYS NOT WORTH LOOKING AT THAT ARE THE LOUDEST.
WHEN DID SHE GET IN?
DUNN
WHAT? YOU COME BACK HERE AND TAKE A LOOK AT ME! COME ON!
HMM...
SO YOU'RE SAYING, WE SHOULD BUY HIM A GIFT TOGETHER?
YEAH, THERE WAS THAT PHOTO INCIDENT AS WELL...SO YOU AND I SHOULD...
I'D RATHER BURN MY MONEY!
AH! HEY!
HIS BIRTHDAY, HUH...?
POOF

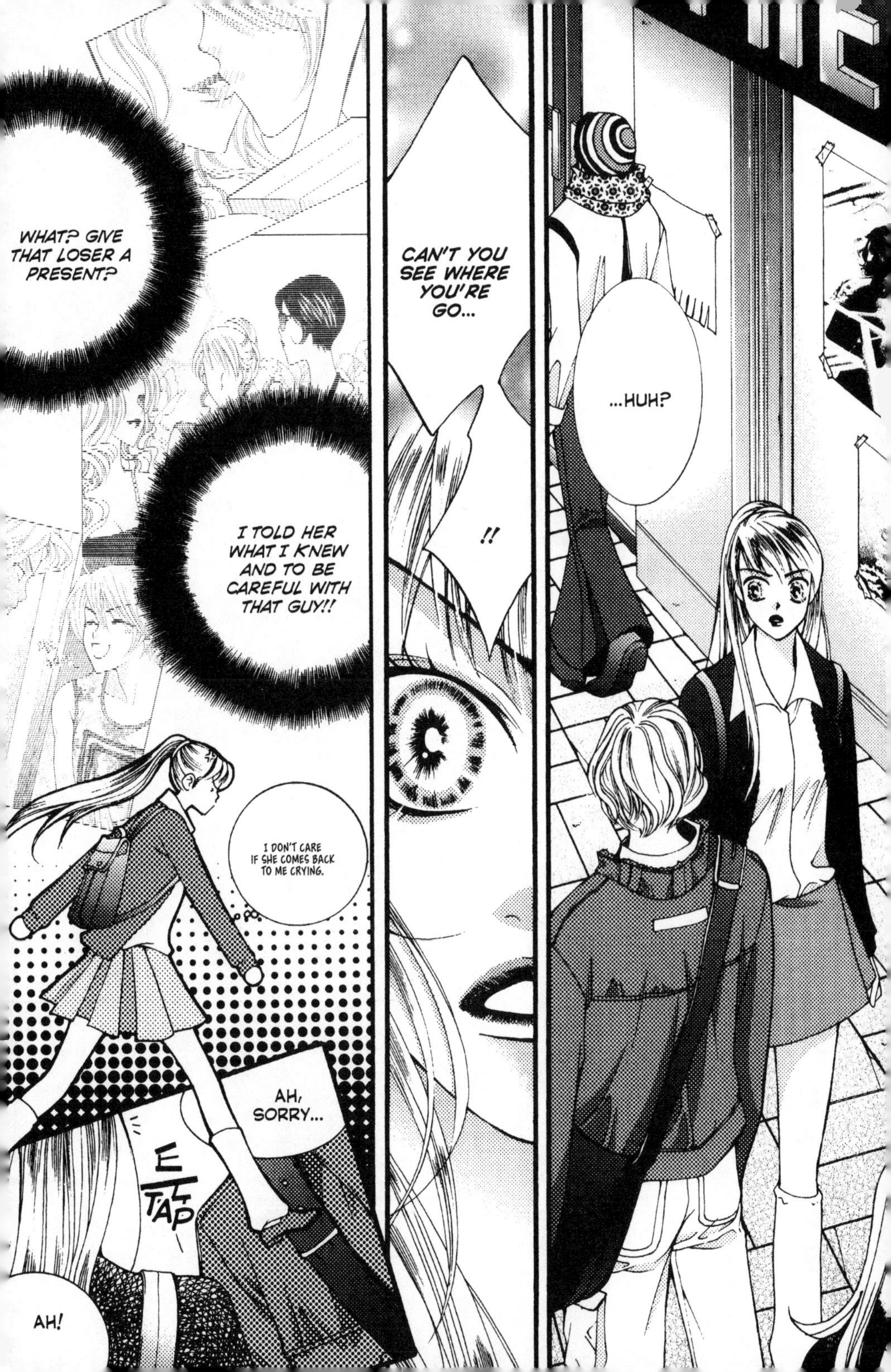
WHAT? GIVE THAT LOSER A PRESENT?
I TOLD HER WHAT I KNEW AND TO BE CAREFUL WITH THAT GUY!!
I DON'T CARE IF SHE COMES BACK TO ME CRYING.
AH, SORRY...
TAP
AH!
CAN'T YOU SEE WHERE YOU'RE GO...
!!
...HUH?

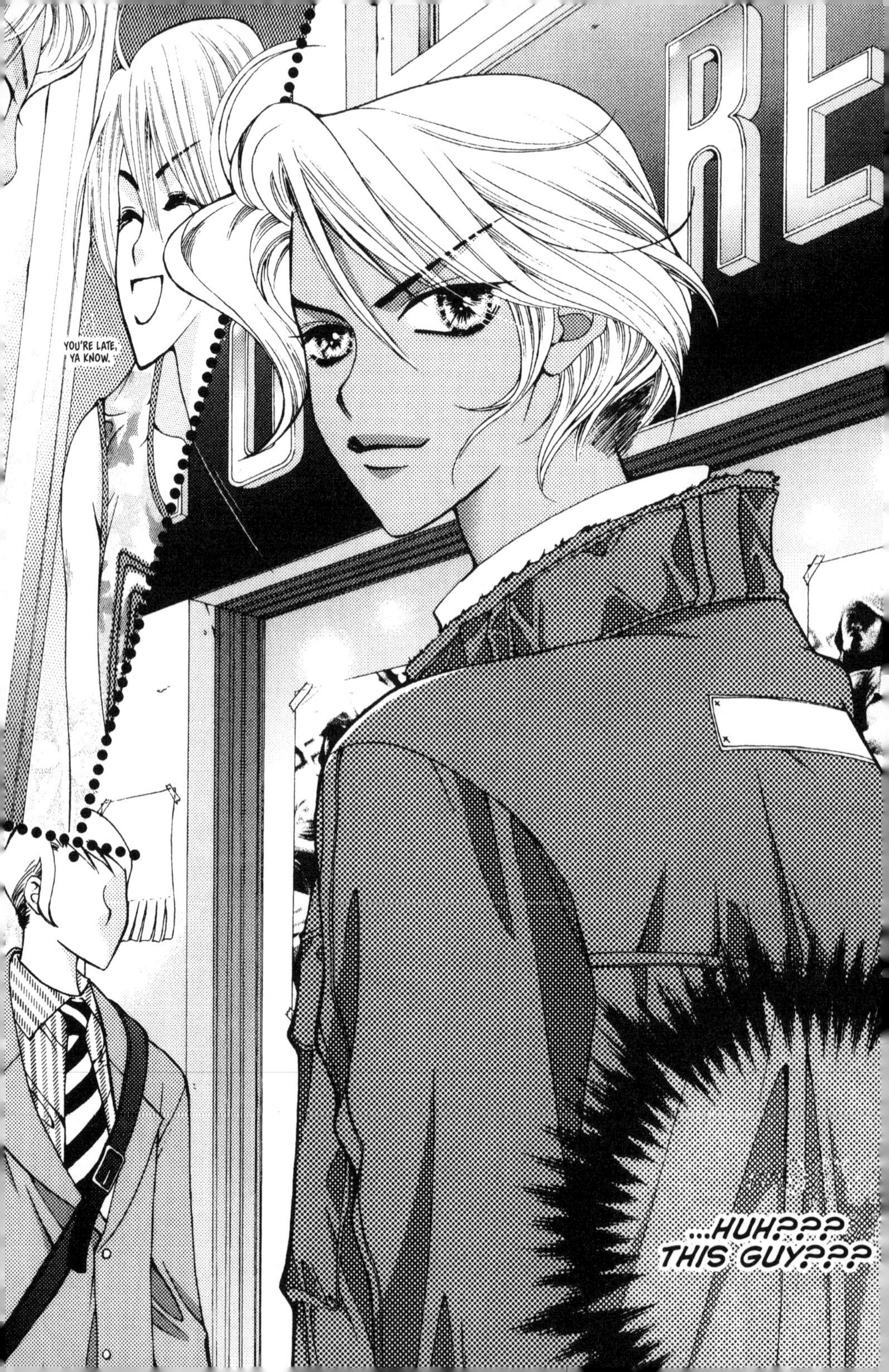
YOU'RE LATE, YA KNOW.
...HUH???
THIS GUY???

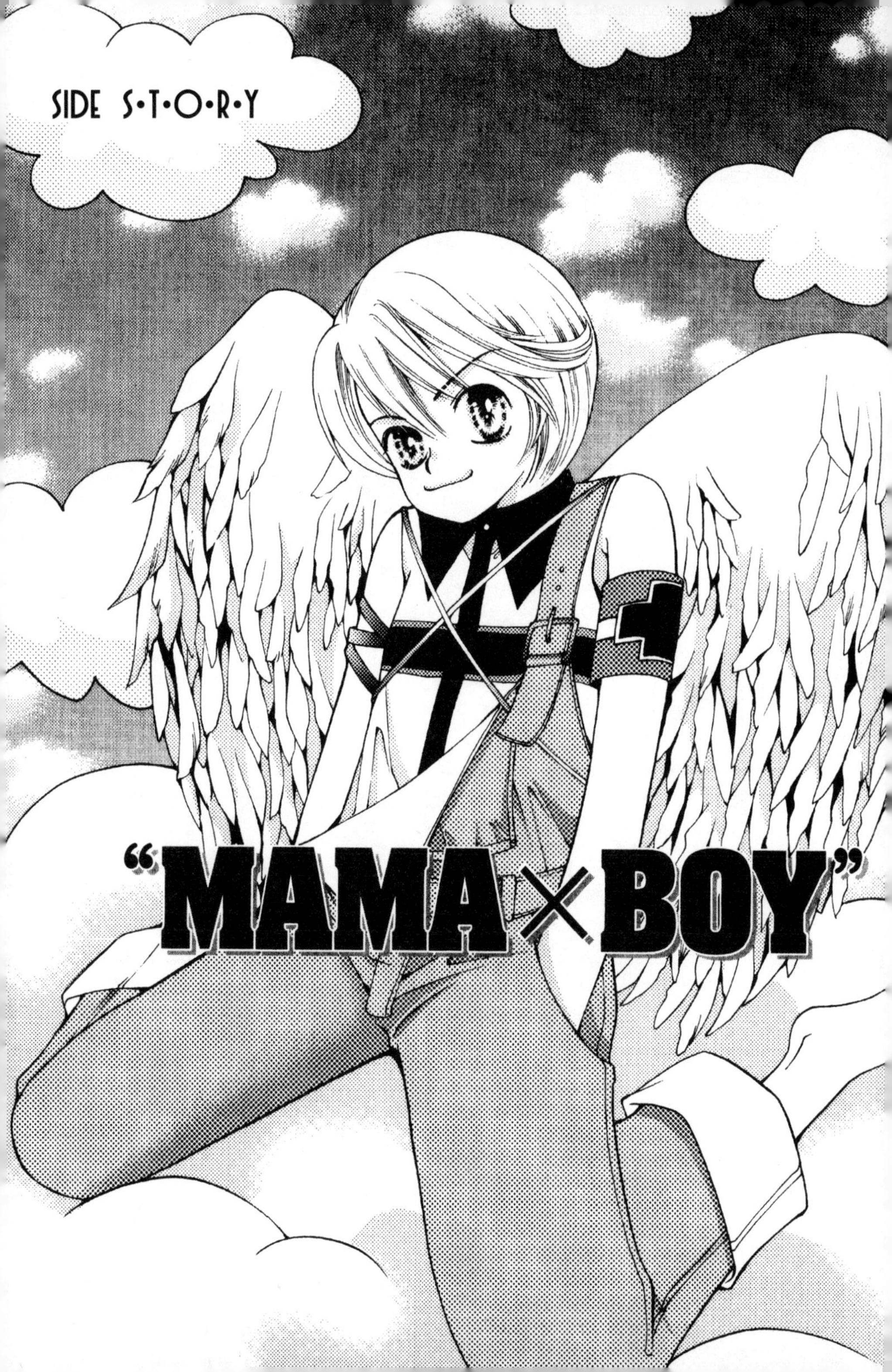
SIDE S•T•O•R•Y
"MAMA × BOY"

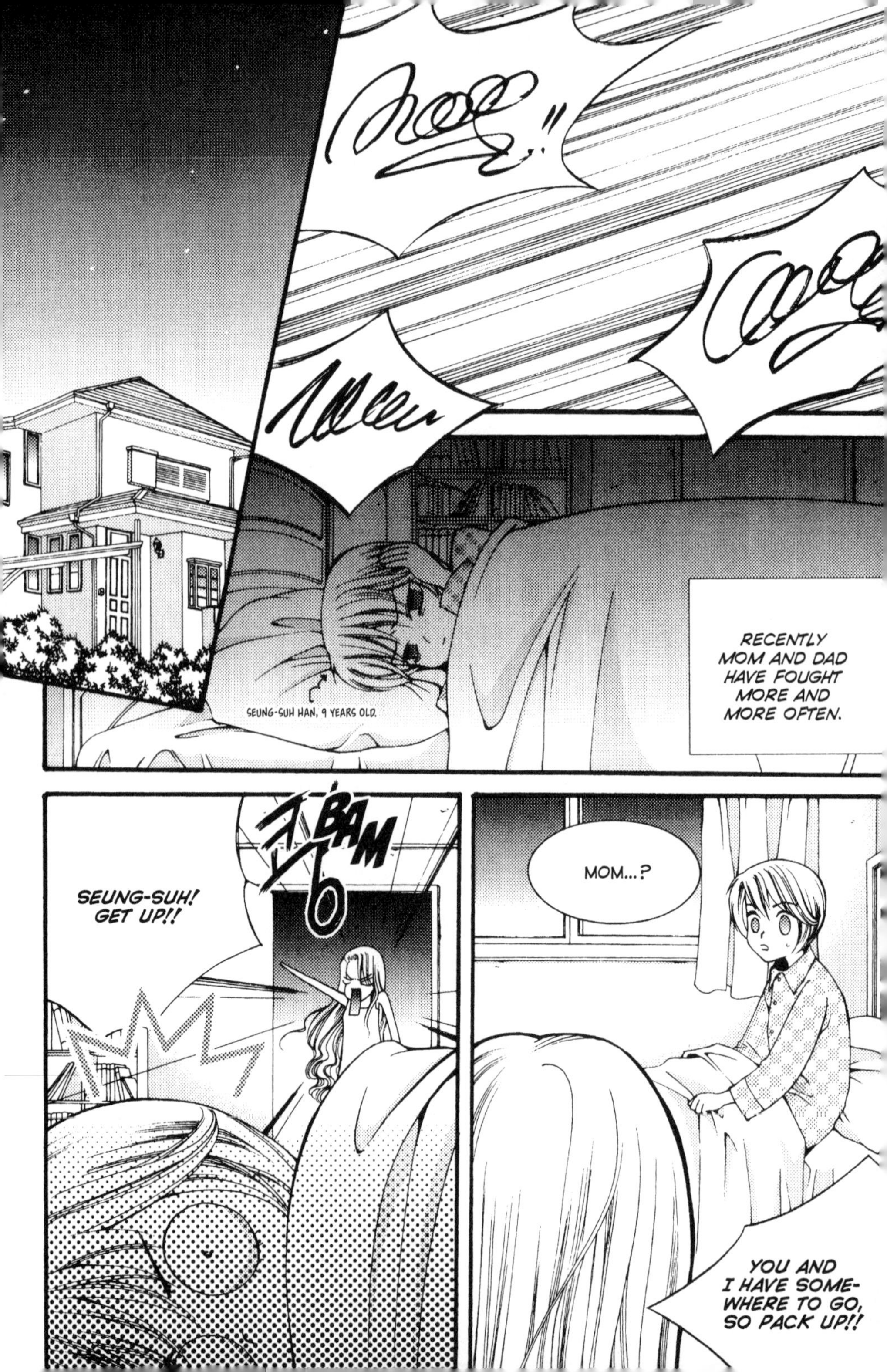
SEUNG-SUH HAN, 9 YEARS OLD.
RECENTLY MOM AND DAD HAVE FOUGHT MORE AND MORE OFTEN.
BAM
SEUNG-SUH! GET UP!!
MOM...?
YOU AND I HAVE SOME-WHERE TO GO, SO PACK UP!!

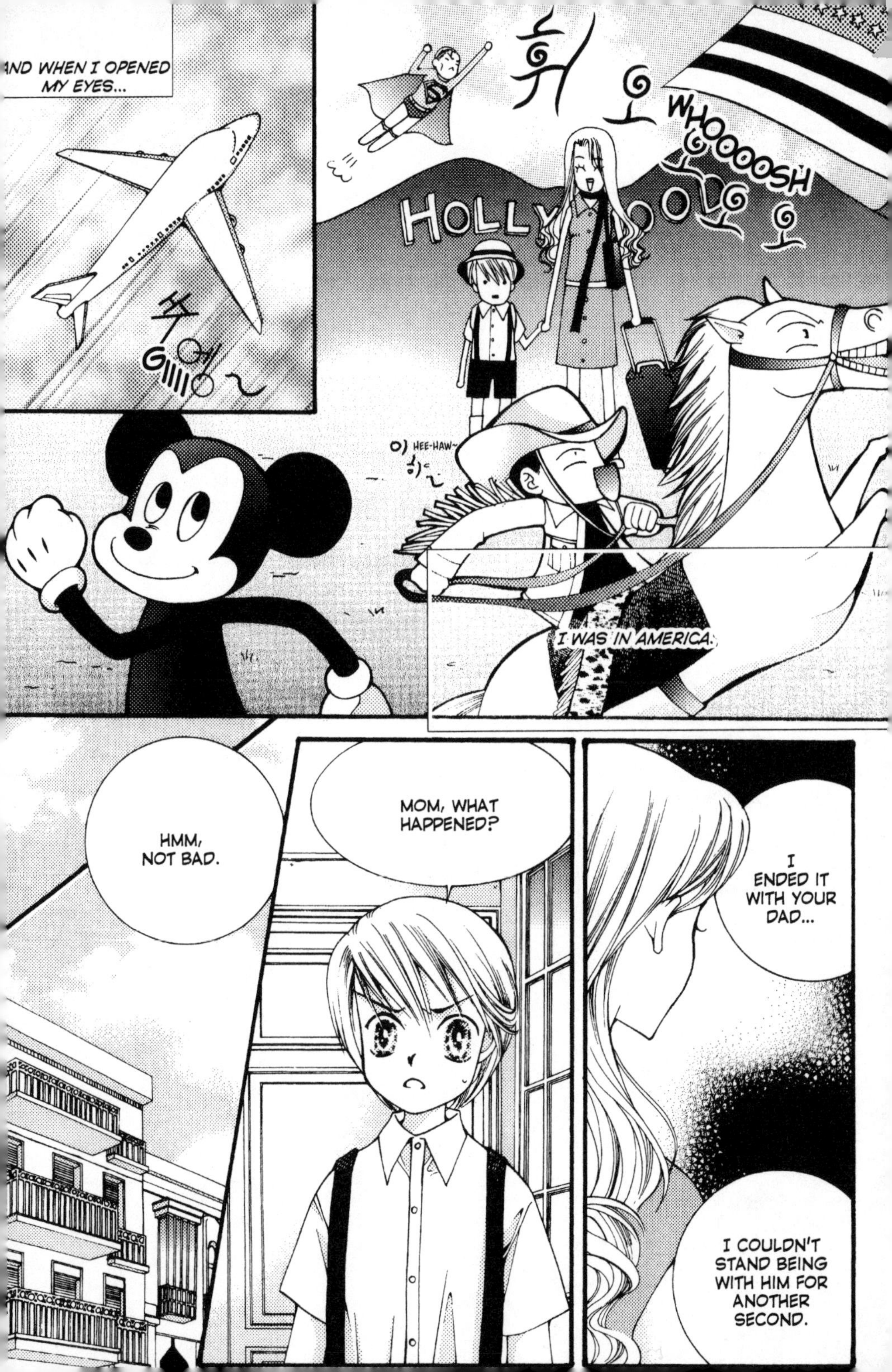
AND WHEN I OPENED MY EYES...
HOLLY
WHOOOOSH
HEE-HAW~
I WAS IN AMERICA.
HMM, NOT BAD.
MOM, WHAT HAPPENED?
I ENDED IT WITH YOUR DAD...
I COULDN'T STAND BEING WITH HIM FOR ANOTHER SECOND.

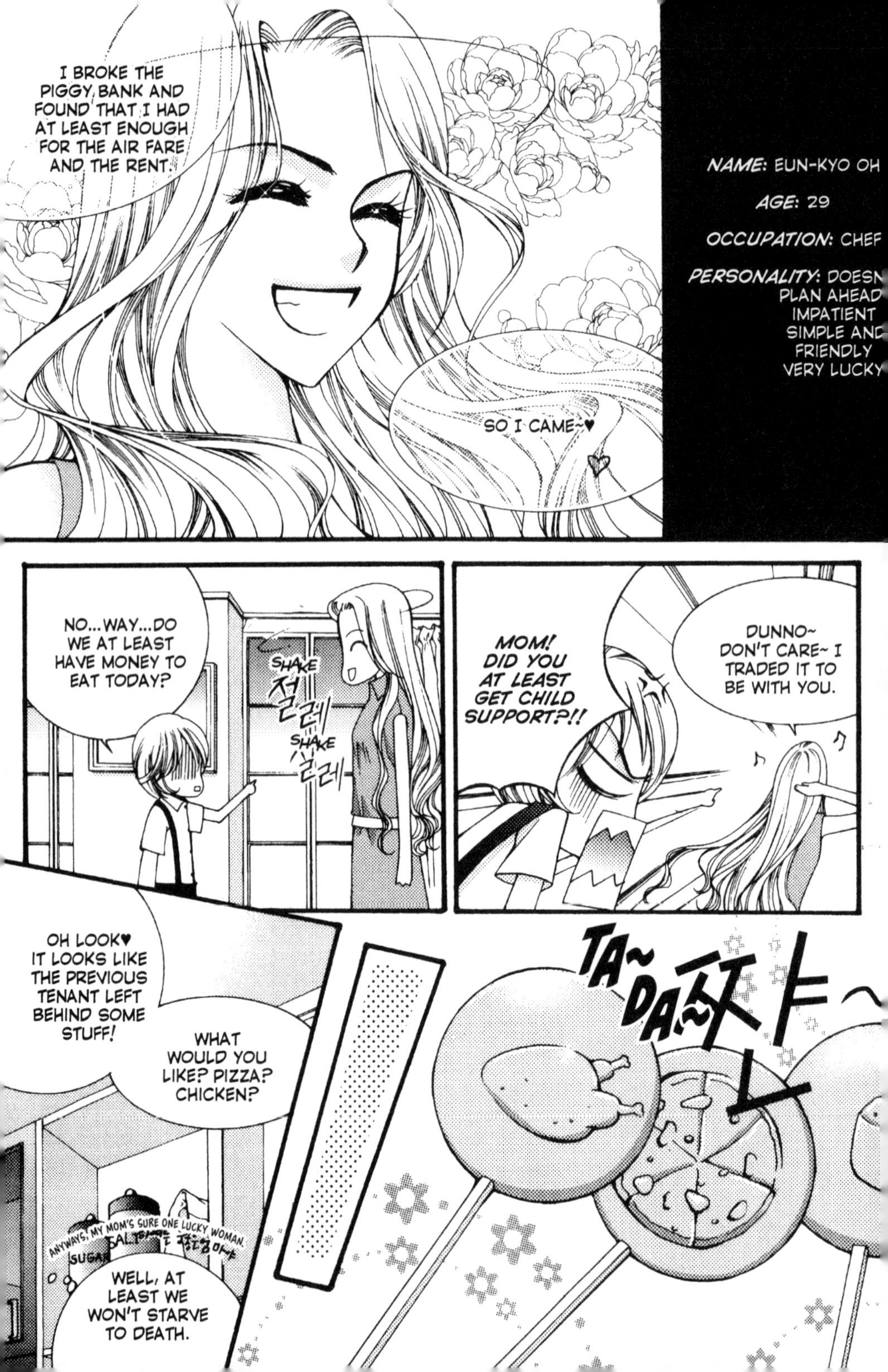
I BROKE THE PIGGY BANK AND FOUND THAT I HAD AT LEAST ENOUGH FOR THE AIR FARE AND THE RENT.
SO I CAME~♥
NAME: EUN-KYO OH
AGE: 29
OCCUPATION: CHEF
PERSONALITY: DOESN PLAN AHEAD IMPATIENT SIMPLE AND FRIENDLY VERY LUCKY
NO...WAY...DO WE AT LEAST HAVE MONEY TO EAT TODAY?
SHAKE
SHAKE
MOM! DID YOU AT LEAST GET CHILD SUPPORT?!!
DUNNO~ DON'T CARE~ I TRADED IT TO BE WITH YOU.
OH LOOK♥ IT LOOKS LIKE THE PREVIOUS TENANT LEFT BEHIND SOME STUFF!
WHAT WOULD YOU LIKE? PIZZA? CHICKEN?
ANYWAYS, MY MOM'S SURE ONE LUCKY WOMAN.
WELL, AT LEAST WE WON'T STARVE TO DEATH.
TA~ DA~

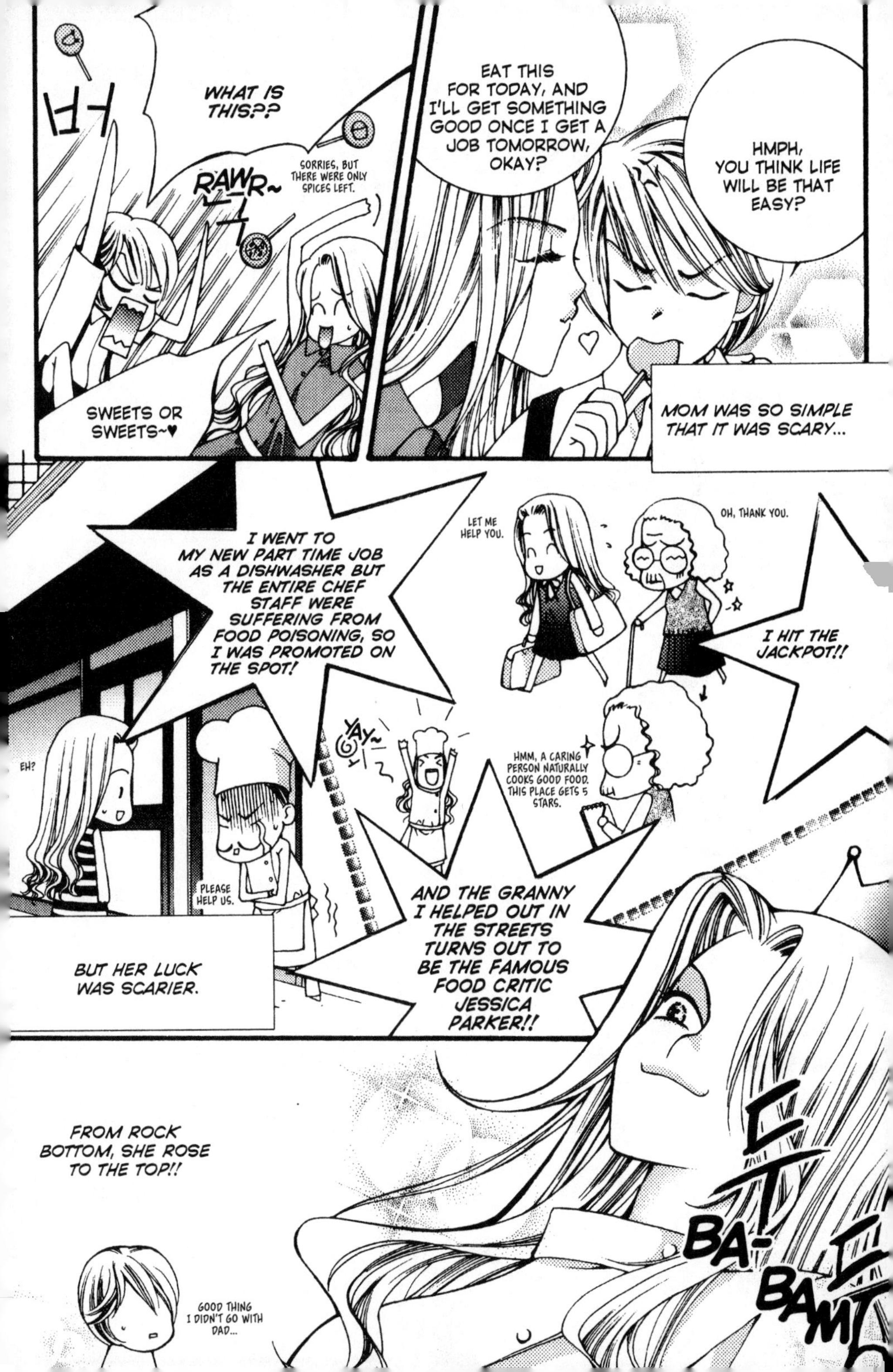
WHAT IS THIS??
RAWR~
SORRIES, BUT THERE WERE ONLY SPICES LEFT.
SWEETS OR SWEETS~♥
EAT THIS FOR TODAY, AND I'LL GET SOMETHING GOOD ONCE I GET A JOB TOMORROW, OKAY?
HMPH, YOU THINK LIFE WILL BE THAT EASY?
MOM WAS SO SIMPLE THAT IT WAS SCARY...
I WENT TO MY NEW PART TIME JOB AS A DISHWASHER BUT THE ENTIRE CHEF STAFF WERE SUFFERING FROM FOOD POISONING, SO I WAS PROMOTED ON THE SPOT!
EH?
PLEASE HELP US.
YAY~
BUT HER LUCK WAS SCARIER.
LET ME HELP YOU.
OH, THANK YOU.
I HIT THE JACKPOT!!
HMM, A CARING PERSON NATURALLY COOKS GOOD FOOD. THIS PLACE GETS 5 STARS.
AND THE GRANNY I HELPED OUT IN THE STREETS TURNS OUT TO BE THE FAMOUS FOOD CRITIC JESSICA PARKER!!
FROM ROCK BOTTOM, SHE ROSE TO THE TOP!!
GOOD THING I DIDN'T GO WITH DAD...
BA-BAM

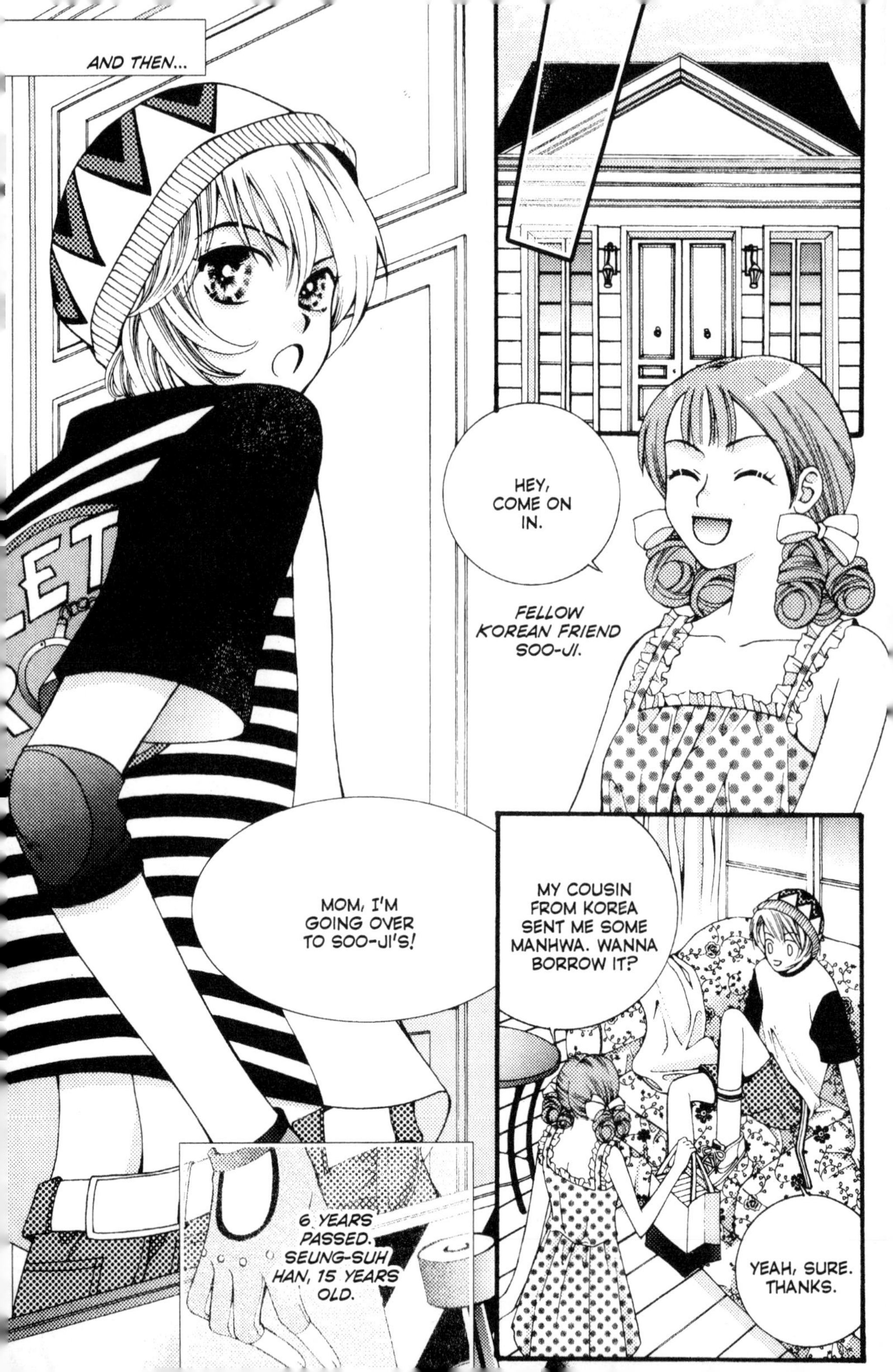
AND THEN...
MOM, I'M GOING OVER TO SOO-JI'S!
6 YEARS PASSED. SEUNG-SUH HAN, 15 YEARS OLD.
HEY, COME ON IN.
FELLOW KOREAN FRIEND SOO-JI.
MY COUSIN FROM KOREA SENT ME SOME MANHWA. WANNA BORROW IT?
YEAH, SURE. THANKS.

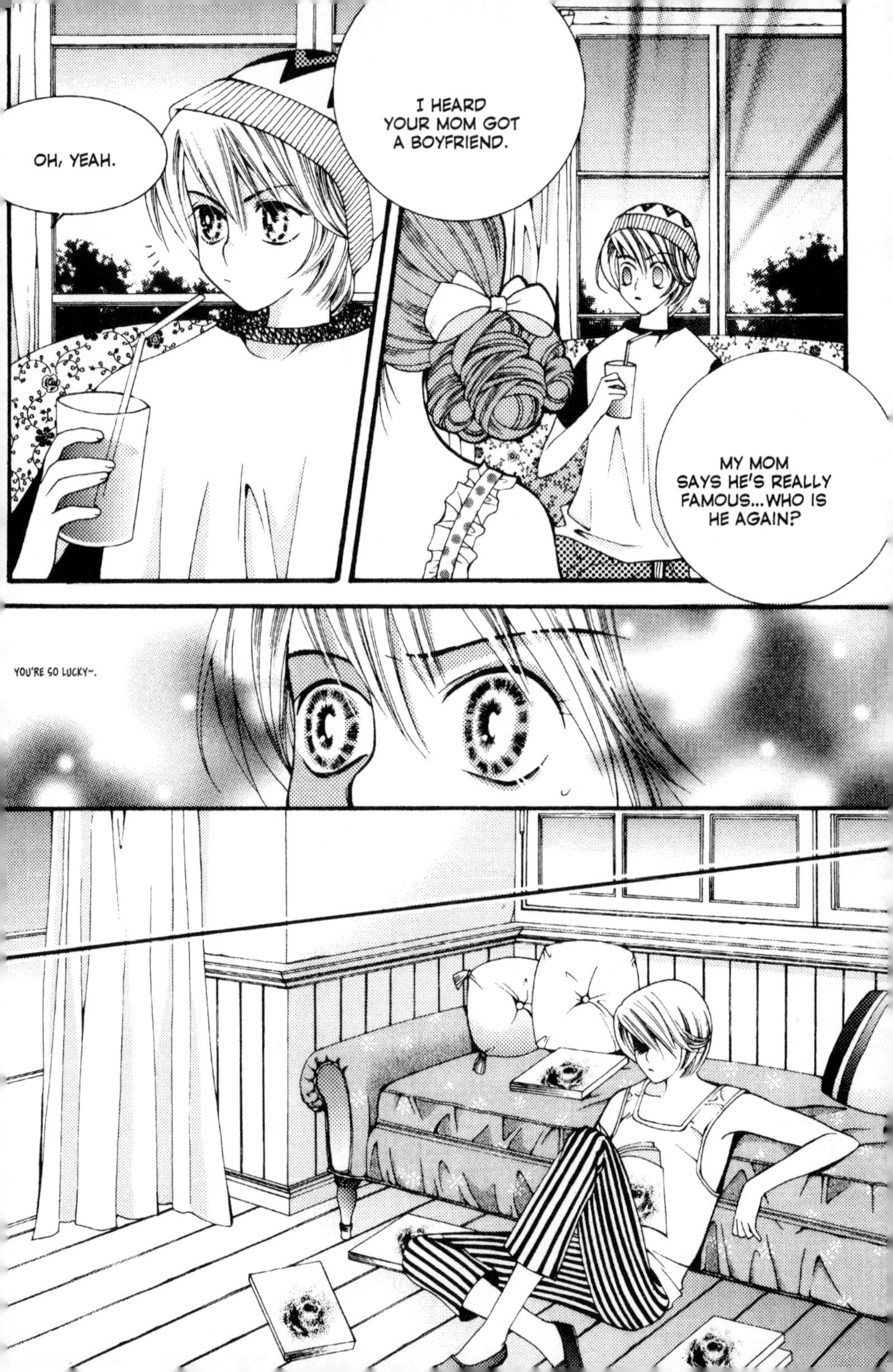
OH, YEAH.
I HEARD YOUR MOM GOT A BOYFRIEND.
MY MOM SAYS HE'S REALLY FAMOUS...WHO IS HE AGAIN?
YOU'RE SO LUCKY~.

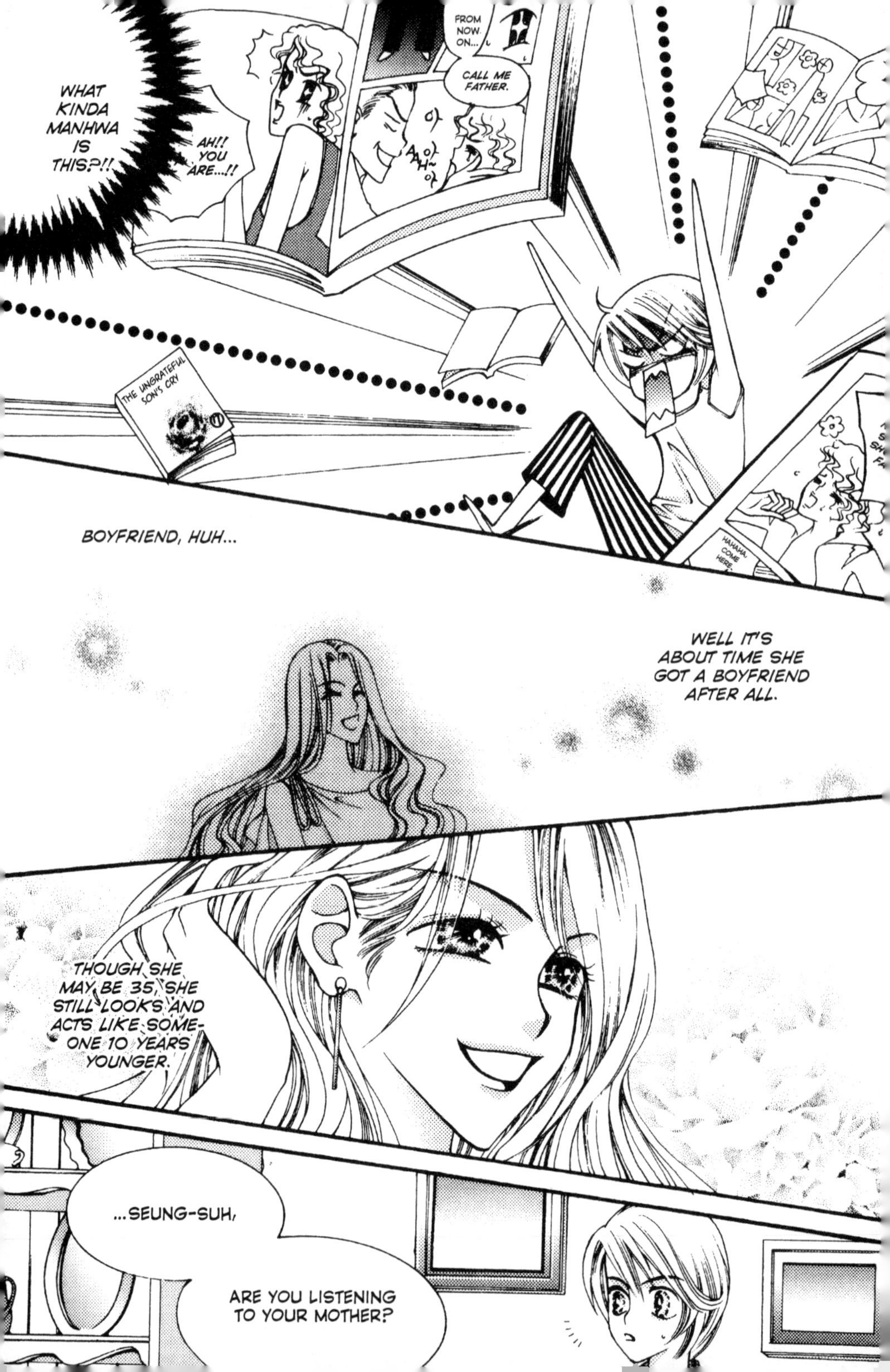
WHAT KINDA MANHWA IS THIS?!!
AH!! YOU ARE...!!
FROM NOW ON...
CALL ME FATHER.
THE UNGRATEFUL SON'S CRY
HAHAHA, COME HERE.
BOYFRIEND, HUH...
WELL IT'S ABOUT TIME SHE GOT A BOYFRIEND AFTER ALL.
THOUGH SHE MAY BE 35, SHE STILL LOOKS AND ACTS LIKE SOME-ONE 10 YEARS YOUNGER.
...SEUNG-SUH,
ARE YOU LISTENING TO YOUR MOTHER?

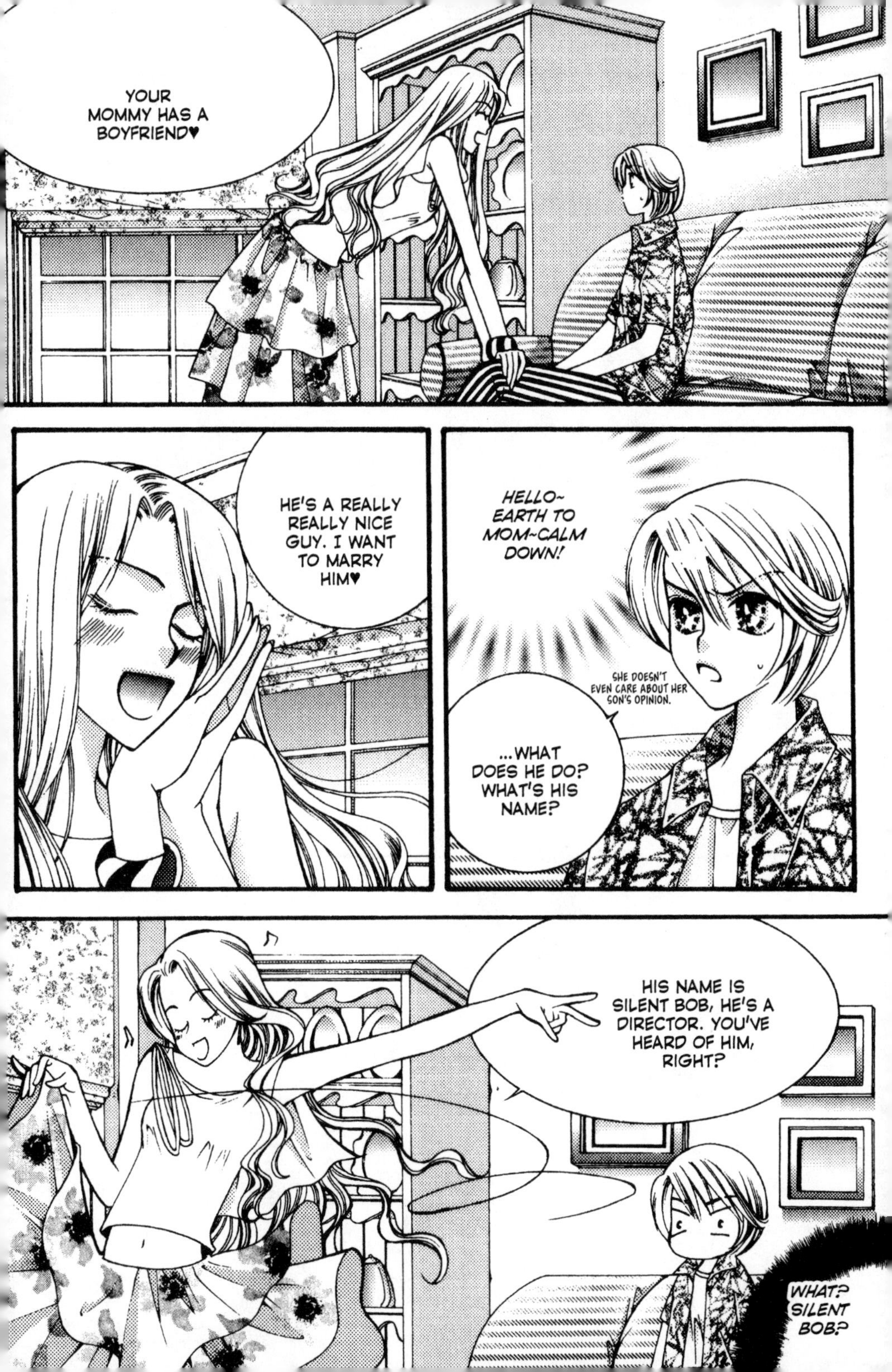
YOUR MOMMY HAS A BOYFRIEND♥
HE'S A REALLY REALLY NICE GUY. I WANT TO MARRY HIM♥
HELLO~ EARTH TO MOM~CALM DOWN!
SHE DOESN'T EVEN CARE ABOUT HER SON'S OPINION.
...WHAT DOES HE DO? WHAT'S HIS NAME?
HIS NAME IS SILENT BOB, HE'S A DIRECTOR. YOU'VE HEARD OF HIM, RIGHT?
WHAT? SILENT BOB?

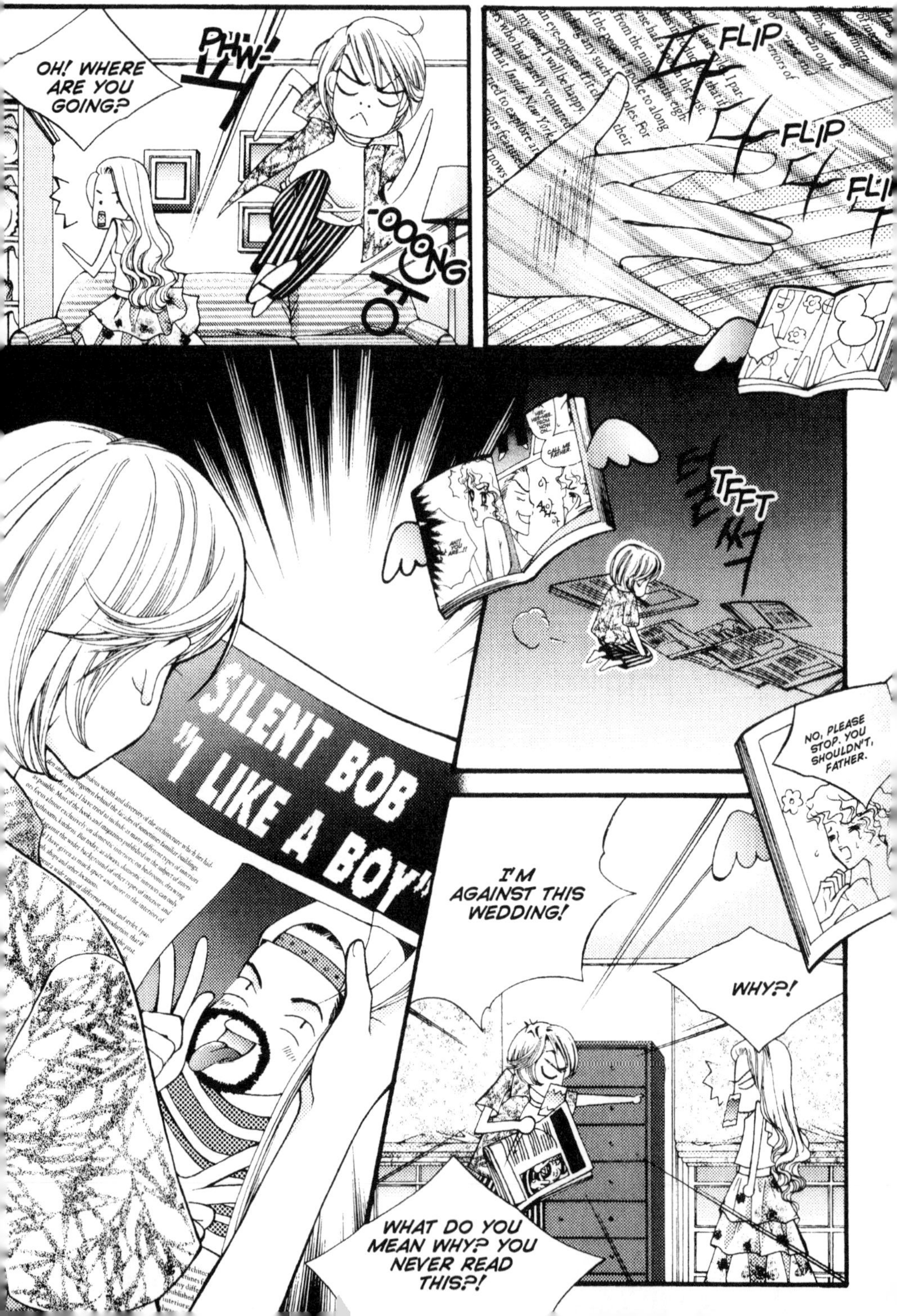
OH! WHERE ARE YOU GOING?
PHW-
-OOONG
FLIP
FLIP
FLI
SILENT BOB
"I LIKE A BOY
TFFT
CALL ME FATHER.
NO, PLEASE STOP. YOU SHOULDN'T, FATHER.
I'M AGAINST THIS WEDDING!
WHY?!
WHAT DO YOU MEAN WHY? YOU NEVER READ THIS?!

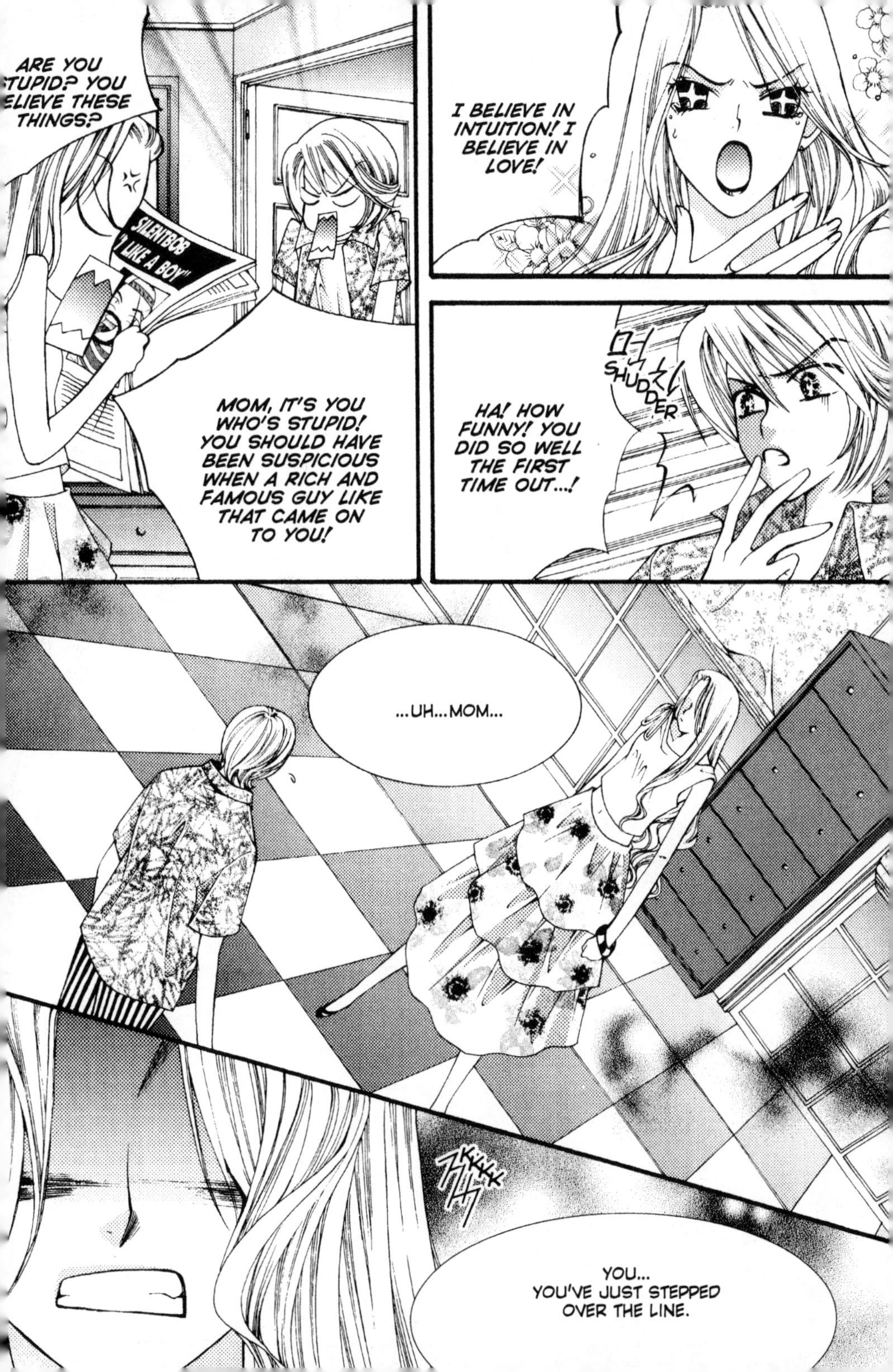
ARE YOU STUPID? YOU BELIEVE THESE THINGS?
SILENTBOB
MOM, IT'S YOU WHO'S STUPID! YOU SHOULD HAVE BEEN SUSPICIOUS WHEN A RICH AND FAMOUS GUY LIKE THAT CAME ON TO YOU!
I BELIEVE IN INTUITION! I BELIEVE IN LOVE!
SHUDDER
HA! HOW FUNNY! YOU DID SO WELL THE FIRST TIME OUT...!
...UH...MOM...
YOU... YOU'VE JUST STEPPED OVER THE LINE.

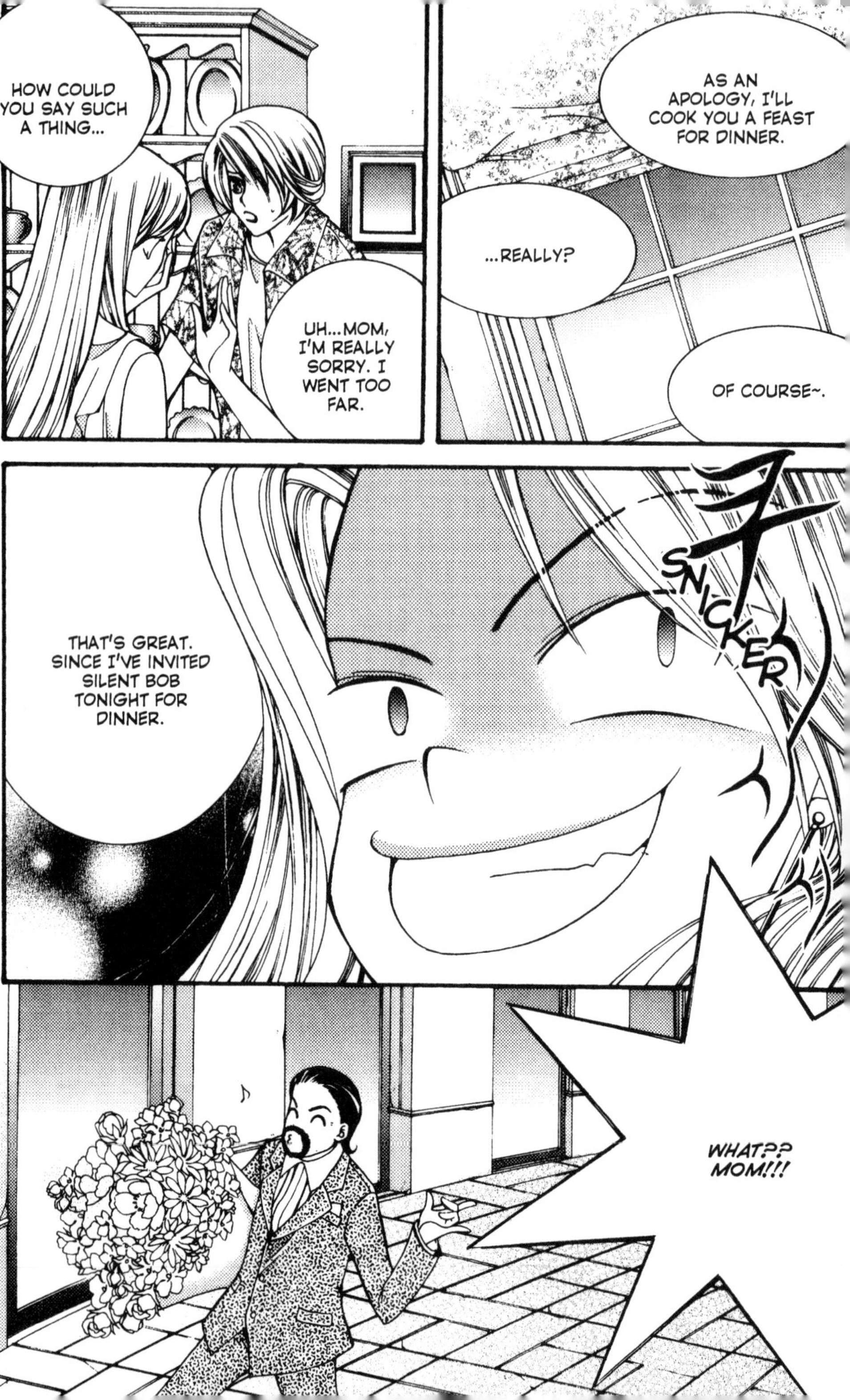
HOW COULD YOU SAY SUCH A THING...
UH...MOM, I'M REALLY SORRY. I WENT TOO FAR.
AS AN APOLOGY, I'LL COOK YOU A FEAST FOR DINNER.
...REALLY?
OF COURSE~.
THAT'S GREAT. SINCE I'VE INVITED SILENT BOB TONIGHT FOR DINNER.
SNICKER
WHAT?? MOM!!!

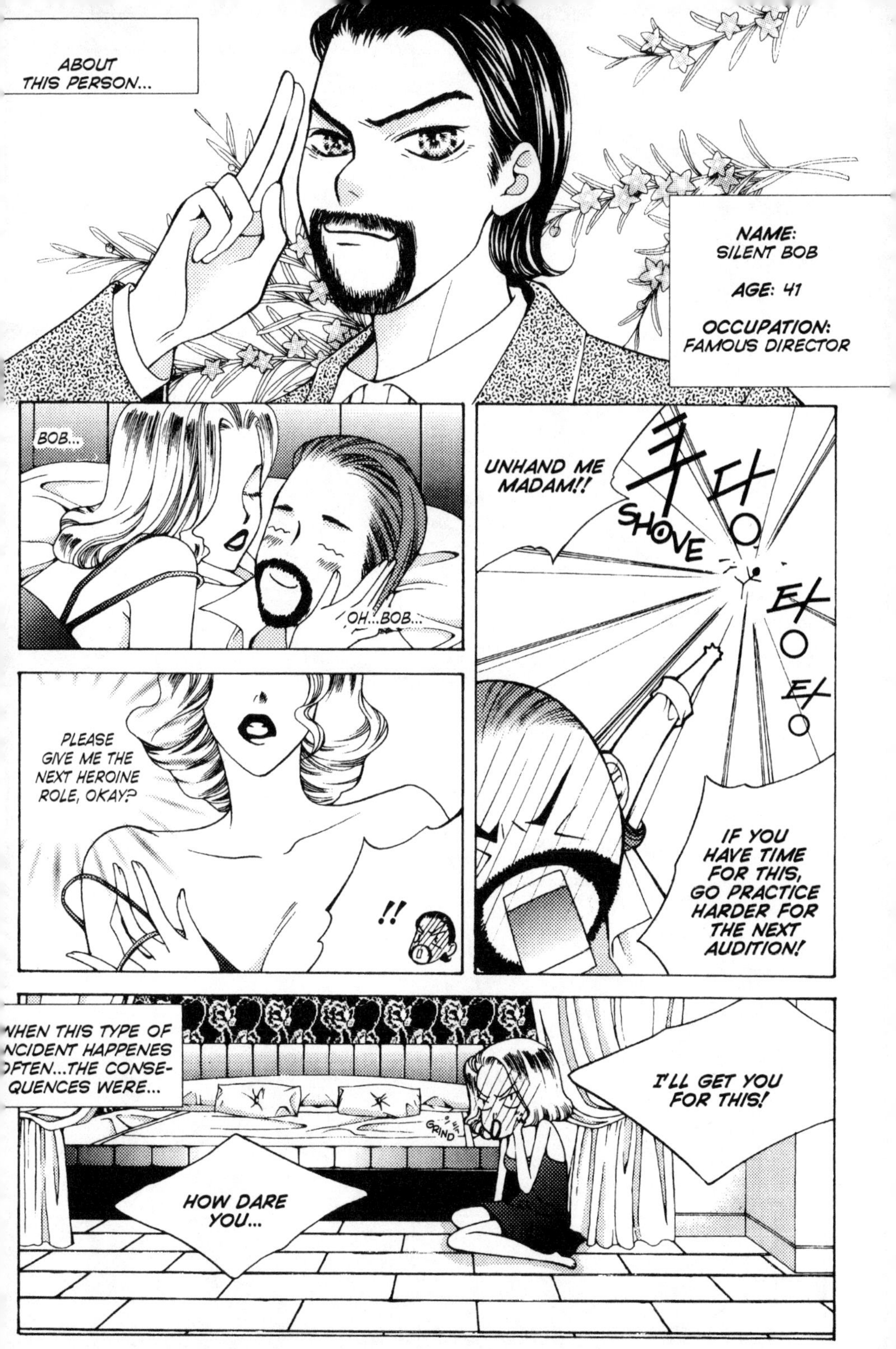
ABOUT THIS PERSON...
NAME: SILENT BOB
AGE: 41
OCCUPATION: FAMOUS DIRECTOR
BOB...
OH...BOB...
PLEASE GIVE ME THE NEXT HEROINE ROLE, OKAY?
!!
UNHAND ME MADAM!!
SHOVE
IF YOU HAVE TIME FOR THIS, GO PRACTICE HARDER FOR THE NEXT AUDITION!
WHEN THIS TYPE OF INCIDENT HAPPENES OFTEN...THE CONSE-QUENCES WERE...
I'LL GET YOU FOR THIS!
GRIND
HOW DARE YOU...

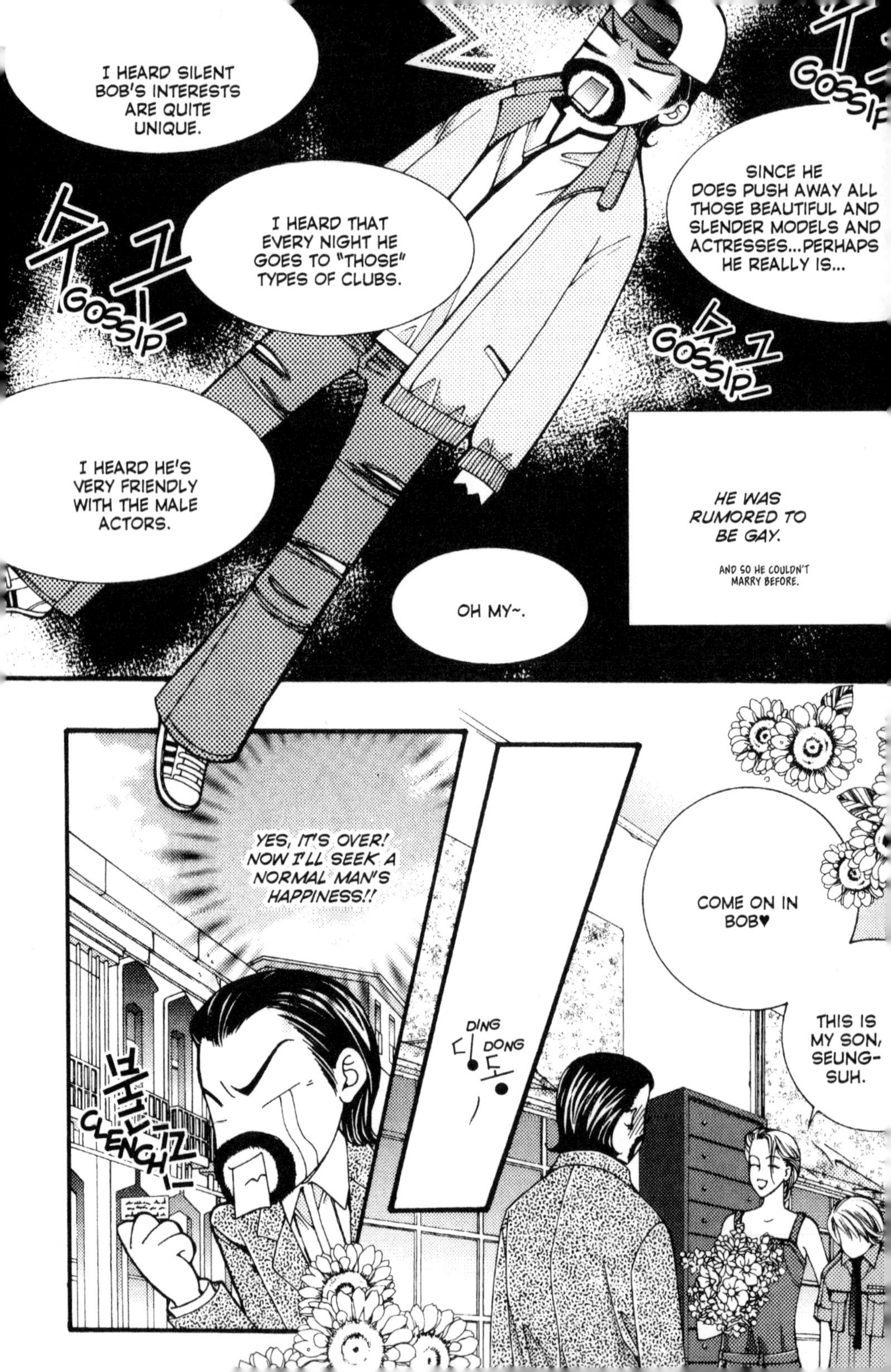
I HEARD SILENT BOB'S INTERESTS ARE QUITE UNIQUE.
GOSSIP
I HEARD THAT EVERY NIGHT HE GOES TO "THOSE" TYPES OF CLUBS.
SINCE HE DOES PUSH AWAY ALL THOSE BEAUTIFUL AND SLENDER MODELS AND ACTRESSES...PERHAPS HE REALLY IS...
GOSSIP
GOSSIP
I HEARD HE'S VERY FRIENDLY WITH THE MALE ACTORS.
OH MY~.
HE WAS RUMORED TO BE GAY.
AND SO HE COULDN'T MARRY BEFORE.
YES, IT'S OVER! NOW I'LL SEEK A NORMAL MAN'S HAPPINESS!!
CLENCH
DING DONG
COME ON IN BOB♥
THIS IS MY SON, SEUNG-SUH.

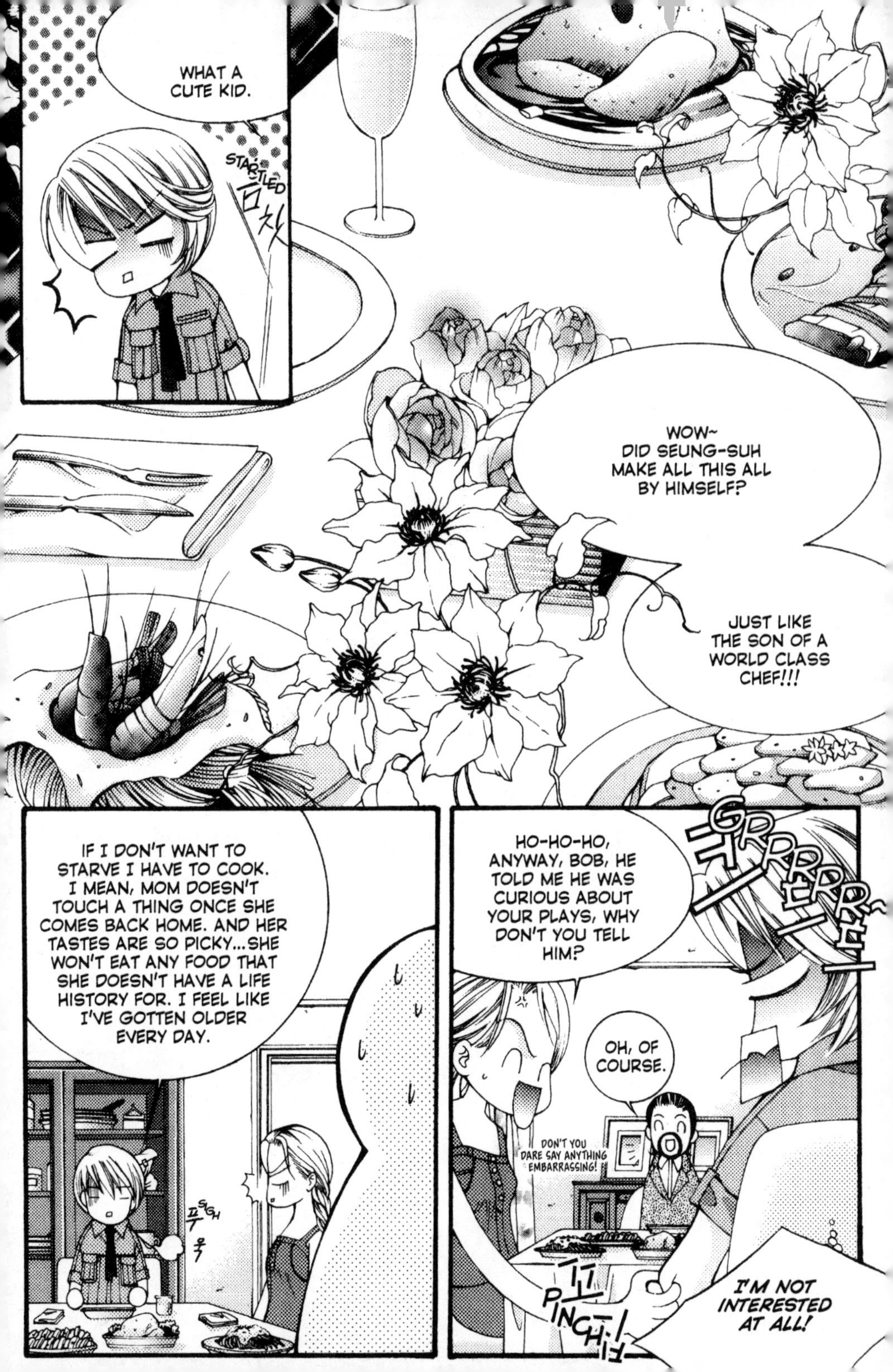
WHAT A CUTE KID.
STARTLED
WOW~ DID SEUNG-SUH MAKE ALL THIS ALL BY HIMSELF?
JUST LIKE THE SON OF A WORLD CLASS CHEF!!!
IF I DON'T WANT TO STARVE I HAVE TO COOK. I MEAN, MOM DOESN'T TOUCH A THING ONCE SHE COMES BACK HOME. AND HER TASTES ARE SO PICKY...SHE WON'T EAT ANY FOOD THAT SHE DOESN'T HAVE A LIFE HISTORY FOR. I FEEL LIKE I'VE GOTTEN OLDER EVERY DAY.
SIGH
HO-HO-HO, ANYWAY, BOB, HE TOLD ME HE WAS CURIOUS ABOUT YOUR PLAYS, WHY DON'T YOU TELL HIM?
GRRRRR~
OH, OF COURSE.
DON'T YOU DARE SAY ANYTHING EMBARRASSING!
PINCH
I'M NOT INTERESTED AT ALL!

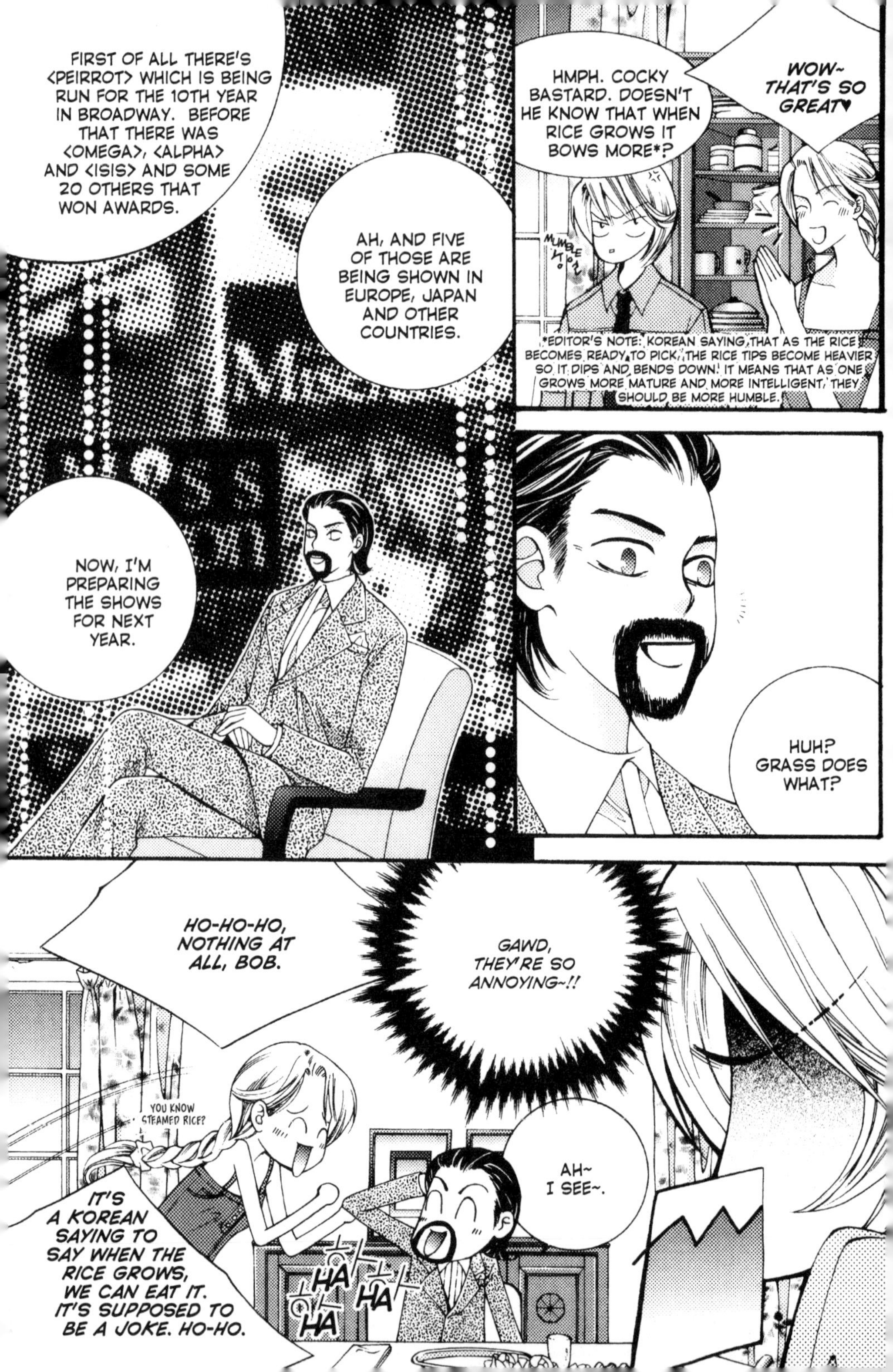
FIRST OF ALL THERE'S <PEIRROT> WHICH IS BEING RUN FOR THE 10TH YEAR IN BROADWAY. BEFORE THAT THERE WAS <OMEGA>, <ALPHA> AND <ISIS> AND SOME 20 OTHERS THAT WON AWARDS.
AH, AND FIVE OF THOSE ARE BEING SHOWN IN EUROPE, JAPAN AND OTHER COUNTRIES.
NOW, I'M PREPARING THE SHOWS FOR NEXT YEAR.
HMPH. COCKY BASTARD. DOESN'T HE KNOW THAT WHEN RICE GROWS IT BOWS MORE*?
WOW~ THAT'S SO GREAT♥
MUMBLE
*EDITOR'S NOTE: KOREAN SAYING THAT AS THE RICE BECOMES READY TO PICK, THE RICE TIPS BECOME HEAVIER SO IT DIPS AND BENDS DOWN. IT MEANS THAT AS ONE GROWS MORE MATURE AND MORE INTELLIGENT, THEY SHOULD BE MORE HUMBLE.
HUH? GRASS DOES WHAT?
HO-HO-HO, NOTHING AT ALL, BOB.
GAWD, THEY'RE SO ANNOYING~!!
YOU KNOW STEAMED RICE?
IT'S A KOREAN SAYING TO SAY WHEN THE RICE GROWS, WE CAN EAT IT. IT'S SUPPOSED TO BE A JOKE. HO-HO.
HA HA HA HA
AH~ I SEE~.

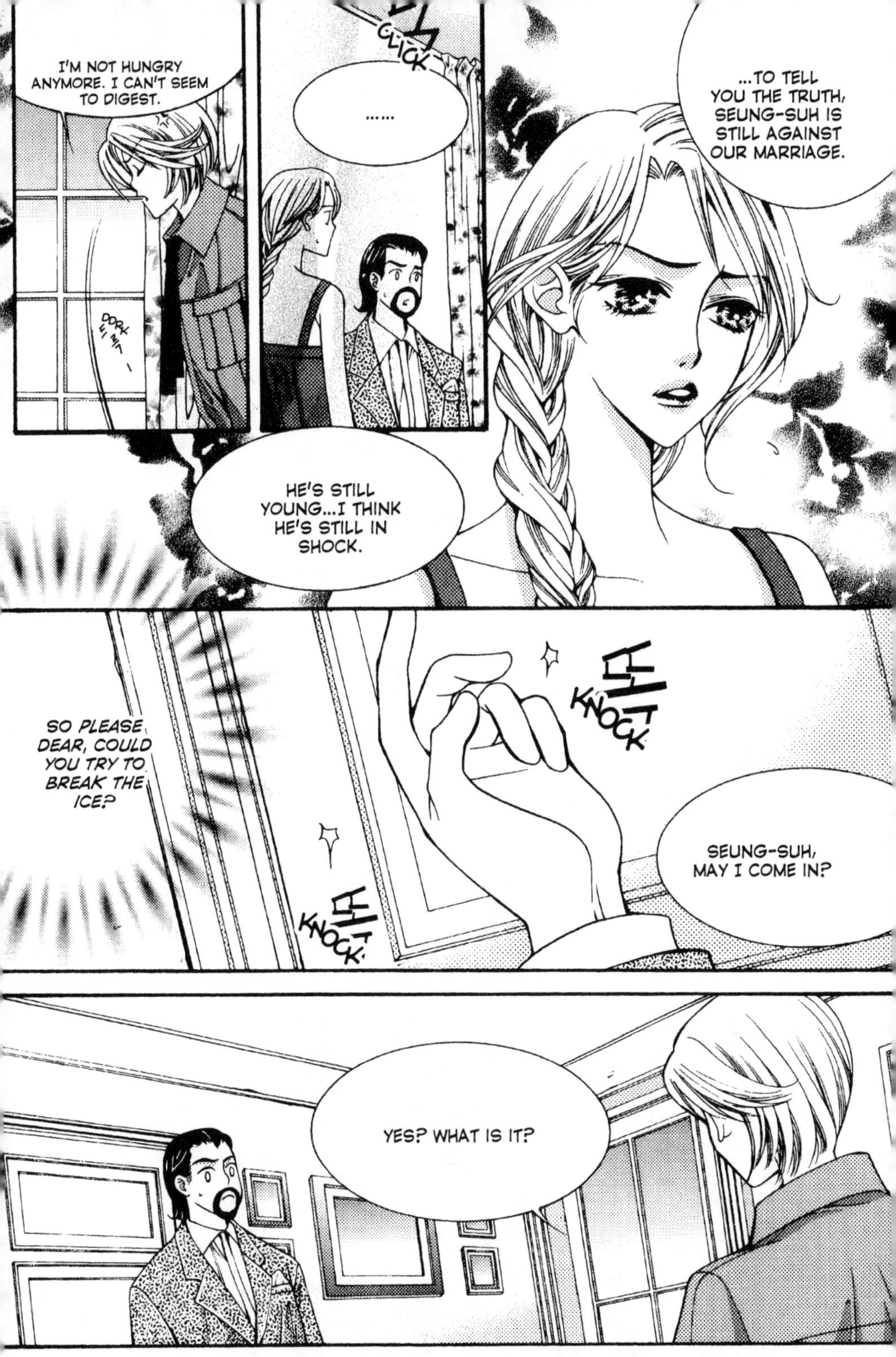
I'M NOT HUNGRY ANYMORE. I CAN'T SEEM TO DIGEST.
CLICK
......
...TO TELL YOU THE TRUTH, SEUNG-SUH IS STILL AGAINST OUR MARRIAGE.
HE'S STILL YOUNG...I THINK HE'S STILL IN SHOCK.
SO PLEASE DEAR, COULD YOU TRY TO BREAK THE ICE?
KNOCK
KNOCK
SEUNG-SUH, MAY I COME IN?
YES? WHAT IS IT?

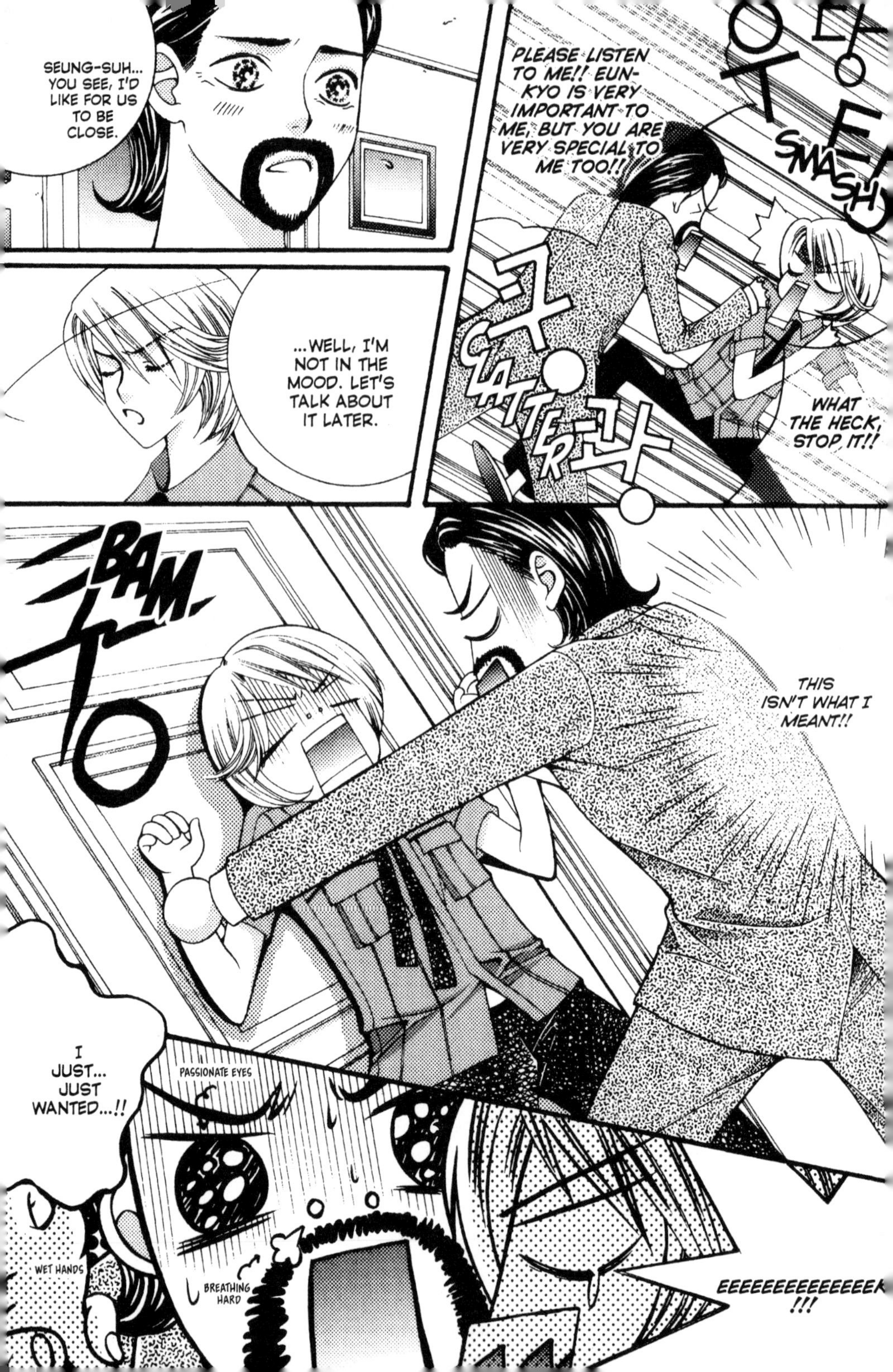

SEUNG-SUH... YOU SEE, I'D LIKE FOR US TO BE CLOSE.
...WELL, I'M NOT IN THE MOOD. LET'S TALK ABOUT IT LATER.
PLEASE LISTEN TO ME!! EUN-KYO IS VERY IMPORTANT TO ME, BUT YOU ARE VERY SPECIAL TO ME TOO!!
SMASH
CLATTER
WHAT THE HECK, STOP IT!!
BAM
THIS ISN'T WHAT I MEANT!!
I JUST... JUST WANTED...!!
PASSIONATE EYES
WET HANDS
BREATHING HARD
EEEEEEEEEEEEEK!!!

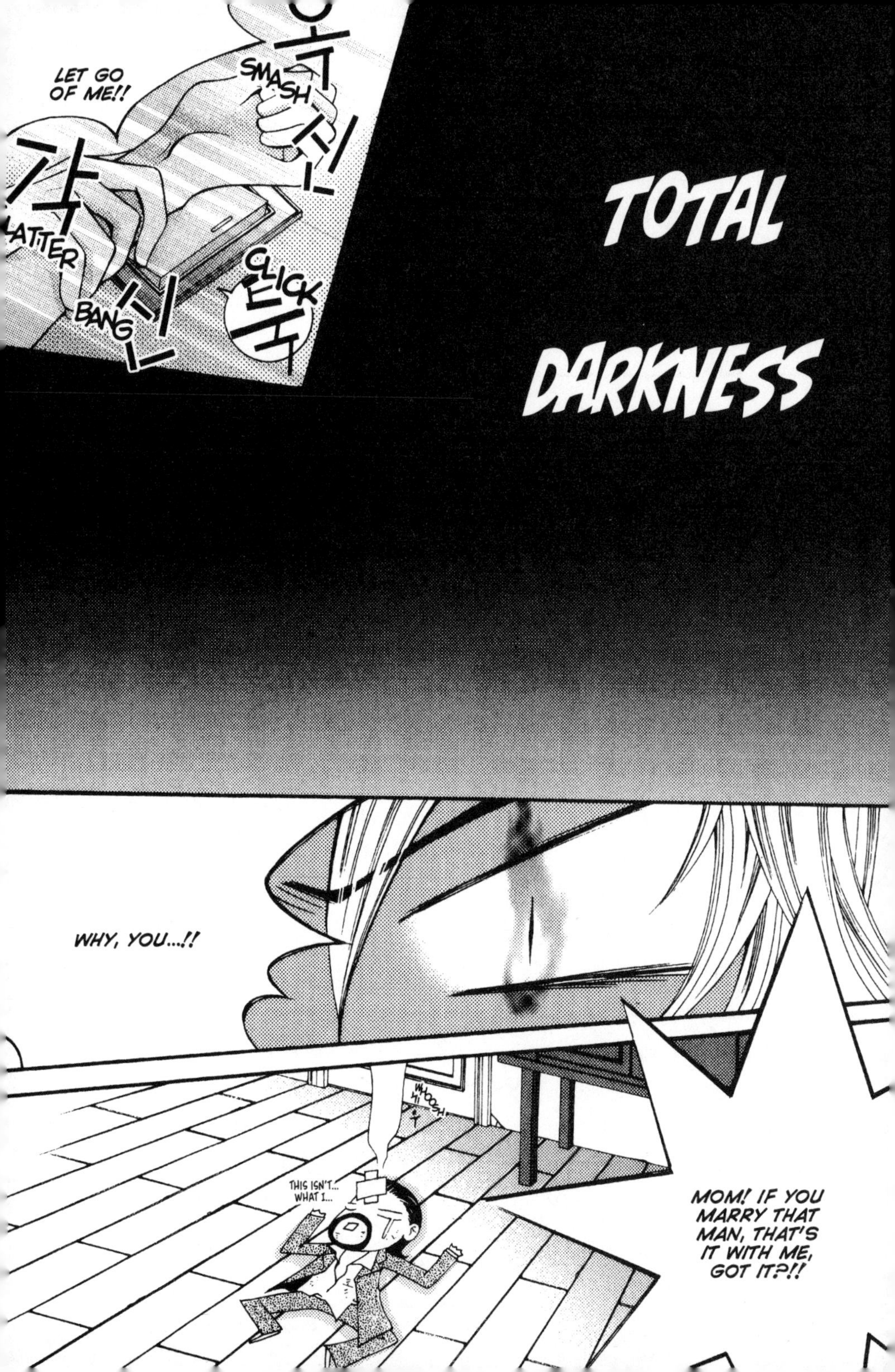

LET GO OF ME!!
SMASH
LATTER
BANG
CLICK
TOTAL DARKNESS
WHY, YOU...!!
WHOOSH
THIS ISN'T... WHAT I...
MOM! IF YOU MARRY THAT MAN, THAT'S IT WITH ME, GOT IT?!!

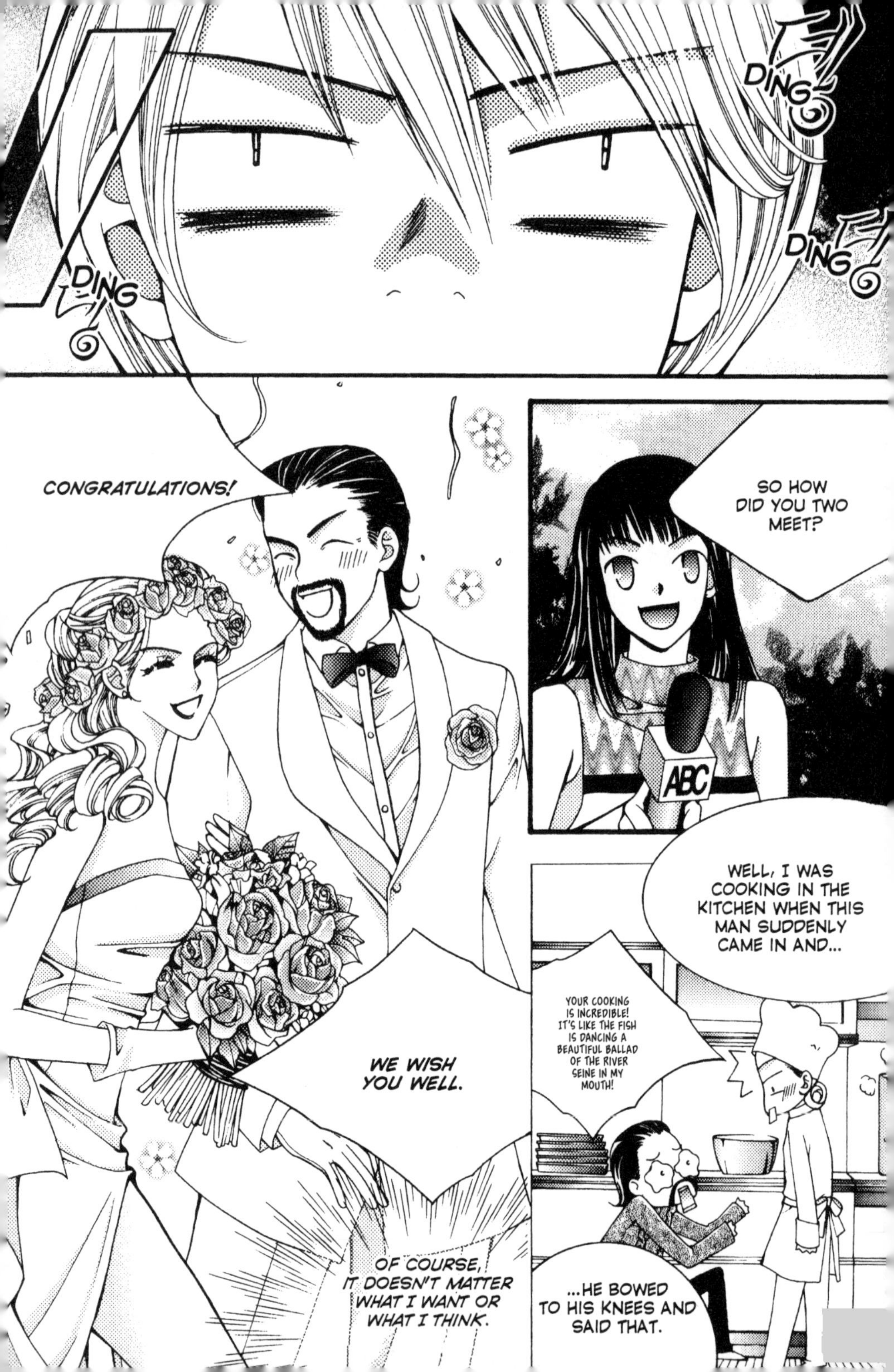
DING
DING
DING
CONGRATULATIONS!
WE WISH YOU WELL.
OF COURSE, IT DOESN'T MATTER WHAT I WANT OR WHAT I THINK.
SO HOW DID YOU TWO MEET?
WELL, I WAS COOKING IN THE KITCHEN WHEN THIS MAN SUDDENLY CAME IN AND...
YOUR COOKING IS INCREDIBLE! IT'S LIKE THE FISH IS DANCING A BEAUTIFUL BALLAD OF THE RIVER SEINE IN MY MOUTH!
...HE BOWED TO HIS KNEES AND SAID THAT.
ABC

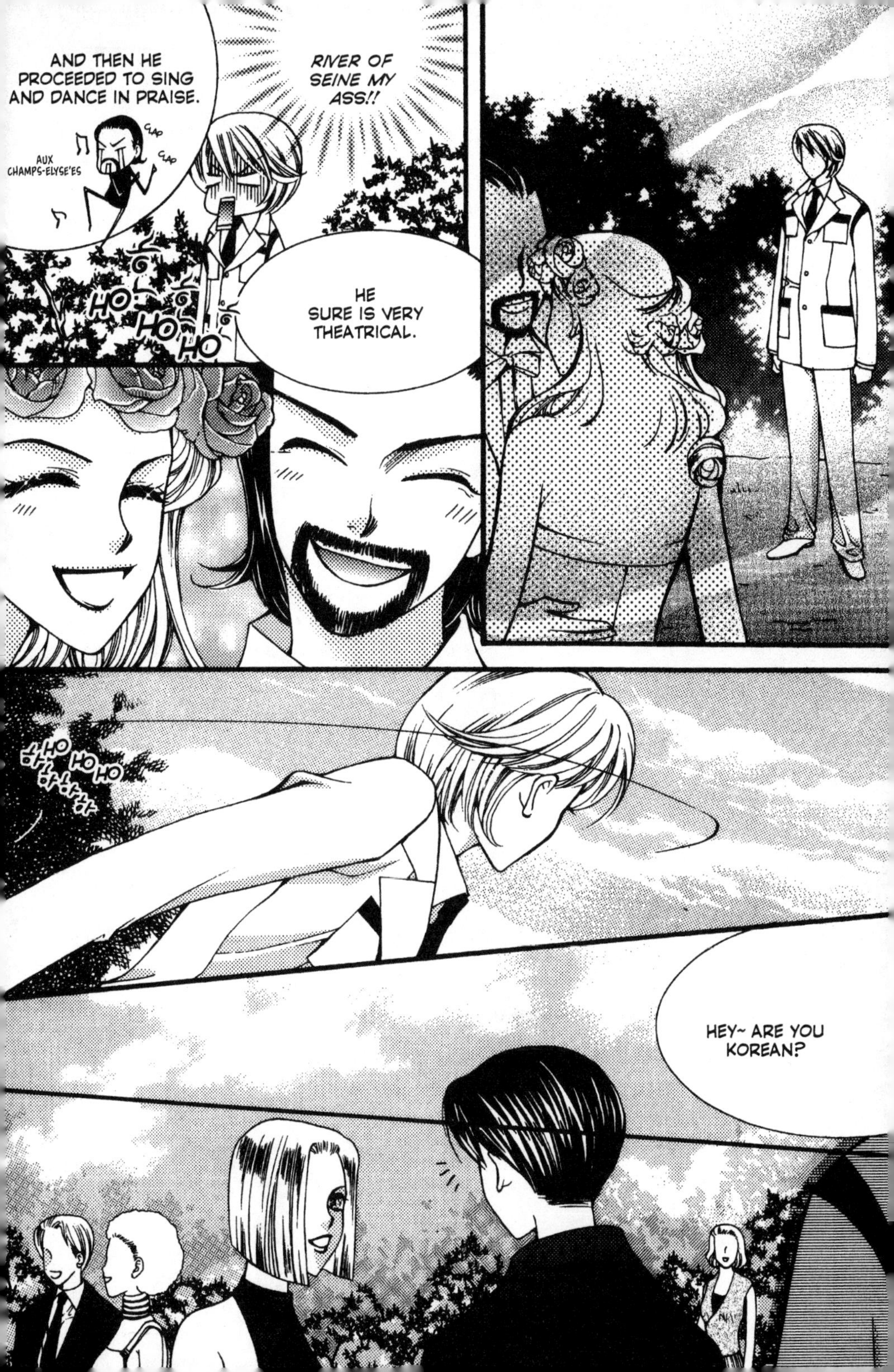
AND THEN HE PROCEEDED TO SING AND DANCE IN PRAISE.
AUX CHAMPS-ELYSE'ES
CLAP
CLAP
RIVER OF SEINE MY ASS!!
HO-HO HO
HE SURE IS VERY THEATRICAL.
하하하하
HO HO HO
HEY~ ARE YOU KOREAN?

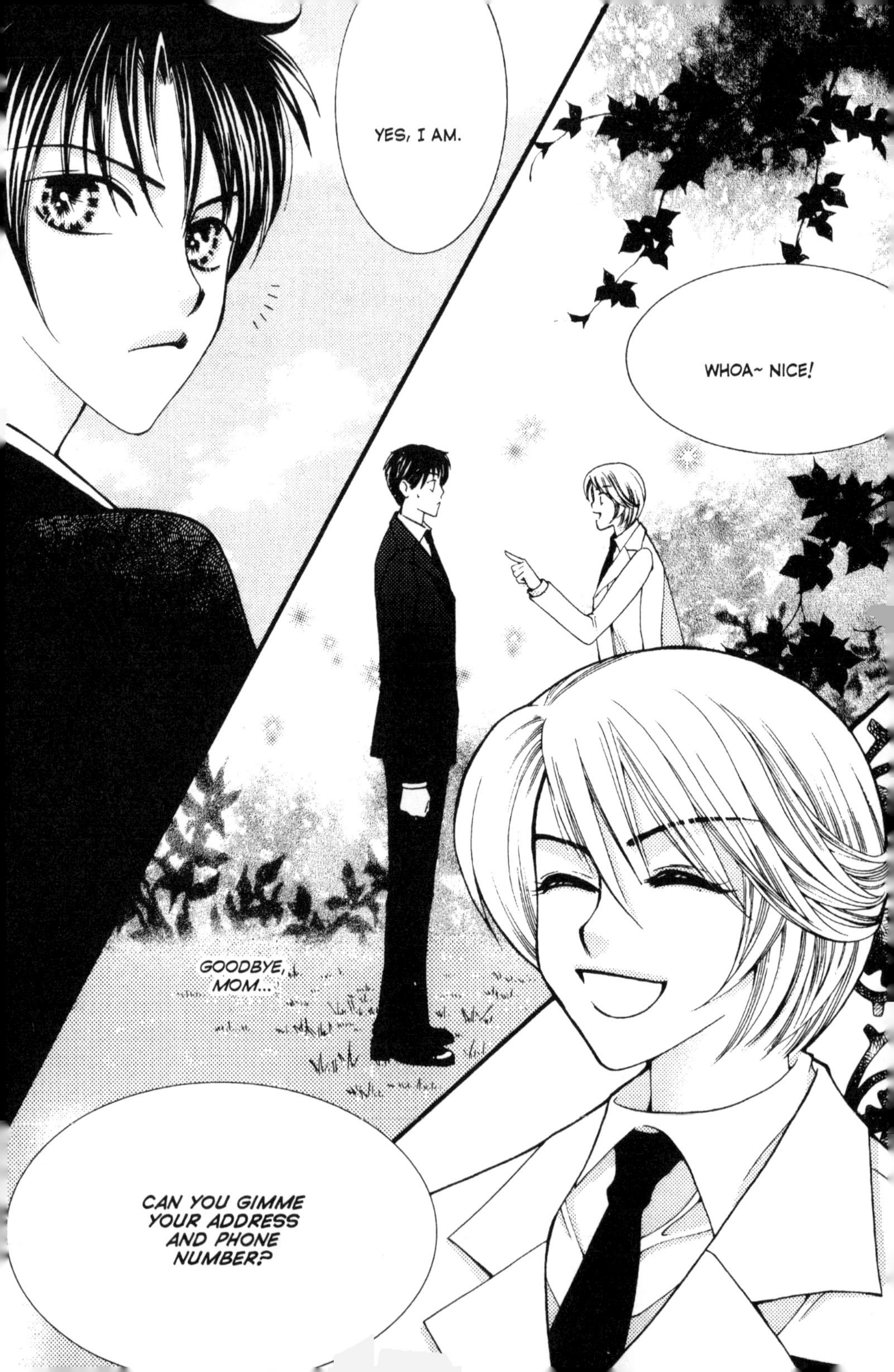
YES, I AM.
WHOA~ NICE!
GOODBYE, MOM...
CAN YOU GIMME YOUR ADDRESS AND PHONE NUMBER?

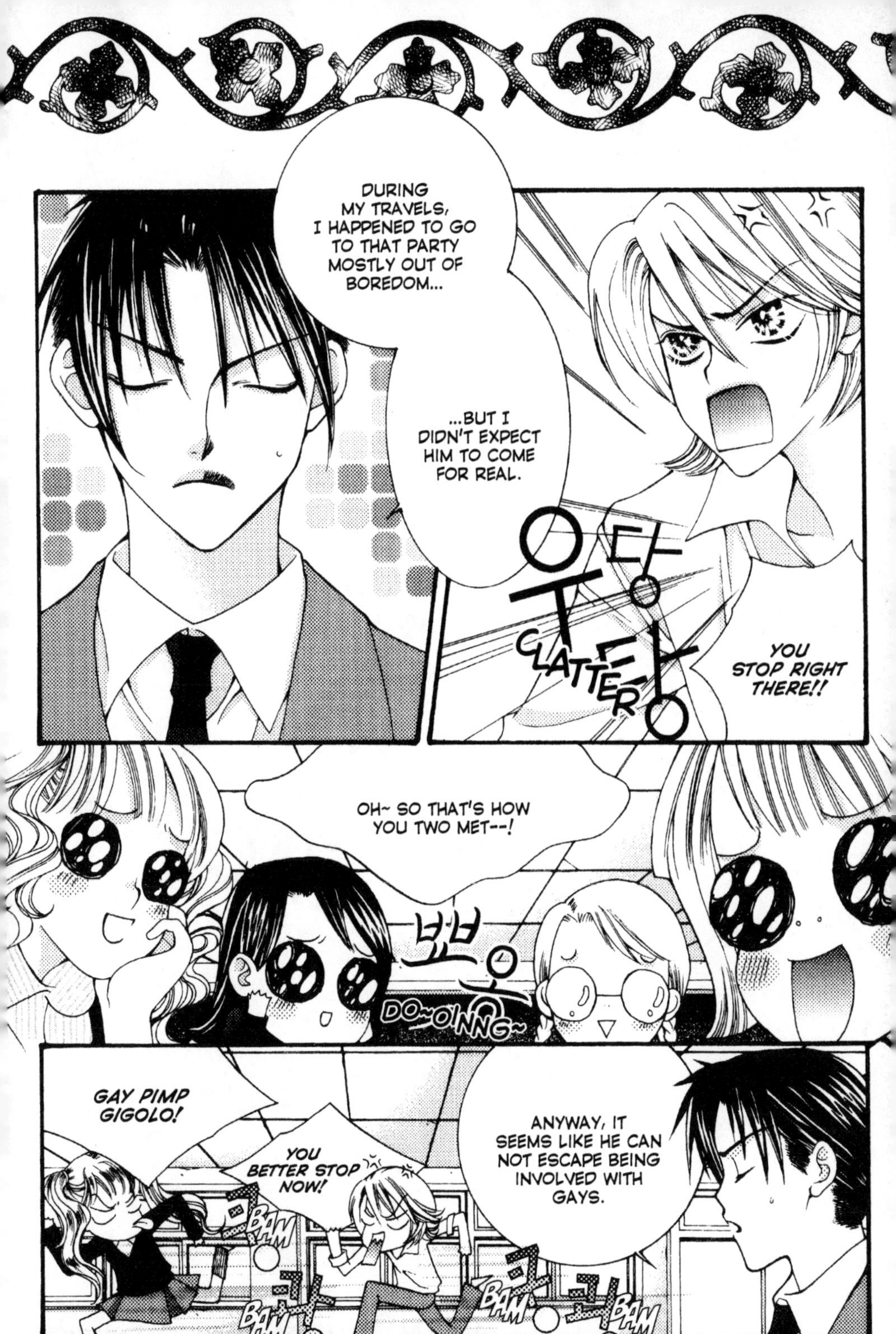
DURING MY TRAVELS, I HAPPENED TO GO TO THAT PARTY MOSTLY OUT OF BOREDOM...
...BUT I DIDN'T EXPECT HIM TO COME FOR REAL.
CLATTER
YOU STOP RIGHT THERE!!
OH~ SO THAT'S HOW YOU TWO MET--!
DO~OINNG~
GAY PIMP GIGOLO!
YOU BETTER STOP NOW!
BAM
BAM
BAM
BAM
ANYWAY, IT SEEMS LIKE HE CAN NOT ESCAPE BEING INVOLVED WITH GAYS.

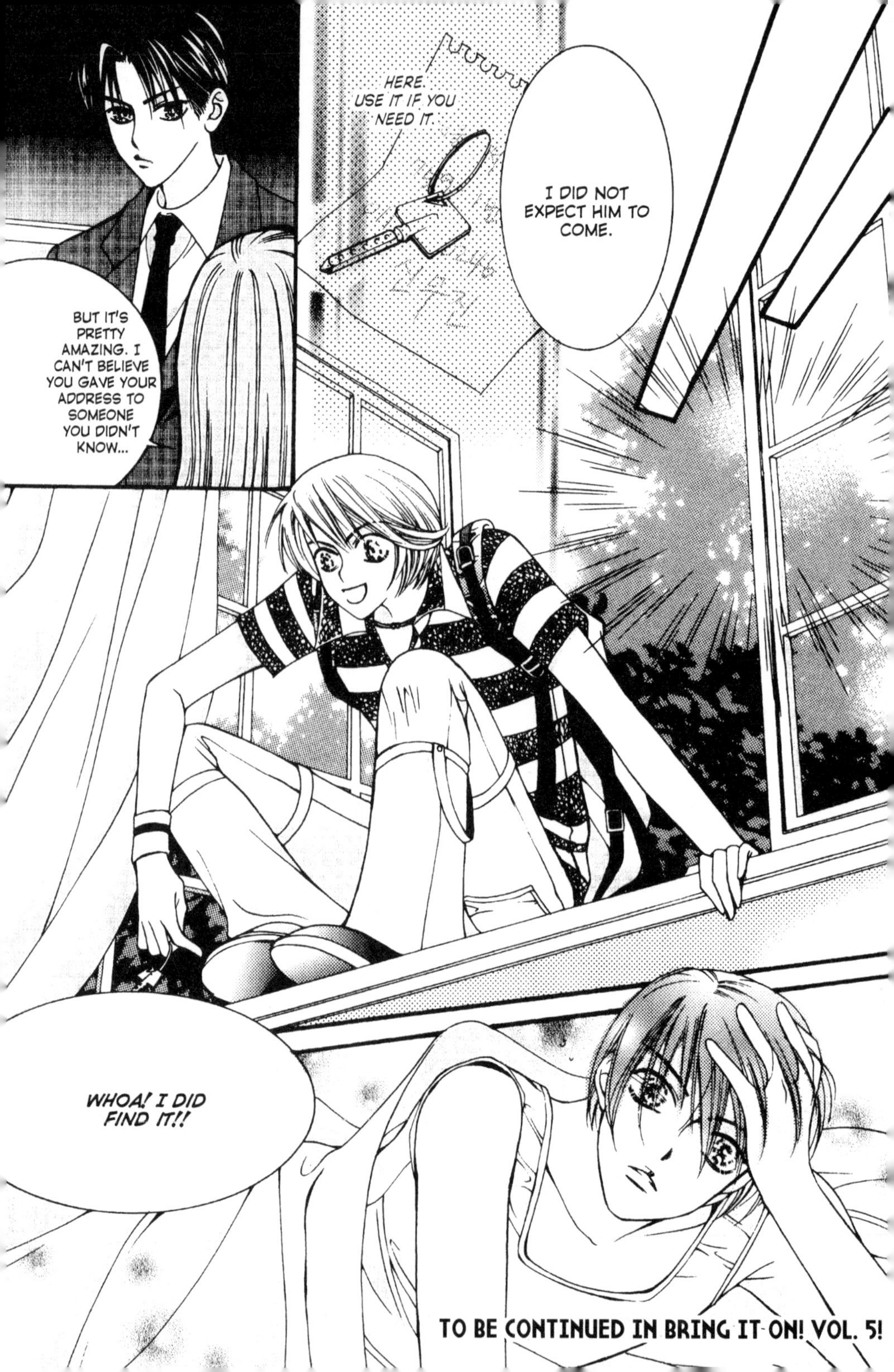
BUT IT'S PRETTY AMAZING. I CAN'T BELIEVE YOU GAVE YOUR ADDRESS TO SOMEONE YOU DIDN'T KNOW...
HERE. USE IT IF YOU NEED IT.
I DID NOT EXPECT HIM TO COME.
WHOA! I DID FIND IT!!
TO BE CONTINUED IN BRING IT ON! VOL. 5!

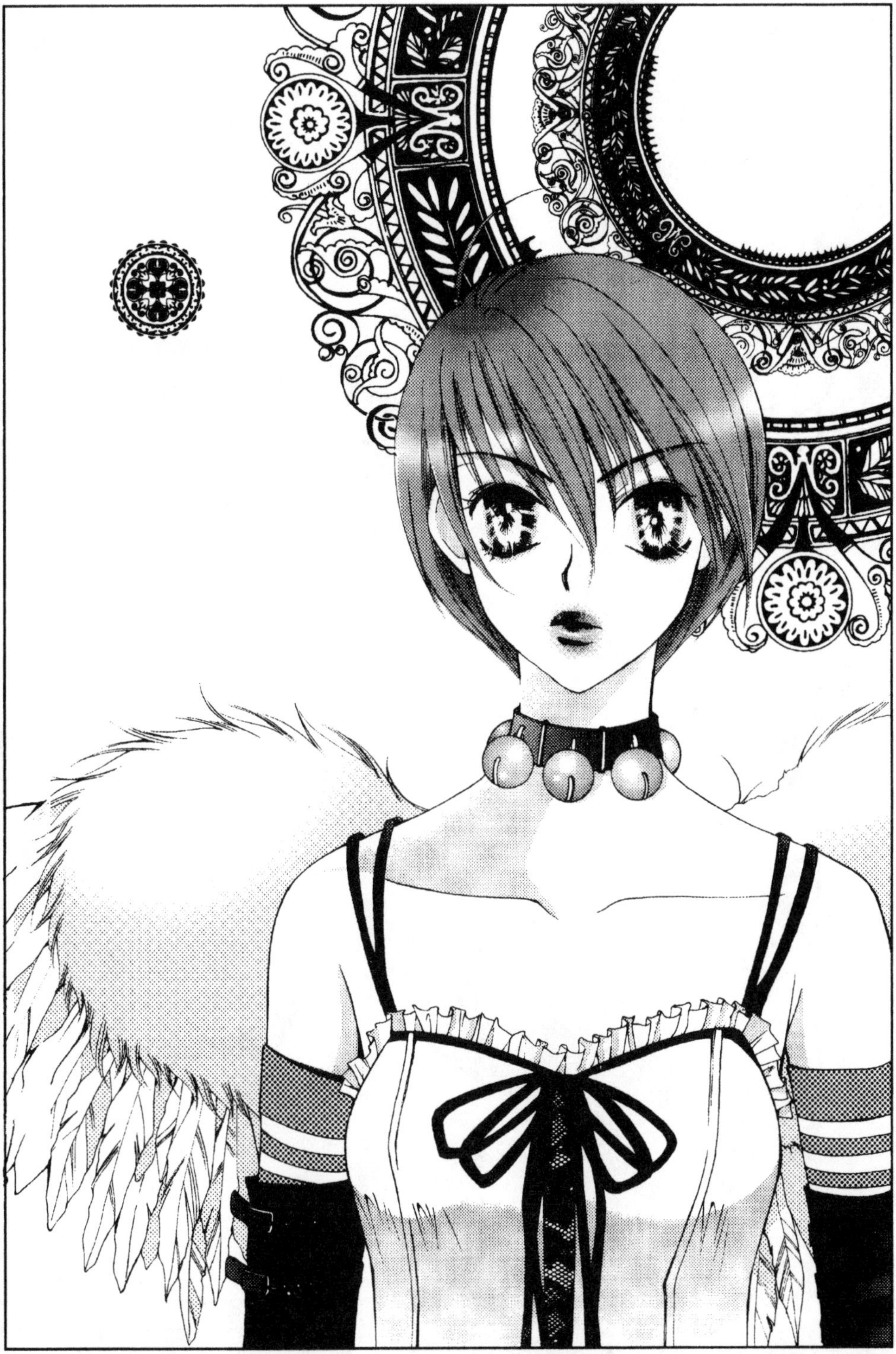

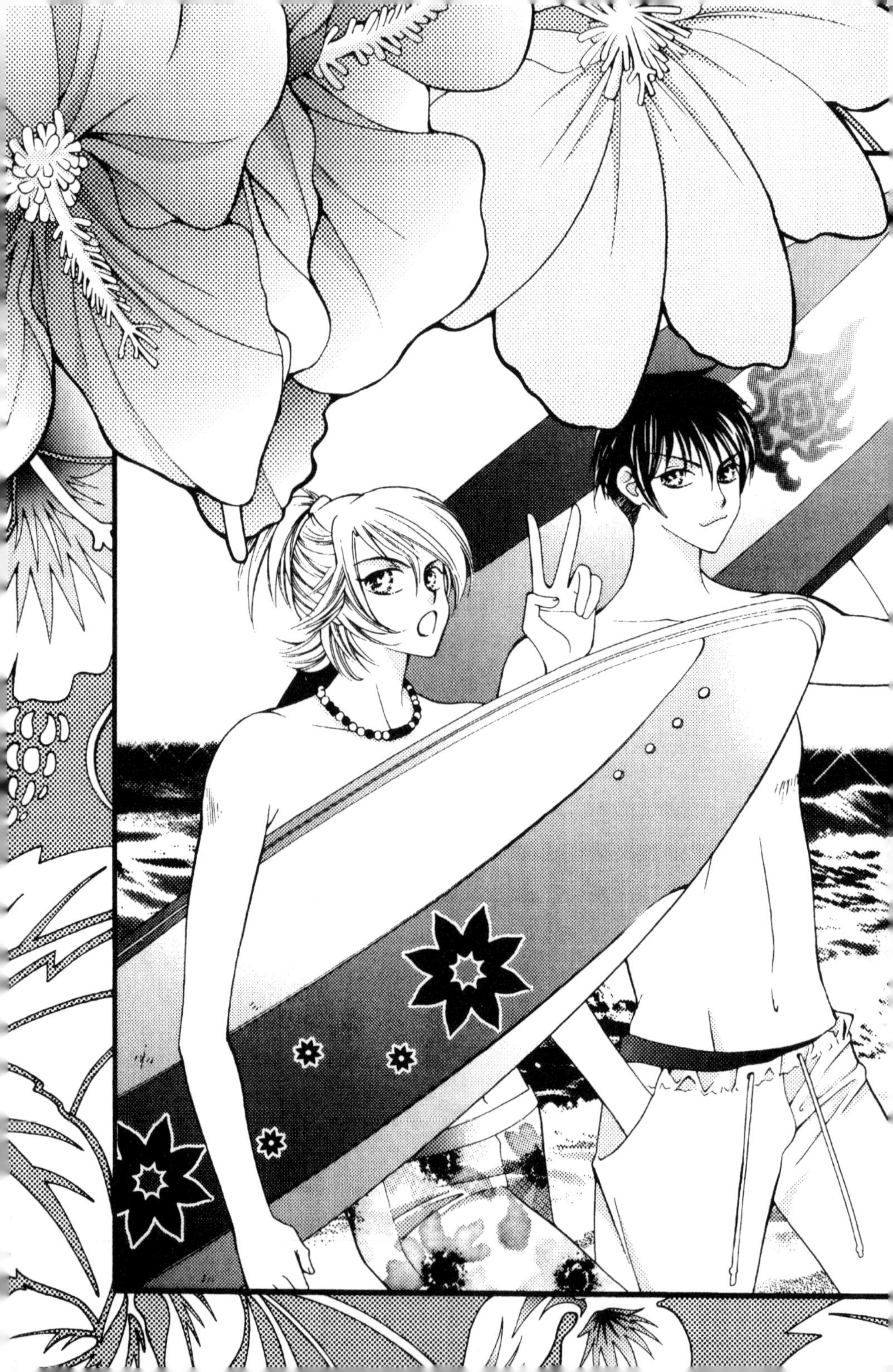

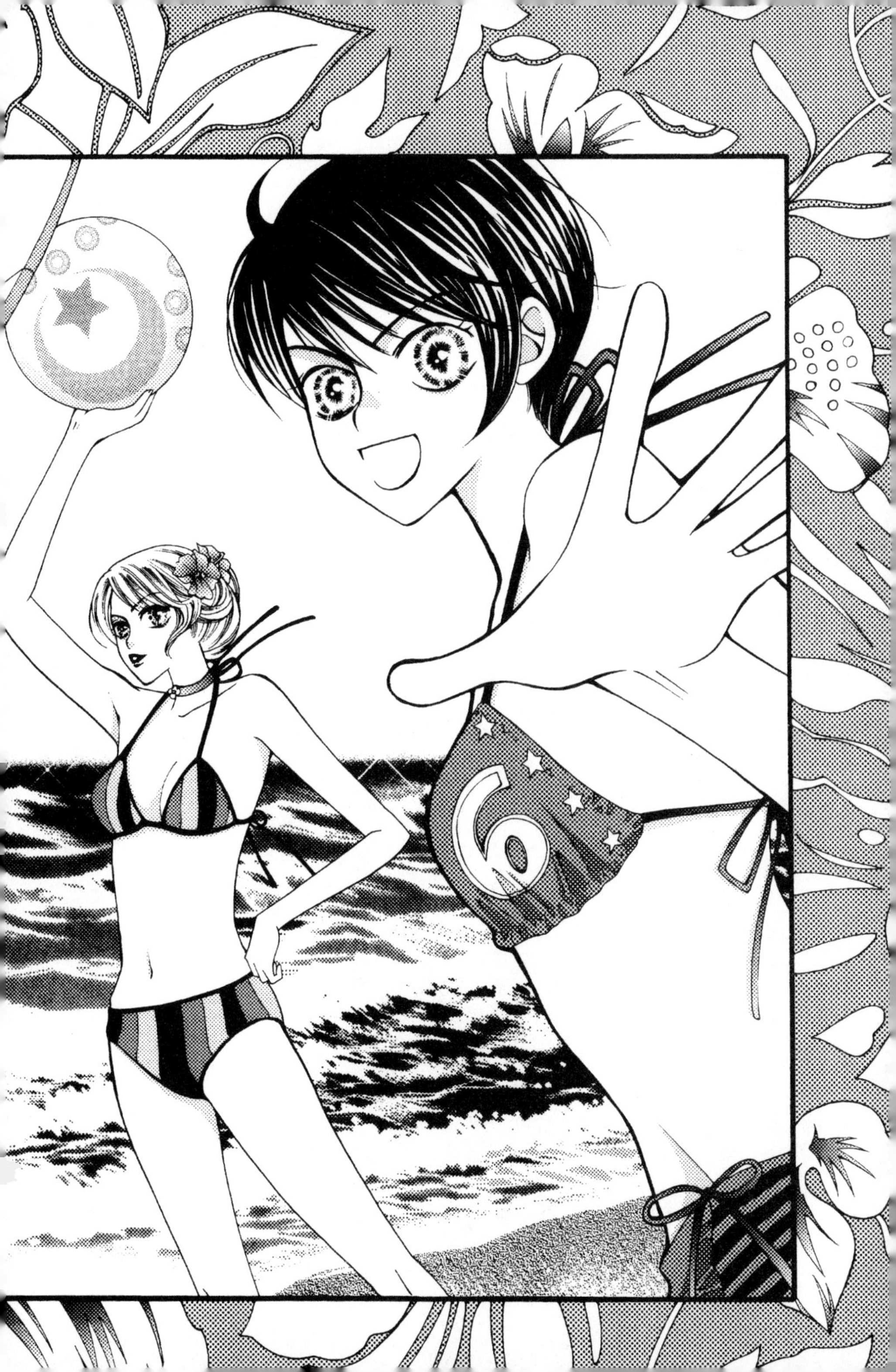

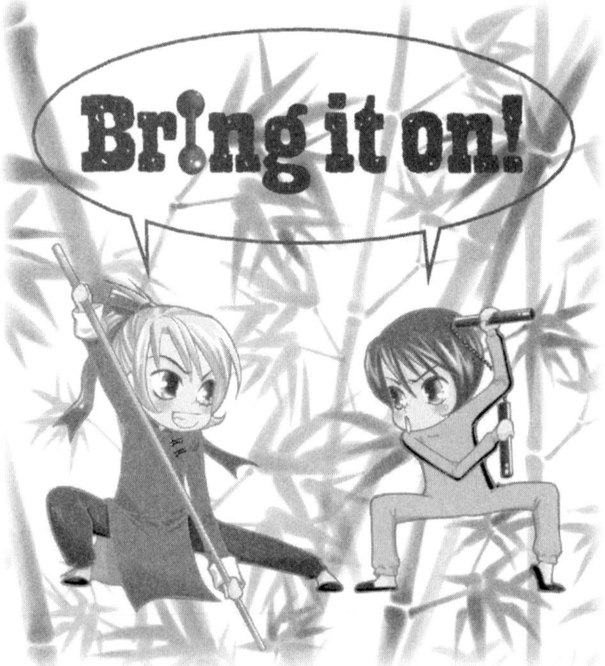
Bring it on!

Goong

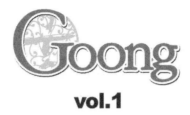

vol.1

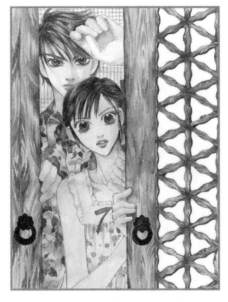

Park SoHee

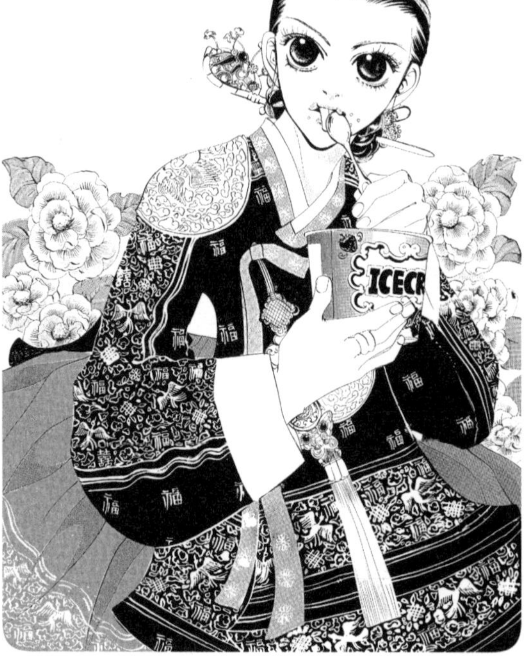
ICECR

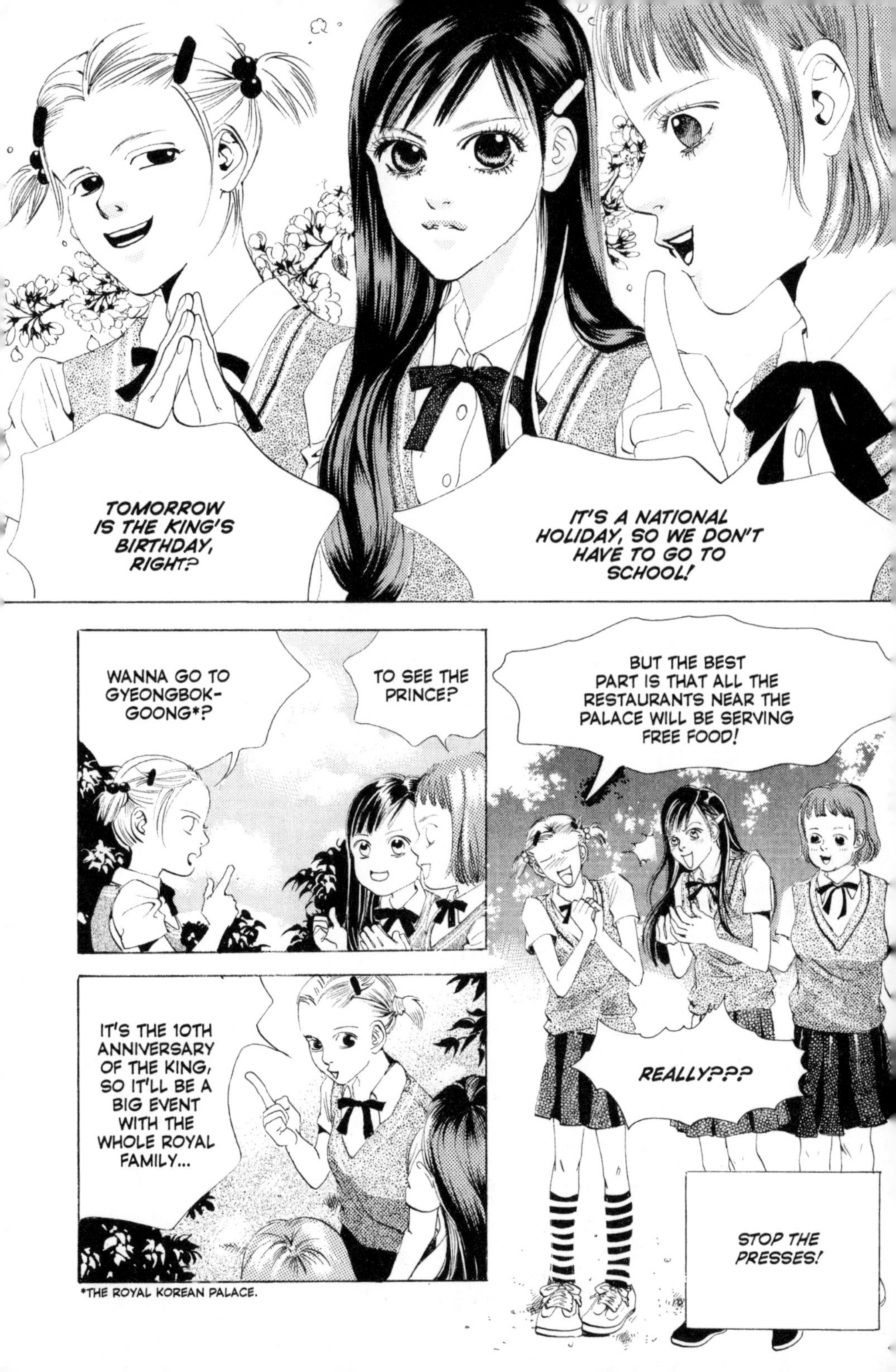
TOMORROW IS THE KING'S BIRTHDAY, RIGHT?
IT'S A NATIONAL HOLIDAY, SO WE DON'T HAVE TO GO TO SCHOOL!
WANNA GO TO GYEONGBOK-GOONG*?
TO SEE THE PRINCE?
IT'S THE 10TH ANNIVERSARY OF THE KING, SO IT'LL BE A BIG EVENT WITH THE WHOLE ROYAL FAMILY...
BUT THE BEST PART IS THAT ALL THE RESTAURANTS NEAR THE PALACE WILL BE SERVING FREE FOOD!
REALLY???
STOP THE PRESSES!

*THE ROYAL KOREAN PALACE.

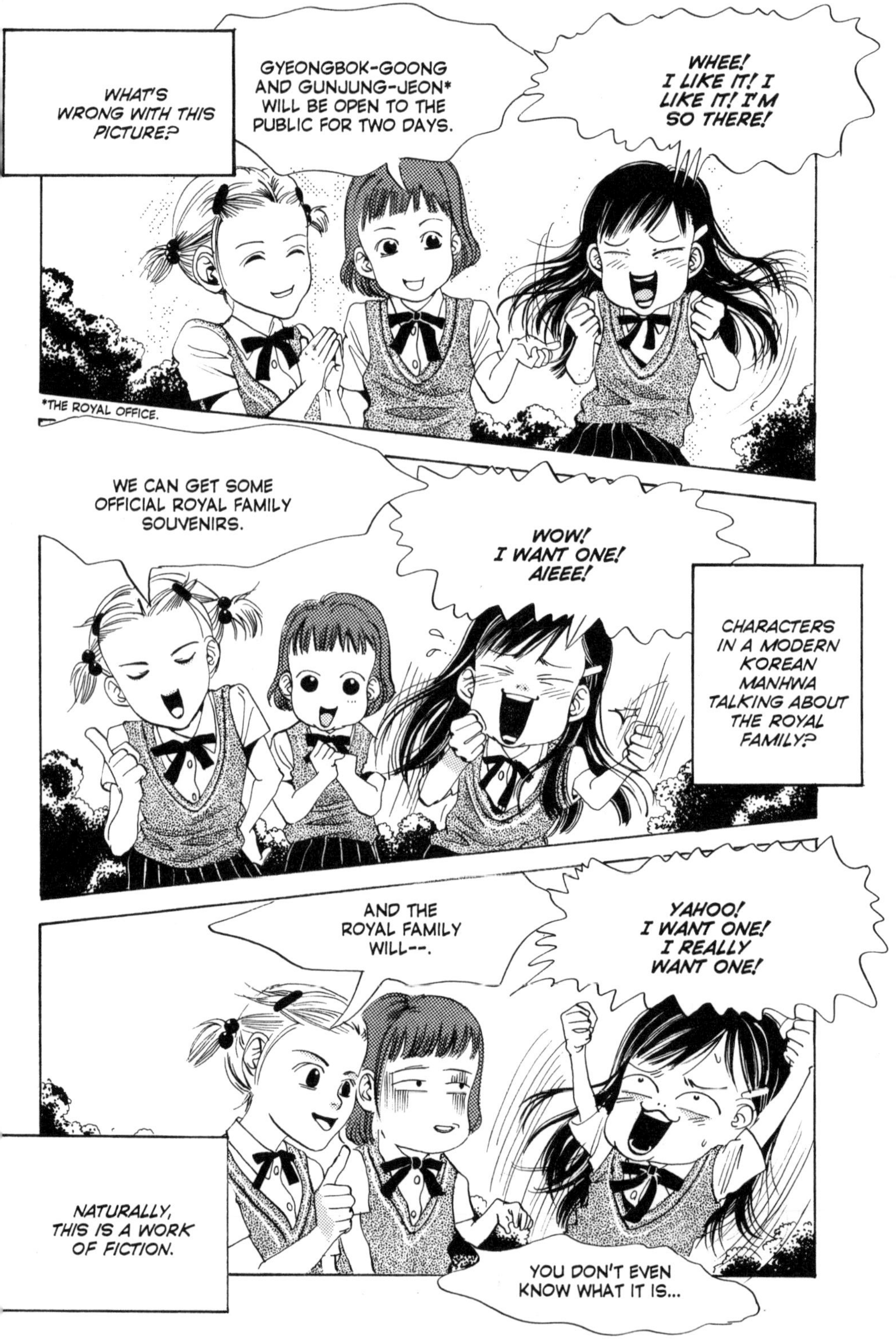
WHAT'S WRONG WITH THIS PICTURE?
GYEONGBOK-GOONG AND GUNJUNG-JEON* WILL BE OPEN TO THE PUBLIC FOR TWO DAYS.
WHEE! I LIKE IT! I LIKE IT! I'M SO THERE!
*THE ROYAL OFFICE.
WE CAN GET SOME OFFICIAL ROYAL FAMILY SOUVENIRS.
WOW! I WANT ONE! AIEEE!
CHARACTERS IN A MODERN KOREAN MANHWA TALKING ABOUT THE ROYAL FAMILY?
AND THE ROYAL FAMILY WILL--.
YAHOO! I WANT ONE! I REALLY WANT ONE!
NATURALLY, THIS IS A WORK OF FICTION.
YOU DON'T EVEN KNOW WHAT IT IS...

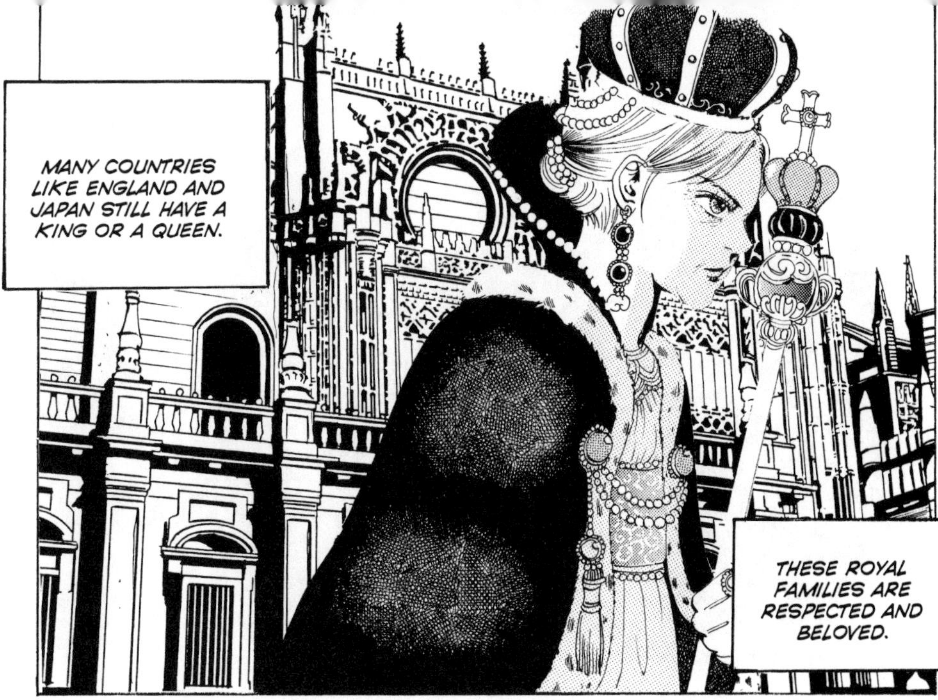
MANY COUNTRIES LIKE ENGLAND AND JAPAN STILL HAVE A KING OR A QUEEN.
THESE ROYAL FAMILIES ARE RESPECTED AND BELOVED.
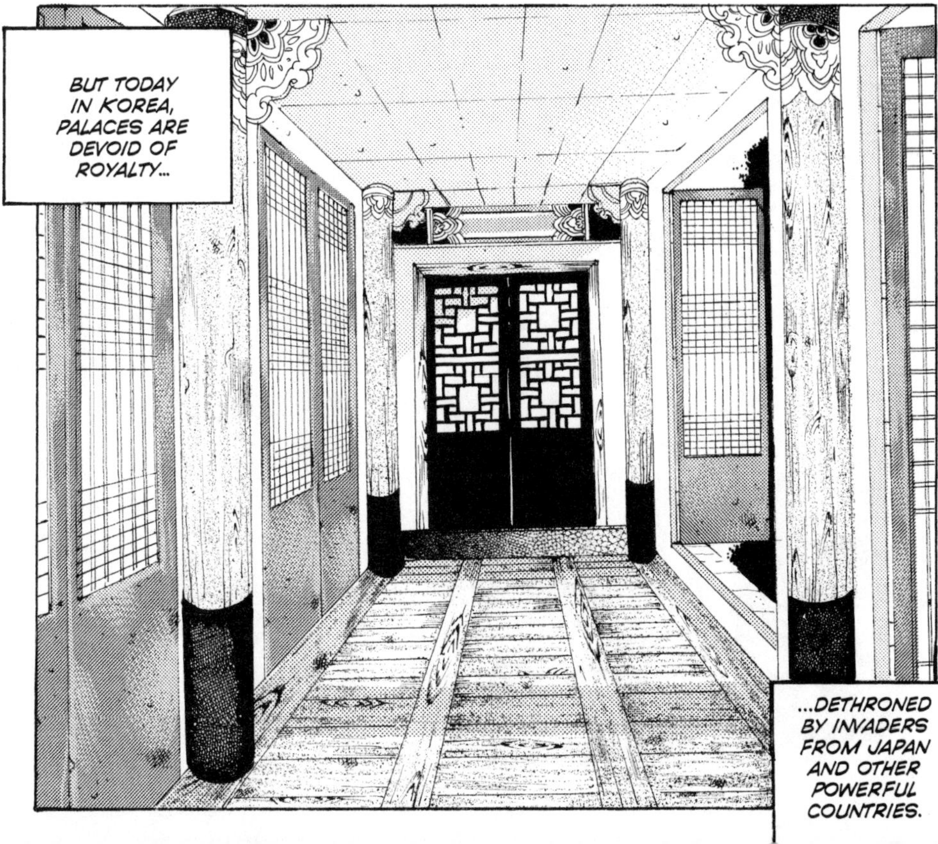
BUT TODAY IN KOREA, PALACES ARE DEVOID OF ROYALTY...
...DETHRONED BY INVADERS FROM JAPAN AND OTHER POWERFUL COUNTRIES.

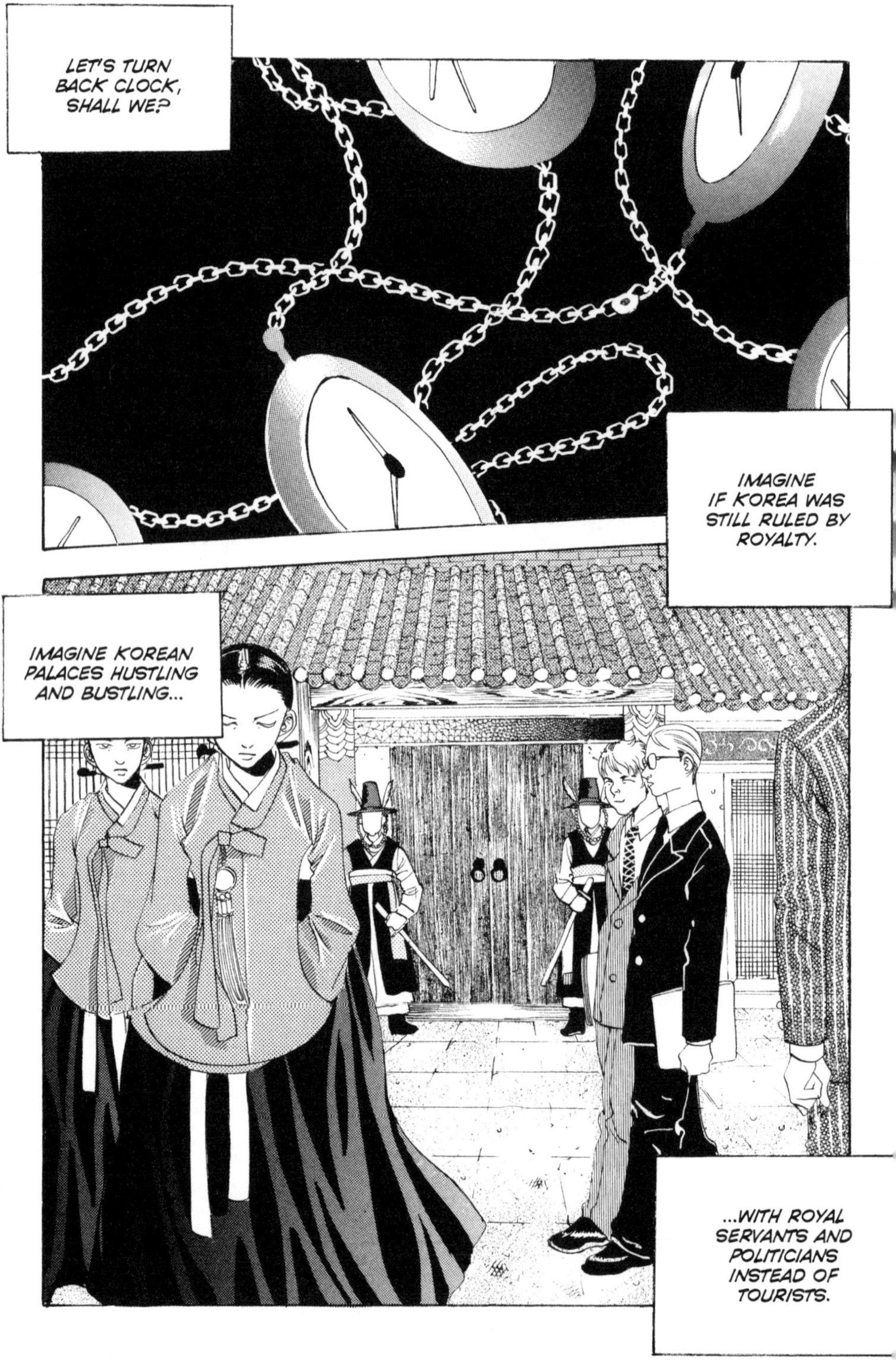
LET'S TURN BACK CLOCK, SHALL WE?
IMAGINE IF KOREA WAS STILL RULED BY ROYALTY.
IMAGINE KOREAN PALACES HUSTLING AND BUSTLING...
...WITH ROYAL SERVANTS AND POLITICIANS INSTEAD OF TOURISTS.

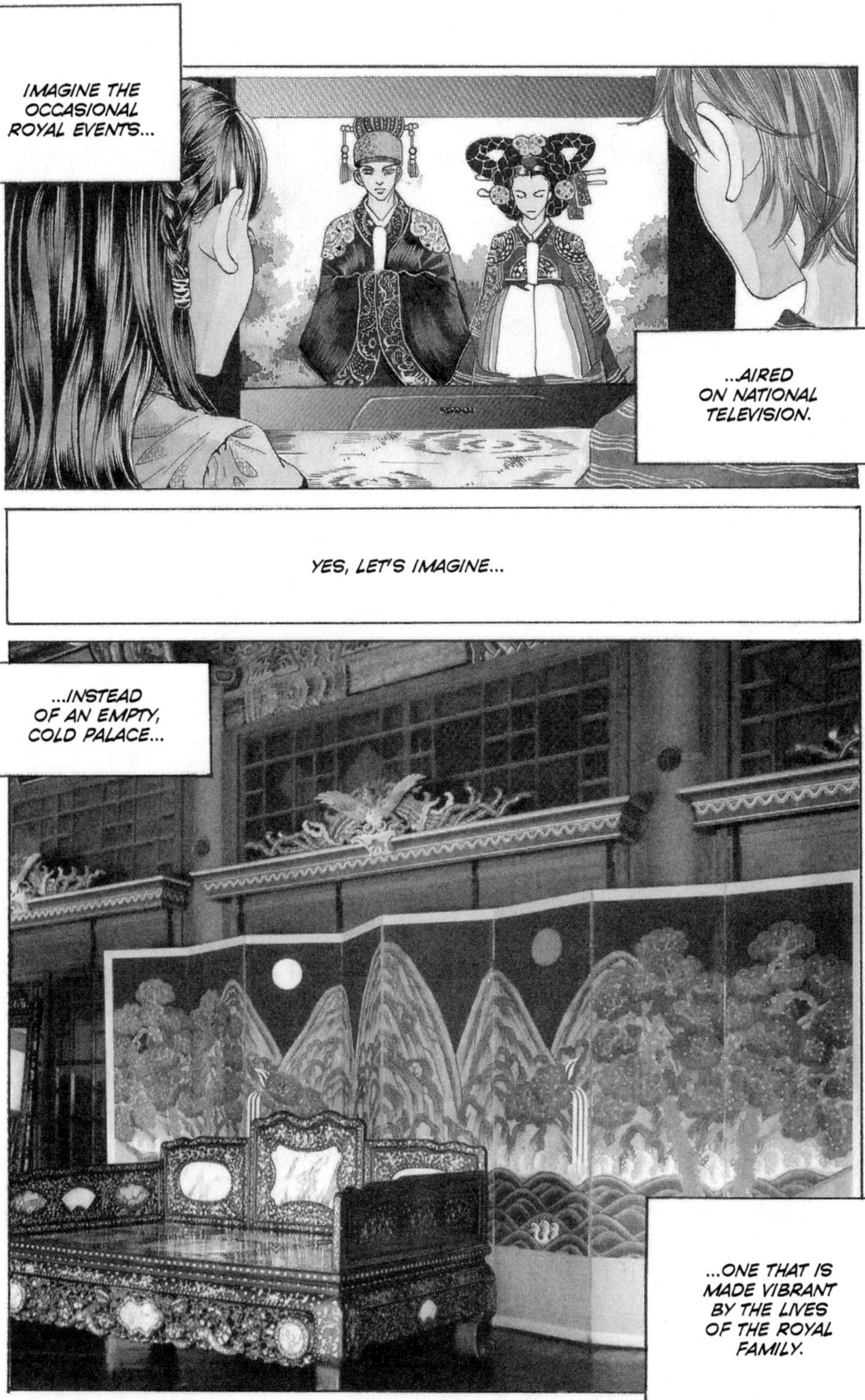
IMAGINE THE OCCASIONAL ROYAL EVENTS...
...AIRED ON NATIONAL TELEVISION.
YES, LET'S IMAGINE...
...INSTEAD OF AN EMPTY, COLD PALACE...
...ONE THAT IS MADE VIBRANT BY THE LIVES OF THE ROYAL FAMILY.

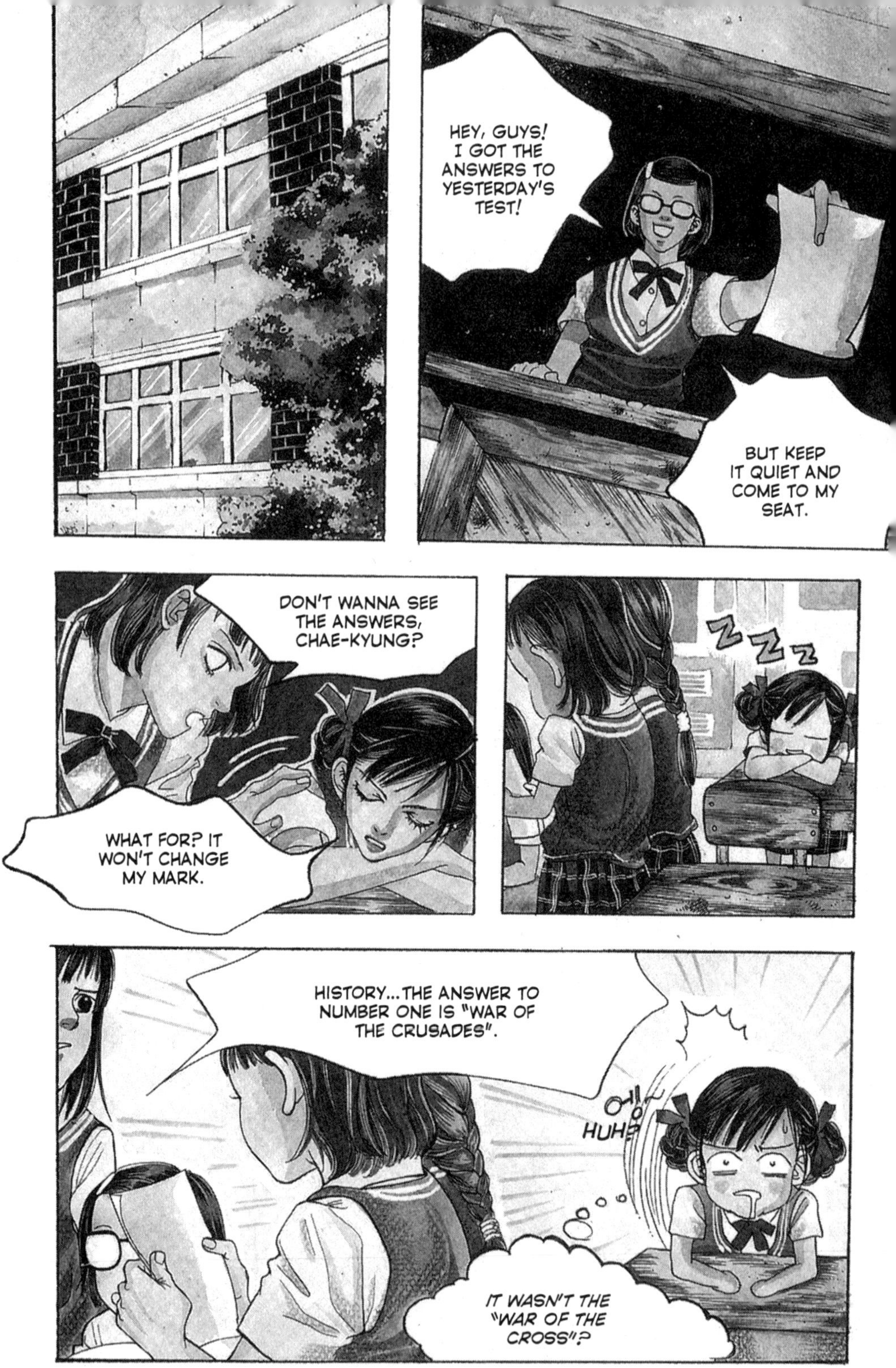
HEY, GUYS!
I GOT THE
ANSWERS TO
YESTERDAY'S
TEST!
BUT KEEP
IT QUIET AND
COME TO MY
SEAT.
DON'T WANNA SEE
THE ANSWERS,
CHAE-KYUNG?
WHAT FOR? IT
WON'T CHANGE
MY MARK.
Z Z Z
HISTORY...THE ANSWER TO
NUMBER ONE IS "WAR OF
THE CRUSADES".
HUH?
IT WASN'T THE
"WAR OF THE
CROSS"?

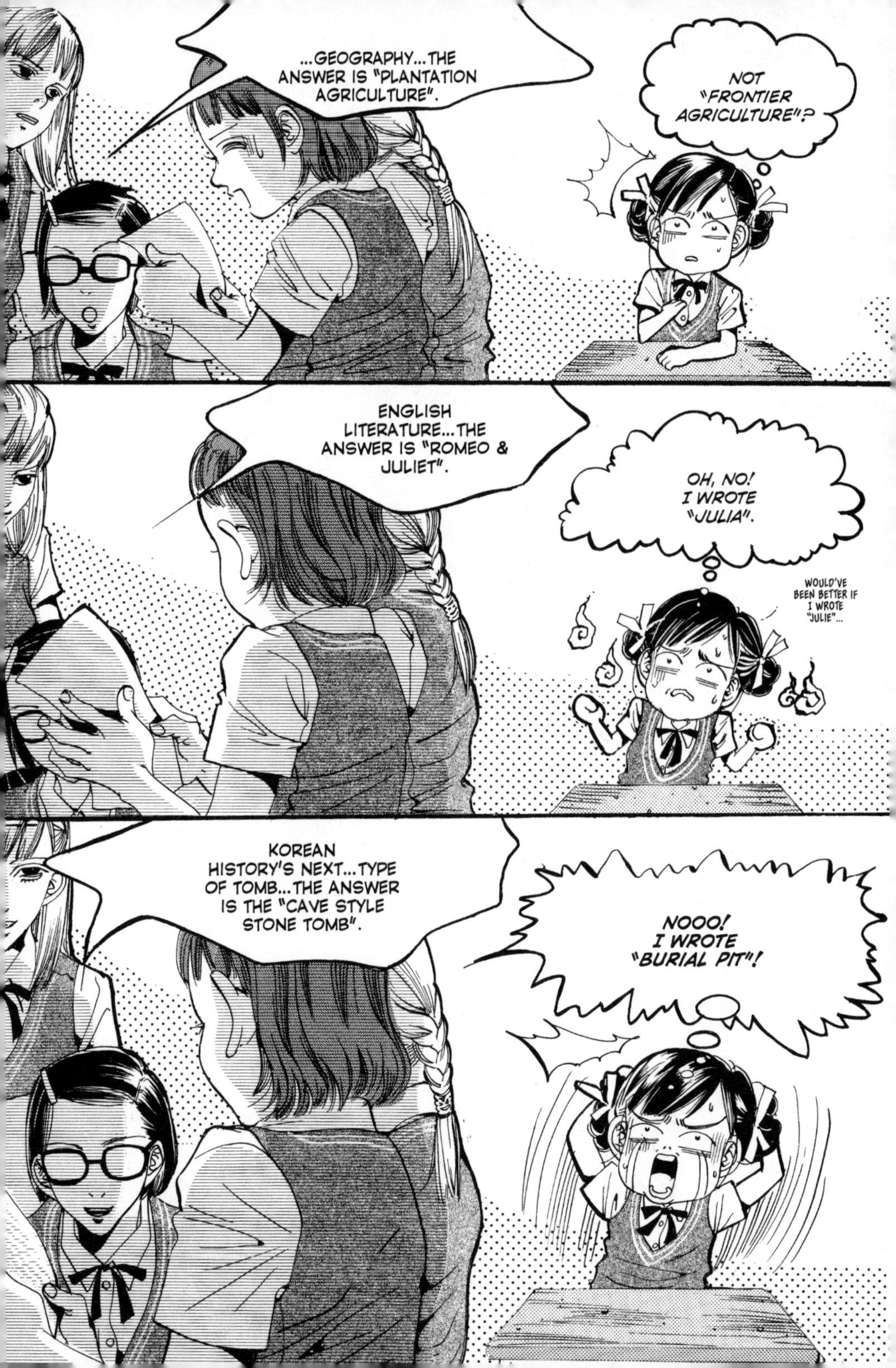
...GEOGRAPHY...THE ANSWER IS "PLANTATION AGRICULTURE".
NOT "FRONTIER AGRICULTURE"?
ENGLISH LITERATURE...THE ANSWER IS "ROMEO & JULIET".
OH, NO! I WROTE "JULIA".
WOULD'VE BEEN BETTER IF I WROTE "JULIE"...
KOREAN HISTORY'S NEXT...TYPE OF TOMB...THE ANSWER IS THE "CAVE STYLE STONE TOMB".
NOOO! I WROTE "BURIAL PIT"!

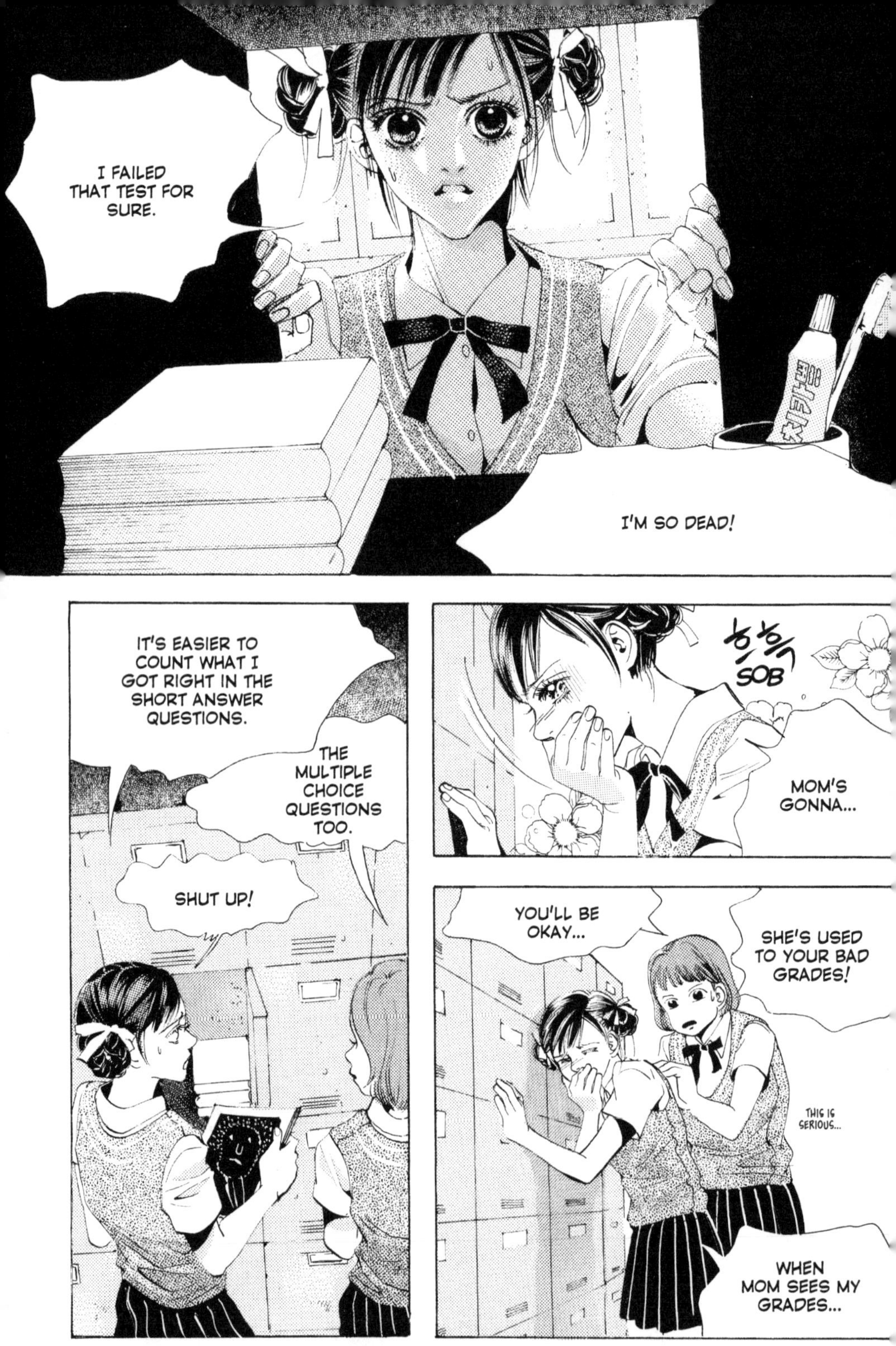
I FAILED THAT TEST FOR SURE.
I'M SO DEAD!
IT'S EASIER TO COUNT WHAT I GOT RIGHT IN THE SHORT ANSWER QUESTIONS.
THE MULTIPLE CHOICE QUESTIONS TOO.
SHUT UP!
SOB
MOM'S GONNA...
YOU'LL BE OKAY...
SHE'S USED TO YOUR BAD GRADES!
THIS IS SERIOUS...
WHEN MOM SEES MY GRADES...

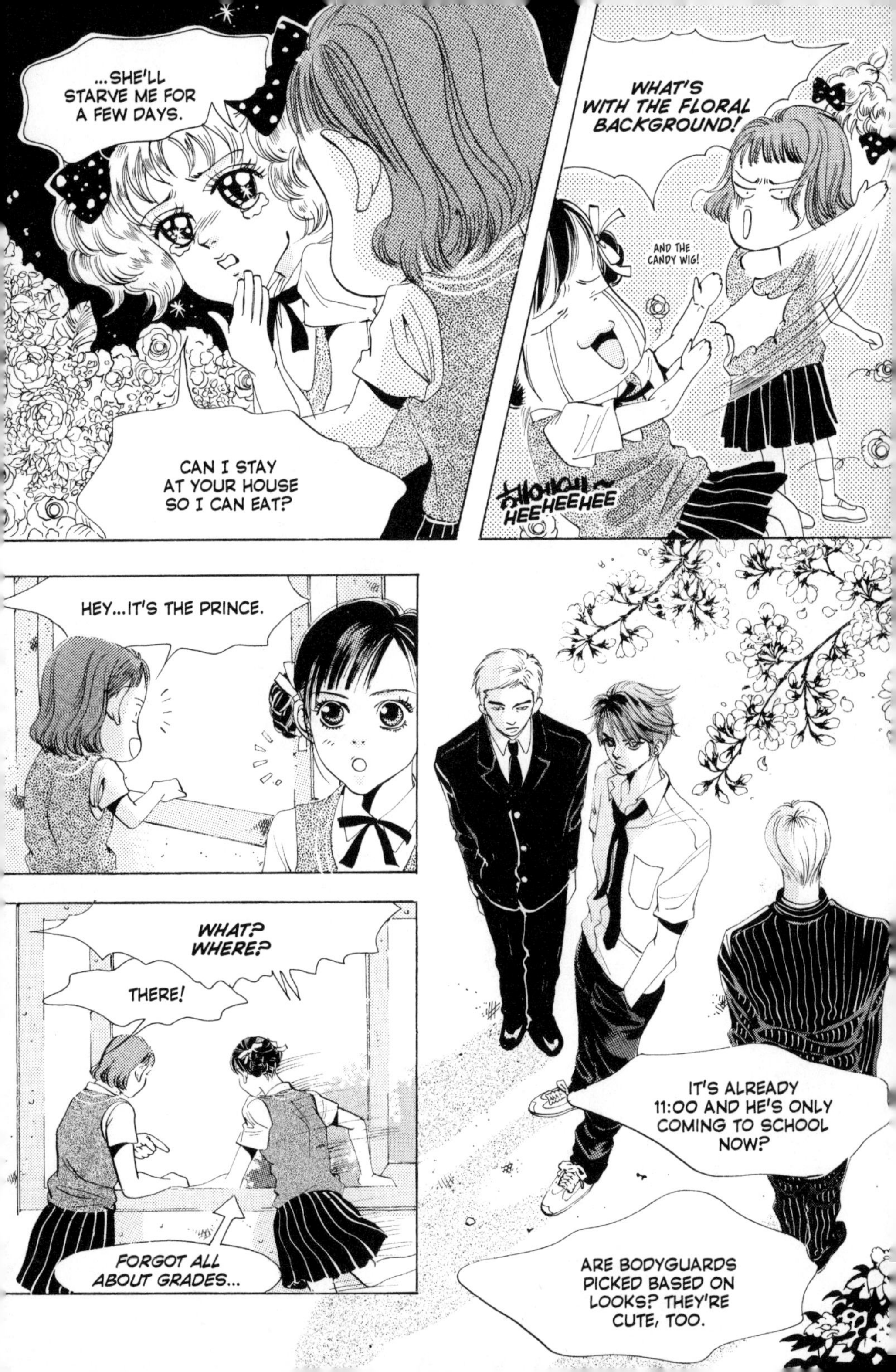
...SHE'LL STARVE ME FOR A FEW DAYS.
CAN I STAY AT YOUR HOUSE SO I CAN EAT?
WHAT'S WITH THE FLORAL BACKGROUND!
AND THE CANDY WIG!
HEEHEEHEE
HEY...IT'S THE PRINCE.
WHAT? WHERE?
THERE!
FORGOT ALL ABOUT GRADES...
IT'S ALREADY 11:00 AND HE'S ONLY COMING TO SCHOOL NOW?
ARE BODYGUARDS PICKED BASED ON LOOKS? THEY'RE CUTE, TOO.

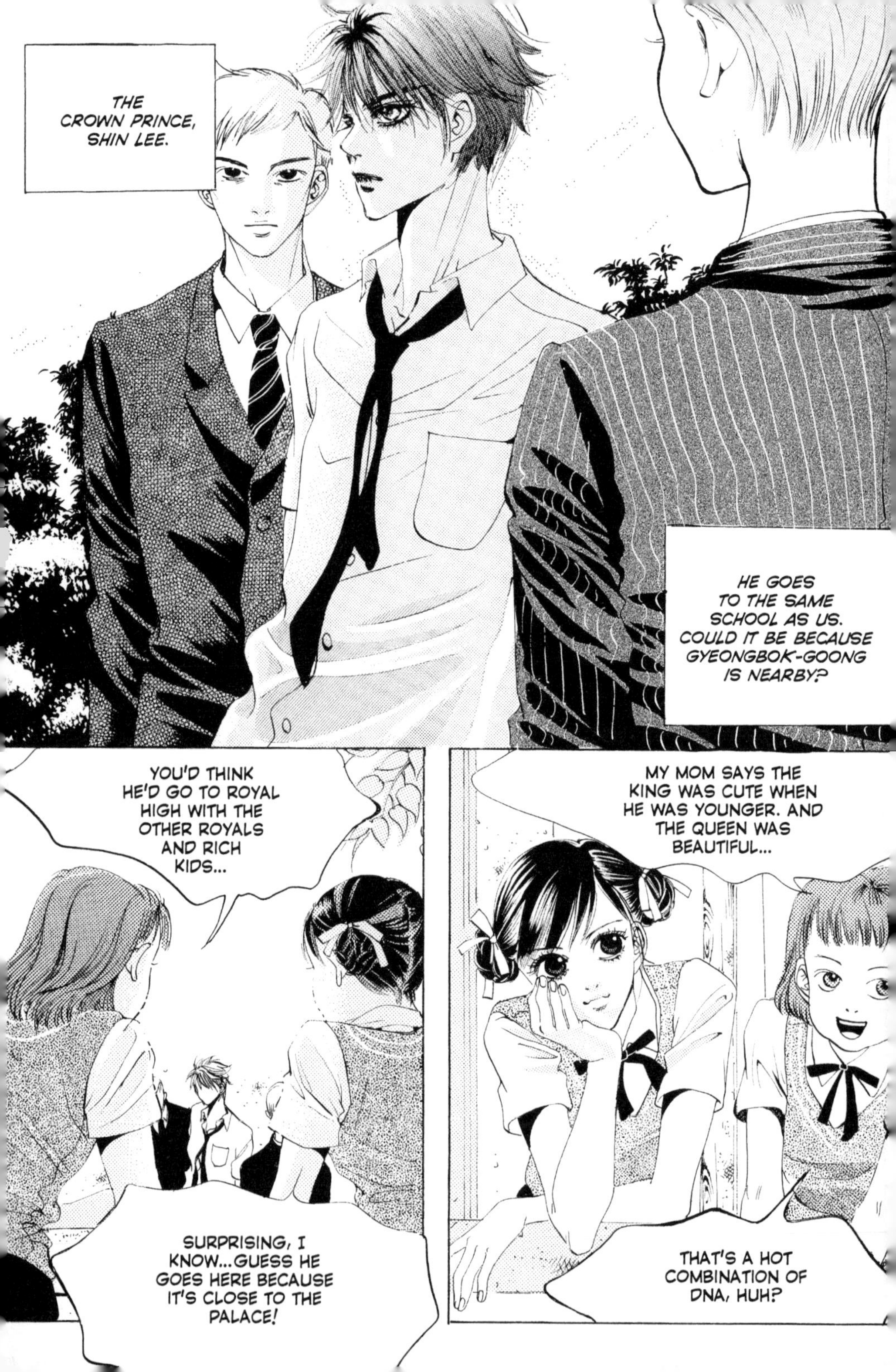
THE CROWN PRINCE, SHIN LEE.
HE GOES TO THE SAME SCHOOL AS US. COULD IT BE BECAUSE GYEONGBOK-GOONG IS NEARBY?
YOU'D THINK HE'D GO TO ROYAL HIGH WITH THE OTHER ROYALS AND RICH KIDS...
SURPRISING, I KNOW...GUESS HE GOES HERE BECAUSE IT'S CLOSE TO THE PALACE!
MY MOM SAYS THE KING WAS CUTE WHEN HE WAS YOUNGER. AND THE QUEEN WAS BEAUTIFUL...
THAT'S A HOT COMBINATION OF DNA, HUH?

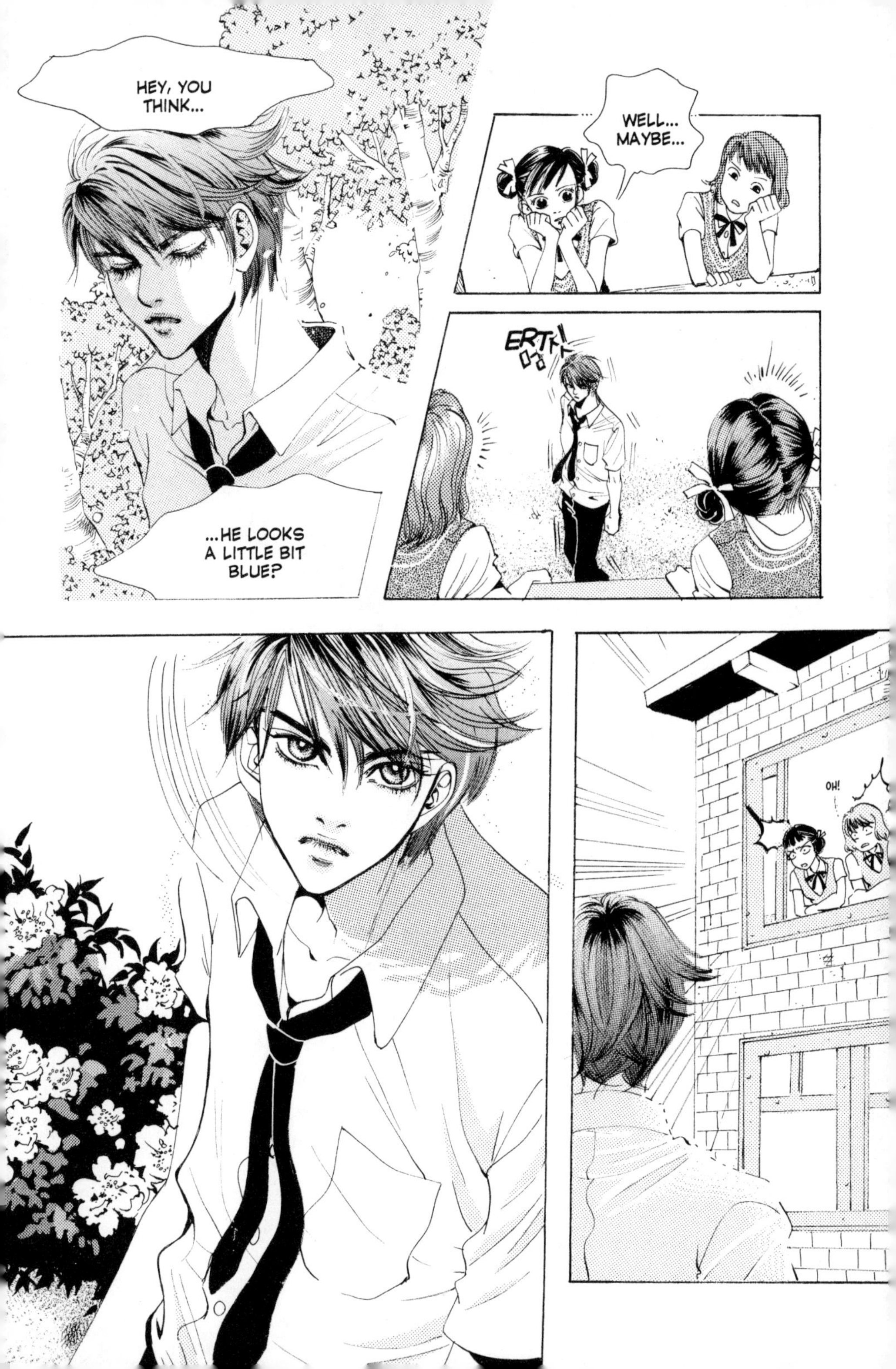
HEY, YOU THINK...
...HE LOOKS A LITTLE BIT BLUE?
WELL... MAYBE...
ERTK!
OH!

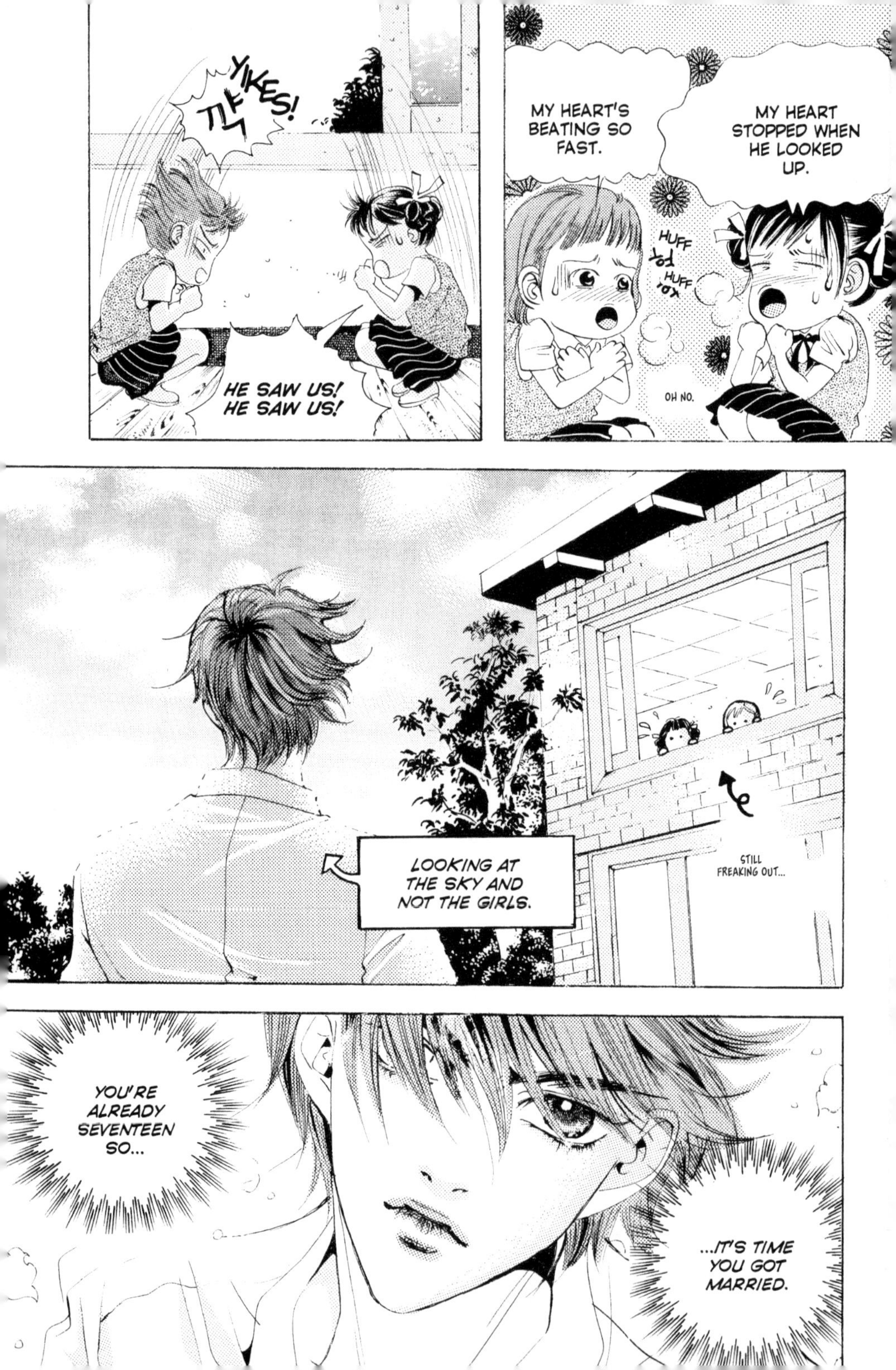
YIKES!
HE SAW US! HE SAW US!
MY HEART'S BEATING SO FAST.
MY HEART STOPPED WHEN HE LOOKED UP.
HUFF
HUFF
OH NO.
LOOKING AT THE SKY AND NOT THE GIRLS.
STILL FREAKING OUT...
YOU'RE ALREADY SEVENTEEN SO...
...IT'S TIME YOU GOT MARRIED.

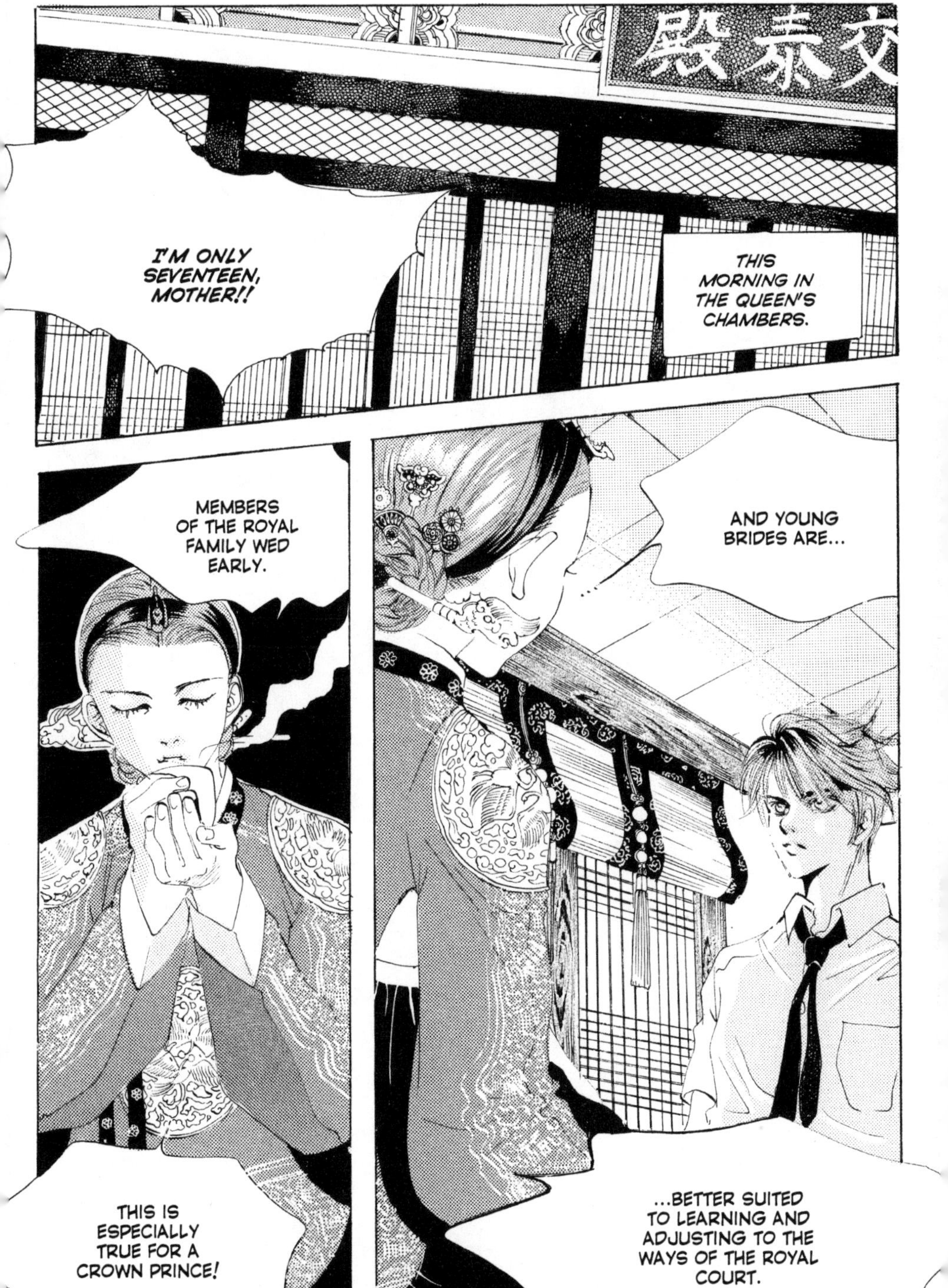

殿泰交
I'M ONLY SEVENTEEN, MOTHER!!
THIS MORNING IN THE QUEEN'S CHAMBERS.
MEMBERS OF THE ROYAL FAMILY WED EARLY.
THIS IS ESPECIALLY TRUE FOR A CROWN PRINCE!
AND YOUNG BRIDES ARE...
...BETTER SUITED TO LEARNING AND ADJUSTING TO THE WAYS OF THE ROYAL COURT.

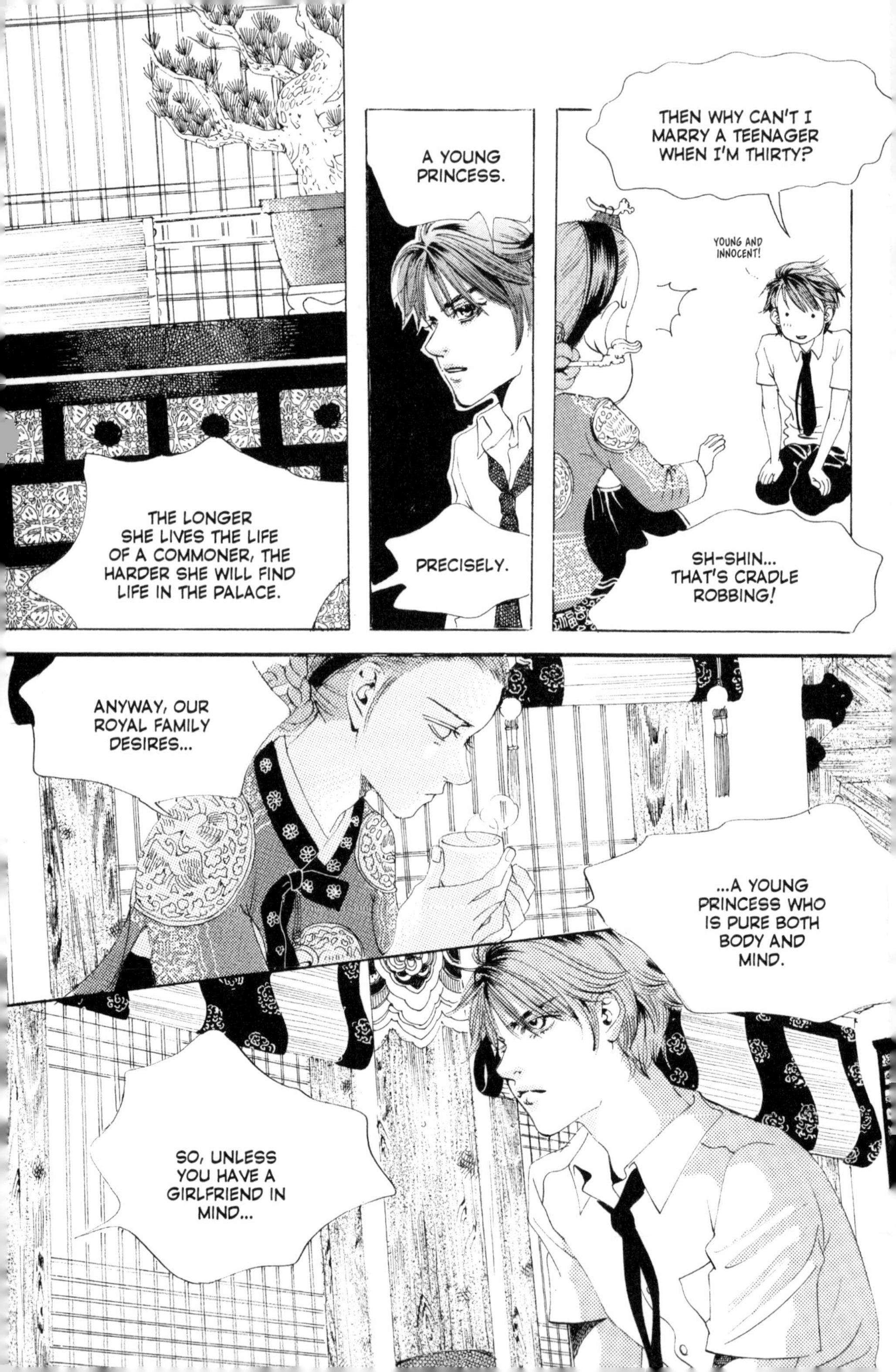
THE LONGER SHE LIVES THE LIFE OF A COMMONER, THE HARDER SHE WILL FIND LIFE IN THE PALACE.
A YOUNG PRINCESS.
PRECISELY.
THEN WHY CAN'T I MARRY A TEENAGER WHEN I'M THIRTY?
YOUNG AND INNOCENT!
SH-SHIN... THAT'S CRADLE ROBBING!
ANYWAY, OUR ROYAL FAMILY DESIRES...
...A YOUNG PRINCESS WHO IS PURE BOTH BODY AND MIND.
SO, UNLESS YOU HAVE A GIRLFRIEND IN MIND...

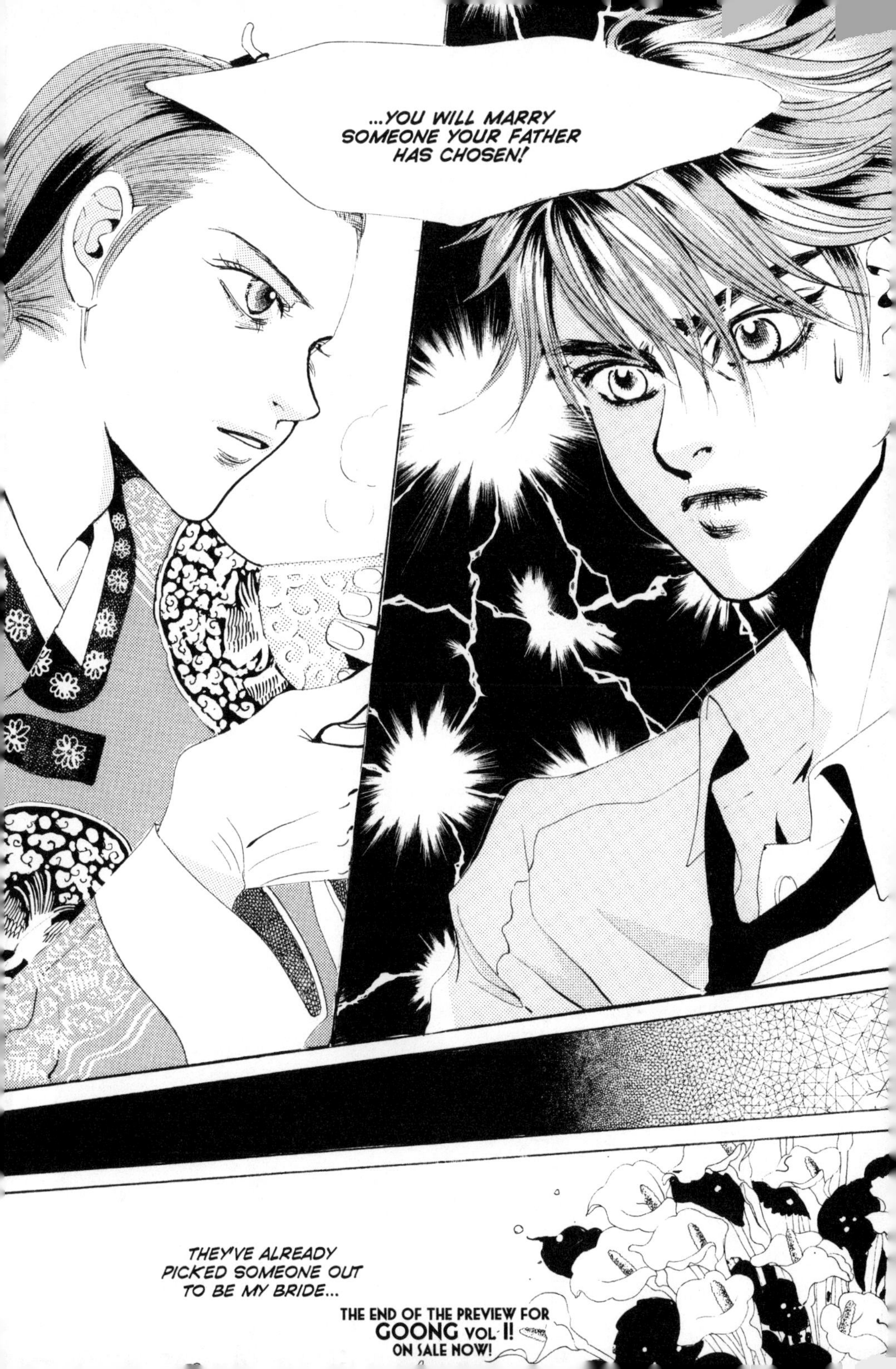
...YOU WILL MARRY SOMEONE YOUR FATHER HAS CHOSEN!
THEY'VE ALREADY PICKED SOMEONE OUT TO BE MY BRIDE...
THE END OF THE PREVIEW FOR GOONG VOL 1! ON SALE NOW!

Bring It On! vol. 4

Story and Art by HyeKyung Baek

Translation: Jackie Oh
English Adaptation: Oliver Strong
Lettering: Terri Delgado · Marshall Dillon

Bring It On!, Vol. 4 © 2002 HyeKyung Baek. All rights reserved. First published in Korea in 2002 by Sigongsa Co., Ltd.

Yen Press
Hachette Book Group USA
237 Park Avenue, New York, NY 10017

Visit our Web sites at www.HachetteBookGroupUSA.com and www.YenPress.com.

Yen Press is an imprint of Hachette Book Group USA, Inc. The Yen Press name and logo are trademarks of Hachette Book Group USA, Inc.

First English Printing: December 2006
First Yen Press Edition: June 2008

ISBN-10: 89-527-4498-5
ISBN-13: 978-89-527-4498-2

10 9 8 7 6 5 4 3 2

BVG

Printed in the United States of America